T0301681

The Financialization of the Firm

The Financialization of the Firm

Managerial and Social Implications

Alexander Styhre

School of Business, Economics and Law, University of Gothenburg, Sweden

Cheltenham, UK • Northampton, MA, USA

Published by
Edward Elgar Publishing Limited
The Lypiatts
15 Lansdown Road
Cheltenham
Glos GL50 2JA
UK

Edward Elgar Publishing, Inc.
William Pratt House
9 Dewey Court
Northampton
Massachusetts 01060
USA

A catalogue record for this book
is available from the British Library

Library of Congress Control Number: 2014959488

This book is available electronically in the **Elgar**online
Business subject collection
DOI 10.4337/9781783478231

ISBN 978 1 78347 822 4 (cased)
ISBN 978 1 78347 823 1 (eBook)

Typeset by Servis Filmsetting Ltd, Stockport, Cheshire
Printed and bound in Great Britain by T.J. International Ltd, Padstow

Contents

Preface and acknowledgments

The capacity and the gift of forgetting have perhaps never been more beautifully and charmingly portrayed than in Kenneth Grahame's *The Wind of the Willows*. After encountering the piper at the gates of dawn, The Friend and Helper, and finding the lost baby otter, Mole and Water Rat are struck by a melancholy that fortunately vanishes into the gentle breeze that suddenly surrounds them:

> As they stared blankly, in dumb misery as they slowly realized all they had seen and all they had lost, a capricious little breeze, dancing up from the surface of the water, tossed the aspens, shook the dewy roses, and blew lightly and caressingly in their faces, and with its soft touch came instant oblivion, for this is the last best gift that the kindly demigod is careful to bestow on those to whom he has revealed himself in their helping: the gift of forgetfulness. Lest the awful remembrance should remain and grow, and overshadow mirth and pleasure, and the great haunting memory should spoil all the after-lifes of little animals helped out of difficulties, in order that they should be happy and light-hearted as before. (Grahame, [1908] 1993: 104–105)

To forget and to move on, these principal human capacities are in many ways helpful as they save us from standing in "dumb misery." Remembrance and recollection are nevertheless useful too, at least on the institutional and collective level. In its own curious and highly personal way, this volume is an attempt to counteract our joint, all-too-human forgetfulness, the "instant oblivion" that at times is necessary to be able continue to live a full life, but that in other cases may prevent us from learning from individual or collective mistakes.

The financialization of the economy and of the firm has been a quite salient mark of the times since at least from the late 1990s and what now is widely described as the Internet bubble. Money-making has always been part of for example, the Wall Street culture and the popular account of the work conducted in such money-dense environments (think of Tom Wolfe's (1987) *Bonfires of the Vanities*), rarely fails to underline this credo. In the late 1990s, the Internet craze included, among many fascinating traits, the conspicuous ambition to make money quickly and seemingly with limited effort; and the finance industry ideology of amassing large stocks of finance capital on the basis of esoteric know-how were no longer a marginal phenomenon. In August 1999, after I graduated from Lund University, I was hired by Chalmers University of Technology in my hometown of Gothenburg. In the period around the turn of the millennium, my department (for reasons not to this day very clear to me), shared some office space with a small but quickly growing Internet-based trading company developed to serve as a market place in the textile industry. The times were great for young, ambitious entrepreneurs in Sweden, a small, export-oriented economy that just a few years earlier had outlived one of its worst finance market crises ever, and were now being fueled by the promise of the relatively novel technological wonder of the Internet and an emerging, buoyant venture capital market. In a very short period, the small company grew from the original four Chalmers graduates in their mid-twenties to something like 40 co-workers including a newly recruited CEO in his forties (I guess), and soon enough the company was rumored to be planning an office in Hong Kong. The attitude and confidence of the four initially quite mellow young entrepreneurs started to change, and the stream of newly hired co-workers showing up in the facilities developed in tandem with the increasing arrogance and self-confidence of the news reporting about the "New Economy" – the new economic regime based on digital media with endless growth potentials and with no more cumbersome ups and downs in the economic cycle (see for example, Neff, 2013). Indeed, as Thomas Frank (2000: 356) remarks, the new economy was "the long summer of corporate love."

While there were many that were willing to believe in the narrative of the promise of the economic possibilities in the Internet age, it was also very difficult to believe that the frantic growth that I and my colleagues witnessed *in situ* would be sustainable. It was, as is often said in hindsight, "crazy times." Among the most spectacular events widely covered in Swedish media in this period was the grandiose failure of Boo.com, a London-based trading site for fashion clothes started by two Swedish entrepreneurs with limited business experience besides running a small publishing house and a successful book-trading site a few years earlier (still in business under the name Bokus). When Boo.com was declared bankrupt in May 2000, it had accumulated an astonishing £178 million in debt, by any standard a remarkable squandering of capital in such a short period of time. In the new millennium, such sums of money (in terms of profits, losses, and economic compensation and bonuses), being cognitively hard for most people to grasp, would be more frequently discussed. After the Internet bubble burst in March 2000, the whole idea of the "New Economy" seemed defunct. The new economy in the case of Sweden brought a new form of entrepreneurship and made it hip, and digital media and Internet were soon institutionalized in the economy and society at large. But the very idea of hyper-accumulation of economic value, the perhaps most radical proposition of the new economy framework, seemed to migrate from the field of digital technologies and media and into the domain of finance.

The new combination of conspicuous greed (or to put it less harshly, the ambition to make money on the basis of entrepreneurial skills and technological know-how) and what Thomas Frank (2000) calls "the conquest of cool," the ability of the field of business to appropriate the coolness otherwise associated with the arts and counterculture (portraying for example, popular culture figures such as Jean-Michel Basquiat, Patty Smith, or Chuck D as "cool," while bankers and business people not so much), represented an entirely new model or even worldview; capitalists now being "cool?" I am glad I was old enough (by the year 2000, I turned 29) not to believe in all this talk about "making the first million before 30," as I could see how some of the best minds of a generation were destroyed by such ambitions. Still, I am happy to have been able to have served as a first-hand witness of the sheer force of the dynamics of capitalism once the hype had taken off. Beliefs do matter, in particular in economic systems based on expectations.

Having said that, while the financialization in the 1990s was spelled "venture capital," the financialization of the first decade of the new millennium until its halt in 2007–2008 occurred in the finance industry. All things being equal, the financialization of small Internet-based firms is relatively limited and confined to the problems of overrating the market possibilities of a smaller group of start-up firms (the venture capital invested in early-stage financing by the mid-1990s represented less than 0.01 percent of the GDP of the EU-15 economies; Deeg, 2009: 566); while the large-scale financialization of the economy orchestrated by the global finance industry tended to penetrate every single economic relation and to migrate globally (see for example Blyth, 2013). Then came 2008, and all of a sudden, everything that had seemed so solid virtually melted into thin air. The free-market solution to everything was not only based on a theoretical framework that seemed porous at best, it did not function practically. Strangely enough, as has been remarked by a series of qualified commentators (for example, Pontusson and Raess, 2012), only a few years after 2008, it seemed as if these events did not happen at all; everything went back to the situation before 2007. But for me, the 2008 financial collapse was a historical event of the same magnitude as the Berlin Wall coming down in November 1989 or the terrorist attacks of September 11, 2001: it was simply an event not so easily forgotten, regardless of all the finance industry actors having much to win in leaving history all behind as soon as possible. Alan Blinder (2013: xvi, original emphasis omitted) observes in his book about the 2008 event and its causes and consequences that "the American people still don't quite know what hit them, and why it happened, or what the authorities did about it." At the same time, there are studies that suggest a change in attitude following the 2008 events. One study showed that while in 2002, 80 percent of Americans agreed in a poll that they "[s]trongly supported capitalism and the free-enterprise system," by 2010 that number had fallen to only 59 percent (Stout, 2012: 10). While I am not in such an authoritative position to claim educational roles on this scale, I still suspect that Blinder is right that many people, myself included, had a hard time understanding what really happened here, amidst the fog of war and afterwards. In many ways, this text is an attempt to clarify for myself how comprehensive and influential the finance industry has become over the last three decades, and particularly since the turn of the millennium.

As the careful reader notices quite early on, this volume relies heavily on literature addressing American (or at least Anglo-American) conditions, and the reason for this is primarily that there are simply more research works on the topic being published in the US than in for example, Sweden. Still, what is true for the US, *mutatis mutandis*, is also true for a small economy like Sweden's (see for example, Deeg, 2009; Djelic, 2001).[1] However, there are important institutional differences between the US and Sweden including differences in the political, legal, and regulatory framework, and in addition, there are important cultural and social traits of the two countries that matter inasmuch as there is strong political support across the political spectrum for what neoliberal intellectuals are fond of referring to as "collectivist solutions" in Sweden. Politically, Sweden has been dominated by the Social Democratic Party and center-right governments have traditionally avoided departing too much from this predominant tradition to recognize the legitimacy of the welfare

---

[1] Macéus' (2014) account of the Swedish government taking over the Carnegie Investment Bank on November 10, 2008, at the height of the financial industry collapse, contains the all-too-familiar elements of a freefalling finance institution: autocratic industry leaders ignoring risks and all warning signals from regulatory authorities; a complex and "feudal" company structure with many divisions and subsidiaries; lavish bonus programs and a widespread preference for extravagant consumerism; an unprecedented risk-taking culture grounded in a milieu increasingly distanced from other industries and the everyday lives of most people; accounting and auditing firms praising the activities that in hindsight were conspicuously poorly functioning and in many ways culpable and morally questionable if not criminal; and the inability to adapt to new information and external demands. It is as if Carnegie had gained a momentum that was impossible to stop, leading to the loss of six billion kronor in stock value for the shareholders when the Swedish government terminated Carnegie's license to operate in the finance market. The case of Carnegie was therefore more or less a blueprint of what was observed in for example the US.

state. In other words, some of the attitudes of American neoliberals, libertarians, and neoconservatives towards the role of the government and its "East-coast intellectuals" are for the most part irrelevant, at times even regarded as evidence of the quirkiness of the American political system from a Swedish perspective. Still, the US has been the politically, economically, and culturally dominant nation throughout the entire period of financialization (while this position is today questioned, primarily by American commentators themselves), and therefore American ideas and policies have in many cases been responded to across the Atlantic and elsewhere. In this view, financialization is of wide interest for a series of societies, economies, industries, and firms.

The term *financialization* being explored in detail in this volume is therefore not only enacted as a technical term, but is also a more general concept aimed at capturing broader socioeconomic and cultural changes since the early 1980s. It is a term that attempts to capture some of what Fernand Braudel (1980) speaks of as *la longue durée*, the more deep-seated cultural and institutional changes in history. I am fully aware I may fail to live up to Braudel's rigorous standards, but I still want the term financialization to mean more than some technical shift in policy. In other words, while this is written as a monograph in the management literature genre, it is also trying to capture some of the more long-term changes whose first implications were witnessed by me and my colleagues in the late 1990s, the emergence of what was once – not very much held back by the failure of previous attempts to "breed the new" – declared to be the *new economy*.

ACKNOWLEDGMENTS

There are a few people I would like to thank who have helped me to bring this project to its conclusion. First of all I would like to thank Francine O'Sullivan, commissioning editor at Edward Elgar Publishing for offering me the opportunity to publish this volume. Second, I would like to thank all my colleagues at the School of Business, Economics, and Law, University of Gothenburg for the inspiring conversations over the years. In particular, my colleagues in the Management and Organization Section who have been good research collaborators and speaking partners over the years. Finally, I would like to thank my family for helping me understand that economic theory and economic research is not a matter of reflecting on esoteric matters but ultimately a quite straightforward analysis of how economic value is generated, allocated, and distributed in this late modern period of time, for many Westerners not so much characterized by a lack of material resources as it is shaped by a complete understanding of the complexity of everyday economy.

Alexander Styhre
Sävedalen
9 March, 2015

1. Introduction: from the managerial capitalism of the society of organizations to the investor capitalism of the ownership society

ON REGIMES OF CAPITALISM

By financialization we mean basically the increased reliance on the finance market and finance capital to secure economic growth in the contemporary economy (Van der Zwan, 2014; Palley, 2013; Krippner, 2005). This shift in competitive capitalism from manufacturing and distribution of physical commodities as being the principal economic activity, to an economy essentially structured on the basis of abstract principles and the accumulation of wealth on the basis of non-tangible assets represents a wide-ranging shift change now being subject to detailed scholarly attention. Rather than starting with an analysis of finance industry statistics, clearly demonstrating the substantial growth of economic value generated in financial services (for example, Crotty, 2008), we can turn an eye to institutional changes. If the post-World War II era until the decline of the Bretton Woods system in the early 1970s (the Nixon Administration dropped out of the system in 1971) has been characterized as what Peter Drucker (1946) once spoke of as the "society of organizations" and Alfred Chandler (1984, 1977) refers to as "managerial capitalism," the era after 1979 when Margret Thatcher was elected Prime Minister in the UK and embarked on a radical political change program, is perhaps better described as what Gerald Davis (2010) speaks of as "the ownership society" (a term widely used by the George W. Bush Administration, 2001–2009; Harrington, 2008) and what Michael Useem (1996) calls "investor capitalism." Since the early 1970s, competitive capitalism has undergone a seismic shift in how economic value is accumulated and how it is distributed and shared (Tabb, 2012). For instance, in the US in 1950 the ten largest employers hired 5 percent of the American workforce, but in 2010 that figure was 2.8 percent (Davis, 2010: 333), indicating the decline in large and stable employing firms. In 1950, eight of the top ten employers were manufacturing firms, while in 2009 they were all in services and retailing, with seven of the largest employers belonging to the latter category. "By March 2009, more Americans were *unemployed* than were employed in manufacturing, and all signs pointed to further displacement in the goods-producing sector," Davis (2009: 27, original emphasis) observes. Moreover, one single retailer, Walmart, employed about as many Americans (1.4 million) as the 20 largest US manufacturers *combined* by 2009 (Davis, 2009: 30). In comparison to the American manufacturing industry, which relies on stable and predictable agreements between unions and employers, jobs in retailing are insecure and lower paid, a condition that has increased the economic inequality in the US. As Davis (2009: 27) states "Large corporations have lost their place as the central pillars of American social structure."

Over the last four decades, the American economy has lost many manufacturing jobs, an effect of the political ignorance derived from the economic advice being given that the offshoring of manufacturing jobs to low-cost countries was part of a "natural" change towards more professional and knowledge-intensive work, and an unwillingness to invest in long-term production facilities when there were possibilities for earning higher rents when investing this capital in the burgeoning finance markets. In many ways, the interwar period was the era of large corporations and industries such as the automotive industry and industry leaders such as Alfred P. Sloan, the legendary Chief Executive Officer (CEO) of General Motors, were the masters of the society of organizations (Mizruchi, 2013). During the last four decades, following the economic decline of the 1970s and the radical shift in policy during the Thatcher and Reagan era of the 1980s, there has been a strong orientation towards the finance industry and the finance market to generate economic value and to coordinate economic activities (Stein, 2011; Stearns and Allan, 1996). Finance market actors today serve the role similar to Sloan and the corporate elites of his generation, to monitor and assess how capital is circulating and accumulating in organizations and networks of organizations. "Nearly three-quarters of the average Fortune 1000 corporation's shares were owned by institutional investors in 2005, with mutual funds making up the most concentrated block," Davis (2009: 33) reports, indicating how large fund and finance companies serve to monitor companies and to align the interests of CEOs and directors with those of finance market actors. As a consequence, the circulation of stocks is substantially higher, indicating that long-term ownership obligations and responsibilities are displaced by an investor culture based on short-term rent seeking: "[w]hereas in 1960, on average, only 12 percent of a New York Stock Exchange-listed company's share would turn over in a year, by 1990 turnover was 46 percent, in 2000, 88 percent, and before the crash of 2008, well over 100 percent" (Tabb, 2012: 53).

In this new ownership society and regime of investor capitalism, companies are being enacted not so much as a bundle of production facilities but as a portfolio of financial resources and legal contracts. Also human beings working in these corporations and competing over work in the era of financialization have started to re-enact themselves in new terms and have started to think of themselves as enterprising subjects consonant with the expectations laid upon them: "[t]he increasing centrality of finance to everyday life also changed people's understanding of their place in society. Traditional corporate employers provided more than a job – they provided a worldview," Davis (2009: 38) says. In ownership society, the overarching worldview being presented to social actors is to think of oneself as an enterprising individual that competes on the basis of the ability to generate economic value and rents for the employing organization (for example, Neff, 2013; Lane, 2010). The financialization of the economy is therefore essentially an intellectual and ideological shift wherein the accumulation of capital and economic rents are the drivers of the economy.

This book examines the financialization of the firm from a management studies and social theory perspective. The volume does not rely on one single unified theoretical framework but makes use of a variety of literatures including organization theory, economic sociology, political science, finance theory, and economics. The book does not aim to present an equally unified and integrated theory of the financialization of the firm, but to examine the various implications of the financialization of the capitalist economy on the firm level and on the level of the co-workers in organizations. While financialization is a quite recent term in the economic sociology literature (Van der Zwan, 2014), arguably introduced by the edited volume of Epstein (2005), it still captures the *longue durée* of the contemporary economic system and in policy, rooted in the 1970s' bear market and the economic turmoil derived from the first and second oil crises of the 1970s. As Krippner (2011, 2005) has argued persuasively, the outcome from all the policies from the Carter Administration onwards has not always been anticipated, or desired, but instead there has been a significant degree of what Robert Merton (1933) speaks of as "unintended consequences of purposeful action" in this story. In addition, there is an element of opportunism in the equation when the hegemonic Keynesian regulatory economic model started to run out of steam and new groups of economists and economic advisers and policy-makers advanced their positions (Mirowski, 2013; Madrick, 2011; Peck, 2010). In Peter Gay's (1986) excellent monograph on the Weimar culture, the "outsiders" of the German society quickly became "insiders" during the short period of the Republic between World War I and the Nazi takeover. Something quite similar occurred in the US during the 1970s and 1980s, when so-called "freshwater" economists at the University of Chicago were increasingly becoming influential in setting the political agenda and in shaping the public mindset regarding the role of the government and the importance of free markets (Jones, 2012). Figures such as Milton Friedman, previously being respected but widely regarded as representing overtly anti-statist and libertarian political views, could now entrench advisory roles in the White House (Burgin, 2012). These changes did not happen overnight but were rather the outcome of a long-term mobilization of conservative and libertarian intellectuals and financiers that were ready to sponsor and fund a new economic theory and policy (Styhre, 2014; Medvetz, 2012; Himmelstein, 1992). This institutional shift is a fascinating story in its own right, and the most conspicuous consequence of this new economic doctrine and policy is the quick expansion of finance markets, that is, the financialization of the economy.

CAPITALISM AS AN ECONOMIC SYSTEM AND REGIMES OF CAPITAL ACCUMULATION

The concept of financialization is deeply entangled with the abstract category of *capital*, and more specifically *finance capital*. In the Western tradition, shaped by Hellenistic philosophy and the Christian and more specifically the Catholic credo, capital qua abstract economic category has historically been treated with great skepticism (Wood, 2002; De Roover, 1974). An inquiry in the financialized economy and the financialization of the firm needs to start with an historical overview of how finance has gradually moved from being a relatively marginal but yet decisive mechanism in economic systems, to become its master and the measure of all things under the sun. Today, finance scholars and pundits at times portray the finance industry as the "motor" of capitalism, or even, when favoring a more neurological metaphor, the "brain" of capitalism. Such metaphors may be regarded as useful and legitimate to varying degrees, and may be more or less justified on the basis of empirical data, but they are nevertheless indicative of a major institutional shift in the economy that has occurred during the last three decades. In the following, an historical view of the relationship between finance capital and capitalism will be provided.

In Max Weber's (1999: 48) account, the capitalist economic system is constituted by a number of key components including "[the] appropriation of the physical means of production by the entrepreneur, freedom of the market, rational technology, rational law, free labor, and finally the commercialization of economic life." In Day's (1987: 142) view, "the birth of capitalism coincides with the emergence of an organized market for short-term credit based on foreign exchange." That is, capitalism is by definition grounded in the organization of a structured market for credit and exchanges of different currencies. Day (1987: 143) dates this event to the second half of the thirteenth century, when there was, he continues, a "remarkable growth" of innovations in the field of "financial and business techniques." Needless to say, modern day capitalism with its emphasis on finance capital originated in a hostile environment dominated by the Catholic Church (Tawney, [1926] 1998; Keen, 1968). For the Church fathers, trade, as opposed to work for one's subsistence, was not in itself treated as being "wicked" but since there was always risks involved in trade, such occupations "nevertheless endangered the salvation of the soul" (De Roover, 1974: 336). In addition, usury and money-lending – of vital importance for economic growth as capital investment propels entre-preneurial activities – was condemned as "sin"; to lend money against interest is to capitalize on time, and time belongs to God. Hence, usury is sinful (De Roover, 1974: 336; see also Le Goff, [1986] 1988):

> The assumption on which all this body of doctrine rested was simple. It was that the danger of economic interests increased in direct proportion to the prominence of the pecuniary motives associated with them. Labor – the common lot of mankind – is necessary and honorable; trade is necessary, but perilous to the soul; finance, if not immoral, it is at best sordid and at worst disreputable. (Tawney, [1926] 1998: 33)

This theological hostility towards capital circulation and accumulation had its root in Hellenic philosophy. Aristotle, undoubtedly the dominant intellectual figure in the medieval period, argued in his *Politics* that money is "sterile," and made a careful distinction between *oikonomia*, "the art of household management," and *chrematistike*, "the art of money-making" (Swedberg, 1998: 30), wherein the latter was less honorable. Scholastic thinkers addressing economic issues including San Bernardino of Siena consequently condemned usury (De Roover, 1974: 344), and well into the reformation period, protestant theologians such as Martin Luther published texts such as *Sermon on Usury* (1520) and *On Trade and Usury* (1524) that condemned usury and profit-making more generally (Tawney, [1926] 1998).

Hard work and poverty had been Christian virtues from its inception. "Blessed are the meek," reads Matthew 5:5, widely understood as an instruction to patiently await future rewards for the toil and hard work in this world, but this conservatism and tolerance or even veneration of poverty and suffering effectively inhibited the development of economic growth and an enterprising culture. A medieval cynic, Benvenuto da Imola (cited in Tawney, [1926] 1998: 8), pointed at the limited choices of the medieval laborer or "entrepreneurs" – to use an anachronistic term – in the era of theological prohibition against usury: "[h]e who takes it [interests on loans] goes to hell, and he who does not goes to the workhouse." However, the period from the twelfth to the fifteenth century was marked by "dramatic developments in economic thought and practice within the framework of a changing society" (Wood, 2002: 206), including the emergence of a new merchant class in the prosperous Italian city-states. According to Wood (2002: 207), these social and doctrinal changes saw that "money became the lifeblood of the state." Wood (2002: 207) goes on to say, "[e]specially in early Renaissance Italy, the theoretical position of wealth and poverty was gradually reversed: wealth was exalted and poverty decried." One of the most important contributions of medieval economic thought was therefore the emergence of the concept of interest and its "[d]ivorce from usurious, and therefore sinful, profit" (Wood, 2002: 207). Theology and economic issues and finance in particular were gradually disconnected.

The Italian merchants located in the glorious city-states on the Italian peninsula were the principal innovators in the field of finance (Braudel, 1992). Levitt (2013a: 141) dates the birth of capitalism to a later period than Day (1987), but nevertheless emphasizes the mercantile roots of the capitalist system. In Levitt's view, the emerging maritime states of the Atlantic rim including Great Britain, Portugal, and the Netherlands, and the merchant classes operating in alliance with the national sovereign for "commerce and conquest, trade and art, wealth and territory," were the drivers of capitalism. The essence of capitalism is therefore not, Levitt (2013a) suggests, its superiority of *production* but instead it is "the superiority in commerce and conquest" that is its *primus motor*. Of particular importance for the mercantilist phase of capitalism was the legal form of the joint-stock chartered company (Levitt, 2013a: 141), a specific form of economic enterprise based on limited liabilities and ultimately backed by the national sovereign as a tool for geopolitical expansion and the accumulation of wealth of the Western economic centers.

Regardless of the precise dating of capitalism, the role of finance capital is of central importance. Arrighi's (2010) seminal study of the expansion of capital from the Italian mercantile city-states of Venice, Genoa, Florence, and Pisa provides some insight into the role of capital in the expansion of differentiated economic systems, from the Italian peninsula to the trading posts north of the Alps (for example, Bruges). In Arrighi's (2010) narrative, the two principal contestants for being the birthplace of Western capitalism were Venice and Genoa, demonstrating two entirely different trajectories in how they were competing over the Euro-Asian trade routes. Unlike many other towns and cities on the Italian peninsula, Venice was not a Roman settlement, but was formed around the turn of the second millennium. In the coming centuries, Venice became a grandiose city-state, a city of many wonders, commercial as well as cultural, developing a sophisticated political system that lasted into the period when Venice was integrated into the new Italian nation state during the *Risorgimento* of the mid-nineteenth century. Venice organized its economic activity into guilds and developed functional finance systems by the second half of twelfth century, so-called *colleganza*. By the twelfth century, the Venetians had managed to accommodate the Church's ban on usury, and the supply of capital enabled further economic expansion (Lane, 1973: 144). In addition, the Venetians enacted double-entry standards (albeit the origin of this standard is disputed, with some scholars believing the practice was first developed in Genoa and Tuscany; Lane, 1973: 104), and developed a system of education in so-called *scuola d'abbaco* (Carruthers and Espeland, 1991: 49), a form of trade schools where the *maestro d'abacco*, "masters of the abacus," trained the sons of merchants in subjects such as Latin, multiplication, division, fractions, and double-entry bookkeeping (Lane, 1973: 141). In 1474, Venice enacted its first rules on intellectual property rights (IPRs), the archaic form of what constitutes modern patenting law (Wilkinson, 2006: 192). In the sixteenth century, Venice was the European center for book publishing, a position taken over by Amsterdam in the seventeenth century and London in eighteenth century (Briggs and Burke, 2009: 46). In short, Venice championed the development of an advanced economic system, eventually reproduced elsewhere.

Unfortunately, these superior abilities to build an advanced city-state and a differentiated economy made Venetian capitalism "parochial and inward-looking" (Arrighi, 2010: 151), that was also combined with a lack of innovation. The Genoese merchants, in contrast, were operating in a much less stable political system with periods of disruption, civil war, and armed conflicts with for example, nearby Pisa, which made Genoese capitalism "subject to strong centrifugal and innovative thrust," according to Arrighi (2010: 151). When the Genoese military-commercial empire in the Mediterranean and Black Sea regions dissolved, this strive to create new means for expanding the commercial activities beyond the city-state intensified. This leaves Arrighi (2010) with two highly complementary models for capital accumulation and economic growth:

> Just as Venice's inherent strength in state- and war-making was its weakness, so Genoa's weakness was its strength. In an attempt to beat Venetian competition, or because they had been beaten by it, the Genoese merchants forced their way into every corner of the European World-economy and opened up new trade routes within and beyond its geographical boundaries. By the beginning of the fifteenth century, they had settlements in the Crimea, Chios, North Africa,

Seville, Lisbon, and Bruges . . . As a result, the Genoese capitalist class came
to control a cosmopolitan commercial and financial network of unprecedented
and unparalleled scale and scope. (Arrighi, 2010: 152)

As opposed to Venice, located at the boundary between the Orient and the
Occident, Genoa had a less strategic position. Still, the Genoans benefit-
ted from being at one of the crossroads of the Mediterranean trade routes.
Liguria was a small region, and in comparison to Tuscany or the Seine
valley, it was not rich, and the city of Genoa was mocked for its provincial-
ism. For instance, in Jacob Burckhardt's ([1860] 1954) magisterial work on
the Italian renaissance culture, an "intellectual bestseller" (albeit *avant la
lattre*) in the second half of the nineteenth century, Genoa is given a most
peripheral role in the modernization of politics, art, and literature:

> Genoa scarcely comes within range of our task, as before the time of Andrea
> Doria it took almost no part in the Renaissance. Indeed, the inhabitants of the
> Riviera was proverbial among Italians for his contempt of all higher culture . . .
> [A]ll who took part in public affairs were at the same time almost exceptionally
> active men of business. (Burckhardt, [1860] 1954: 64)

An intellectual's contempt for the merchant and businessman cannot
overshadow the fact that the Genoans, a seafaring people, were familiar
with "the many cultures that circled the sea" (Epstein, 1996: 162), and that
Genoese culture was mercantile: "[i]ts richest citizens were merchants, and
the business of the city was trade" (Epstein, 1996: 161).

The commerce bred in the city fostered the profession of notary and
several hundred skilled, secular masters of Latin and the law that constituted an educated class that served both the commune and the church
and thus advanced Genoa as a center for finance capital (Epstein, 1996:
161). The first deposit banks had been developed in Tuscany in cities
such as Florence, Siena, and Lucca, and thereafter they spread to Genoa
and Venice (Kindleberger, 2007: 42). Still, Genoa was the site where
the first chartered bank, Casa di San Giogio, was established in 1407
(Kindleberger, 2007: 47). The bank had a sophisticated organization and
governance structure, and Niccolò Machiavelli described the bank as "a
state within the state" (Calomiris and Haber, 2014: 67). The bank's financial competence, political relations, and international connections made it
a trusted business partner for not only merchants but also many European
monarchs. During the Thirty Years' War (1618–1648), for instance, Philip
II of Spain relied on Genoese bankers "to pay his troops and naval forces"
(Calomiris and Haber, 2014: 67).

The Genoese commercial and financial class, suffered from the weak
and conflict-torn Genoese state, always at risk of disintegrating. For

this reason, Genoans were more effective in developing trade routes and commercial centers beyond its immediate geopolitical territory than their Venetian competitors. A poem by Genoa's foremost poet, known under the name "The Anonymous," testifies to this deterritorialized expansion of Genoese finance capital.

E tanti sun li Zenoexi
E per lo mondo si distexi
Che und'eli van o stan
Un'altra Zenoa gè fan

Which translates roughly as:

And so many are the Genoese
And so spread out through the world,
That wherever one goes or stays
There, he makes another Genoa

The political volatility of the Genoese city-state made Genoa the first modern capital lending center. Bruges in Flanders was the first major site for the Genoese expansion, and by the second half of the fifteenth century, Antwerp gained a more prominent role (Kindleberger, 2007: 37). With Genoese finance market actors leading the way, Italian bankers developed branches in Avignon, Barcelona, Bruges, and later in Lyon, Besançon, Antwerp, Amsterdam, London, and Hamburg during the medieval period (Kindleberger, 2007: 43). Not until the period after 1640 did the finance market initiative move north of the Alps, to the Netherlands and Amsterdam (dominating the 1640–1780 period), and thereafter to Great Britain and London (1780–approx. 1920) (North, 1991; North and Weingast, 1989). Arrighi (2010) summarizes his argument, pointing at the differences between Venice and Genoa:

> [T]he Venetian and the Genoese regimes of accumulation developed along divergent trajectories, which in the fifteenth century crystallized into two opposite elementary forms of capitalist organization. Venice came to constitute the prototype of all future forms of "state (monopoly) capitalism," whereas Genoa came to constitute the prototype for all future forms of "cosmopolitan (finance) capitalism." (Arrighi, 2010: 153)

Venice is still today a venerated city of spectacular (but unfortunately decaying and ultimately sinking) beauty, visited by millions of tourists annually. Genoa, having fewer grand sites, remains an easily forgotten but still intriguing city in the northern Mediterranean region, hosting a major port. Today, the city is perhaps best known for its gastronomical innovation *pesto* and for indirectly influencing everyday language (albeit arguably unbeknown to many) as the French name of the city, Gênes, being the root of the word *jeans*, a term derived from the fabric produced in the Ligurian metropole. Still, we all owe to the Genoans the innovation of the international finance system being today the lifeblood of the capitalist regime of accumulation, especially in the period of financialization. As we will see in the following sections, the Genoese innovation of finance capital being disconnected from a particular national state and its sovereign or government, originally serving as the "lender of last resort," has been the leitmotif of the financialization of competitive capitalism during the recent period. As we have moved from "managerial capitalism" to "investor capitalism," finance capital has gradually become detached from actual tangible assets and has taken on a virtual existence on its own as being what regulates virtually a wider set of social and economic relations.

MANAGERIALISM AND FINANCIALIZATION: REGIMES OF VALUE CREATION AND VALUE EXTRACTION

In early 2002, in the period of the Enron scandal (detailed below), the following joke was circulating on Wall Street:

> Enron Venture Capitalism: you have two cows. You sell three of them to your publicly listed company, using letters of credit opened by your brother-in-law at the bank, then execute a debt/equity swap with an associated general offer so that you get all four cows back, with a tax exemption for five cows. The milk rights of the six cows are transferred via an intermediary to a Cayman Island company owned by the majority shareholder who sells the right to all seven cows back to your listed company. The annual report says the company owns eight cows, with an option on one more. (Enron joke, cited in Froud et al., 2004: 886: original emphasis omitted)

Anthropologists and other scholars studying jokes and humor (for example, Billig, 2005; Sanders, 2004) tend to regard jokes as a mechanism that enables one to express what is otherwise complicated to give voice to, what evades representation (for a selection of studies of joking and humor in organizations, see Korczynski, 2011; Westwood and Rhodes, 2007; Terrion and Ashforth, 2002; Grugulis, 2002; Hardy and Philips, 1999). "[J]okes are expressive of the social situation in which they occur," Douglas (1999: 152) proposes. In addition, for Douglas (1999: 155), the joke contrasts again *the rite*; the rite "imposes order and harmony," while the joke "disorganizes" – "Essentially, a joke is anti-rite" (Douglas, 1999: 152). For scholars examining jokes and humor, a joke is "never just a joke," but provides a gateway into the collective's cognition, norm systems, and morality. The "Enron Venture Capitalism" joke is thus indicative of the new regime of value extraction practices that were gradually established in not only the American energy company Enron but in the finance industry at large in the era of financialization.

Tabb (2012) uses the term *social structure of accumulation* (SSA) to denote the integrated institutional structures that dominate during different phases of growth and capital accumulation. An SSA, Tabb (2012: 25) writes, is the creation of "relatively lasting accommodations between capital and labor, the United States [Tabb's nation of analysis] and rest of the world, capital and state, capitalists and other capitalists, and citizens and their governments." Tabb (2012: 26) suggests that an SSA "typically lasts about three decades," and by the beginning of the second decade of the new millennium we are, Tabb 2012: 26) proposes, at the end of the "free-market global neoliberalization." This SSA has the following characteristics: "a free-market ideology, decline in coverage by the social safety net, more individualistic citizen-state relationships, deregulation, harsh capital-labor relations, and reduced financial regulation of banks" (Tabb, 2012: 27). Prior to the free-market global neoliberalization SSA, the "national Keynesian SSA" dominated after the World War II, but this system based on the regulation of markets, the growth of the economy and the welfare state, and a redistribution of economic resources, started to decline in the period from the late 1960s and with notable events such as the US abandonment of the Bretton Woods post-war financial regime and the oil price increase by the Organization of Petroleum Exporting Countries (OPEC) of the early 1970s (Tabb, 2012: 29). While proponents of finance theory and its political implication, the deregulation of finance markets and the accumulation of capital in the finance industry are prone to make claims that finance is the primus motor of the economy as it more effectively allocates resources to high-growth industries, the data speak against such a rosy view of finance: real global growth was 4.9 percent in 1950–1974, 3.4 percent between 1974–1979, and 2.3 percent in the 1990s, Tabb (2012: 31) reports. In addition, as will be detailed in the following chapters, the financialization of the economy is associated with a decline in real wages and the increase of household debt: "[b]etween 1973 and 2007 real wages went down by 4.4 percent, in contrast to the 1947–73 increase of 75 percent" (Tabb, 2012: 39); "[h]ousehold debt was little more than half the gross domestic product in 1981. It was equal to 100 percent of GDP in 2007" (Tabb, 2012: 34). Therefore, rather than thinking of economic growth in the era of financialization as being propelled by the increased understanding of underlying capital accumulation mechanisms in terms of for example, higher human capital investment and more accurate theories about finance, or caused by investment in productive capital such as machinery or tools, the economic growth is primarily based on increased debt, per se being both the cause and effect of financialization (Montgomerie, 2009).

Under all conditions, the shift to the new SSA, the SSA of financialization, brought a new idea of how economic value is both created and extracted, and distributed in the economy and in firms. While mainstream neoclassical economic theory speaks of value creation in terms of a realistic epistemology, as what actually exists as a substance or "foundational value" (Andersson et al., 2010), heterodox economists and social scientists enact economic value as what is being created in the very accounting apparatus that is bound up with firms' operations. In this view, value creation is less a matter of being an *actual event* as it is the outcome from calculative practices and financialized operations that do not rely on common-sense distinctions such as between real and synthetic, actual and virtual, economic values. Say Erturk et al. (2010):

> It does not make sense to think of value as being created or destroyed by a firm. More accurately, value is made material within accounting regulations and conventions which refract current market prices onto the balance sheet of firms and results in trading and holding gains and losses. Under these conditions, value is not only mutable but also relational insofar as it reflects the often volatile exchanges and sentiments within markets over time. (Erturk et al., 2010: 547)

As a consequence, the traditional view that economic growth is a matter of value creation and accompanying activities to extract value from economic activities is gradually displaced by the view that value extraction occurs independently of actual value creation. "[L]ittle attention has been paid to the tension between how value is created and how value is extracted in modern-day capitalism," Lazonick and Mazzucato (2013: 1094) argue, and add that in the era of financialization, there is an "increasing separation between those economic actors who take the risks of investing in innovation and those who reap the rewards from innovation" (Lazonick and Mazzucato, 2013: 1094). In the era of managerial capitalism, capital owners invested in firms that produced goods and services that were traded in the market and the value created derived from both the innovations being produced by such firms, and the difference between aggregated development and production costs per unit and the market price generating a yield. This generic economic model is no longer fully applicable as new modes of value extraction short-circuit the balance between value creation and value extraction. In the era of financialization, the firm is no longer primarily conceived of as a bundle of productive resources that can generate income when used effectively and being skillfully integrated, but instead the firm becomes a portfolio of financial assets that can be used to generate economic value. In this new regime, the deregulation of the financial markets have been the key to the new ways of extracting additional value out of what was previously seen as for example, a production unit. Such deregulatory activities are in turn justified and made legitimate by the advancement of neoclassical finance theory that enacted markets as superior mechanisms for pricing and allocating resources. This is particularly true for finance markets operating on liquid assets such as currencies, stocks, and derivate instruments. However, as the events of 2008 revealed, many newly developed finance assets such as collateralized debt obligations (CDOs) (Bluhm and Wagner, 2011) and mortgage-backed securities (MBSs) (McConnell and Buser, 2011) were substantially less liquid than assumed in bear markets and in situations where the capitalization of finance institutions (that is, risk-taking) are at an extreme level. Regardless of these theoretical inconsistencies, the era of financialization is determined by the ability of certain groups to advance its positions regarding their share of the economic value extracted from firms: "[f]inancial deregulation and the spread of stock-related pay have enabled investors (especially of private equity) and top corporate executives to secure ownership of assets just before major innovation-related gains are capitalized into them," Lazonick and Mazzucato (2013: 1106) argue. Financialization is thus strongly correlated with the growth of economic inequality, ultimately based on institutional changes: "[a] set of socially devised institutions related to corporate governance, stock markets, and income taxation have permitted this concentration of value extraction in a few hands" (Lazonick and Mazzucato, 2013: 1108).

The exemplary case *par excellence* of how value creation and value extraction diverges in the era of financialization is the Texas energy company Enron. The literature examining the case of Enron is enormous (see for example, Bratton and Levitin, 2013; Ailon, 2012; Tourish and Vatcha, 2005; Craig and Amernic, 2004; Cullinan, 2004; Watkins, 2003; Seeger and Ulmer, 2003) and it is beyond the scope of this book to once again reiterate how one of the most admired and praised companies of the 1990s "new economy" suddenly appeared to be a fraud, leaving many business school professors, experts, and media pundits in the embarrassing situation of not having been able to anticipate how far the Enron executives and board of directors had stretched their moral standards. Enron's innovation was the "the financialization of energy," Froud et al. (2004: 889) write. The somewhat dull energy market was here coupled with new financial innovations and new accounting procedures enabling value creation and value extraction at a new level in the industry. In the period from the mid-1990s to its bankruptcy in 2002, Enron managed to grow at a spectacular pace: "Enron tripled sales revenues in 3 years from US$9 to US$31 billion between 1995 and 1998 and then tripled sales revenues again from US$31 to US$100 billion from 1998 to 2000" (Froud et al., 2004: 891). The so-called *new economy*, propelled by the commercialization and development of information media and the Internet, was characterized, Froud et al. (2004: 892) suggest, by an increased separation between technological innovations on the one hand, and turnover growth and rising stock prices on the other. In the period 1995 to the information technology bubble burst in 2000 – after the NASDAC index peaked at 5,060 in March 2000, by midsummer the index stood at 3,600 and finally bottomed at less than 1,200, losing more than three-fourths of its value (Baker, 2013: 52) – the firm was increasingly enacted as the site of value creation not in terms of actual accomplishments but in terms of the economic value that could be extracted from the yet-to-come innovations. As a consequence, the by now customary divergence between substantial value and market values, and the growth in intangible assets on the firms' balance sheets was justified on basis of *expectations*. In the case of Enron, combining energy industry and financial and service industry features, the value extracted very much benefited a small group of executives and directors:

> In 2000, US$430 million was paid out in annual bonuses, and a further US$320 million was paid to 65 executives under the Performance Unit Plan . . . In all, US$750 million was paid out in cash bonuses when the company's net income for the year was US$975 billion and the Senate Sub Committee was suitably critical of the board for allowing management to enrich itself with "lavish" bonuses which were not in the shareholders' interest. (Froud et al., 2004: 897)

When Enron eventually proved to use inadequate market reporting and accounting procedures, not only was Enron declared bankrupt, but also Enron's principal accounting firm, Anderson, did not survive the scandal. The case of Enron was the first major scandal that was followed by a number of smaller but still significant cases (for example, WorldCom) of how value creation and value extraction has been cut loose from underlying actual activities and assets in the firm, and where new advanced forms of financial engineering were used to enrich certain stakeholders (White, 2010; Stiglitz, 2009; Sikka, 2009). By the end of the day, the financialization of the economy and companies such as Enron is indicative of the shift in the institutional and regulatory setting being justified on the basis of finance theory and neoclassical economic theory, and its axiomatic belief in the market as being more efficient in pricing assets than any other mechanism. As will be discussed in the forthcoming chapters, there is quite substantial evidence that the new regime of value creation, based on intangibles and synthetic financial assets including derivatives, and value extraction, benefiting a smaller group of capital owners, in many ways have destabilized the economy. After 1980, the number of financial bubbles, collapses, and frauds has grown substantially (Blinder, 2013; Gorton, 2010; Black, 2005), partly because of the time it takes to implement new regulatory frameworks (Abdelal, 2007; Singer, 2007) but also because the very idea of value creation and value extraction has changed. These institutional changes will be detailed in this volume.

OUTLINE OF THE BOOK

This book is composed of this introduction, two parts including two and three chapters respectively, and one final summary chapter. In the first part of the book, Chapter 2 introduces the concept of financialization and Chapter 3 discusses the short-, mid-, and long-term consequences of the new financialized economic regime. The second part of the book addresses firm-level consequences, including corporate governance practices (Chapter 4), new regimes of management control based on the use of external auditing and rating services (Chapter 5), and the changes in workplace control and economic compensation (Chapter 6). In the final chapter, some theoretical implications are discussed and consequences for managerial practice will also be addressed.

PART I

The great financialization

2. What is financialization?

In this chapter, the concept of financialization will be critically examined and related to a variety of changes in the environment of the firm including macroeconomic changes during the 1970s, the shift in policy on economic and regulatory issues, the growth of new academic disciplines including finance theory as a special branch of neoclassical economic theory, and the growth of a neoconservative and neoliberal ideology in the Anglo-American world. All these changes suggest that financialization is overdetermined by a series of interrelated events and changes whose aggregate consequences could not really be foreseen by any actor being part of the policy-making and decision-making leading to today's financialized economy. Therefore, when examining the financialization of the economy, there is not much room for conspiracy theories (possibly appealing to left-leaning analysts and commentators), nor for Hegelian-style acclaims of the irresistible advancement of an increasingly rational society based on reason, clarity and *Vernuft* (possibly favored by right-leaning analysts and commentators), but rather the explanation for the financialization of the economy is to be sought in the various down-to-earth attempts to handle day-to-day matters and concerns, taken together leading to new possibilities but also to new problems and what economists speak of as externalities (Krippner, 2011). Such a view of history, pointing at the long-term effects, the thickness and ambiguities of history-making, what the Prussian General Carl von Clausewitz referred to as *Nebel des Krieges*, the "fog of war," and the accompanying difficulties involved when entangling historical conditions in *ex post facto* analyses, opens up for a more complex narrative than the more coherent neoclassical economic theory explanation. In the neoclassical economic framework, a few basic mechanisms and principles are capable of comprehending everything under the sun – for example, in the case of speaking of "effective human capital investments in finance training" to explain the unprecedented growth of the finance industry – or a more critical account speaking about the deregulation of the first national and then global finance markets as being the elites' hijacking of political and regulatory bodies (such theories fail to explain why a broad variety of governments on various points at the political scale have favored finance market deregulations). Instead, like everything human, the construction of finance markets is the outcome of a blend of political action, human collaboration, controversies and debates, ideological framing of problems and solutions (not always neatly coordinated in time and space), and a variety of other factors that determine the present economic system, including various calculative practices, tools, and technologies put to work (Williams, 2013; MacKenzie, 2012, 2006, 2004; Pryke, 2010; Vollmer et al., 2009; Preda, 2009a, 2009b; Zaloom, 2003; Willman et al., 2001). Students of financialization should therefore seek to discern a variety of traces and pathways that intersect the finance market to be able to grasp its full institutional and practical complexity; and they should also be more concerned regarding the question of whether the present regime of financialization is beneficial for all of us or if it produces negative effects and externalities. That is, the outcome from a study of financialization is therefore not so much a matter of creating a tribune where various groups and individuals are to be judged but more of a forward-oriented analysis aimed at identifying challenges for the future. Financialization is not of necessity problematic in its essence, but there may be consequences of financialization that are less appealing, including the economic inequalities that co-evolve with the growth of financial activities, or the intense competition between individuals caused by financialized performance-reward systems. The student of financialization in short needs to ask: *What is financialization?* and *What are the implications for the firm?*

ON FINANCIALIZATION

The Marxist economist Rudolf Hilferding spoke of the dominance of finance capital in the advanced capitalist economy already before World War I, and treated money *qua* capital as a commodity that *per se* embodies value while at the same time being differentiated from all other commodities "by being the equivalent of all of them and thus expressing their value" (Hilferding, [1910] 1981: 33). Liberals such as the lawyer Louis D. Brandeis ([1914] 1967), subscribing to other analytical frameworks and addressing more practical issues, were equally concerned about the "money trusts," the widespread use of interlocking board membership across finance institutions and corporations, and oligarchic tendencies in American capitalism in the period:

> The dominant element in our financial oligarchy is the investment banker. Associated banks, trust companies and insurance companies are his tools.

Controlled railroads, public service and industrial corporations financial are his subjects. Though properly middleman, these bankers bestride as masters of America's business world, so that practically no large enterprise can be undertaken successfully without their participation of approval. (Brandeis, [1914] 1967: 3)

The capacity of money to influence and shape economic and social relations was thoroughly examined by Hilferding's and Brandeis' contemporary, the social theorist George Simmel in his classic work *The Philosophy of Money* (Simmel, [1900] 1978). In the interwar period, not the least characterized by dramatic economic events such as the hyperinflation of the Weimar Republic in the 1920s, and the Wall Street Crash of 1929 and the Great Depression, the role of money supply, interest rates, and economic stimulus to stabilize the economy were attended to and examined by economists. In the post-World War II period, the path-breaking and pragmatic Keynesian economic theories, advanced in *The General Theory of Employment, Interest and Money* (Keynes, 1953), served as the dominant theoretical framework for policy-making and the institutional build-up in the new high-growth capitalist Western economies. Not until the 1970s would the Keynesian framework prove to be incapable of handling all sorts of economic challenges, arguably, as the economist Michał Kalecki (1942) predicted (a proposition also advanced by the Italian Marxist theorist Antonio Gramsci in his essay "Americanism and Fordism," written in the 1929–1930 period), on the basis of declining profit levels in industry. To cut a long story short, the decline of the Keynesian framework paved the way for the financialization of the economy, a term that for example, Hilferding ([1910] 1981) may have been comfortable using.

Krippner (2005: 174) defines financialization as "a pattern of accumulation in which profits accrue primarily through financial channels rather than trade and commodity production." Similarly, Orhangazi (2008: 863) addresses financialization as "[t]he increase in the size and significance of financial markets and financial institutions in the modern macroeconomy." Onaran et al. (2011) add that financialization denotes many different occurrences, conditions, new policies, and practices, on societal, corporate, and household levels:

> The notion of financialization covers a wide range of phenomena: the deregulation of the financial sector and the proliferation of new financial instruments, the increase in household debt, the development of the originate-and-distribute model of banking, the emergence of institutional investors as major players on financial markets, the boom (and bust) in asset markets, shareholder value orientation and changes in corporate governance (of non-financial business), and a spectacular rise of income in the financial sector and of financial investments. (Onaran et al., 2011: 637)

This bewildering variety of phenomena covered by the concept of financialization makes it a contested and complicated analytical term. Practically speaking, financialization denotes a change in the "patterns of accumulation" including a series of new policies, regulatory changes, and institutional shifts, including:

> [S]hifts in central bank policy toward a near-exclusive focus on price stability, large increases in financial flows for households both internally and in domestic financial markets, improved financing for households and elements of consumption and elements of consumption/credit driven growth, changes in corporate governance and attempts to align managerial incentives with shareholder interest via stock option plans, and an increased influence of financial institutions and institutional investors. (Skott and Ryoo, 2008: 827)

As Martin (2002: 8) aptly remarks, in the literature, financialization "[s]tands simultaneously as subject and object of analysis – something to be explained and a way of making sense out of what is going on around us." This implies that it is complicated to develop and maintain an analytical framework and vocabulary that is independent of the changes occurring during more than three decades, and consequently, Martin (2002: 11) argues, "economic fundamentals – measurement of growth, inflation, productivity unemployment, consumer confidence, money supply – become flustered under the financial gaze." Thus financialization cannot be understood as a "discrete process" but must be "traced by its rhizomatic manifestations throughout social and cultural life," Haiven (2014: 5) adds. Block (2014) also stresses the integration and normalization of financial issues in everyday life:

> Over the last century, everyday life in the developed societies has been transformed by a process of financialization. Consumption of goods, services, housing, and education now critically depend on access to credit. The consolidation of retirement as a predictable life course event now nearly involves everybody in a financialized process of everything – either through private saving or private programs or a combination of the two – claims on resources for years when they will not receive income from work. (Block, 2014: 4)

Critical theorists in the Gramscian tradition would claim that financialization is hegemonic, but Martin (2002: 11) advances an alternative view and suggests that "as a new package of principles of political economy, financialization may not have been given due time to ripen intellectually before it as taken out of the box." That is, rather than representing a set of principles, theories, and practices that have been widely recognized and adopted by social actors and institutions, financialization is instead the outcome from entrepreneurial and enterprising activities conducted by a new class of professional finance industry actors and their allies favoring free-market capitalism over Keynesian or post-Keynesian regulated economies. Deeg (2009) here speaks of financialization as a "self-reinforcing process" to some extent being out of the control of policy-makers and regulatory agencies:

> [F]inancialization began with the removal of capital controls and early moves to deregulate markets in the US and Europe in the late 1970s but especially 1980s. To considerable degree, financialization becomes a self-reinforcing process as market actors used new freedoms to expand financial markets and create new financial product markets. As markets expanded, new financial actors such as institutional investors, hedge and private equity funds emerged that further reinforced financialization. (Deeg, 2009: 554)

In a way, financialization, despite its enormous influence on the economy and society for more than three decades, is still in its infancy.

Traditionally, economic value derives from either individuals producing commodities or offering services (for example, health care services), or through the distribution channels that are developed. The first major economic centers in medieval Europe were dominated by merchant classes and their trade over large distances. In the era of financialization, the dominance of production and distribution is broken and the production of economic wealth is primarily taking place within the very circulation of capital per se. Economic value is extracted and generated within the new circuits of capital. Krippner (2005: 176) here makes the key distinction between an "activity-centered view" (for example, the talk about the "post-industrial society" and the decline of for example, manufacturing in the Western world), and an "accumulation-centered view" emphasizing "where profits are generated in the economy." This shifts the focus from more general and overarching statements regarding the nature of economic value and stresses the very activities that serve to secure and reproduce economic rents. Krippner (2005: 179) agrees that the line of demarcation between financial and non-financial sectors of the economy is "ambiguous," but still argues it is important to maintain such an analytical distinction when examining how economic wealth is generated in new circuits and domains. Moreover, Krippner (2005: 181) points at four different meanings of financialization in the literature:

- The use of shareholder value corporate governance, that is, a specific regime of managerial control in organizations aimed at reducing the so-called agency costs in all governance.
- The dominance of capital-markets over bank-based finance, denoting an institutional and industry-based change from traditional

   companies to a new category of enter-prising professional capital
   firms operating on the basis of new procedures and standards.
● The increased power of the *rentier* class, being more of a social
   theory of the consequences of financialization where for instance
   Marxist economists have stressed the role of capital-owning classes
   in different phases of the economy.
● The "explosion of financial trading associated with the proliferation
   of new financial instruments" (Krippner, 2005: 181), that is, the
   development of what Crotty (2009) speaks of as the "new financial
   architecture," the development of a series of new products and
   instruments enabling further value extraction and (in theory) a more
   effective sharing of risks.

As indicated above, these four views, representing individual institutional
arrangements and conditions, are individual modalities of the same underlying condition, that of the finance markets today playing an increasingly larger role in regulating non-financial firms and institutions and in
extracting economic value from non-financial activities. Krippner (2005:
199) thus concludes that her central empirical claim is that "accumulation is now occurring increasingly through financial channels." In a more
recent publication, Krippner (2011: 3) asserts that "there is little question
that the US economy has experienced a remarkable turn towards financial activities in recent years." Krippner (2005: 199) continues: "[d]uring
the 1980s and 1990s, the ratio of portfolio income to corporate cash flow
ranges between approximately three and five times the levels characteristic of the 1950s and 1960s. The ratio of financial to non-financial profit
behaves similarly." In addition, during the last three decades, there has
been a development of what Tabb (2012) refers to as the "second banking
system" that today plays a key role in accumulating the economic value in
for example, the US economy:

> The non-bank financial system and the products they buy and sell are widely
> seen as a second banking system that grew apart from, but not unconnected to
> the older financial system. The shadow banking system includes hedge funds,
> private equity groups, money market funds, and pension funds, among others,
> and features sources involving the use and reuse of collateral posted with banks
> and other to finance transactions that show up as non-balance-sheet funding.
> (Tabb, 2012: 93)

By the eve of the financial collapse of 2008, the shadow banking system
stood at US$25 trillion, "more than twice the size of the traditional
banking system" (Martin, 2014: 246). In Europe, the same figure was
9.5 trillion euros. This second banking system tended to marginalize

traditional financial institutions based on certain professional practices and norms: "[i]n 1977 commercial banks in the United States held 56 percent of all financial assets, thirty-two years later, the banks' share had fallen to just 20 percent of total assets" (Tabb, 2012: 96). Moreover, "[w]hile half a century earlier three-quarters of finance sector debt was on the books of banks, savings and loans [institutions], and finance companies, by 2008 these traditional financial institutions were responsible for only 18 percent of the total" (Tabb, 2012: 40). These changes in the finance industry and the banking sector was dependent on new pro-business policies in Washington and the rise of the neoconservative and neoliberal political shift in for example, the US and the UK in the 1980s. Martin (2002: 28) points at increased proportions of new laws and regulations for the finance industry during the Clinton years of the 1990s, the take-off period for the unprecedented accumulation of economic value in the finance sector in the new millennium: in the period 1979–1992, "just over 600 laws were passed per session" in the seven sessions of Congress, whereof "34 pertained specifically to finance." During the Clinton years (1993–2000), the number of new laws fell to 293 whereof "on average 94 finance laws were passed" increasing from around 5 percent to 25 percent of all legislation. Also Democratic presidents and Labour governments in the UK endorsed and encouraged the expansion of the finance industry and the finance market.

In order to increase the economic value creation and value extraction, the second banking system developed a new set of financial instruments and assets that leveraged both the yield and the risk and that effectively financialized a variety of economic assets. These new innovations included the use of securitized assets: "[s]ecuritized assets, many originating in the traditional banking system, were important to the explosion of finance. In 2006 banks issued $1.8 trillion in securities backed by mortgages, credit cards, auto loans, and other debt. More than half of the credit card and student loans in the country were securitized" (Tabb, 2012: 96).

Securitization allowed the new financial institutions to "increase their asset velocity through leverage," and to "reuse their capital many times over by moving assets off their balance sheets" (Tabb, 2012: 97). In other words, securities brought long-term contracts (at times lasting for 30 or 50 years) such as mortgage loans back into the circulation of capital and therefore further adding to the economic growth. "Between 1980 and 2007 derivate contracts of all kinds expanded form $1 trillion globally to $600 trillion," Tabb (2012: 100) adds. The immediate effect was an increased accumulation of economic value in the new financial institutions: in 2004, the finance sector accounted for 40 percent of all "domestic corporate profit"; in 1964, it was 2 percent (Tabb, 2012: 42). While this remarkable and often quite swift expansion and multiplication of the capital base through derivate instruments and securities may seem dangerous from a common-sense view, the new finance theory, and its spokesman, the economist, Tabb (2012: 100) say, lend credence to the view that "these were safe instruments." Unfortunately, what worked in theory fell short in practice, many of the leveraged finance market actors discovered in the 2007–2008 period: "[b]y spring 2010, 93 percent of subprime mortgage-backed securities issued in 2006 were downgraded to junk status" (Tabb, 2012: 138).

As a consequence of these institutional and regulatory changes, firms today make their profits not so much on the basis of their ability to produce goods and services but through the financial operations that can be associated with these activities. "[F]igures demonstrate that there has been a steady rise in the ratio of financial assets of NFCs [non-financial corporations], which was accompanied by a raise in their financial income," Orhangazi (2008: 864) reports. In 2004, General Motors announced that "66% of its $1.3 billion quarterly profits came from GMAC [GM's financial services]," and a day before, Ford Motor Company declared "a loss in its automotive operation," fortunately mediated by a "$1.7 billion in net income, mostly from its financial operations" (Lin and Tomaskovic-Devey, 2013: 1293). Deeg (2009) lists five significant changes in firm governance that derive from the financialization of the economy:

> First, firms are no longer restricted (by either regulation or market structure) in their financing options to domestic markets; second, there is a general shift in firm financing patterns from bank to market and self-finance; third, firms in this system are increasingly subject to a common set of rules of financial transparency and financial practices; fourth, firms in this system are subject to increasingly common corporate governance rules and practices, such as shareholder value, minority shareholder protection, etc.; fifth, firm strategies and restructuring are increasingly subject to influence outside of firm management or corporate insiders, especially by financial market actors (notably institutional investors, hedge and equity funds), which leads to a more active market for corporate control and restructuring via takeovers, mergers and acquisitions. (Deeg, 2009: 554–7)

During more than three decades, the institutions of managerial capitalism have been displaced by the new institutional framework of investor capitalism, emphasizing the central role of finance markets and finance industry actors, leading to an entirely new understanding of the firm.

Drivers of Financialization

The question then is how the concept of financialization came about and what are the macroeconomic changes, the institutional shifts, and political agendas that have collectively produced this new economic regime granting so much authority to the abstract concept of finance capital? While for example, Krippner (2011) takes a moderate view of financialization, treating it by and large as the outcome from uncoordinated action with unintended consequences; other commentators take a more politicized view. Palley (2013) and Levitt (2013a) advocate the view that financialization is the foremost effect of neoliberalism, the political and economic doctrine that advanced free (that is, unregulated) markets as the most efficient way to organize economic transactions and exchanges. Palley (2013: 5) argues that "neoliberalism is an ideology of elite interests, and it serves to shift economic power and income from labor to capital," and consequently financialization "reinforces this shift and further changes the redistribution of income at a more disaggregated level by increasing the managers' share of the wage bill, increasing the share of interest income, and increasing the financial sector's share of profit income" (Palley, 2013: 5). The departure from the Keynesian doctrine and the embracing of free-market solutions to economic challenges leads to a number of new political priorities, including: (1) the "abandonment of the commitment to full employment, which was replaced by a focus on low inflation," and (2) "severing the link between wages and productivity growth" (Palley, 2013: 6). In this new, neoliberal economic "growth model," Palley (2013: 6) argues, "credit and asset price inflation" replace "wage growth" as the engines of demand growth. This claim is supported by empirical evidence pointing at the increase in economic inequality, the rise of household debt, and the slower rate of capital accumulation in the era of financialization. Orhangazi (2008: 883) provides data for the 1973–2003 period and suggests that the findings demonstrate "a negative relationship between financialization and capital accumulation, especially for large firms." In addition, the data support the view that financialization has negative implications for "firm investment behavior" (Orhangazi, 2008: 883).

For Marxist theorists, the connection between financialization and neoliberalism, or more specifically, the economic doctrines developed by a set of quite heterogeneous economists including Friedrich von Hayek and later Chicago economists such as Milton Friedman and George Stigler, sharing a commitment to unregulated markets as being effective "spontaneous orders" (in Hayek's phrasing), is of long pedigree, stretching back to Rudolf von Hilferding's ([1910] 1981) *Finance Capital.* For Quiggin (2010: 21), Hayek and his Austrian colleague Ludwig von Mises "were dogmatic supporters of laissez-faire," and over the years Hayek managed to establish an intellectual and political community sharing his view of the need to counteract the regulated and state-controlled economy (Burgin, 2012; Jones, 2012). In these free-market doctrines, the finance markets play a pivotal role for Hayek, Sotiropoulos et al. (2013: 102, original emphasis omitted) suggest: "Hayek's perspective renders capital markets central to the organization of capitalism as a system of exploitation. Finance has a crucial role in disciplining economic behaviour according to the inner norms of the system." In other words, in this Marxist view, "the logic of capital" operates through not so much its ability to "forecast the future" – if that would be the case, we would not have seen the sharply increased amount of bubbles and economic crises as have been reported over the last three decades (see for example, Mirowski, 2013; Gorton, 2010; Stiglitz, 2010; Black, 2005) – as it aims to "discipline the present" (Sotiropoulos et al., 2013: 102, original emphasis omitted). While Marxist explanations easily overate the ability of key actors to orchestrate and direct social and economic systems (Krippner, 2011), free-market protagonists' enactment of the finance market as a mechanism disciplining *all other* markets is an interesting hypothesis that has also been translated into for instance shareholder value programs and similar governance principles, where finance market actors are inscribed with certain rationalities allegedly beneficial for all other economic actors.

In the following, three interrelated, yet to some extent individual changes in the political and economic landscape will be examined to further explore the conditions under which free-market protagonists could advance their positions and doctrines. First, macroeconomic changes in the 1970s and 1980s will be examined. Second, the growth of a new finance theory framework serving to justify the belief in the market as an efficient mechanism for allocating resources and coordinating economic action is addressed. Third and finally, the shift in the political landscape in the 1970s and the decline of the Keynesian welfare state policy are covered, paying specific attention to the two leading countries for the neoconservative and neoliberal "revolution," the UK and the US.

MACROECONOMIC CONDITIONS: 1980s' CAPITAL INFLOW AND ITS CONSEQUENCES

In the 1970s, the Western economies ran out of steam as the profit in industry declined when the cost of energy increased sharply during the two oil crises. In the UK, there were harsh conflicts between the government and the trade unions, increasingly radically claiming a greater share of the fruits of their labor. Already in the mid-1960s, the profit rates started to decline in American industry: "[f]rom 1965 to 1973, the profit rate in manufacturing fell by nearly 41 percent while that of the private business sector fell by 30 percent" (Van Arnum and Naples, 2013: 1160). The economic decline in the manufacturing industry led to a bear market in the US that in fact was worse than during the depression: "[t]he American stock market lost nearly half of its value between 1972 and the end of 1974" Stein (2011: 102) writes. In order to handle the economic downturn, leading to both high unemployment and soaring inflation – a new phenomenon referred to as *stagflation* – advocates of monetarist policies, proposing that the supply of money and high-interest rates should curb inflation, gained influence as the Keynesian economic policies that had dominated in the post-World War II period lost much of its credibility and prestige. Addressing a television audience on 12 August, 1975, US President Gerald Ford announced that, "[i]nflation is our domestic public enemy No. 1" (cited in Stein, 2011: 112). Ford's successor, President Jimmy Carter inherited the inflation problem and named Paul Volcker, the new chairman of the Federal Reserve, to handle it. Volcker embarked on a new monetarist, high-interest policy – leading to what is referred to as the "Volcker shock" – that he himself did not really believe in the theoretical (that is, monetarist) level, but that had the merit of stabilizing the economy as inflation went down.[1] "Volcker's announced plan to keep interest rates high until inflation was eliminated expedited capital inflows, and the dollar rose dramatically throughout the mid-1980s," Van Arnum and Naples (2013: 1161) write. As a consequence, from the low-inflation policy, interest rates rose and financial profitability increased: "[n]ot surprisingly, domestic firms began shifting from expanding production capacity to investing in financial assets" (Van Arnum and Naples, 2013: 1160). Unfortunately, Volcker's policy did not work as intended, and it took more than two years to reduce the inflation level to below the 4 percent level in 1982. But the price to be paid for this defeat was substantial: during 1982, GDP fell 2.2 percent and the unemployment rates were the highest since the Great Depression (Stein, 2011: 265). This policy, Stein (2011: 237) claims, "injured the economy." By limiting the money growth in the economy, wage increase was made impossible and the unemployment rates grew. The Fed assumed that once inflation was reduced, the economy was expected to return to its previous equilibrium. That would not be the case. Perhaps unintendedly, the new Fed monetary policy was

---

[1] According to Stein (2011: 228), "Most Fed officials believed the monetarist were simplistic, calling them 'the chiropractors of modern economics.'"

simultaneously an "anti-labor policy" (Van Arnum and Naples, 2013: 1162) as manufacturing jobs were eliminated (Smil, 2013; Bluestone and Harrison, 1982). The new Reagan Administration was not very concerned about the decline of the manufacturing industry:

> The high interest rates yielded a high dollar, which priced U.S. manufacturing out of the world markets. Instead of fingering the dollar, pundits questioned U.S. industry's ability to compete with foreign companies. But unlike government and the service sectors, productivity in manufacturing increased over 3 percent in 1984 and 1985. The expensive dollar aborted an industrial renaissance. The dollar's overall value rose 63 percent from 1980 to March 1985 – the equivalent of taxing U.S. exports by 63 percent and providing U.S. import with an equivalent subsidy. (Stein, 2011: 269)

Rather than seeking to restore the competitiveness of the manufacturing industry, there were other industries like the finance industry that advanced their positions. In addition to changes in the American economic policy, there was also a shift in the global capital flows. The high-interest rates in the US and high-overseas savings in export-oriented countries such as Japan but also significant savings in the US created a supply of capital in the American economy. For instance, the American Savings and Loan Associations' financial assets equaled $21 billion in 1949, $138 billion in 1965, and $249 billion in 1979 (all in 1967 constant dollars). Open-end mutual funds equaled $46 billion in 1978. Only in the relatively short period between 1978 and 1983, mutual funds "expanded over fivefold to $291.5 billion" (Stearns and Allan, 1996: 704). Money market mutual funds equaled $2.4 billion in 1974 (when they originated) but grew to $10.8 billion in 1978 (Stearns and Allan, 1996: 704). Over the post-World War II period, internal savings in the US accumulated a stock of capital, and when the new Reagan Administration announced its new laissez-faire policy, downplaying the role of governmental regulation, new possibilities for financial operations opened up:

> By promulgating a strong laissez-faire ideology, the state signaled to the business community that it intended to limit its role in the economy. By changing how antitrust laws would be enforced, it specifically disturbed the institutional arrangements set up to monitor and limit mergers. In such a normative vacuum innovations are likely to occur. (Stearns and Allan, 1996: 706)

For instance, a new category of finance industry professionals realized that they could exploit the lowly rated stock-listed American companies, now being large-scale conglomerates as executives and directors had sought to spread the risks by horizontal diversification. The new relaxed regulatory control of the finance market permitted these new finance industry professionals to issue junk bonds that in turn financed their acquisitions of corporations: "[b]etween 1983 and 1989, nonfinancial corporations issued $160 billion of junk bonds to the public. The sum accounted for more than 35 percent of total public bonds offerings. About two-thirds of these issues were associated with restructurings (i.e., leveraged-buyouts and acquisitions)" (Stearns and Allan, 1996: 706).

The leveraged buyout wave that swept through the American economy in the mid-1980s was thus a new form of advanced finance engineering wherein underpriced listed companies were bought and sold off piece by piece. The use of junk bonds was one of the first new financial instruments in the new era of financialization.

In addition to the internal savings, the high-interest rate, the overrated dollar, and the American export deficit, high-overseas savings in, for example, Asia, made capital flow into the American economy in early 1980s. The inflow of capital was $85 billion in 1983, $103 billion in 1984, $129 billion in 1985, and $221 billion in 1986 (Krippner, 2010: 157). The Reagan Administration found itself in a situation where it could take advantage of an international stock of capital, and the inflow of savings financed the substantial budgets deficits during the Reagan presidency. Data from the *1989 Economic Report of the Presidents* provides the following budget deficits: $208 billion in 1983, $185 billion in 1984, $212 billion in 1985, and $221 billion in 1986 (Krippner, 2010: 169). The inflow of capital thus enabled the Reagan Administration to have the cake and eat it too: budget deficits and increased military spending became two defining marks of the Reagan era's economic policy. In the 1980s, the American economy was thus cash-rich and in combination with reduced regulatory control, new laissez-faire policies, and the emergence of the new class of finance industry actors, the era of financialization could take off. However, prior to such changes, there were important theoretical and political footwork being conducted in for example, the universities and political quarters.

THE NEW FINANCE THEORY

"We are all Keynesians now," President Richard M. Nixon declared in the early 1970s (Jones, 2012: 221). Nixon left office in disgrace but in hindsight his presidency was much more radical than any Democratic president to come would be (Crotty, 2012: 83). This famous statement by a Republican, pro-business president, was perhaps the zenith of the Keynesian economic program that dominated in the post-World War II period. Keynes' economic theory was a pragmatic and action-oriented program to create economic growth on the basis of economic stimulation, and consequently Keynesianism was associated with the welfare state and its institutions. Similar to the neoliberal economic policies being in vogue in the 1990s and the new millennium, Keynesianism in various forms was enacted by governments both to the left and to the right.

In 1947, the Austrian economist Friedrich von Hayek had founded the Mont Pèlerin Society (MPS), an economic and political organization aimed at promoting economic freedom and liberalism. Hayek was one of Keynes' principal opponents and he had published a much-debated work during the end of World War II, *The Road to Serfdom*, wherein he denounced all kinds of collectivist solutions to economic problems. In contrast to Keynes, justifying the state as the regulator of the economy, Hayek had a firm belief in the market as being the most efficient mechanism for allocating resources and for the circulation of information. Hayek, born in Austria and being part of the so-called Austrian School of Economics that included economists such as Eugen Bahm-Böwerk, Ludwig von Mises, and Joseph Schumpeter, managed to attract a variety of intellectuals to the MPS including the Austrian philosopher of science Karl Popper, to a group that was supposed to serve as a forum for the exchange of ideas and joint thinking. As numerous commentators have remarked, MPS members would, from the mid-1970s, claim a series of Nobel Prizes in economics sciences, beginning with the Hayek himself in 1974, but during the period until the late 1960s, the MPS members were widely treated as conservative extremists and the MPS was essentially a "club of losers" (Peck, 2010: 40). In what Kotz (2013: 397) refers to as "The Golden Age of Capitalism," the 1948–1973 period, Hayek's warning that the growth of the welfare state would lead to "serfdom" seemed utterly unsupported by empirical evidence or even absurd as the economy grew at an unprecedented rate and the economic benefits derived from such accomplishments were more evenly distributed than ever before: "[t]he free-market theorists' warnings of economic disaster should government interfere in the market seemed misplaced, and the old free-market theory appeared to be permanently consigned to the proverbial dustbin of outmoded ideas" (Kotz, 2013: 397).

However, the MPS included not only European intellectuals to the center-right wing but also American libertarian economists such as Milton Friedman, Aaron Director, and George Stigler, all at the University of Chicago. The Austrian School of Economics was based on reasoning and argumentation and not so much on a mathematization of economic theory, but the Chicago economists' favored a "positive economic theory" and Friedman developed a monetarist economic theory that strongly questioned the Keynesian explanations of for example, the Depression in the 1930s. Rather than being the outcome from a decline in demand as suggested by Keynes, Friedman proposed a monetary explanation, suggesting that the shortage of capital was the principal driver of the Depression. Mainstream economists were still hard to convince, and monetarism has never been truly adopted by what at times are called "saltwater economists," economists working in formerly Keynesian milieux in universities such as the Massachusetts Institute of Technology (MIT), Yale, Harvard, and Princeton. Chicago monetarism still became part of what was known as *supply-side economics* during the Thatcher Government and Reagan Administration.

A common explanation for the decline of the credibility of Keynesianism – today, the term post-Keynesianism is widespread in economics quarters, indicating the crisis of the theory in the 1970s – was the new condition of stagflation, inflation plus high unemployment, but commentators such as Mirowski (2005: 86) suggests that there were a number of political and economic conditions that contributed to the new situation where supply-side economics could be advanced. In Mirowski's account, the neoliberal, Hayekian critique of government qua central planner not always necessarily doing good and acting wisely, struck a chord among certain voters, and the neoconservative revolution of the Reagan era was very much based on the popular narrative of East-coast liberals squandering hard-earned tax money piped into Washington from the American heartland to finance various questionable liberal projects. As Mirowski (2005: 86) notices, one "standard complaint" about Keynesianism is that it "looked at the government as if it were totally benevolent and it would engage in fiscal and monetary policy for the good of all, with no thought as to its own persistence and viability." This assumption became a principal target for neoliberal intellectuals, questioning such assumptions of benevolence. In contrast, neoconservatives and supply-siders advocated tax cuts, reduced public spending, and deregulation as key political objectives. In order to justify high degrees of public spending in the Reagan years, the supply-side economics view postulated that tax cuts would lead to increased economic growth as the money being released from public spending would create a "virtuous spiral" in the economy, wherein more tax money would be collected on a broader basis. When critics objected that tax cuts for the richest income groups would undermine the state and federal budgets, supply-siders responded that this money would "trickle down" the economic system and benefit not just a few groups but virtually everyone. "*Supply side economics* argued that reducing taxes can unleash enormous gains in economic efficiency," Taylor (2010: 222, original emphasis) summarizes. The so-called Laffer curve (named after Reagan's economic adviser Arthur Laffer) predicted a relationship between tax cuts

The financialization of the firm

and economic growth, and therefore supply-siders were convinced that "[c]utting taxes would get rid of the fiscal deficit and . . . [and] give a big boost to economic growth" (Taylor, 2010: 250–251). In addition, in this new regime, tax cuts should preferably be complemented by deregulation of markets to enable further economic activities: "[s]upply-side economics suggested that the most important obstacle to economic growth reflected institutional features of markets that interfered with incentives to invest rather than insufficient demand, as under the Keynesian paradigm" (Krippner, 2010: 155).

In addition to the political changes and the new economic policy, there had been a development of a new finance theory in the decades preceding the economic decline of the 1970s. Within the neoclassic economic framework, a new generation of economists studied finance markets and advanced the idea of "efficient markets," a truly Hayekian idea that finance markets are capable of accommodating *all available* information and that this information is present in the pricing of the commodities and assets being traded. The so-called *Efficient Market Hypothesis* (EMH) is strongly associated with the University of Chicago economics department and more specifically with Eugene F. Fama, a 2013 Nobel Memorial Prize in Economic Sciences laureate. While the EMH was not theoretically credible – how, for instance, would the EMH explain the ability of certain traders to exploit information imbalances, information economics scholars such as George Akerlof (1970) would ask – but the idea of markets being capable of accommodating information was of key importance in advancing what critics would later speak of as *market fundamentalism*, the belief that markets are always the most efficient mechanism for organizing economic transactions. EMH is thus the most explicit statement in the Hayekian tradition of thinking, the jewel in the crown of the emerging neoliberal/libertarian/neoconservative economic doctrine. Regardless of later research being published by Fama himself, indicating that markets are probably not that perfectly efficient after all, the EMH served a key role in advancing the market as the solution not only to a few economic activities but for *all forms* of economic exchanges and social concerns. When former chairman of the Federal Reserve Alan Greenspan was testifying before the US Congress in the fall of 2008, following the collapse of the finance industry and the bailout that cost the American taxpayers an estimated US$1.75 trillion or 12.1 percent of the GDP (Blyth, 2013: 45), Greenspan had to admit that his firm belief in markets taking care of themselves, an idea directly derived from the EMH, was not as robust as he had previously assumed. At the very, very highest executive level of the regulatory and administrative apparatus of Western capitalism, engaging narratives not accompanied by solid empirical evidence can play a key role in shaping policy and regulatory control.

For the new political cadre taking office in the late 1970s and early 1980s, the new finance theory was aligned with their political convictions that collectivist solutions to social problems belonged to the past, and since they were "socialist" approaches anyway, they were not credible in the eyes of the new leading figures like Prime Minister Thatcher and the long-standing critic of communism President Reagan. Thatcher was unusual in the world of politics as she officially declared her belief in the writings of Hayek, and she once brought a copy of Hayek's *The Constitution of Liberty* (1960) to a cabinet meeting to announce, "This is what we believe!" Reagan, having his background in entertainment and in the Hollywood film industry, was less of an ideologue than the hard-nosed Margaret Thatcher, and was more inclined to tell invigorating stories about "Morning in America" (as Reagan's campaign slogan promised), but these two leaders followed similar principles and shared a stock of underlying theories and doctrines guiding their politics. In a way, in the Thatcher and Reagan eras, economic theory and politics tended to converge into a politico-economic framework that was eventually adopted by the Labour Party Prime Minister Tony Blair and the Democrat President Bill Clinton in the 1990s. Welfare state Keynesianism was thus displaced by the market-based neoliberal state.

POLITICAL CHANGES

In the UK, the economic decline in the 1970s was accompanied by fierce struggles between trade unions and industry, and state-owned industries were claimed to be inefficient in delivering goods and services to its clients. Thatcher had received some media attention when she was school minister and had made the massively unpopular decision to withdraw free milk for school children, that won her the nickname "Maggie Thatcher, milk snatcher" – an event that taught Thatcher the lesson to choose one's conflicts with great care. Thatcher's political program, including the new political program to sell off state-owned corporations and to deregulate markets, was not easily digested by even her own party, the Conservative Party, and Thatcher was in many ways a radical in the sense of breaking with conservative norms regarding governance and political programs. For a long time, there was criticism from the right and she was eventually ousted in the early 1990s when her poll tax program failed to receive recognition. Among Labour Party voters, Thatcher remains still a deeply discouraging figure, and when she passed away in April 2013, there was a gush of texts and commentaries being published in liberal and left-leaning British newspapers testifying to how she failed to unify the UK; for Conservative voters, in contrast, Thatcher remains for the most part a saintly figure that, with current Prime Minister David Cameron's words, "[m]ade Britain great anew." However for the working class voters in the British Midlands and other industrial regions that were struck hard by her policies, the heritage of Thatcher and Thatcherism is a scattered working class society. Statistics testify to her influence in these communities: "[t]here were five million in poverty in 1979; by 1992, the number was closer to fourteen million" (Jones, 2011: 62). In addition, foreigners visiting the UK in the 1980s noticed for the first time in years homeless people on the streets, and during the Thatcher era, in the period 1984–1989, the number of homeless Britons increased by 38 percent (Jones, 2011: 10). The Thatcher Government also significantly reduced the welfare state benefits, including greatly reduced work accident insurance, unemployment insurance, and sickness insurance compensation:

> After the coming of the Thatcher government in 1979, benefit levels fell drastically up to 1985, then gradually to 1995. In 1995, work accident insurance, with 20% replacement level, was less than half of its level in 1930; unemployment insurance, with 24%, to about two-thirds of the 1930 level; and sickness insurance, with 20%, was about the same level as in 1930. (Korpi and Palme, 2003: 433).

The most conspicuous evidence of the new policy was perhaps the Thatcher–trade union struggles in the 1980s, when the miners' strike lasted for a long period of time and ended with state-owned mines being closed down and with mass unemployment in the former mining towns and districts. Conversely, for Thatcher's admirers, the new government reinvigorated the economy and there was substantial economic growth reported, even if analysts point at mixed results as the UK benefited from both the newly found North Sea oil and a general economic upswing in the 1980s (Healy, 1992). In many ways, Thatcher's Britain is a story very different from the American unfolding of the political changes. In the UK, Thatcher was very much a one-woman army fueled by convictions and demonstrating a remarkable persistence, by and large unaccompanied by any wider institutional changes. In the US, the neoconservative moment had been growing as a subterranean phenomenon for decades, and when Reagan took office in early 1981, it was more of a culmination of a long wave of institutional change and mobilization in both the "pro-business lobby" and the center-right political community.

In the American industry, profit rates declined steadily until the mid-1970s from its peak in 1966, when the after-tax profit rate for all non-financial corporations in the US was 13.7 percent (Akard, 1992: 601). Between, 1975 and 1981, the period of increased mobilization and consolidation in the pro-business community, manufacturing cost increases exceeded price increases by 3.3 percent per year, a cumulative difference of 23.1 percent (Prechel, 1994: 733). In the business community, otherwise having a long tradition of respect for the trade unions and their need for negotiating industrial relations (Mizruchi, 2013), the "profits squeeze" was attributed to "excessive" wage costs created by organized labor in the tight labor markets of the 1960s. In addition, the "generous government cushions" in the labor market such as unemployment insurance, social security, and minimum wage laws were blamed for reducing "labor discipline."[2] Furthermore, the business community through the government increased the costs of production by imposing excessive taxation and an overregulation of business activity (Akard, 1992: 601). At the same time, the business community felt underappreciated and were blamed for all sorts of social evils in the late 1960s and 1970s. A memorandum written by Judge Lewis E. Powell in 1971, just prior to President Nixon's nomination of him to the Supreme Court, testifies to this sense of resentment in the business community: "few elements of American society today have as little influence as the American business man, the corporation and even the millions of corporate stockholders" (Lewis E. Powell, cited in Asen, 2009: 272).

In order to change this situation and to create a new pro-business culture in America, prominent business leaders and lobbying groups representing all segments of capital mobilized in the 1974–1981 period, which began as a quite defensive pursuit to restore the power of American industry. Eventually after 1978, the mobilization entered a more triumphant phase, leading to the Economic Recovery Tax Act of 1981, the cornerstone of the "pro-market economic program" of the first Reagan Administration that resulted in a "significant limitation of the fiscal capacity of the state

---

[2] Various forms of employment protection have been commonly portrayed as the systems that inhibit the efficiency of the labor market in the pro-business and free-market neo-classic economic literature guiding policy over the last three and a half decades. Such regulations are therefore claimed to lead to structural unemployment above its "natural level." Consequently, much effort has been invested in deregulating labor markets and to marginalize trade unions. Sarkar's (2013) analysis of panel data from the 1990–2008 period from 23 OECD countries provides no empirical support for this conjecture: "The panel data models find no short-term or long-term positive relationship between long-term unemployment and employment protection" (Sarkar, 2013: 1345). Similar results are presented by Glyn et al. (2006) and Peck and Theodore (2000). Sarkar (2013: 1345) continues: "This study casts serious doubt on the orthodox standpoint that strictness of employment protection hurts labour through increased unemployment," and thus suggesting that, "The policy prescription should be employment generation by other means."

to enact new interventionist programs" (Akard, 1992: 603). Prior crises in the Western capitalist economic system had resulted in the expansion of "state administrative and fiscal capacities" (Akard, 1992: 600) and the extension of labor right legislation and various state-backed, neocorporatist arrangements in core industries. At the same time, prior to the mid-1960s the American automotive industry was very much regulating itself, relying on the so-called "Treaty of Detroit," a contract between the United Auto Workers and General Motors and what Davis (2010: 335) speaks of as "the Magna Carta of the society of organizations." After 1966, this neocorporatist regime was increasingly complemented by government initiatives:

> Before the passage of the national Traffic and Motor Vehicle Safety Act in 1966, the automobile industry was completely unregulated by the federal government . . . Ford Motor Company did not even have a full-time lobbyist. By the mid-1970s, nearly every aspect of the automobile was regulated, including exhaust levels, fuel efficiency and safety: a major share of the car industry's research and development became devoted to compliance with government directives, while the cumulative impact of eighteen government mandated specifications adopted between 1968 and 1974 was estimated to have increased the retail, price of the average car by $300. (Vogel, 1983: 27)

The 1970s economic stagnation and high-inflation economy deviated from this historical pathway for a number of reasons. First of all, while the federal government, industry, and trade unions had jointly negotiated their mutual interests, there were no longer any firm trust in the state in playing this intermediary role as there were, Akard (1992: 601) writes, "[an] early universal antagonism towards the more than 25 major pieces of federal legislation enacted between 1965 and 1975 regulating workplace safety, environmental pollution, and product quality." Vogel (1983: 24–25) emphasizes "[t]he mutual distrust and antagonism that developed between the regulators and the regulated during this period [1965–1975] has no parallel outside the United States, traditionally considered the most conservative or pro-business capitalist democracy." In addition, in the period 1970–1975, these laws and regulations were enforced by a growing cadre of federal regulatory personnel, growing from a staff of 9,707 in 1970 to 52,098 in 1975 and making direct federal expenditure increase fivefold during the period (Akard, 1992: 601). The business community thus had enough of collaborative efforts in the face of these "new economic realities" and therefore chose to create its own collaborative networks to reduce the market power of labor and the administrative and fiscal capacities of the state. This new mobilization of the business community increased sharply the activities in Washington: between 1968 and 1978, the number of corporations with "public affairs offices" in Washington increased five-fold, from 100 to more than 500 (Vogel, 1983: 30–31). The number of lawyers in Washington also increased by 62.5 percent between 1972 and 1978, reaching 26,000 by the end of the period, "in large measure due to the increased corporate demands for legal representation" (Vogel, 1983: 31). One major accomplishment of the pro-business community was the passing of the bill reducing capital gains taxation in 1978, being, Vogel (1983: 39) suggests, a "classic piece of class legislation." The bill "[p]rovided direct financial benefits for businesses as a whole and virtually no benefits to middle and lower income taxpayers," and was therefore an "extraordinary political achievement for business: it represented the most important redistributive policy initiated by business in more than a decade" (Vogel, 1983: 39). Two years later, this wide-ranging work, including many interest and industry organizations was crowned with the election of Ronald Reagan as president, explicitly endorsing a pro-business and free-market agenda but also reaching out to the growing neoconservative communities in primarily American suburbia. "The political success of business in the late 1970s fully paralleled those enjoyed by the public interest movement a decade earlier," Vogel (1983: 38) contends.

While much of Reagan's economic policy was based on neoliberal and free-market ideologies (that is, various forms of anti-Keynesianism and monetarist policies advocated by his economic advisers, including Milton Friedman), it is impossible to fully explain the presidency of Reagan (as well as his Republican followers, Bush *père et fils*) without recognizing the neoconservative movement. High (2009: 476) remarks that neoconservatism is not a "coherent movement" as its "ideological sources" are diverse, and this has given neoconservatism its "markedly protean character." In Himmelstein's (1992: 14) view, neoconservatism embodies at least three quite distinct traditions, including: (1) *economic libertarianism*; (2) *social traditionalism*; and (3) *militant anti-communism* (Himmelstein, 1992: 14). One of the standing concerns for market liberals is how to align and bring into harmony economic liberalism assuming that "the market is always right," and social traditionalism that looks with great skepticism at markets that peddle for instance pornography and alcohol and that seem to produce enormous economic inequalities that threaten to shatter traditional ways of life.

McGirr's (2001) book about neoconservatism in southern California in Orange County sketches the contours of this social traditionalism. After the World War II, many veterans settled in the sunny south, and being trained in military discipline and hosting anti-communist beliefs – a standpoint easily spilling over to a critique of all kinds of collectivist solutions to social problems, thus putting communism, socialism, and social democracy in the same basket – this growing suburban community was not only concerned about the spread of Russian, Chinese, and Latin American communism, but were also very much worried about the decline of the America they grew up in during the interwar period. In the 1960s, the citizens right movement, the sexual revolution, and a general liberalization of everyday life had caused much controversy and many struggles, and for these conservative communities, the East-coast liberals and Washington politicians were partly responsible for this alleged decline of the moral fabric of the republic. The neoconservatives were biding their time and the first attempt to make it into the White House was when the arch-conservative Arizona Senator Barry Goldwater declared his presidential campaign in 1964. For the mainstream political commentators and the political elites, Goldwater was widely regarded a crackpot and an extremist and Goldwater never managed to win the election, but a new aspiring politician, the Governor Ronald Reagan, known to the Americans and the world as "the Errol Flynn of B-movies," endorsed Goldwater's campaign. Reagan's public speech in support of Senator Goldwater is still today a minor classic for neoconservatives.

Reagan had a background in the Actors' Guild in Hollywood and he had supported Senator Joseph McCarthy's paranoid search for unAmerican activities in the film industry in the 1950s. In conservative quarters, Reagan was a rising star embodying all-American values and was charismatic, engaging, and welcoming in his attitude. In 1968, the fabled year of student protests in Paris and elsewhere and the Soviet invasion of Czechoslovakia, the Republican Richard M. Nixon was elected president in the US and took office in early 1969. Nixon's Republican presidency was in many ways the last period of Keynesianism welfare policy, and when Jimmy Carter was elected president after a short intermission with Gerald Ford (Nixon's vice president after Spiro Agnew's resignation and the only person that served both as American president and vice president without being elected by the Electoral College) taking over after Nixon's disappearance from public political life after the Watergate scandal, the first attempts were made to deregulate markets and to adopt pro-business policies. Carter announced in a State of the Union address that "government could no longer solve people's problems" (cited in Jones, 2012: 254), a claim that would be repeated time and again during the three coming decades. The naming of Paul Volcker as the chairman of the Federal Reserve in 1979 was another key event in opening up for free-market economic policies. The Federal Reserve's new high-interest policy in combination with the deregulation of the finance market, starting in 1980, led to the first major finance market crisis in the mid-1980s, in the American Savings and Loans industry set up to provide home mortgage loans for average income groups (Black, 2005). In the 1980s, the finance industry underwent a significant restructuring – between 1979 and 1994, over 4,500 independent banks (36 percent of all banks) closed in the US (Panitch and Gindin, 2012: 173) – leading to a concentration in commercial banking. This concentration in turn led to a new role of the Federal Reserve as a lender of last resort for the US finance industry. Already in 1982, Paul Volcker (cited in Panitch and Gindin, 2012: 179, original emphasis omitted) announced, "[i]f things get bad, we can't stay on the side or we'll have a major liquidity crisis . . . We are not here to see the economy destroyed in the interest of not bailing somebody out." Twenty-five years later, in 2008, this declaration was turned into actual policy as the US government rescued the finance industry from collapsing.

One of the key elements of the neoconservative narrative was the anti-statist position that the state or any other international organization should not interfere within the lives of American citizens (see for example, Hart, 2014). Washington politicians should not use tax money to finance all kinds of projects they favored, and there is a deep-seated skepticism in neoconservative quarters regarding the role of the Federal government and the smug East Coast liberals and cosmopolitan class dominating in Washington. Another key element is the use of the term "elite" to denote less of the capital-owning class (that is, the richest stratum in society) as it instead increasingly denotes *cultural* and *political* elites. In this narrative, of central importance for the influence of neoconservatives, a billionaire capitalist in the American heartland has more in common with an agricultural worker in Wyoming than with an East Coast liberal Yale graduate living in Manhattan and having a cosmopolitan outlook. The billionaire and the agricultural worker share norms and values, their love of God and their country, and they are both concerned about how their money is squandered by federal politicians and agencies. In this story, the sheer access to capital resources and personal wealth is effectively downplayed. As detailed by Thomas Frank (2004) in *What's the Matter with America?*, a treatise that critically discusses why the super-rich and the working poor both share a commitment to neoconservative beliefs and the Republican Party, the neoconservative think tanks, and media pundits – perhaps best represented by Rupert Murdoch's *Fox News* channel – has been very successful in nourishing the idea that the Washington elites only care for themselves and their own interests, and consequently the role of the state needs to be minimized. As many commentators also have remarked, this critique of the state is more ornamental as the federal budgets and state agencies have been very much involved in various market creation activities that benefit the very same capital owners that declare their skepticism regarding the role of the state. The term "the Neoliberal State" has been used to denote this new role of the state as the creator and ultimate guardian of free markets.

Funding the Free-market Institutes and Think Tanks

One important aspect of the neoliberal and neoconservative mobilization in the 1970s and 1980s was the funding of research institutes and think tanks that would legitimize and advance a free-market policy agenda in American politics. Neoconservative intellectuals and political leaders such as William E. Simon, the Treasury Secretary in the Nixon and Ford Administrations, was one key figure in the funding of academic research committed to a pro-business, free-market agenda, and being skeptical towards government interventions into the world of business. Simon articulated, Asen (2009: 264) argues, "a coherent vision of a reinvigorated conservative political network that included think tanks, media organizations, and policy actors," and served a key role in bridging policy-making, business, activist networks, and in developing "efficacious strategies in each realm and making connections among them" (Asen, 2009: 264). In neoconservative circles, Simon is a heroic figure (see for example, Schumacher and Hutchinson, 2003), perhaps not as well-known as some other high-profile free-market proponents such as Milton Friedman, but still a main contributor to the re-establishment of conservatism as a political force in American politics.[3]

In his book *A Time For Truth* (1978), Simon presented his neoconservative agenda and he argued that businesspeople "suffer at the hands of a liberal ruling elite" (William E. Simon, cited in Asen, 2009: 276), and propagated against what Simon regarded as the "disastrous transfiguration of equality into egalitarianism." These liberal elites are, Simon argued, "fundamentally anti-democratic" in the methods they use to enforce the "orthodoxy" of egalitarianism. Egalitarianism is a term that is based on a "collectivist myth," Simon argued, articulating an idea that also Margaret Thatcher endorsed, that of "society" as being a figment of the minds of liberal elites: "[t]here is no such thing as the people . . . There are only individual citizens with individual wills and individual purposes" (William E. Simon, cited in Asen, 2009: 278). To counteract the dangers of egalitarianism and to protect the right to freedom endowed by the Founding Fathers of the American constitution, Simon advocated that funds should

---

[3] To this date, The William E. Simon Foundation provides support for "programs that are intended to strengthen the free enterprise systems and the spiritual values on which its rests: individual freedom, initiative, thrift, self-discipline, and faith in God" (cited in Schumacher and Hutchinson, 2003: 286).

be channeled to academic researchers that shared a commitment to the neoconservative cause. Using pseudo-military terms to underline the gravity of the situation, Simon spoke of these intellectuals as "conservative counterintelligentsia":[4]

> Rather than making unrestricted grants to private universities on the basis of their academic reputation, [pro-business advocators such as William Simon] suggested that corporations to be more discriminating: they should channel funds to schools, departments, institutes or faculty that are likely to support corporate objectives and values. While there are relatively few instances of funds being withheld from educational or research institutions because of their "anti-business" reputations, there has been a substantial increase in the amount of private and business funding earmarked for particular projects and programmes. (Vogel, 1983: 38)

High (2009: 484) argues that the neoconservatives "[c]ould never have sustained political careers without developing a network of pressure groups and think-tanks." By the mid-1970s, in the midst of the economic crisis derived from the shortage of oil, there was a wave of new think tanks and institutes being funded by private financiers. The American Enterprise Institute, the "flagship" of conservative think tanks, saw its budget increase tenfold from $0.9 million in 1970 to $10.6 million in 1983, and the Hoover Institution at Stanford University, being close to bankruptcy in the early 1960s, had expanded its annual budget from $1.9 million in 1970 to $8.4 million by 1983 (Himmelstein, 1992: 147). In addition, new think tanks and policy institutes were founded in the 1970s on the basis of donations of businessmen, including the neoconservative Heritage Foundation started in 1973 with a several hundred thousand dollar donation from the industrialist Joseph Coors; by 1983, the Heritage Foundation had a budget of $10.6 million (Himmelstein, 1992: 147). The John M. Olin Foundation was founded in 1977 and was financed by the Olin Corporation that spent around $5 million a year to support "scholarship in the philosophy of a free society and the economics of a free market" (Himmelstein, 1992: 149). The director of the Olin Foundation, William E. Simon, would later

---

[4] This vocabulary follows a militant anti-communist tradition in the neoconservative community, where for instance neoliberal intellectuals, in particular economic and political theorists, Jones (2012: 120) argues, were fond of portraying themselves as "foot-soldiers in the fight against communism." The emerging American neoconservatism of the 1960s and 1970s were also increasingly concerned not so much about the expansion of Soviet-style totalitarian communism but with the liberal ideas at the heart of the American republic, a political agenda that was never really seen as being the same thing as orthodox communist politics but that nevertheless was envisaged as a threat to "freedom" in its emphasis on egalitarianism.

play a key role in making Rochester University in the state of New York something like a branch of the University of Chicago economics department (Nikh-Khah, 2014), by recruiting agency theorist and shareholder value champion Michael C. Jensen. Corporate grants also fostered new institutes, including the Institute for Contemporary Studies, established in San Francisco in 1974, and the International Institute for Economic Research in Los Angeles, created in 1975. These institutes played an "extremely important role" in publishing studies of the costs associated with the "expansion of government regulation," but also in promoting public policies aimed at "strengthening the supply side of the American economy" (Vogel, 1983: 38).

These new think tanks and institutions were not passively contemplating the political and economic system but were actively involved in shaping the political agenda. When Reagan took office, a substantial amount of high-level appointees were recruited from these new think tanks and institutes. In Reagan's first term alone, "fifty came from Hoover, thirty-six from Heritage, thirty-four from AEI [American Enterprise Institute], and eighteen from the Center for Strategic and International Studies" (Himmelstein, 1992: 150–151). As opposed to this neoliberal and neoconservative mobilization of capital and intellectuals advancing the philosophy of free-market enterprising, organizations on the left of the Washington Consensus such as the Economic Policy Institute, relying on trade union funding, were disadvantaged (High, 2009: 484). It would then be a fair assessment to say that the neoliberal and neoconservative shift in policy was bound up with capital funding and support from industry. Already in the 1950s, private financiers had paid for Hayek's work at the London School of Economics, and a similar arrangement was made with Ludwig von Mises at New York University, so the close connections between financiers and free-market intellectuals had a long-standing tradition.

THE NEW POLICIES PUT TO WORK

There were substantial differences between the UK and the US, and the UK did not have the advantage of holding the favored currency and could not attract the same amount of foreign savings as the US. The Thatcher Government's agenda included confrontations with the unions that were widely regarded as being too aggressive in advancing their demands, the privatization of state-owned corporations, and the deregulation of markets. The Reagan Administration, instead, focused on tax cuts for the higher income groups and the relaxing of regulatory control of markets and industry. The British privatization program and the American tax reforms were thus the two pillars of the new economic and political order. Thatcher addressed the joint interests and shared political agendas at an early stage: "[w]e are both determined to sweep away the restrictions that hold back enterprise" (Margaret Thatcher, speech at the White House, February 26, 1981, cited in Troy, 2009: 70). On both sides of the Atlantic, the new office-holders went to work.

For the Thatcher Government, the trade unions were targeted as the principal enemy of the "economic freedom" that Prime Minister Thatcher wanted so dearly to restore. Vogel (1996: 52) suggests there were also political reasons for this strategy: "[t]he Thatcher group believed that union power was partially responsible for the country's economic woes . . . The Thatcherites also struck at unions for political reasons, to weaken the Labour Party's support base." A series of employment acts were introduced by the Thatcher Government, severely limiting the power of organized labor. In addition, several large unions "had their assets 'sequestrated' (i.e, seized) for failing to comply with the new codes of conduct" (Healey, 1992: 9). Partly as a consequence of this new legislations, union density in the UK fell from its peak at 58 percent by the end of the 1970s to 45 percent by 1990 (Healey, 1992: 9). Thatcher and her government would even go so far as to implement economic policies – by then the so-fashionable program of supply-side economics and monetarism – they did not fully believe in to weaken the unions:

> The Thatcher government never believed for a moment that [monetarism] was the correct way to bring down inflation. They did however see that this would be a very good way to raise unemployment, and raising unemployment was an extremely desirable way of reducing the strength of the working classes . . . What was engineered – in Marxist terms – was a crisis of capitalism which re-created the reserve army of labour, and has allowed the capitalist to make higher profits ever since. (Sir Alan Budd, a top UK Treasury civil servant, cited in Palma, 2009: 837)[5]

In addition to the weakening of the trade union's influence in the British economy, the privatization of public companies was given priority by Thatcher. "Privatization . . . was one of the central means of reversing

---

[5] In the US, the inflation-fighting policy came to overshadow many other economic and industrial policies and objectives, and the concern for unemployment rates in particular. In the Clinton era, for instance, inflation had fallen from the relatively low level of 3 percent to the even lower level of 2.6 percent during 1993, and yet the Federal Reserve under the direction of Alan Greenspan raised interest rates because "[i]t believed that an unemployment rate below 6.2 percent would set off inflation" (Stein, 2011: 282).

the corrosive and corrupting effects of socialism . . . privatization is at the centre of any programme of reclaiming territory for freedom," Margaret Thatcher writes in her memoirs (cited in Kinderman, 2012: 42). Simmons et al. (2008) suggest that Thatcher advanced a most radical agenda as state-owned firms were widely accepted in the political mainstream in many countries in the Organisation for Economic Co-operation and Development (OECD): "[p]rior to Margaret Thatcher's ascent to power in the United Kingdom, state-owned firms were widely accepted in both developed and developing countries. No government had ever engaged in a sustained program of selling off state-owned enterprises" (Simmons et al., 2008: 27–28). In addition, in the medium run, some of the industries being privatized did better under private management and some did worse, but there were few "glaring disasters" until the privatization of British Rail – but this came at the very end of Britain's privatization program (Simmons et al., 2008: 27–28). In being relatively successfully transferring state-owned enterprises to private owners and consortia, Thatcherism served to legitimize the economists' claim that private ownership was desirable over state-controlled firms. As a consequence, less free-market-oriented economists "[j]umped on the bandwagon to argue that there were, in fact, very few natural monopolies, and hence most state-owned industries in most countries were inefficient and would benefit from being sold" (Simmons et al., 2008: 28). Privatization of public firms was therefore perhaps the most lasting effects of the free-market policy of Thatcherism.

However, not everyone was impressed with this transfer of public assets to private ownership, and for instance Judt (2010) claims that the Thatcher-era UK privatizations resulted in a "net transfer" of £14 billion from "the taxpaying public to stockholders and other investors." An additional £3 billion in fees to bankers handling the privatization project should be included in the calculation, Judt (2010: 110–111) suggests. If the state discounts all risks and then lowers the price of an asset to the level where private owners are interested in taking over the activities, it is not really an indication of the superior effectiveness of market transactions, Judt (2010) and others suggest, but free-market advocates treated a transfer from public to private ownership as being an inherently rational process. Moreover, as also has been frequently remarked, selling assets to private owners that are critical to the functioning of society including railway systems and other infrastructures is building moral hazard into the economic system as the private owner can always reap the economic benefits in good times and be assured that the state will never let basic infrastructures collapse during crises and economic downturns. This "too big to fail"-logic was frequently referred to when the finance industry corporations were bailed out by the American Troubled Asset Relief Program (TARP) enacted by Congress in 2008.

Nevertheless, the British privatization program was exemplary in advancing a new policy where "the state is rolled back" in the new neoliberal vocabulary, and in the US, the Reagan Administration implemented a tax reform in the mid-1980s that played a key role in what Swank (2008) speaks of as the "US-driven diffusion of neoliberalism." While taxation has served the role to redistribute income from high-income groups to lower income groups, the Reagan tax reforms were "the archetype of the shift to the neoliberal tax paradigm" (Swank, 2008: 77), stressing efficiency over redistribution. After the reform, earners in the middle fifth of the American income strata would pay 9.8 percent of their income in payroll taxes, while the comparable figure for the top 1 percent was 1.4 percent. For the middle fifth, the rate of total federal taxes fell only 0.7 percent in the period between 1979 and 1989, while the comparable figure for the top 10 percent income group was 3.3 percent and for the top 1 percent income group, 8.1 percent (Madrick, 2011: 170–171). Corporations and the richest income level benefited the most from these tax cuts. Reagan was widely announcing less expansive government spending but his budget deficits during the 1983–1987 period were on a 5.9 percent average. The spending of tax money was less focused in the poor and the middle classes and more focused on military mobilization (Crotty, 2012: 84). The shift in taxation policy and the emphasis on the trickle-down effects wherein economic growth would be propelled by the sheer amount of money in circulation, the principal idea of supply-side economics, became, Swank (2008: 95) proposes, an international standard for policy-makers in the Western world. Just like Thatcher had introduced privatization of public companies as a method to limit the state's role, Reagan abandoned the Keynesian tradition to use taxation to counteract and reduce economic inequalities. In the new neoliberal and neoconservative doctrine, economic inequality was no longer a political concern as competition between individuals was regarded as the motor of economic growth. In addition, a series of academic work published in the 1960s, including Gary Becker's human capital theory (for example, Becker, 1968) and Mancur Olson's (1965) theory of "free-riders" in collective action, provided an entirely new vocabulary for policy-makers. For instance, in Becker's theory, economic inequality is not a matter of social class or certain groups being discriminated or otherwise unfavored, but is faithful to a rational choice theory, with less desirable income patterns being the outcome from unsuccessful or misconceived human capital investments. That is, the finance industry worker entering the profession in Wall Street at a minimum salary of say $300,000 is making a better human

capital investment than the school teacher working in the public school
system making $50,000 a year. Thatcher declared, "[c]lass is a communist
concept. It groups people together and sets them against each other"
(Margaret Thatcher, *Newsweek* Interview, 1992, cited in Mirowski, 2013:
117), underlining the fierce resistance among neoliberals to recognize that
there are any collective structures at all in society. For neoliberals (but less
so for neoconservatives, emphasizing the local community and its shared
tradition, worldview, and morals), there is nothing but enterprising individuals and these individuals are solely and individually responsible for
their own economic well-being. Needless to say, this hard-core rational
choice theory was not easy to digest for a series of academic researchers,
policy-makers, and interest groups, but human capital theory remains one
of the backbone theories in the neoliberal toolbox.

   "Man is not free unless government is limited," Ronald Reagan
announced (cited in Troy, 2009: 21). In practice this did not mean so
much to cut down on federal activities (and certainly not to reduce federal
budgets) as it meant the government working actively to support business.
Under Reagan, the government accelerated the deregulation of business,
and financial market deregulation was "especially dramatic" (Crotty,
2012: 85). The new brew of finance market deregulation, high employment, regressive tax cuts, and aggressions on unions leading to a reduction
of unionization in the US (Jacobs and Myers, 2014) – a central objective
in the establishment of the "economic freedom" that first Hayek and later
Friedman had called for – led to a sharp rise in economic inequality. While
the UK and the US cases display a few differences derived from historical
conditions and institutional idiosyncrasies, they both underline the centrality the new free-market ideology and economic freedom (defined in
the negative as the absence of state-regulation and oversight) over political freedom. On both sides of the Atlantic, many of the "most important
advisers, government colleagues, and supporters" of the new governments
were recruited from the neoliberal, free-market, and pro-business community and networks (Jones, 2012: 268).

   In their analysis of the diffusion of neoliberal policies in the 1980s and
1990s, Simmons et al. (2008: 47) persuasively argue that "simple coercion" is rarely the main mechanism driving policy diffusion. There are
testimonies that the institutions of the Washington Consensus including
the International Monetary Fund (IMF), the World Trade Organization
(WTO), and the World Bank, had tried to impose neoliberal policies in
certain areas of the world, but these prescribed policies have rarely worked
exactly as intended (Fairbrother, 2014; Babb, 2013). Instead, there is a
certain fashion element in policy-making just as in everything else human.
Thatcher and Reagan thus offered an alternative to the post-World War

II Keynesianism policy, and also in countries where social democrats and socialists were elected presidents and prime ministers, bits and pieces of the new Anglo-American policy were adopted. Deregulation of previously controlled markets, the interest in privatizing certain industries, and not the least the deregulation of the national, regional, and global finance markets entered the policy-makers' agendas. Simmons et al. (2008) write:

> In economic policy, it appears, what is fashionable in economic theory plays a big role in what is implemented. This suggests a straightforward learning model, in which policymakers assess the cold, hard evidence and base policy decisions on it, may not depict the process accurately. When countries view the policy experiments through rose-colored lenses, they are more likely to replicate those experiments. When countries have vocal proponents for fashionable new policies around, they are more likely to follow them. (Simmons et al., 2008: 47–48)

Moreover, the advancement of academic theories and spokespersons for the new policy, especially in the discipline of economics, a domain of professional technocratic expertise that has advanced its position greatly during the last few decades, has played a central role in legitimizing what once seemed as radical right-wing policies (for example, trade union confrontations): "[w]e see evidence that ideological trends shape the spread of capital account liberalization. We see evidence that academic movements shape the diffusion of government downsizing and privatization," Simmons et al. (2008: 48) conclude. While the new policies of Thatcherism and Reaganomics represented a seismic shift in policy and did arguably produce economic growth and opened up for new groups and interests, there were also significant side-effects and externalities that became salient in the era. Next we turn to the effects of the new neoliberal and neoconservative programs.

LONG-TERM SOCIAL AND ECONOMIC CONSEQUENCES

The conflict between the Federal Reserve chairman Paul Volcker's fighting of inflation and the deficit spending of Ronald Reagan was mediated by the inflow of foreign investment capital, especially from Japan. This capital financed a debt-based consumption boom at all levels in the American economy – "by consumers, corporations, and the U.S. federal government" (Tomaskovic-Devey and Lin, 2011: 543). In combination with new regulatory control of the finance markets, the inflow of capital made the finance markets a much quicker and (still) safer way to secure returns than investing in the traditional industries, for example, manufacturing. This emphasis on finance market investment had two effects. First, there was a decline in the American industry and in the relatively short period of 1980–1985, "the US trade deficit increased by 309 percent – from $36.3 to $148.5 billion" (Sell, 2003: 80). The Reagan Administration was only mildly concerned about such structural changes as these were accompanied by economic theories regarding the "global shift," where "low-value adding" and "dirty" industries were "naturally" offshored to low-cost countries as advanced economies should increasingly engage in high-growth innovation-based industries (Milberg and Winkler, 2010). In the eyes of Reagan's economic advisers, the loss of manufacturing industry was not a worrisome tendency. Second, the quick inflow of capital into the new and emerging finance markets increased the volatility in interest rates and stock market performance, and this encouraged the creation of new financial instruments including "variable rate mortgages, credit default swaps, and mortgage-based and other derivative securities" (Tomaskovic-Devey and Lin, 2011: 545). Finance market investment provided faster yields than investment elsewhere and money piped into the finance industry was transformed into new, more advanced, but also easily calculable and less liquid financial instruments. In addition, in the 1980s, the leveraged buyout wave that swept across the American industry made CEOs and directors more aware of the importance of generating shareholder value as proposed by agency theorists, and therefore larger proportions of the value generated in non-financial firms were fed back into the finance industry rather than benefiting other constituencies: "investment in new productive capital became less attractive and financial investment became more attractive . . . Institutional investors encouraged corporate CEOs to adopt the aspects of agency theory they preferred, focusing on short-term stock market value goals and tying executive compensation to stock prices" (Tomaskovic-Devey and Lin, 2011: 546). The immediate effect was that finance market actors could benefit from a massive inflow of capital and, as a consequence, the compensation to this new class of professional workers soared: in the sector, employee compensation went from "being above average for the economy overall" to about "60 percent higher than in the rest of the economy" (Tomaskovic-Devey and Lin, 2011: 553). Despite the American finance industry employing a relatively limited amount of individuals, by 2008, "[a]lmost a quarter of the GDP and more than a quarter of the profits accumulated in the finance sector" (Tomaskovic-Devey and Lin, 2011: 553). In nominal terms, that represents a transfer of between 5.8 and 6.6 trillion 2011 dollars in income into the finance sector, mostly as profits (Tomaskovic-Devey and Lin, 2011: 553). While free-market protagonists are always fond of explaining such changes on the basis of individual decisions, and speak of "invest-ment in human capital" as the driver of finance market efficiency, there is evidence of wide-ranging legal, regulatory, and institutional changes that have benefited the finance market expansion in the period after 1980. However, Tomaskovic-Devey and Lin (2011: 553) do not assume the win-win narrative derived from successful human capital investment to be a credible explanation but suggest that this growth in size, turnover, and compensation in the finance industry is effectively someone else's loss. Studies (for example, Orhangazi, 2008; Stockhammer, 2004) show that financialization actually "reduced nonfinancial firms' capital investment in new productive assets and increased the share of their cash flow diverted to the finance sector as increased profits" (Tomaskovic-Devey and Lin, 2011: 553).

The perhaps most conspicuous effect of the accumulation of economic resources in the finance industry is the growth of economic inequality. Fortunately, there is quite detailed empirical evidence of how a larger proportion of the accumulated economic wealth in the American economy is located in the top income groups and primarily in the 1 percent or 0.1 percent income group. In the US, corporate income tax served to reduce the distribution to shareholders and the income to the state could be invested in counteracting economic inequality (Piketty and Saez, 2003: 13). In the Reagan years, such taxation was substantially reduced as part of the pro-business program. When examining the statistics, the income distribution after 1980s represents a return to almost the pre-World War I levels: "[i]n 1915 the top 0.01 percent earned 400 times more than the average; in 1970 the average top 0.01 percent income was 'only' 50 times the average; in 1998 they earned about 250 times the average income" (Piketty and Saez, 2003: 13). Piketty and Saez (2003) also report that individuals in the P90-95 and P95-99 fractals rely mostly on labor income – capital income is less than 25 percent in these income groups – while the top percentile, the capital owning class, derive most of their income in the form of capital income (Piketty and Saez, 2003: 17). The reduction of eco-nomic inequality between 1914 and 1945 was thus based on the reduction of capital income through progressive taxation. As neoliberal and neocon-servative economic and fiscal policies were implemented in for example, the US in the 1980s, the effect was to "[a]gain produce in a few decades levels of wealth concentration similar to those at the beginning of the century" (Piketty and Saez, 2003: 24). For instance, from 1986 to 1988 the income reported for the highest income groups rose sharply, an immediate effect of the large top marginal tax rate cuts of the Tax Reform Act of 1986 (Piketty and Saez, 2003: 31). Moreover, Piketty and Saez (2003) suggest that the huge increase in income for the top income groups since the early

1980s is not observable in European countries that have been part of the same technological shifts during the period, and consequently, it is primarily fiscal policy that explains the growth of economic inequality (Piketty and Saez, 2003: 34). In summary, Piketty and Saez (2003) demonstrate that even until the ninety-ninth percentile, it is labor income that is the principal source of economic resources, but for the top 1 percent capital income accounts for a substantial share of the taxable income. In addition, the return to economic inequality levels of the early twentieth century is essentially the effect of policy.

While Piketty and Saez (2003) are concerned to report empirical material without making any far-reaching policy recommendations, Hacker and Pierson (2010) address what they refer to as the "winner-takes-all inequality" after 1980. In their view, economic inequality derives from "fundamental shifts in four core areas of U.S. policy" related to financial markets, corporate governance, industrial relations, and taxation. This shift in policy has been "powerfully driven by this political-organizational transformation," Hacker and Pierson (2010: 154) suggest. Today, the top 0.1 percent of the American population has seen their share of income grow from 2.7 percent to 12.3 percent of all income, a fourfold increase (Hacker and Pierson, 2010: 155). Between 1979 and 2005, "the average after-tax incomes of the richest 1 percent of households rose nearly by 230 percent" (Hacker and Pierson, 2010: 157). This shift in the income structure is a long-term trend that seems to be unrelated to either the business cycles or the color of the administration in the White House. In addition, regardless of what Reagan's economic advisers and other commentators have predicted, few of the economic benefits of economic growth at the top of the income pyramid has trickled down to benefit lower income groups. As taxes have been a very effective method to counteract economic inequality and the uneven distribution of income, it is no wonder that supply-side economics and neoliberal policies emphasized the reduction of taxation. Reagan's tax reforms were thus followed by substantial tax cuts by George W. Bush two decades later, a reform that "haemorrhaged trillions of dollars of government revenue" (Crotty, 2012: 85), and that has been estimated to cost "$5.4 trillion over a decade" (Crotty, 2012: 98). Stein (2011: 293) argues that these tax cuts "were solutions looking for problems" and had a relatively modest impact on the economic growth that justified them (Crotty, 2012), as they were primarily benefiting taxpayers earning more than $200,000 per year; the 15.5 percent payroll tax that is the main tax for 80 percent of the American taxpayers was not affected, and median payroll, income, and sales taxes paid by this group in 2006 was higher than in 1966 (Stein, 2011: 294). Hacker and Pierson (2010: 183) emphasize that this new policy has strongly benefited the richest 1 percent of the income percentile, primarily benefiting from the declining role of the corporate income tax and the real estate tax. Government officials such as the Treasury Secretary in the George W. Bush Administration, Henry "Hank" Paulson, declared that economic inequality is caused by "market forces" that are beyond the control of government and the political system, but Hacker and Pierson (2010) suggest that the deregulation of financial markets, the reduction of corporate tax, and the tax reforms of Republican presidents are all examples of new policies that have created economic winner-takes-all inequalities: "[p]olicy – both as what governments have done and what, as a result of drift, it has failed to do – has played an absolutely central role in the rise of winner-takes-all economic outcomes . . . A winner-takes-all politics accompanied, and helped produce a winner-takes-all economy" (Hacker and Pierson, 2010: 196). Rather than being the outcome from some market-based *force majeur*, economic inequality is the outcome from political processes and policy-making, Volscho and Kelly (2012) argue. In their view, economic inequality is the consequence of neoconservative shifts in policy and the Republican Party's stronger position in Congress (Volscho and Kelly, 2012: 693). "The idea that government cannot effectively redress economic inequality simply does not ring true compared to empirical reality," Kelly and Enns (2010: 856) conclude.

What may be even more discouraging is that once economic inequality has been established in a certain society it is likely to stay, Kelly and Enns (2010) propose. In their view, economic inequality "may be self-reinforcing," with economic inequality generating "political inequalities" that in turn "prevents the poor from using the democratic process to push for government action that would increase their well-being and reduce economic inequality" (Kelly and Enns, 2010: 855). Contrary to common-sense thinking, evidence shows that economically disfavored groups tend to become more conservative and side with interests that do not benefit themselves: "both the rich and the poor respond to rising inequality by shifting in a conservative direction" (Kelly and Enns, 2010: 859). In addition, policies that are supported by high-income groups are more likely to be enacted than in the case when they are supported by low-income groups, evidence suggests (Kelly and Enns, 2010: 857). This is what Thomas Frank (2004) again speaks of as the "Kansas problem" (using his home state Kansas in the US Midwest as an example of this shift towards a more conservative, anti-statist worldview), the evidence of lower and mid-income groups voting for the Republican Party that discredit the welfare state that such groups would benefit from.

Perhaps the US is in many ways leading the way in terms of economic policy, but international comparisons suggest that the change in income structure is less dramatic elsewhere. At the same time, growing economic inequality in the era of financialization seems to be more or less a global phenomenon. In their study of 16 OECD countries, Alderson and Nielsen (2002: 1248) found that ten countries have experienced an upswing in inequality in the 1967–1992 period. Very much aligned with the research referred to above, Alderson and Nielsen (2002) suggest that there is no exogenous force (for example, technological shifts) that has caused the growth in economic inequality:

> [We] find only modest evidence in support of the idea that increasing inequality is an inherent feature of postindustrial development, that is, that there is a systematic propensity for the most developed countries to experience an upturn in inequality beyond a certain level of development. Clearly, the inequality experience of the advanced industrial countries in recent decades has been shaped by more than processes of economic development alone. (Alderson and Nielsen, 2002: 1272)

More specifically, the deregulation of international finance markets and the relaxing of capital control, leading to more direct investment has affected economic inequality in three ways: (1) by accelerating deindustrialization, leading to a shift from well-paid and secure manufacturing jobs to lower paid work in retail and services; (2) by weakening the bargaining position of labor; and (3) by "altering the distribution of income between labor to capital and the demand for unskilled labor" (Alderson and Nielsen, 2002: 1261). In other words, the free market for capital investment may have been beneficial for economic effectiveness, but the working population being dependent on their income has not benefited as the distribution of income has emphasized and favored income from capital ownership. In the era of financialization, just like in the case of the mid-1980s American tax reform, the policy changed from a concern for redistribution of income to capital market efficiency. The concern for the welfare state was discredited and the free-market policies that its proponents claimed were benefiting everyone, if not directly at least indirectly through the virtues of market efficiencies, generated substantial income growth in the top income groups. Few of the benefits trickled down the system as the otherwise remarkably liquid capital appeared to have inertia once it was registered as capital income. The most conspicuous effect of the financialization of the economy is thus the growth in economic inequality. This economic inequality was not an unavoidable feature of the financial system but was rather grounded in policies and ideologies that tend to benefit certain groups more than others.

Ailon (2014) argues that in a historical perspective, the finance industry could be rendered legitimate only after it could demonstrate that it was clearly separated from mere "gambling" and other activities operating under the "stigmatizing shadow" of chance and future uncertainties. The key to this process of legitimation was to carefully separate *risk* from *uncertainty*, that is, to distinguish analytically, as Knight did in his seminal work *Risk, Uncertainty, and Profit* (1921), between "predictable and non-predictable, or more correctly, probabilizable and nonprobabilizable (or calculable and non-calculable) forms of indeterminacy" (Reddy, 1996: 224). "Financial risk" was thus codified as a "calculable, manageable entity" (Ailon, 2014: 612) at the very heart of finance's professional expertise.[6] The mathematization and abstraction of finance, today being at an unprecedented level as certain derivatives composed of layers of interrelated assets are both very complicated to understand and to price, also for financial traders (for example, Bluhm and Wagner, 2011; Spatt, 2014), unfortunately dissociate the finance market actor from the social world these assets ultimately represent. "As financialization spreads and deepens, a distinct social prism takes root along with it. Given the dominance of financial markets, the social perspective they breed has a broad sociological significance," Ailon (2014: 615) proposes. For instance, the shareholder value ideology, the proposition that the free cash flow, the capital left after all other costs have been covered by the firm, can legitimately be claimed by the shareholders, is part of this "financialized" worldview where "the financial engagement displaces social awareness" (Ailon, 2014: 615):

> [A]s corporations are perceived in abstract form as stock prices or shareholder values, or as part of certain indexes and so forth, financial actors lose any sense of moral and social responsibility for the lives of the employees whose workplaces are frequently restructured as a means of boosting these stock prices in an insatiable market. (Ailon, 2014: 614)

Also Tabb (2013) stresses how the finance industry has taken on a new role in the financialized economy, leading to new views of the firm and new attitudes towards how to balance long-term economic growth and short-term financial yields:

> "[w]hen the financial sector moves beyond lubricating the wheels of commerce to dominate the real economy, problems develop. Companies are seen as

---

[6] The conceptual and empirical literature on the development of different specialisms in risk management and its practical use is quite extensive. The literature includes studies of financial risk management in the finance industry (Langley, 2013; Amoore, 2011; Millo and MacKenzie, 2009; Kalthoff, 2005; Willman et al., 2001), in internal audits (Spira and Page, 2002), and consumer credit assessment (Marron, 2007).

portfolios of financial assets to be bought and sold, reorganized, merged, spun off, or closed down for short-term profits and tax benefits. (Tabb, 2013: 527)

In this perspective, financialization is not a form of specific, technical, and professional expertise operating within narrowly defined domains of juris-diction in the financial markets, but is rather a regime of abstract thinking penetrating to most spheres of social life. "[T]he same technological means that enhance financial connectivity also enhance social forgetting and 'dis-sociation'" (Ailon, 2014: 615). Following Martin's (2002) interest for what he speaks of as the "financialization of everyday life," Ailon (2014: 615) suggests that the present regime of financialization needs to be understood in terms of the "social forgetting" and "social dissociation" that these various institutional, cultural, and behavioral changes of financialization breed. Seen in this view, the triumph of a financialized worldview is also the triumph over society, and tragically, also the triumph of finance over itself; there is something eschatological about this auto-destructive ten-dency of the finance industry to maintain a condescending and ignorant view of what occurs outside of the finance industry (see for example, Ho, 2009), almost treating the wider society as an atavism and a reminiscence of the world of yesterday, dragging behind the visionary leadership of global financial institutions.

Was Everyone Happy with the New Economic Regime?

For hardcore neoliberals and free-market acolytes, economic inequalities are not a major concern as they theoretically speaking do little more than mirror individual human capital investment decisions and the market's valuation of such investments. At the same time, this group of academic researchers, policy-makers, and think tank pundits regard such outcomes as being "natural" and unavoidable, they have to grapple with this natu-ralist thesis. As Philip Mirowski (2013: 56) aptly remarks, it is a thorny problem for neoliberals how to "maintain the pretense of freedom as noncoercion when, in practice, it seems unlikely that most people would freely choose the neoliberal version of the state." That is, if the market today deregulated and guarded by state-based control and monitoring activities, is the naturally and overwhelmingly superior way to allocate resources and organize transactions, why is it then that it does not just effortlessly and without all the political support and theoretical justifica-tion, come to dominate all other economic forms? (Mirowski, 2013: 73). The empirically observable strong reliance on the state and state agencies to serve as market-makers that discount risks and lower entry barriers, and so forth, that is, all the political and regulatory artifice that surrounds the "naturality" of the market, are thus based on two opposing institutional logics. While neoliberal intellectuals are always regressing to explain everything they regard as undesirable as the presence of the state and the government, other key groups that do not fully share the commitment to free-market transactions may be more recalcitrant in accepting such ready-made explanations.

For instance, neoliberals and libertarians had, at least in the US, to side with neoconservatives to orchestrate the shift to the new regime, and these neoconservative groups were not necessarily sure that markets per se were inherently rational. Troy's (2009) praise of Ronald Reagan and his presidency admits few mistakes on Reagan's part, and the volume also avoids most of the more thorny economic problems of the Reagan presidency, but at one point Troy remarks that the charming and positive Reagan were not always capable of anticipating what kind of world and society he and his allies were creating when they opened the Pandora's box of free-market liberalism. As Troy (2009: 115) points out in an otherwise celebratory account of Reagan, blinded by their critique of the Left, Reagan and the neoconservative community were "unable to connect the dots between the capitalist resurgence they celebrated and the cultural upheaval they mourned." They thus failed to anticipate how many of the policies they implemented and corporate practices they encouraged would "neutralize or undermine" many of the traditional values and structures they held in esteem and cherished. The free-market policy to some extent contributed to the destruction of family values, traditionalism, and a sense of community as job opportunities disappeared and blue-collar communities were uprooted at the same time as, some critics would claim, greed and selfishness were acclaimed as virtues of the new era – attitudes and norms traditionally rejected by conservatives praising stability and reciprocity. Bartolini et al. (2014: 1026–1027) report that "[a]ll available measures of well-being, both subjective and objective, point to a decrease in well-being in the USA over the past decades." In contrast, Bartolini et al. (2014: 1027) continue, European self-reported happiness "seem to exhibit a rising trend." Bartolini et al. (2014: 1034) speculate whether these figures are caused by "hyperconsumerism" and its demands for longer work hours, providing only "additional market products" that in fact may only poorly "substitute for other sources of well-being." Moreover, Americans spend "an increasing portion of their leisure time on activities very intense (and expensive) in term of use of market goods and services" (Bartolini et al., 2014: 1034). In Bartolini et al.'s (2014: 1034) disheartening conclusion, the late modern American reacts to an "impoverished human landscape brought about by years of rapid economic growth" by engaging in "compensatory hyperconsumerism."

In addition, the neoliberal adage that "the market is always right" was not of necessity self-evident for groups that were concerned about the moral fabric of the republic and being concerned about the trade of all kinds of goods and services that seemed poorly tuned to the neoconservative credo.[7] Again, for many center-right commentators, the alliance between free-market advocators and neoconservatives is in many ways a puzzling phenomenon, and perhaps it is the persistent anti-statist rhetoric of neoliberal intellectuals that managed to win the neoconservatives over to their side. No matter whether this alliance will stand fast in the future, it was a collaborate effort that was key to the shift in policy from welfare state Keynesianism to the free-market financialization of the state, the firm, and the individual.

SUMMARY AND CONCLUSION

The concept of financialization is a complex theoretical term comprising a variety of practices, institutional changes, and policies prescribing how firms and industries are to be treated as bundles of financial resources. In addition, the drivers of the financialization of both the Anglo-American economies and the global economies include various factors such as macroeconomic conditions, regulatory frameworks, and demographic changes. As a consequence, financialization is a theoretical term that is more associative than denotative, that is better used to sketch overarching economic and social changes than to capture one precise shift in practice or policy. Still, the term is highly useful when exploring both the growth and increased significance of the finance industry and the finance market, and how non-financial firms have increasingly engaged in finance market

---

[7] For libertarian economists such as Milton Friedman, the market was not only always right, it also – which is a radical point – rewards "moral behavior." For the older generation of Chicago economists like Frank Knight, the moral landscape of capitalism was bleak, while Hayek did not either believe that the market necessarily rewarded merit. Hayek's market advocacy was based on the idea that "markets provided an ethically neutral arbiter, and that this was preferable to any system that tried to determine outcomes in the basis of a preconceived notion of good" (Burgin, 2012: 188). With habit of the economists trained in neoclassical economic theory, Friedman abandoned all such qualifications and complications, and provided a more straightforward argument that markets "promoted virtuous behavior" (Burgin, 2012: 188). As a corollary to this proposition, again, "any attempt to interfere with them on ethical grounds should therefore be subject to doubt" (Burgin, 2012: 188). Despite some neoconservatives not being fully convinced, Friedman's advocacy of laissez-faire and the morality of capitalism provided the foundation for "much of the Republican's Party's policy platform in the decades that followed"(Burgin, 2012: 187). Friedman served as a political and economic adviser for the arch-conservative Barry Goldwater in 1964, and in the Nixon and Reagan Administrations.

activities and themselves being treated as financial assets and being disciplined by finance market control, primarily through shareholder value creating policies. In the next chapter, the role of the finance industry in the new regime of investor capitalism will be examined in more detail, and specific attention is given to the role of finance market deregulation to enable a free circulation of finance capital and how such policies and regulatory frameworks are easily underrating the risks of free-market regimes.

3. Finance industry prominence: causes and consequences

INTRODUCTION

In 2005, the British Prime Minister Gordon Brown declared in his budget statement before the parliament that he expected the growth of the economy to be between 3 and 3.5 percent during the year, and in 2006 the figure was estimated to be between 2.5 and 3 percent, figures twice or three times as high as what was calculated in the euro area and in Japan. As an effect of this growth, Brown remarked, Britain and North America have "over the last eight years grown at twice the rate of most G7 competitors, our living standard also rising twice as fast" (Prime Minister Gordon Brown's Budget Statement in 2005, cited in Erturk et al., 2012: 7). In hindsight, this statement was indicative of the "misplaced optimism before 2008" (Erturk et al., 2012: 10) regarding economic growth and employment in the financialized Anglo-American economies. On 15 September, 2008, Lehman Brothers, one of the "Big Five" on Wall Street, filed for bankruptcy. This event had repercussions throughout the entire global financial system and during a few dramatic weeks the financial market ended up in a stalemate when it became clear that the finance industry would be unable to stabilize itself without the support and primarily the capital provided by national states (Blinder, 2013; Barofsky, 2012; Friedman and Kraus, 2012; Stiglitz, 2010; Sorkin, 2009). For free-market advocates, this was a most embarrassing and discouraging event for two reasons: first, the finance industry had been widely portrayed as operating in the most pure and thus most efficient of all capitalist markets, capable of not only producing economic wealth on its own but also to discipline and monitor all other markets; one market to rule them all, in other words. How this supposedly inherently rational industry, the principal argument for all the deregulatory efforts and policies over the last four decades, allegedly employing "the brightest" and "the smartest" of the elite university graduates (Ho, 2009), failed to live up to such high hopes still today remains a mystery to many of the free-market advocates.[1]

Second, the very idea of market efficiency and the market as the supreme mechanism for settling disputes and organizing economic transactions, the very Euclidian anchoring axiom in the free-market doctrine, was badly torn by the events of 2008. Among the many reactions in the bewildering amount of commentaries, books, papers, and blog posts addressing the 2008 finance market collapse, some called for a new financial order and regulatory regime and pointed at the need for sobering up to be able to avoid future bubbles in the finance market. At the same time, the events of 2008 were quickly forgotten regardless of a significant amount of tax money that was committed to secure the interests of finance market actors. As Mirowski (2013) demonstrates, a few years after 2008, it was more or less the case as if the events of 2008 never really happened. In 2013, five years after the Lehman Brothers bankruptcy, Eugene F. Fama, the father of the EMH, the anchoring point for much free-market policy-making (Bryan and Rafferty, 2013: 132–133; Centeno and Cohen, 2012: 328; Mizruchi and Stearns, 2005: 292), was awarded the Bank of Sweden's Nobel Memorial Prize in Economic Sciences for his "studies of finance markets." The role of EMH as a guiding star for over four decades of free-market policy-making was not emphasized in the committee's decision. The economics profession's mainstream explanation was that the events of 2008 were more or less a bump in the road of the neoclassical economic theory highway, and as they could point at the limited effect on the stock-markets, they proposed that there was no reason to implement either new "economic theories," or new regulatory approaches (Mirowski, 2013). The hegemony of neoclassical economic theory and its accompanying policy programs was manifested in broad daylight the years following that grim fall of 2008. Free-market protagonists indeed did not let the chance to blame the state for the event go to waste, and a poor design of the regulatory control and the state's role in promoting a subprime home mortgage market became favorite explanations. The greed and risk-taking, including the widespread use of quite spectacular off-the-balance-sheet vehicles, was not treated as an important factor to consider. As always, in this understanding, when the market fails, it is the state that is to blame. "Never forget: for neoliberals, the preordained answer to any problem, economic or otherwise, is more markets" (Mirowski, 2013: 332).

This chapter will address some of the implications of the strong reliance on finance markets and the finance industry in the era of financialization. While the events of 2008 pointed at the need to critically examine a number of the practices and policies in the finance industry, this chapter

[1] As Mirowski (2013) emphasizes, many of these free marketeers could as usual take refuge in the comfortable and all-too-familiar idea that the government and its policies and regulations were ultimately to blame for the collapse of the finance market (see also Blyth, 2013).

will not again repeat what happened during the first eight years of the new millennium but rather address some of the suggestions for changes that were proposed when the immediate crisis was handled.

SOCIOLOGICAL AND NEOCLASSIC VIEWS OF THE MARKET

The Sociological Perspective

In the economic sociology view, there is no "market" per se, but the concept of the market is instead a linguistic marker that social actors make use of for our own convenience to denote a variety of activities, practices, resources, and materialities put to use. In the neoclassic view of the market, the market is the supreme information processor, effectively sharing available information in the pricing of assets, but in the economic sociology enactment of the market, the market is "built from the bottom up," and consequently markets are not natural or primordial economic sites but are to be conceived as human accomplishments. Whether these markers are efficient or not is an empirical question and not an operative principle, and empirical evidence in many cases suggests that markets are all-too-human constructions demonstrating many flaws and shortcomings. Not the least the presence of bubbles and bursts over history in the era of financialization makes the neoclassic view of the market complicated. While mainstream economists assume that markets always already exist as some original site for economic exchanges, economic sociologists are concerned with understanding how markets are made and reproduced. Such a model of the market as what is made and created rather than what is excluded from the analysis opens up for a performative view of economic transactions (MacKenzie, 2006). For instance, markets include a variety of resources and practices including machines, tools, technologies, calculative practices, valuation and commensuration activities, information exchanges, regulatory frameworks, the production of texts and documents, and so on. As Esposito (2013: 108) remarks, "economics is included within the object it describes . . . [but] it must observe the economy from the inside, and this as though it were an external observer." As there are few such standpoints from the outside of the economic system, the analysts must start from the point of view that they are in the midst of a constant assembling of market devices (Callon et al., 2007) and market practices that simultaneously constitute and are the effect of market transactions and exchanges. More specifically, any actor operating on a market relies on what Zuckerman (2012) speaks of as a *principle of self-recursion*: it is not the *value* per se, the "objective" or "foundational" value of a certain commodity that determines the decision whether to buy or sell for example, a financial asset, but the *perceived value* of the asset in the eyes of *other* market actors. Zuckerman (2012) uses the example first used by John Maynard Keynes of a beauty contest organizer that selects young women to participate not so much on the organizer's own preferences but on basis of what she thinks *others* would regard a beautiful woman, that is, personal preferences and valuations are less useful than, in this case, a general understanding of societal and local beliefs regarding female beauty. Zuckerman applies this general "second-order observation logic" (see for example, Luhmann, 2000: 64) to finance markets. In the case where financial returns are based on "buying at a low price and selling high," while at the same time prices are determined by the "prevailing valuation," market participants acting rationally should anticipate trends in how the market actors price the asset rather than to calculate some "objective value of assets" (Zuckerman, 2012: 234). That is, they should look at the movements in the price volatility rather than fixed pricing points. Based on the principle of self-recursion, the concept of per-formativity is central to the operations in economic action, Esposito says:

> The operators decide not only on the basis of what they know and what they want, but also on the basis of how the others will observe their decisions and how they will act. They recognize that it is the behavior of others, that will ulti-mately determine whether their decision is right or wrong. (Esposito, 2013: 111)

All skilled market-based action is thus based on the capacity to anticipate the actions of others, and consequently economic action and the market at large, the aggregated effect of economic action, is performativity pro-duced: "[e]conomic operations generate the reality in which they operate and the unpredictability they face as a result" (Esposito, 2013: 112). The second corollary is that economic action becomes so when someone *defines* an action as being economic: "[e]very behavior, object, or institu-tion becomes economic only when economics define it as such," Esposito (2013: 113) argues (see also Reay, 2012: 76).

Cheng and Xiong (2014) offer one fine example of the performativity of finance actors in the case they refer to as the "financialization of com-modity markets." In the 2000–2008 period, *commodity futures*, a financial instrument aimed at predicting future commodity prices, was widely circulated. In this period, the price volatility of many commodities also "spiked," Cheng and Xiong (2014: 7.2) write. Cheng and Xiong (2014: 7.2) suggest that processes of financialization have transformed the com-modities market through the ability to inform the market mechanisms that Cheng and Xiong (2014) refer to as "risk-sharing" and "information discovery." Examining the case of the oil market, Cheng and Xiong (2014: 7.19) account for how a series of "economic fundamentals" indicated a peak of the economic cycle in October 2007. At this point in time, the S&P 500, the FTSE 100, DAX, and Nikkei equity indices reached their highest points, and in March 2008, the Bear Stearns collapse further contributed to a less assuring view of the state of the global economy. At the same time, in the first half of 2008, the oil price was pushed up by more than 40 percent. Cheng and Xiong (2014: 7.19) argue convincingly that the growth of the emerging economies, whereof China made a prognosis suggesting a slowdown of its economic growth, would not sufficiently explain the soaring oil price. Rather than being explained on the basis of elementary yet robust economic mechanisms including an upward moving intersection of supply and demand curves, Cheng and Xiong (2014: 7.19) suggest that capital was transferred from the declining US real estate market (showing evidence of major changes being underway in the summer and fall of 2007) to the commodities market, which in turn led to a speculation on the price of crude oil. This is where the performativity of finance market actors becomes salient. As oil the prices went up, the European Central Bank (ECB) motivated an increase in its key interest rate in early July 2008, just before the bust in oil prices; "the large increase in commodity prices in early 2008 . . . may have temporarily influenced people's expectations of global economic strength and thus commodity demand by distorting price signals" (Cheng and Xiong, 2014: 7.19). Speaking against many economic fundamentals, the ECB acted on the basis of commodity market indica- tors, thus serving to amplify finance market speculation, derived from declining return-on-investment prospects in the real estate market and causing an inflow of finance capital into commodities markets, into "real economy" effects when the cost for finance capital was raised through the ECB's higher interest rates; finance market operations therefore have performative capacities. When commodity prices are inflated for the benefit of the (successful) finance market speculator, someone suffers the consequences as the cost to acquire finance capital increases. When for example, finance market actors and commentators speak about "the market" in anthropomorphic terms as a freestanding and autonomous actor *sui generis*, this rhetoric veils the inner working of markets as being based not so much on structural and systemic traits as on individual action and specific groups' interests (Carruthers and Kim, 2011).

The Neoclassic and the Heterodox View

In contrast to this sociological view of the market, based on the idea of performativity, in the neoclassical economic tradition of thinking, economic transactions are enacted as things that occur in the equilibrium wherein many actors negotiate contracts and exchange goods and services and intangible assets such as financial assets. In this view, the market is always already in place. Practically speaking, economists know that there is a great deal of effort put into creating markets and in for example, states discounting risks in policy-making to enable private initiatives, but the problem is that neoclassical economic theory and its reliance on mathematical modeling fail to take into account such processes. Instead, *ex hypothesi*, markets are always already in place, and there are no particular reasons for integrating market-making per se into the models. This proposition makes neoclassic economics not so much a science in the Newtonian tradition of being based on a combination of empirical data and robust theoretical modeling but is better described as being in a Copernican stage. Nikolai Copernicus failed to see, as Kepler did later, that the astral bodies did not move in circles but in *ellipses*, as Copernicus was relying on the dominant Platonist dogma of the aesthetics and rationality of the circle and the sphere (Hallyn, 1990). For a philosopher of science like Isabelle Stengers (1997: 21), this breakthrough finding makes Kepler a true hero of scientific investigation as he actively used empirical data and mathematical modeling to calculate the *actual trajectories* of astral bodies, not assuming them to be circular from the beginning and using data to prove the model to be true.

It is important to notice that the category of economists is a large and in many ways heterogeneous group, representing many theoretical and methodological orientations and expressing various political concerns and preferences (Breslau, 2013; Reay, 2012, 2007; Fourcade, 2009). Hyman Minsky is one important post-Keynesian economist not sharing the firm belief in the market as the ultimate processor of information (for an introduction to Minsky's work and life, see Mehrling, 1999). In his work *Stabilizing an Unstable Economy* (1986), Minsky argues that the empirical fact that there has been recurrent instabilities and crises in the capitalist economic system since at least the mid-1960s (not to mention the events after the publication of Minsky's work and his death in 1996) is rendered insignificant in what Minsky refers to as the "neoclassical synthesis." As Minsky (1986: 99) rightly points out – following (but without recognizing it) Max Weber's proposition that scientific disciplines are sets of *theoretical* problems – "questions that are meaningful in the world are often nonsense questions within a theory." In standard economic theory, the question "Why is our economy so unstable?," of great interest for a variety of actors and not the least the layman dependent on economists' explanations, is a "nonsense question," Minsky argues. "Standard economic theory not only does not lead to an explanation of instability as a system attribute, it really does not recognize that endogenous instability is a problem that a satisfactory theory must explain," Minsky (1986: 99) proposes. He continues:

> Within the neoclassical theory, fluctuations, disequilibrium, and financial trauma can only occur because of shocks or changes imposed from outside the system. Thus, a great deal of what happens in history is explained as the result of institutional failures in unique historical circumstances. Dominant events such as the Great Depression of the 1930s cannot be explained as the result of systemic characteristics so long as the world is viewed through the binders imposed by neoclassical theory. (Minsky, 1986: 139)

In other words, the neoclassical synthesis enacts the economic system a self-regulating and naturally occurring system that are brought into disequilibrium only by external pressures, including political decisions, the work of unions, and other "institutions" that are theoretically positioned outside of the economic system. For Minsky (1986), this theoretical model undermines any comprehensive understanding of the dynamics of economic systems: "[i]t may be that what the neoclassical theory ignores, namely institutions, and in particular financial institutions, leads to the observations it cannot explain" (Minsky, 1986: 101). We can here illustrate this point with reference to the trading of property rights in markets: "[m]arkets by definition involve the exchange of property rights. But governments define property rights. Studies of markets that ignore politics – or contests about what governments should do – therefore overlook a powerful explanation" (Jacobs and Myers, 2014: 768).

While the new generation of finance theorists operating in the neoclassical economic tradition would generally understand the market as a superior mechanism for pricing assets and propose that the reliance on market transactions is what ultimately constitutes the resilience of the economy, Minsky (1986) draws exactly the opposite conclusion: it is the finance market and the finance industry actors that bring in mechanisms (for example, rent-seeking) that casts the economy into a process of perpetual change and that on a systemic basis produce crises and economic collapses. This is what Mirowski (2010) speaks of as the "inherent vice" of markets. Says Minsky (1986): "[t]he multi-billion corporations, which dominate our economy, borrow in a wide array of financial markets and from many different institutions in order to carry out their operations and fulfill their financial contracts . . . In our economy, nonfinancial corporations have many of the liability management attributes of banks" (Minsky, 1986: 42).

Mehrling (2011: 67) argues that the basic problem in a "capital-using economy" is that *illiquidity* is a "fact of life" inasmuch as "long-lived capital assets are the source of so much realized cash flow." Such capital generates a cash flow only over an extended period of time, which means that illiquidity is always a problem for the economy as a whole, and therefore also for the individual agent operating within the economy. In the case where the money market and the capital market are "intertwined" as in the case of the US, the problem of illiquidity is handled through various hedging operations, securing the owners' of capital assets access to liquid assets. But hedging operations, Minsky argues, can easily be overtaken by speculating finance actors, making the financial system inherently fragile and unstable. "Why this tendency towards fragility?," Mehrling (2011: 68) asks. "The reason ultimately is the liquidity preference of wealth holders," he responds. Capital owners want to secure their access to cash flow and when money markets and capital markets are folded into one another, it is increasingly difficult to distinguish *speculative* from *productive* credit (Mehrling, 2011: 48). As the neoclassical synthesis takes a most positive view of the calculative practices of the finance industry, proponents of the finance-led economy of the era of financialization fail to see how the finance market is based on the ability to change position and to make profit on basis of Zuckerman's (2012) principle of self-recursion; the innate dynamics and instability of the finance market is thus the blind-spot of the neoclassical synthesis (Minsky, 1986: 140). Worse still, as have been observed at countless occasions during the last four decades, "theory lends legitimacy to policy" (Minsky, 1986: 139): "[t]he neoclassical synthesis put blinders on policy makers by restricting the legitimate options to manipulating government spending and taxation and operating upon the money supply" (Minsky, 1986: 139–140).

Minsky thus represents what Mehrling (1999: 138) refers to as a "hyper-modern institutionalism," wherein it is *institutions*, not *markets*, that need to be examined. The institutions of the economy "do not merely organize the stuff of some pre-existing real world; they are the only real world there is," Mehrling (1999: 138) writes. He continues: "[f]inancial relationships are not about mediating something else on the 'real' side of the economy; they are constitutive relationship of the whole system. The veil of money is the very fabric of the modern economy" (Mehrling, 1999: 138). For Minsky, the blind faith in the market's ability to "stabilize itself" leads to one financial crisis after the other, and the first casualty is competitive capitalism as managerial capitalism evolves into what Minsky came to call *money manager capitalism* (Mehrling, 1999: 131); when state subsidies and the rescue activities implemented benefit large-scale organizations, "big business went out, but big finance came in" (Mehrling, 1999: 131).

Needless to say, Minsky is commonly portrayed as a heterodox economist, not subscribing to the mainstream, predominant neoclassical

economic theory view. Yet, his analysis, firmly anchored in formal neoclassical economic theory and its methods, have been very influential
during the last period of time, and after the finance industry collapse of
2008 in particular. Minsky's (1986) critique of the idea that only external
forces can destabilize the economic system is of great importance for the
understanding of the substantial critique of all kinds of political regulation and the work of labor organizations such as unions, that is, the "free-
market capitalism program." Such political action is not only unfavorable
for the proponents of the neoclassical synthesis – they represent a violation
of the theoretical framework *par préférence* at its very core. Consequently,
Minsky (1986) argues, there are many things in the economic system that
cannot be explained on the basis of the predominant theory, and many
concerns and issues that are easily detected on an empirical basis are portrayed as anomalies or as insignificant events. Still, the work of Minsky
(1986) is commonly located in the fringes of economic theory.

Finance Theory as Market-maker

While mainstream finance theory economists treated Minsky as an
"eccentric crank" (Martin, 2014: 218) and dismisses basically anyone not
sharing their convictions as "economic Luddites" (Martin, 2014: 192),
Minsky would rise to prominence during the 2008 rescue activities, long
after Minsky's death in 1996. Larry Sumners, a leading American economist former chief economist of the World Bank, and Barack Obama's
economic adviser, listed Hyman Minsky as one source of influence in the
work to restore the finance markets in the fall of 2008 (Martin, 2014: 191).
Minsky's contribution lies in his ability to connect the national, regional,
and global finance market and the macroeconomy while still recognizing
the role of the government, what Martin (2014) refers to as the *sovereign*.
A key concern for the new generation of finance theorists was that the
"everyday central banking practice remained annoyingly ambivalent
towards the so-called 'neoclassical' theory," Martin (2014: 219) writes.
"How could modern orthodox microeconomics hold its head up as queen
of the social sciences if it could not even win over its own policy-makers?"
(Martin, 2014: 219). Then again, the major innovations of the new theory
of finance markets, including the theory of portfolio balance, the Capital
Asset Pricing Model (CAPM), and the theory of option pricing, were
eagerly adopted by finance market practitioners, naturally interested in
making sense of what they were doing and in acquiring tools and heuristics that could guide their day-to-day work (Martin, 2014: 221). As the
new theories were brought into the everyday work in financial trading
while being less recognized in policy-making quarters, finance theory were

increasingly focusing on the pricing of securities on private markets while ignoring macroeconomic conditions and the role of the government as the lender of last resort. "By ignoring the essential link between the financial securities traded on the capital market and the monetary system operated by the sovereign and the banks, academic finance built a theory of finance without the macroeconomy just as neoclassical macroeconomics [had previously] built a theory without finance," Martin (2014: 221) argues. This ignorance of the role of the government was in part caused by the esthetic criterion of purity in economic models favored in neoclassical economic theory, where economists "felt no need to complicate things with the additional dimension of liquidity" (Martin, 2014: 221–222). In addition, free-market beliefs and anti-statism ideologies contributed to the new orthodoxy: "I don't see that the private market, in creating this wonderful array of derivatives, is creating any systemic risk . . . However, there is someone around creating systemic risks: the government," Economist and Nobel laureate Fisher Black (cited in Martin, 2014: 223) declared. These kind of "anti-authority fantasies" (Martin, 2014: 223) were frequently articulated in the 1980s, 1990s, and in new millennium. As neoclassic economic theory was increasingly treated by economists as "the theory of everything" at the end of history (that is, after what was understood as the final triumph of market liberalism) economists "were proudly marching out under the respective banners to fight the good fight and evangelise their gospel" (Martin, 2014: 222).

This general belief in the innate rationality of markets was further emphasized in the case of finance markets, ultimately based on calculative practices and the capacity to render assets liquid to enable trade. For orthodox economists, the combination of markets and calculative practices created a strong instrumental orientation in the processes of information and *eo ipso* the pricing of assets that they had much faith in. But beneath the instrumental and calculative veneer of finance trading, also finance markets accommodated information inconsistencies and shortage, and bounded rationality. "Money is a social relation created from prospective promises," Pixley (2012: 10) argues. She continues: "[r]ational calculation is only retrospective, unable to 'see' beyond the chasm separating the future from promise made in the present." As a consequence, this social relation is based on "uncertain outcomes," Pixley (2012: 11) argues, making "rational calculations" on the basis of historical data incapable of fully predicting outcomes. Therefore, finance is "inherently emotional and relational." Pixley (2012: 11) here uses the term "future-oriented emotions" and "institutionalized emotions," which arise from the "uncertainty of money." "Distrust and trust motivate all financial action," Pixley (2012: 11) summarizes. This social and emotional embedding of money must not be ignored when examining finance markets. In addition to such a view of money, Martin (2014) argues, which Minsky (1986) understood, that what was missing from the new body of finance theory was the insight that *liquidity* – which came to a halt in the fall of 2008 – is a distinct property of credit, either represented by money or as "inert bilateral credit" (Martin, 2014: 221). Credit is thus the connecting point between finance markets and the macroeconomy, and when credit runs short, the finance market closes down unless the sovereign makes a move to restore functional finance markets by acting as the lender of last resort. When ignoring the role of the sovereign – the state and the government – as a significant, yet not always active participant in finance markets, "modern academic finance had ended up as a formal, mathematical theory of money in Utopia, a world with an infinite array of substitutable claims, with no mention of sovereign money," Martin (2014: 222) claims. But as this Utopia was based on the fragile fundament of increased debt and excessive risk-taking – anomalies for free-market protagonists as markets were claimed to regulate themselves and to uncompromisingly punish individual actor's excessive risk-taking. By 2008, heterodox theorists such as Minsky were dusted off to once again reconnect finance markets to their mothership, the sovereign state.

THE NEW FINANCE MARKET ARCHITECTURE

Beginning in the early 1980s, the national and global finance markets have been deregulated to enable capital investment to flow freely across national borders and regions. Today, widespread international agreements have secured a situation wherein capital is increasingly liquid and capable of flowing into markets with high-rent potentials (Lépinay, 2011; Eichengreen, 2008; Singer, 2007; Abdelal, 2007). In addition, in the finance markets there has been a series of deregulatory policies implemented in for example, the US. Perrow (2010) comments on the gradual shift in policy in the US during the decade preceding the 2008 events:

> In just ten years, 1998–2007, the U.S. economy experienced a series of deregulatory acts that is, as Simon Johnson of MIT observed, "a river of deregulatory policies that is, in hindsight, astonishing" (Johnson, 2009). Financial firms and their think tanks and professional associations proposed and lobbied for these changes, and in some cases played a major role in drafting the legislation. (Perrow, 2010: 316)

Other commentators were equally concerned about this expansion of the finance market and its accompanying decline of regulatory control:

"[n]othing has contributed to imbalances in the economy so much as the outlandish expansion of financialization, although the imbalances have also promoted financialization," one commentator, Michael Perelman, remarked (2008, cited in Zalewski and Whalen, 2010: 758). James Crotty (2009: 564), a University of Massachusetts economist, uses the term the *New Financial Architecture* to refer to the "integration of modern day financial markets with the era's light government regulation." This new financial architecture included a few different components, including: (1) new financial instruments; (2) reduced regulatory control; (3) the reliance on credit ratings that underrated the risk-taking; and (4) increased debt-based consumption. These four components will be addressed below.

New Financial Instruments

The inflow of capital into the American economy and the pro-business, anti-statist policy of the Reagan era made the finance industry the "industry of the decade" in the 1980s. Finance had previously been a somewhat dull professional domain of expertise, closely related to accounting, but the new conditions and the newly developed finance theory within the neoclassical economic framework facilitated opportunities for a new professional category of knowledge workers to emerge. Derivatives, MBSs, CDOs, and credit default swaps (CDSs) are examples of some of the new financial instruments that were developed to enable further value extraction from underlying assets, for example, home mortgages (Blinder, 2013; Lépinay, 2011). In theory, such new instruments complement other financial assets and make capital more liquid as they serve to spread risks better and to reduce transactions costs. The implementation of a long series of new financial instruments led to the sharp growth of the accumulated value of financial assets: "[t]he value of financial assets in the US grew from four times GDP in 1980 to ten times GDP in 2007" (Crotty, 2009: 575). In nominal terms, the global market for the new category of financial instruments called derivatives rose from US$41 trillion in 1997 to US$677 trillion in 2007 (Callinicos, 2009: 74). Such financial assets are not *per se* complicated to trade and can serve a key role in a sound financial market, but problems occur when they grow in proportion to other assets and the risks increase dramatically. In addition, these new financial assets (for example, CDOs) are complicated to price and consequently they are more illiquid than, say, a stock being directly related to an underlying asset (MacKenzie and Spears, 2014b: 424). Crotty (2009) discusses this pricing problem:

> The relation between the value of a CDO and the value of it mortgages is complex and nonlinear. Significant changes in the value of underlying

mortgages induce large and unpredictable movements in CDO values. Rating agencies and the investment banks that create these securities rely on extremely complicated simulation models to price them. It can take a powerful computer several days to determine the price of a CDO. (Crotty, 2009: 567)

Bluhm and Wagner (2011: 217) argue on basis of lengthy mathematical modeling and calculations that CDOs are "highly complex" and therefore need a "certain repertoire that includes valuation teams, booking capabilities, monitoring facilities, etc." If such a repertoire is not in place and fully functional (as could be the case for, for example, smaller institutions), "then it is not recommended to invest in CDOs" Bluhm and Wagner (2011: 217) state. In short, Bluhm and Wagner (2011: 218) summarize, "it takes a lot to be successful in the CDO investor space." During the 2008 crisis, CDOs could be only sold at an enormous loss, indicating that this particular financial asset demands a stable and even a growing finance market:

> The assets in CDOs are illiquid. Since they are rarely traded they cannot be marked to market or revalued as market price change . . . When hedge funds owned by the investment bank Bear Stearns incurred large losses on subprime mortgages in late June 2007, the bank began to auction the most highly rated among them, but called the auction off when bids were only 85–90 percent of face value. (Crotty, 2008: 176)

Colander et al. (2009: 253) explain this pricing problem and its consequential illiquidity on the basis of the absence of historical empirical data that can be used to calculate the value of an asset over the economic cycle: the absence of such data series made the underlying theoretical foundations regarding for example, risks and default probabilities, of these products "highly questionable."

As MacKenzie and Pardo-Guerra (2014: 157) argue, successful innovations, also in the finance industry, are "nearly always bricolage": innovations are commonly not the "mechanical implementation of a grand plan nor simply logical deduction from existing scientific theory (or, in the case of finance, from economics)" (MacKenzie and Pardo-Guerra, 2014: 157), but are based on the creative and ad hoc reuse of existing resources to provide tools and calculative practices that have proven to "work" in real life settings. Therefore, to be successful in pricing and trading financial assets is not so much a matter of demonstrating "[a]n explicit ideological commitment to a particular idea of the market place" (MacKenzie and Pardo-Guerra, 2014: 157), as it is to be able handle local situations and "immediate problems," as well as to recognize "wider goals" in the community. In the case of the Gaussian copula model developed by the so-called quants hired by Wall Street finance institutions to price derivatives such as CDOs, these mathematically skilled innovators "[w]ent for what 'worked,' not for what was culturally homogeneous, 'pure' or 'beautiful'" (MacKenzie and Spears, 2014a: 410). The problem was still that this pricing and risk-assessment model "worked" quite differently in the rating agencies, regulating the financial markets as many traders were forbidden either by regulation or by organizational mandates to buy anything other than investment-grade securities (MacKenzie and Spears, 2014b: 428), and in the finance institutions. In the rating agencies, a financial asset was rated *once*, and a grading of the financial asset was issued; in the finance institutions, in contrast, the same financial assets were subject to a constant monitoring of risks, calculated value, and returns on the asset. In short, these two forms of organizations operated within different temporal horizons and under different objectives.

The innovation of the Gaussian copula model, not being "a single, unitary model" (MacKenzie and Spears, 2014a: 398) but a bricolage of elements, was integrated into what MacKenzie and Spears (2014a) refer to as an *evaluation culture*, based on a "[d]istinctive set of assumptions about what 'the economic world' is made of, together with a mechanism of socialization into those practices and beliefs" (MacKenzie and Spears, 2014a: 395). Being something different than the isolated and autonomous *homo ecomomicus* actor of neoclassic economy theory, members in evaluation cultures always needs to participate in *shared* calculative practices, also to pursue self-interested goals:

> Culture and rationality are not opposed, even if rationality is constructed as the pursuit of narrow self-interest. Even the most selfishly rational actor needs to calculate what is in his or her best interest, and that calculation of necessity partakes in the material culture of finance. Because such culture differs, and because there is no a priori way to be entirely sure which practices are the most efficacious, even a fully reflexive, rational actor cannot stand outside of finance's culture and evaluations. (MacKenzie and Spears, 2014b: 428)

In this view, to be able to trade complex derivatives, there is a need for shared methods to price the financial assets, and therefore the work of highly paid quantitative analysts (so-called "quants") hired by for example, investment banks, are needed not just to try to "capture the way the world is," but also to achieve the "uncoordinated action" that occurs when many actors participating in the trade use the same calculative practices (MacKenzie and Spears, 2014b: 437). That is, the mathematical models used to price derivatives are, again, *performative* insofar as they enable uncoordinated action through their very use. This is also the reason why, MacKenzie and Spears (2014b: 437) argue, investment banks – "those apparently most capitalist of institutions" – quite frequently give away, free of charge, "models in whose development they have invested much time and money."

Despite all the efforts to develop and distribute robust models for calculating the risks of derivatives such as CDOs, by February 2009, it was estimated that "almost half of all the CDOs ever issued had defaulted" (Crotty, 2009: 567). The excessive risk-taking involved in the quick expansion of CDOs was also accompanied by a massive concentration of the ownership of these new financial assets, further increasing the systemic risk. In the US, the seven largest commercial banks held 98 percent of the industry's derivatives (Crotty, 2008: 173). In addition, there was a widespread use of new advanced information technology-based applications when trading financial assets. Lenglet (2011: 47) reports that by the end of August 2009, "large banks recognized that approximately 80 percent of their total equity trading flows in some markets was being processed by algorithms." This so-called *robot trading* based on the use of advanced mathematical modeling and calculations represents the most recent step towards a full automatization of financial engineering, shortening the time to make transactions but also eliminating human reflection and attention altogether from the trade. Under "normal conditions" such trading may work as anticipated, but as soon as there is any turbulence in the system, there are few mediating mechanisms that stabilize the system.

Reduced Regulatory Control and Relaxed Money Lending Routines

In addition to the finance industry itself inventing new ways to "slice and dice" and repackage underlying financial assets into new financial instruments, policy-making during the last four decades has widely embraced the neoclassical view of the market as what is both inherently rational and capable of regulating itself. As a consequence, policy has been directed to reduce governmental oversight and control and to let market actors (for example, credit rating agencies (CRAs) themselves take care of their own regulatory control, a concept that rests on the idea of the risk of lost "market credibility" of the CRAs in the event of inadequate ratings. As indicated by Perrow (2010), a deregulatory finance market wave swept through Washington in the decade preceding the 2008 events. In 1984, 1990, and 2005, Congress passed laws "exempting certain financial contracts from the standard provisions of the Bankruptcy Code" (Sissoko, 2010: 6), and the New Deal regulatory framework of the 1930s was eliminated step-by-step, leading to the repeal of the Glass-Steagall Act in 1999. In the critical account by Stiglitz (2009: 333) of the policy-making under Alan Greenspan's leadership of the Federal Reserve (see also Jabłecki and Machaj, 2009; Batra, 2005), the elimination of the Glass-Steagall Act served to spread risk-taking from investment banking to commercial banks, institutions that "should have acted in a far more prudential manner," Stiglitz (2009: 333) says. Federal Reserve officials and other policy-makers maintained the free-market belief until the crisis could no longer be denied, and these policies did not in any way anticipate the degree of risk-taking in the financial institutions. Timothy Geithner, the New York Federal Reserve chairman, and Hank Paulson's successor as Treasury Secretary in the George W. Bush Administration, stated in 2006 that the current financial system was more resilient as there was less risk "concentrated in banks," and that the "probability of systemic financial crises" would therefore be lower. In the same year, the IMF made a similar proclamation, praising the "dispersion of credit risks" as what served to stabilize the financial system (Crotty, 2009: 567). However, as the regulatory control was relaxed as markets were expected to be self-regulatory and able to look after themselves, the financial institutions took excessive risks as they overrated the value of their assets: "[f]rom 1973 to 2003, the US Securities and Exchange Commission (SEC) limited investment bank leverage to 12 times capital. However, in 2004, under pressure from Goldman Sachs chairman and later Treasury Secretary Henry Paulson, it raised the acceptable leverage ratio to 40 times capital and made compliance voluntary" (Crotty, 2009: 574).

In addition, using so-called *off-balance sheet vehicles* (White, 2009; Arnold, 2009), a highly questionable procedure, banks could further leverage their capital stock but also make an already instable system even more vulnerable to a downturn in the economy and a recalculation of the value of the assets held (Blinder, 2013). "[A] huge quantity of subprime mortgage-backed securities was held off-balance sheet, in 'structured investment vehicles,'" White (2009: 394) remarks. Crotty (2009: 574) stresses that commercial banks "appeared to be adequately capitalized" as they "overestimated the value of on-balance-sheet assets" at the same time as a high percentage of their most "vulnerable assets" (later relabeled "toxic assets" in the TARP rescue campaign) were hidden in off-balance-sheet vehicles. The consequence was an excessive level of leverage and enormous risk exposure, and many European banks had a leverage ratio of 50 or more before the 2008 crisis. By the end of 2008, many large banks had "[s]een their equity position evaporate to the brink of insolvency and beyond, only massive government bailouts kept these 'zombie banks' alive" (Crotty, 2009: 574).

The starting point for this expansion of and increased risk-taking in the finance system was the creation of a subprime housing market, a government initiative where the finance institutions Freddie Mac and Fannie

Mae initially served a key role (Gotham, 2006). This initiative *per se* cannot explain the collapse of the global finance market but was definitely part of the story as it served to increase the stock of mortgage loans that was transformed into financial assets and soon enough traded globally (Fligstein and Habinek, 2014). The US housing market boom, starting in the late 1990s and taking off in the 2002–2005 period, was fueled by sub-prime mortgage lending, which in turn increased the trade of CDOs and other MBSs These financial engineering operations translated subprime risks into sources of profit for the mortgage originators (White, 2009: 394). In the 1998 to 2001 period, the subprime mortgage loans accounted for 10 to 15 percent of annual mortgage originations in the US; by 2006 such loans accounted for "[m]ore than one third of all mortgage origina-tions" (Jarsulic, 2013: 24). In the 2001–2006 period, more than US$4 trillion of subprime mortgage loans were originated. While it is true that this market creation is derived from political decision, it does not explain all the risk-taking in the finance industry during the last decades (Blinder, 2013: 18–19) and is therefore just another opportunity to blame the gov-ernment for everything under the sun that goes wrong.[2] In contrast, Polillo (2011: 457) suggests that the new finance regime provided access to capital in market niches historically marginalized by the credit system (hence the term *subprime* mortgages),[3] but that the instituted norms regarding creditworthiness and ultimately the "moral authority" of money were violated in the process (see also Fourcade and Healy, 2013; Poon, 2009).[4]

---

[2] As Wisman (2013: 930) points out, the US housing market and the consumer behavior data demonstrate that the role of the real estate industry in the era of financialization needs to be carefully examined: "[i]n spite of shrinking average household size (2.9 in 1973 to 2.5 in 2003), the average home size in the USA almost doubled, rising from 1,400 square feet in 1970 to 2,700 square feet in 2007, and whereas home-owners paid about twice their family income for a home, by 2007 they were paying five times." In addition, although median household income fell slightly between 1999 and 2005 in the US, the average house price rose by 42 percent (Wisman, 2013: 933), a condition that indicates the oversupply of finance capital in the real estate market.

[3] Fourcade and Healy (2013: 565) here use the neologism *Lumpenscoretariat* to denote people that receive low so-called FICO credit scores on their loan applications.

[4] Ailon (2012) demonstrates how *Wall Street Journal* editorials addressing the cases of the corporate scandals of LTCM and Enron have served the role of promoting the "legiti-macy and popularity of finance" (Ailon, 2012: 255) and how issues such as risk have been addressed within a new framework of understanding, no longer being what should be mini-mized given certain "risk-avoidance functions" of actors but being examined on basis of a combination of "indeterminacy" and "hyper-responsibilization" (Ailon, 2012: 265). What Ailon (2012) refers to as "the risk-management discourse" advanced by *Wall Street Journal* commentators "works backwards," Ailon (2012: 266) suggests: "First a disaster, then the explanation of the causes in an earlier transgression of probabilities. First the unforeseen happen, then all the things that would have been known are assembled; first indetermina-tion, then hyper-responsibilization." Such a "retrospective risk-management narrative," where things that were unknown by the time of the decision made are *ex post facto* treated

The rise and fall of the American subprime mortgage market is therefore indicative of the seemingly paradoxical process in financial expansion of simultaneous *homogenization* and *differentiation*, where local economic conditions (for example, the Californian housing market) is bound up with global capital flows and the use of derivate instruments and securities to even out local risks:

> Subprime mortgages, while they circulate in global markets, are local currencies tied to the purchase of real estate. They were explicitly devised to make previous criteria of credit assessment irrelevant because of the purported power of those who bundled them in derivate instruments to parcel out risk. Mortgage-backed securities held the promise of erasing inequalities in risk and increasing homogenization; instead, they created a conflict over creditworthiness, indeed a crisis over what constitutes the moral authority of money. This conflict implicated and destabilized local circuits of money in perhaps unprecedented ways, representing a victory for wildcat banking of epic proportions. (Polillo, 2011: 457)

The subprime mortgage market was the creation of the finance industry itself, and similar to the finance innovation of junk bonds in the 1980s, championed by Michael Milken and others (Singer, 2007: 85), was designed to disrupt instituted standards of creditworthiness to be able to extract economic value from also the last niches of the mortgage market not yet exploited. And just as in the case of the junk bond market, speculation in combination with lenient regulatory control was the driver of the expansion of these contracts:

---

as if they should in fact have been known (that is, the "hyper-responsibilization") serve to "solidify a sense of financial market-justice" (Ailon, 2012: 266). As a consequence, effective risk-management is what the market rewards, but it is simultaneously based on a notion of justice that is only possible to define retrospectively, after the fact and in accordance with the outcomes. This represents a performative view of justice; justice is what is actually produced under specific conditions. In other words, retrospective risk-management narrative does little to explain *how* and *why* certain risk-management practices are rewarded or punished, and can only in hindsight explain what happened and why. The narrative is thus based on a sense of ontological indeterminacy or even fatalism, and a morality of responsibilization; actors could not have foreseen certain events and outcomes, yet they must expect to be held responsible *ex post facto*. As Power (2013: 530) examines, this way to enact finance markets and their operations leads to a new view of fraud, shifting from the "detection of *actual* frauds" to the "design of systems oriented towards fraud risk." This in turn leads to a "normalization of fraud," including a new conceptualization of fraud from being an exceptional and extraordinary occurrence to "one risk among many to be managed" (Power, 2013: 534). That is, in the new financial architecture, a curious blend of indeterminacy, moral obligations to carry responsibilities regardless of the possibilities for making adequate predictions, and a tolerance for working in an environment where a variety of risks are to be constantly managed and monitored, need to be developed by the finance market actor or anyone collaborating with finance market actors.

Few holders of [subprime] mortgages could afford to pay the higher rates they would likely face in two years. In the true bubble mentality, they were essentially betting on rising house prices. If their house values rose enough, they could refine their mortgages to years later, pay off their old ARMs [adjustable-rate mortgages] (thus avoiding higher mortgage rates) and even take some cash out of the deal. (Blinder, 2013: 70–71)

To repeat, in the 1997–2006 period, housing prices rose with a factor of 4.5 faster than US Consumer Price Index (White, 2013: 104). In October 2005, then Chairman of the Council of Economic Advisers Ben Bernanke, eventually chairman of the Federal Reserve, delivered a speech before Congress wherein he testified that the recent upswing in housing prices was evidence of a vital, well-functioning economy: "[h]ousing prices have risen by nearly 25 percent in the past two years. Although speculative activity has increased in some areas, at a national level these price increases largely reflect strong economic fundamentals" (cited in Mian and Sufi, 2014: 78).

Mian and Sufi (2009) offer a detailed statistical analysis of the subprime mortgage market, using US postal codes to examine how certain neighborhoods that historically were excluded from the market were suddenly made eligible for housing loans in the 2002–2005 period. "This pattern is prevalent in almost every city in the United States," Mian and Sufi (2009: 1492) say. The analysis reveals that the 2002–2005 period is the *only period* in the 18 years examined in which mortgage growth and income growth are negatively correlated (Mian and Sufi, 2009: 1453). Apparently, the risk taking appetite and/or the routines for calculating creditworthiness was changed and/or modified in the period, and that is precisely what Mian and Sufi's (2009: 1453) analysis suggests: "[w]e show that subprime ZIP codes are more likely to be denied credit prior to the expansion in subprime mortgages. However, from 2002 to 2005, denial rates for subprime ZIP codes fall disproportionally." This relaxation of earlier credit-rationing constraints coincides with a few additional interesting conditions: first, the period in which credit growth becomes negatively correlated with income growth "[c]oincides exactly with the expansion of subprime mortgage securitization" (Mian and Sufi, 2009: 1453). Second, the increase in the rate of securitization is much stronger in subprime ZIP codes compared to prime ZIP codes during the 2002–2005 period. In addition, the relative increase is "[d]riven primarily by securitization sold to financial institutions not affiliated with the mortgage originator" (Mian and Sufi, 2009: 1453–1454). In other words, the subprime loans were to a higher extent repackaged into securities compared to other loans, and thereafter they were sold to other financial institutions on the global financial market (Fligstein and Habinek, 2014). The consequences of this credit expansion into previously unchartered markets and complemented by a new category of securities, became quite apparent after 2005. When the mortgage holders could not pay their loans in the 2006–2007 period, the default rate increased "significantly more" in subprime ZIP code areas (Mian and Sufi, 2009: 1454). "This result hints at moral hazard on behalf of originators as a factor contributing to the expansion of credit supply, although we believe more research is needed on this precise mechanism," Mian and Sufi (2009: 1454) argue. In their summary, Mian and Sufi (2009: 1454) state that unless a moral hazard explanation applies, that is, that the subprime lenders and issuers of securities were aware of the fragile construction of this category of financial instrument and sought to spread the risks, these actors made estimates predicting high-housing market price growths that eventually proved to be faulty. That is, lenders either, at worst, consciously inflated the mortgage market and used securities to reap the short-term financial benefits and to distribute the risks, or, at best, participated in an expansion of mortgage credit markets to subprime neighborhoods across the US to be able to speculate on increased housing prices in the 2002–2005 period.

After the subprime mortgage market burst and the Great Recession arrived, the top 10 percent of the net-worth income group increased their share of the wealth in the economy from 71 percent in 2007 (up from 66 percent in 1992) to 74 percent in 2010 (Mian and Sufi, 2014: 25). This tendency to make the rich stay rich while the poor get poorer is explained by the fact that the richest 10 percent held financial assets that performed much better during the recession than housing (Mian and Sufi, 2014: 23). In many cases, these financial assets were senior claims on houses. The finance markets were saved by the government, but homeowners were not in the position to take advantage of such privileges. Instead, in many states where the legislation did not require a juridical foreclosure saw real estate prices falling more than 40 percent, while the comparative figure in states that demanded juridical foreclosure stayed at 25 percent. As the ability to skip mortgage payments without being immediately foreclosed upon "acts as a type of unemployment insurance" (Mian and Sufi, 2014: 67), legal protection against too early foreclosures would have helped some more of the homeowners to outlive the finance industry crisis. Deregulatory juridical policies thus supported a quick liquidation of subprime mort-gage loans, benefiting the financial institutions but leaving homeowners without any mechanisms that stabilized the situation and counteracted the decline in housing prices. The subprime mortgage market and the accompanying juridical framework thus systematically concentrated risk on those "the least able to bear it," that is, the low-income groups that relied on subprime mortgage contracts (Mian and Sufi, 2014: 30). As homeowners holding low or non-existent levels of equity in their homes after the 25 to 40 percent pricefall on real estates struggled to balance their economy, private consumption was cut down to rebalance budgets and to secure a long-term stability in household spending. The US Census Bureau provides statistics that confirm a change in consumption patterns in the third quarter of 2008, after the Lehman Brothers bankruptcy. Over the period for which monthly data are available from the US Census Bureau, "retail sales had their worst percentage drop in October 2008, and their second worst drop in December 2008, and their third worst drop in November 2008" (Kahle and Stulz, 2013: 282). Kahle and Stulz (2013: 281) provide data that suggest that the financial crisis was a "common shock" that equally affected private consumers and impaired all kinds of firms regardless of whether they were dependent on credit or not. In other words, it was not the impaired access to capital that caused the Great Recession that followed the finance market collapse but a general decline in demand caused by new levels of uncertainty in the period. An additional consequence of the expansion and collapse of the subprime mortgage market was therefore, calculated by Mian and Sufi (2014: 66), the loss of 4 million jobs between March 2007 and March 2009, accounting for roughly 65 percent of all jobs lost in the sample during the period. In the worst cases, homeowners would first lose their homes in the event of foreclosure, and thereafter their jobs because of a decline in private consumption. These tragedies occurred on an everyday basis in states such as California and Florida, which both experienced up to a 50 percent rise in housing prices in the first years of the new millennium. At the same time "troubled assets" – in many cases securities constructed on the basis of mortgages originating in the subprime market – were generously taken over by the American taxpayers from finance institutions in distress. Ben Bernanke's assurance a few years earlier that "speculative activity" was a minor concern and that price levels reflected "strong economic fundamentals" was in sharp contrast with the bleak realities facing these unfortunate homeowners.

Martinez-Moyano et al.'s (2014) study of the gradual loss of internal control in the finance industry sheds some further light on the processes leading to what Vaughan (1996: 153) speaks of as the "normalization of deviance." Based on interviews with 70 finance industry regulators and finance industry actors, Martinez-Moyano et al. (2014: 328) suggest that identifying any violations of rules takes time, and that the assessment of the impact of these violations takes even longer, especially when "the transactions are complex and potential legal problems are ambiguous." In a culture where short-term profit maximization overrules all other organizational objectives, rule violations become normalized and are widely regarded in lenient and forgiving terms by managers, directors, and co-workers as "[t]rivial technical violations or bypassing of 'obsolete' rules incomparable with current business realities" (Martinez-Moyano et al., 2014: 328). Over time, this negligence of formal regulation leads to a structural and pervasive erosion of the regulatory control of the industry (see also Clark and Newell, 2013). External regulators try to prevent rule violations through a combination of inspection, market surveillance, and enforcement (Martinez-Moyano et al., 2014: 328), but if what MacKenzie and Spears (2014a, 2014b) refer to as the evaluation culture of the finance industry treats such activities as illegitimate or outmoded, evidence of negative attitudes toward rules can be found. "In some areas, including financial markets, rule enforcement erodes when the short-term benefits of production diminish concerns about unspecified, distant risks from rules or procedural violations," Martinez-Moyano et al. (2014: 333) argue. They continue: "[b]eliefs, cognitive assumptions, formal and informal procedures, and rewards for completing transactions versus maintaining tight internal controls reinforce the bias towards completing transactions and away from equally mindful enforcement of rules." In other words, eroding rule compliance is rooted in local organizational and industry cultures, and accompanying managerial practices and routines (see for example, Macéus, 2014). "Flexible" and "pragmatic" rule following are part of any industry and organization (Ortmann, 2010; Young, 1999), but when violations of key rules become normalized, managerial initiatives and regulatory enforcement are needed to restore standards. In the finance industry, a firm belief in the financial market as being capable at self-regulating among actors and a culture privileging the generation of profits over all other objectives and concerns arguably tolerated a normalization of deviance from prescribed standards (Martinez-Moyano et al., 2014).

Needless to say, the consequences of these financial operations were quite dramatic and served to restructure the entire finance industry. When the whole subprime market and its interrelated financial activities crashed in the fall of 2008, the "Big Fourteen" of the Wall Street finance industry were reduced to the "Big Nine" as Merrill Lynch, Wachovia, Washington Mutual, and Bear Stearns (acquired by JP Morgan Chase before September 15, 2013, the day of the Lehman Brothers bankruptcy) merged with other finance actors, and Lehman Brothers filed for bankruptcy. In the two-year period from late 2007 to late 2009, a total sum of US$2.64 trillion in finance assets disappeared from the "Big Fourteen/Big Nine" finance industry actors (Blinder, 2013: 166–167), and the US and world economy was thrown into what has been frequently referred to as the Great Recession (Pontusson and Raess, 2012).

The aftermath
In the aftermath of the 2008 events, Alan Greenspan had to admit in a
Congressional hearing in October 2008 that he was "shocked" to learn that
his worldview guiding most of his professional career crumbled in front of
his and others' eyes. Chairman of the House Committee on Government
Oversight and Reform Henry Waxman (D-CA) dryly concluded that, "[i]n
other words, you found that your view of the world, your ideology, was
not right. It was not working." However, no matter how costly the bailout
and the TARP rescue activities of the George W. Bush Administration
were (today, the money has been paid back by the beneficiaries), the
free-market acolytes lost the war but won the peace. At a certain point, it
appeared as if there would be a shift in policy and some kind of substantiated learning from the 2008 events, but instead, by and large the same
people do basically the same thing half a decade after 2008 (Blinder, 2013;
Mirowski, 2013). As Paul Krugman, the Princeton economist and well-
known *New York Times* columnist and Nobel laureate, comments, officials
like Timothy Geithner, Treasury Secretary during the last months of the
George W. Bush Administration, are still faithful to their beliefs and see no
major need for altering the system that is still theoretically credible in their
eyes. As Paul Krugman pointed out (cited in Crotty, 2009: 578), Timothy
Geithner and other representatives of the Federal Reserve and the George
W. Bush Administration made clear from the very outset that "they still
have faith in the people who created the financial crisis." Not only did
they make such public declarations, they also maintained the familiar free-
market argument that "governments do a bad job in running banks" – "as
opposed, presumably, to the wonderful jobs the private bankers have
done," Krugman snapped (cited in Crotty, 2009: 578) – in an attempt to
justify the financial bailout activities with few requirements on the finance
market decision-makers. "This was bad analysis, bad policy, and terrible
politics," Krugman claimed (cited in Crotty, 2009: 578). Joseph Stiglitz
(2009: 331), another Nobel laureate, tells an entirely different story than
Geithner, stating that "the banks were supposed to be the experts in risk
management, they not only didn't manage risk; they created it." Blinder
(2013), writing a few years after Stiglitz (2009), points at the broader
picture and how a series of factors contributed to the Great Recession:

> The Americans built a fragile house of cards, piece by piece, starting in the late
> 1990s and continuing right up until disaster struck in 2007. The intricate but
> precarious construction was based on asset-price bubbles, exaggerated by irre-
> sponsible leverage, encouraged by crazy compensation schemes and excessive
> complexity, and aided and abetted by embarrassingly bad underwriting stand-
> ards, dismal performances by the statistical rating agencies and lax financial
> regulations. (Blinder, 2013: 80)

The question for the future is then: why could no one predict the outcome from the excessive risk-taking and the risk-exposure in the finance industry and counteract these risks, and – perhaps even more puzzling – what can we learn from these events? Colander et al. (2009: 260) suggest that the sheer belief in the neoclassical theory of market rationality belongs to what Lakatos (1970) speaks of as "the core of the scientific program" of finance theory, and consequently this basic and foundational assumption cannot be questioned. This leads to a series of *ad hoc* hypotheses being added to the axioms of the theory:

> In much of the macroeconomics and finance literature, there is an almost scholastic acceptance of axiomatic first principles (basically, the building blocks of an intertemporally optimizing representative agent with completely rational expectation formation) independent of any empirical evidence. Even dramatic differences between the model's behavior and empirical data are not taken as evidence against the model's underlying axiom. Quite in contrast to what one would expect of an applied science, most of the contemporary work in macroeconomics and finance is thus characterized by pre-analytical belief in the validity of certain models that are never meaningfully exposed to empirical cases. (Colander et al., 2009: 260)

Barofsky (2012) served as an officer under Treasury Secretary Hank Paulson in the George W. Bush Administration to implement the TARP activities, and he points to the "more of the same" tendency in the finance industry. The top banks are now, Barofsky (2012: 229) says, 23 percent larger than they were before the crisis and today they hold more than US$8.5 trillion in assets, a rise from 43 percent to 56 percent of the US GDP in only five years. These banks and financial institutions today control 52 percent of all industry assets, a figure that was a mere 17 percent only four decades ago. While Wall Street continues to do what it has been doing for the last few decades, someone had to pick up the bill for saving the finance market institutions, and that would be the state and the taxpayers in the countries hosting banks that were part of the global finance system and its exchanges of what proved to be "troubled assets." It is noteworthy that the US government was anxious to save the finance industry to stabilize "world capitalism," there were few initiatives to cushion the rest of the economy from the finance industry-generated worldwide near-collapse. It is almost as if that idea never crossed the policy-makers and politicians' minds:

> The financial rescue . . . did nothing to reverse the damage to the real US economy. The recession that began in December 2007 was the most severe since the Great Depression. Real GDP declined, and it currently remains below capacity; more than eight million jobs were lost during 2008–2009.

Fiscal stimulus measures, widely recognized to be inadequate when enacted in 2009, reduced the depth of the real contraction but were insufficient to produce the sustained growth necessary for rapid employment growth. (Jarsulic, 2013: 39)

To repeat: the Great Recession that followed the events of 2008 led to a 6.3 percent decline in payroll employment in the US – "the largest by far of any postwar recessions" (Biven and Schierholz, 2013: 62) – while at the same time the average family income fell by 3.7 percent between 2007 and 2009 (median income fell by 5.3 percent, testifying to the "long right-hand tail" of income distribution in the US economy). The main price paid by the American taxpayers was apparently not the cost for the much-debated TARP program as the finance industry could quite easily repay their debts, but the wider effects on employment and income in the non-financial sectors of the economy. Speaking about the US, Barofsky (2012) stresses the quite immediate consequences for the individual in the American economy:

The economic "recovery" that has been heralded in some quarters pales in comparison to the damage wrought on the economy [by the financial institutions]. Nearly nine million jobs were lost as a result of the financial crisis along with 3.5 million homes, accompanied by a loss of $7 trillion in housing wealth. The poor have suffered the most, with the poverty rate increasing from 12.5 percent to 15.1 since 2007. (Barofsky, 2012: 226)

It is therefore deeply ironic that free-market protagonists who dislike collective solutions are now preaching the need for "economic austerity" (that is, the reduction of public spending) in order to pay the bill for the excesses in the finance markets (Schui, 2014). In many European countries, not necessarily sharing the Anglo-American belief in free-market capitalism but entertaining what at times is called *embedded liberalism economies*, banks held assets worth more than the national GDP (Blyth, 2013). In France, the three biggest banks held assets worth nearly two and a half times French GDP, and in 2008 the top two German banks had assets equal to 114 percent of the German GDP. Similar figures have been reported from many countries in the eurozone (Blyth, 2013: 83). As EU members cannot, unlike the US, print money to bail out their banks, the taxpayers are expected to carry the burden to save the banks. Hence, economic austerity has been preached by free-market protagonists.

The theoretical argument in favor of economic austerity is based on the assumption that if the government "cuts spending and reduces borrowing, private actors will increase to fill the gap" (Konzelmann, 2014: 731). This hypothesis in turn rests on the assumption that consumer and business decisions are based on rational decisions about the future, regardless of "how uncertain that might be" (Konzelmann, 2014: 731). In addition, proponents of austerity assume that "public sector profligacy" and "private sector parsimony" (and vice versa) are *interactive* and that the one excludes the other by some inherent self-correcting mechanism (Konzelmann, 2014: 732). If that would be the case, economic systems would be self-stabilizing and making government intervention unnecessary. Unfortunately, this hypothesis has not been supported by empirical evidence. As Konzelmann, (2014: 732) argues, "there are few signs of any such tendency towards automatic stabilization." An economic policy based on austerity is thus resting on frail empirical grounds (see for example, Konzelmann, 2014: 726) – it is a "politicized" concept.

Blyth (2013: 15) is quite explicit regarding who will carry the costs for saving the banks from themselves: "'[w]e have spent too much' those at the top say, rather blithely ignoring the fact that 'spending' was the cost of saving their assets with the public purse." Konzelmann (2014) says that this new policy was advocated by the same finance industry actors that previously benefited from government rescue activities, surprisingly shortly after the events of 2008:

> In 2010, after bank bailouts and emergency stimulus measures had apparently averted financial collapse, there was a policy *volte-face* to one of austerity. This was partly due to a similar *volte-face* on part of the financial markets having cried out for a rescue in the wake of financial crisis, they now felt emboldened – to challenge countries that were subsequently burdened with high levels of public debt. (Konzelmann, 2014: 732–733)

At the same time as taxpayers are told to "tighten their belts" and to tolerate a more austere fiscal policy, the people who created the financial mess of 2008 have demonstrated preciously little interest in "contributing to the cleanup" (Blyth, 2013: 15). "Austerity is a great policy for the banks because the people who are to pay for the mess are not the same who made it," Blyth (2013: 50) suggests (see also Lysandrou, 2013; Pontusson and Raess, 2012). Also Konzelmann (2014) stresses how economic austerity has been in the explicit interest of finance industry actors, actively participating in policy-making to secure their interest:

> [I]n the aftermath of the 2008 financial crisis, economic policy has been increasingly dictated by financial market traders, with their own interest at heart and with very little loyalty to any national social or political economy. They are demanding austerity as evidence that governments are capable of managing their deficits and are serious about repaying their debts. (Konzelmann, 2014: 734)

The consequences from this new economic policy, where the costs caused by private finance institutions operating on a global market are carried by the national taxpayers, are significant. Tabb (2013) suggests:

> What we see as a financial and fiscal crisis is best understood as an intensification of class struggle over who shall bear the cost of the crisis the banks and other financial speculators have caused with the acquiescence and often encouragement from of politicians and regulators who have promoted a social structure of accumulation premised on corporate-led globalization and financialization that cannot be sustained. The current global depression signals the need for a new regulatory regime for the world system. There is no technical fix to what is a political struggle with enormous consequences. (Tabb, 2013: 537)

Taken together, the new regulatory regime was based on armchair thinking and any evidence of moral hazard and excessive risk-taking derived from the animal spirit that even hardcore neoclassical economists recognize has been ignored, overlooked, or interpreted as being consonant with predominant beliefs. The outcome was a collapsed finance industry and a wounded reputation of economists and policy-makers, but as time passed these actors were biding their time to be able to continue as if nothing ever really happened. That tacit has been very effective, and today mainstream media and the wider public possibly remember 2008 as a hazy moment where something happened but no one really fully understood what, and then all of a sudden that too was history (Blinder, 2013). By 2010, Goldman Sachs was listed by *Fortune* as the sixth most "Admired Company in America," the only Wall Street firm on the list (Mandis, 2013: 9).

The Role of Credit Rating Agencies

The role of CRAs will be discussed in greater detail in the chapter addressing auditing and external control of organizations, but in this context, the role of CRAs is more explicitly related to the new financial architecture. In the stream of books being published after the great debacle of 2008, the contribution by Friedman and Kraus (2012) rejects the popular "too big to fail" explanation (Strahan, 2013; Sorkin, 2009), assuming that finance market actors were conscious of the risks they juggled but opportunistically anticipated that the state would pay in the case of a major systemic breakdown. For Friedman and Kraus (2012), such an explanation touches on conspiracy theories and also underrates the importance of the professional belief in markets as being the superior processors of information. However, Friedman and Kraus (2012) still stress that finance market regulators were ignorant of the role of CRAs including the "Big Three," Standard & Poor, Moody's, and Fitch, having legal monopolies since the

1970s to rate financial assets and the issuers. In this explanatory framework, the regulators were guilty of what Friedman and Kraus (2012) refer to as an *economism*, a doctrine that "blinded" the regulators. This *economism* included the belief that markets are, in the default position, "perfect, such that market participants are, in effects, omniscient" (Friedman and Kraus, 2012: 2). More specifically, succumbing to what Friedman and Kraus (2012: 149) name *price fetishism*, a key element in the EMH that assumes that market prices are always right and there are no opportunities for manipulating prices in unregulated markets. This assumption is not empirically credible as there is ample evidence of market actors both manipulating market information and prices (see for example, Spatt, 2014) and being brought to justice for doing so, and yet Friedman and Kraus (2012) see this strong belief in the accuracy of market pricing as being the principal underlying fallacy explaining the system breakdown in 2008. "In the case of accounting regulators, the underlying assumption was not that capitalists' *behavior* should be left alone, but rather than market *prices* somehow have the ability to overcome human limitations and accurately predict the future," Friedman and Kraus (2012: 149) summarize.

There was much evidence that CRAs were incorrectly rating assets as being safe investments, in some cases only days prior to filed bankruptcies, but again, after the dust had fallen, the very same three rating agencies continued to execute a very central role in the global financial system. Reports issued by Standard & Poor or Moody's are still treated as factual evidence in mainstream media. The new financial architecture did not give very much space to regulatory authority, but privately owned corporations, at times very unwilling to report their financial performance data to the wider public (Partnoy, 1999), are given the license to issue assessments that guide the industry. The free-market ideology thus enacts privately owned businesses as credible market-makers, regardless of the moral hazard being built into the system where such market-makers rely on fees from the very same companies they rate. In this view, free-market capitalism becomes something like a Moebius-strip where it is theoretically and practically impossible to distinguish the inside from the outside. In the traditional model of separation of powers into market-based actors and regulatory agencies, there is an institutional line of demarcation between the inside and the outside of the market, but in the new financial architecture, both financial institutions and their raters are part of the same market structure. This arrangement represents a major shift in policy during the era of financialization, from the reliance on state-controlled regulatory agencies to market-based self-correction.

The Growth of Debt

The fourth element of the new financial architecture deals not so much with the finance market and the finance industry per se, but points at the consequences of the supply of capital and the value extraction practices in the finance industry. The period after 1980 has demonstrated a remarkable growth in debt and in debt-based consumption on all levels; on household, state or municipality, and the federal levels (Lazzarato, 2012; Hyman, 2011). In the US in 1981, household debt was 48 percent of GDP; in 2007 it was 100 percent. Private sector debt was 123 percent of GDP in 1981, and by late 2008, it was 290 percent (Crotty, 2009). Stockhammer (2013) stresses that the level of household debt in the US has increased faster than in the business sector, indicating that the finance industry has been able to reach into new market segments: "[w]hile the business sector has increased debt from 52 percent of GDP (in 1976) to 77 percent (2009), with household debt has increased from 45 percent (1976) to 98 percent (2009), with a clear acceleration in the early 2000s" (Stockhammer, 2013: 513).

Jones (2011: 158) reports similar growth figures for the UK: in 1980, the ratio between debt and income was 45, while in 1997 it had doubled, and by the end of 2007 it soared to "an astonishing 157.4." Expressed differently, between 2000 and 2007 consumers in the UK spent £55 billion in excess of their income on the basis of the access to the generous supply of credit card financing and bank loans. Also the finance industry itself had leveraged its risk by taking on debt: the level of debt rose from "22% of GDP in 1981 to 117% in late 2008" (Crotty, 2009: 575). While the sheer level of debt is not a problem *per se* (Graeber, 2011) as debt tends to follow demographic patterns (Aglietta, 2000), nor is it indicative of a well-functioning and expansive economy (La Porta et al. 2000: 18), there are reasons to believe that the increase of debt is co-produced with the financialization of the economy and the growth of the finance industry. Montgomerie (2009: 2) argues persuasively that the expansion of household debt in the US is intimately bound up with the development of asset-backed securities, which "facilitated widespread private credit creation by consumer credit issuers." As Tabb (2012) shows, the expansion of securitized assets was not a marginal phenomenon in the American finance industry:

> [s]ecuritized assets, many originating in the traditional banking system, were important to the explosion of finance. In 2006 banks issued $1.8 trillion in securities backed by mortgages, credit cards, auto loans, and other debt. More than half of the credit card and student loans in the country were securitized. (Tabb, 2012: 96)

Montgomerie (2009) suggests that household debt filled the growing gap between income and expenditure:

> Unsecured debt is relevant because practices of debt-based consumption integrated ongoing socioeconomic transformation experienced by middle-income households, namely, wage stagnation and declining social support, into processes of financialised expansion. Therefore, the everyday politics of debt-based consumption contributed to the social consolidation of financialised growth in the US economy. (Montgomerie, 2009: 2)

This position is shared with Barba and Pivetti (2009) that stress the causality of the decline in productivity growth and real wages on the one hand, and household debt on the other hand. Barba and Pivetti (2009: 127) refer to this phenomenon as "the substitution of loans for wages:"

> [R]ising household debt should be seen as the counterpart of the conspicuous redistribution of income that has taken place in the USA since the beginning of the 1980s ... the rising household debt is viewed as the response to falling or stagnant real wages and salaries – and even as the response to rising wages that were, however, persistently not keeping pace with productivity growth. (Barba and Pivetti, 2009: 122)

The linear causality of financialization and debt, that is, that the first leads to the second, is questioned by Montgomerie (2009: 3), suggesting instead that "unsecured debt levels among median-income households bolstered financialisation, not the other way around." This expansion of financialization was caused by several changes in American society and in the finance industry. The new neoliberal and neoconservative "pro-business" policies gaining ground in the 1980s and 1990s led to, Montgomerie (2009: 4) argues, "stagnating real wage growth and receding non-wage benefits combined with dwindling state support and rising costs of living costs." Also Wisman (2013) stresses the relations between stagnating wages, increased economic inequality, and the rise of debt in his analysis, making economic inequality, by and large an effect of policy decisions derived from ideological convictions, the key driver of the increase in debt and financialization more largely. Between the mid-1970s and 2005, the 0.01 percent of the highest income group saw their income as a percentage of aggregated income soar from 0.9 percent to 6 percent, a ratio "surpassing the previous extreme level attained in 1929" (Wisman, 2013: 923). As this highest income group demonstrates a declining marginal consumption function, that is, they dedicate a lower proportion of their income on consumption vis-à-vis lower income groups, these increases in income could be reinvested:

The windfall of income and wealth accruing to an elite was far greater than could readily be spent, even on the most lavish consumption, leaving them and their money managers with the challenge of locating ways to place these increased assets to maximum effect. But due to stagnating wages, those who spent most or all of their income had a far smaller share of total income to spend and thus profitable investment potentials in the real economy was limited. (Wisman, 2013: 924)

The general unwillingness to invest in the real economy would have led to an economic decline in the period, but this tendency was moderated by a high level of household consumer demand, "paid for by their reduced saving, greater debt and longer work hours" (Wisman, 2013: 925). Between 1980 and 2008, despite declining real wages and rising economic inequality, consumption as a percentage of US GDP rose from 63 percent to 70 percent. The orthodox neoclassical economic theory explanation for this growth is that the policy to fight inflation paid off in the form of households being more willing to consume, but as Wisman (2013: 929) remarks, that this thesis has "not fared well empirically." At the same time, to finance the growth in household consumption total household debt as a percentage of GDP, "[i]ncreased from about 45 percent in 1975, to about 70 percent in 2000, to 96 percent in late 2007" (Wisman, 2013: 933). In addition, in the period between 1970 and 2002, the "household work hours rose about 20 percent in the USA"; in contrast, in the European Union demonstrating lower degrees of economic inequality, "the work hours fell 12 percent" (Wisman, 2013: 936). In other words, while high-income groups reinvested their capital income in the expanding finance industry, the so-called real economy was running on the basis of debt-based household consumption and more hours worked.

As credit became easily available, households turned to unsecured debt "to plug the gap between income and expenditure" (Montgomerie, 2009: 4) to maintain welfare levels, a phenomenon that has been referred to as *debtfare*. In fact, household survey data reveal that unsecured debt levels were above income levels as early as 1992 (Montgomerie, 2009: 3), that is, prior to the expansion of unsecured debt enabled by the use of securities. "[I]n the lowest income quartile the share of families with credit card debt rose from 11.9% in 1983 to 30.3% in 2004, while the share of families with installment loans tripled over the same period," Barba and Pivetti (2009: 117) add. In many cases, households ended up in a situation where the option to "work a good credit score" disappeared if consumers wanted to own "the material items they felt entitled to" as residents of the US (Peñaloza and Barnhart, 2011: 759). Consequently many informants in Peñaloza and Barnhart's (2011: 759) study were "optimistic" regarding their ability to uphold their private consumption despite the data revealing stagnating real wages speaking against such scenarios. In this milieu of a new and less strict financial self-discipline and a more liberal attitude regarding debt and consumption, the expansion of securities issued by the finance industry served to further increase the supply of capital (Montgomerie, 2009).

Moreover, in the finance industry, being more leniently regulated under the banner of pro-business policy, banks no longer acted as *intermediaries* between savers and borrowers, but increasingly relied on deposits taking and savings to raise capital. In order to "increase their asset velocity through leverage" (Tabb, 2012: 97), banks used securitization to "[r]educe capital reserves and recapitalize their balance sheets by reselling assets to open markets" (Montgomerie, 2009: 5). The immediate consequence of this new, high-risk, high-capitalization, and high-velocity strategy was the expansion of debt: "[i]n 1995, total securitised pools were US$200 billion and tripled over seven years to US$600 billion. Securitised unsecured debt pools reached their peak immediately prior to the onset of the global credit crash in 2007 at US$690 billion" (Montgomerie, 2009: 7). The leading US policy-makers including Alan Greenspan and his allies at the US Treasury Department were not particularly concerned about the increased levels of unsecured debt. Instead, they understood household borrowing, based on their favored neoclassical economic models of the relationship between interest rates, inflation, and employment, as being indicative of households being in the fortunate position to reap the benefits from liberalization and competitive markets (Montgomerie, 2009: 10). Such "a sanguine view of escalating household borrowing" (Montgomerie, 2009: 10) was self-gratifying and turned a blind eye to the externalities of the free-market policies Greenspan et al. endorsed and held in esteem, all based on abstract theoretical reasoning, ultimately founded on a general idea about market efficiency.

In contrast to this free-market policy, Barba and Pivetti (2009: 130) suggest that for any capitalist economy, in a long-run perspective, it is "decidedly more appropriate" to recourse to public debt than to recourse to household debt for "sustaining aggregate demand and activity levels." In March 2010, the US Federal Reserve board reported that 11.3 million American homes, accounting for 24 percent of the US total, "[h]ad an upside down mortgage worth more than the home," Peñaloza and Barnhart (2011: 743) report. Such figures indicate that housing prices have outpaced real wage growth, a condition that is complicated to maintain in an economy relying on private consumption. As aggregated household debt is more complicated to control than public debt, an economy characterized by high levels of household debt becomes fragile and vulnerable, a condition that Onaran et al. (2011) argue caused the 2007–2009 financial crisis:

> The effects of financialization regarding income distribution at the expense of wage earners, the consequent reliance on debt fuelled by the housing bubble to maintain consumption and growth based on low physical investment has led to a risky and fragile economy. This is exactly the mechanism that underlines the financial crisis of 2007–2009. (Onaran et al. 2011: 657)

Again, the policies of Alan Greenspan and his policy-makers and regulators favored capital accumulation benefiting a small group of constituencies at the expense of long-term economic stability and growth of the economy.

As a consequence of the free-market economic policy, many American households today encounter a harsh reality where there is little room for hairsplitting academic debates. Nearly half of the US (and UK) population have not participated in pension savings, and one-third of US households reported they have used loans to pay for basic living expenses such as rents, mortgage payments, groceries, utilities, or insurance (Montgomerie, 2009: 12). In addition, a 74 percent increase in "health insurance premiums for the average US family" had forced 29 million Americans to take unsecured consumer loans to cover costs for medicine: "roughly half of all personal bankruptcies are due in part to medical problems" (Montgomerie, 2009: 17). All these changes have led to a situation where "middle-class households are effectively crushed under a mountain of debt" (Montgomerie, 2009: 13). In Montgomerie's (2009: 13) conclusion, rather than being the beneficiaries of efficient markets and liberalized economies, as suggested by US policy-makers and politicians, the middle-class households were "[f]odder for financialised expansion." The most significant change in household savings is that families facing increased difficulties to live up to the material standards prescribed in the "American way of life" have to take on debt to be able to continue to consume "beyond the limits of income" (Montgomerie, 2009: 14). As both Montgomerie (2009: 14) and Martin (2002: 11) propose, such a relaxed view of household debt is indicative of the underlying post-industrial or post-Fordist "just-in-time production economy," wherein "[w]e live in a perpetual present without a buffer for the future" (Martin, 2002: 11). "In the consumer credit boom . . . prudence and thrift are displaced by new moral and calculative disciplines of responsibly and entrepreneurially meeting, managing, and manipulating ever-increasing outstanding obligations," Langley (2008: 135) proposes.

One of the consequences of the just-in-time income/debt balancing is that there is a relatively narrow window where the individual consumer can legitimately execute his or her decisions. The debt-based financialized economy is in other words embedded in moral norms and beliefs. Consumers that accumulate too little debt are not effectively handling their economic resources and do not contribute to the economy and economic growth. In contrast, consumers that fail to act in accordance with the neoclassical rational choice model underlying finance market operations are pathologized (Mehta, 2013). Speaking of consumers more generally, Mehta (2013: 1243) suggest that vulnerable consumers may "pay higher prices, purchase inappropriate products, or fail to make a purchase at all despite it appearing to be in their best interests to do so." In the field of *behavioral economics*, such decisions are treated as deviations from a prescribed norm, that of the axiomatic form of rational choice theory, and consequently there is a perceived need for a rehabilitation of these consumers. This methodological and theoretical reductionism, rendering the individual the autonomous and isolated subject – "the atomized and self-regarding individual" (Mehta, 2013: 1245) – unfortunately "[d]istract attention from facets of the individual's environment, such as characteristics of markets and the behaviours of firms, and also the set of norms and beliefs underpinning the economic system" (Mehta, 2013: 1244). Rational choice theory assumes that human reasoning and decision-making is instrumental in orientation and structured in accordance with a mathematical logic (Mehta, 2013: 1246), and deviations from such calculative rationalities are widely treated as a suboptimal decision that needs to be corrected and/or theoretically explained. Still, as social and cultural factors would be able to explain why for instance certain vulnerable customers accept unfavorable short-term money loan conditions, the strict adherence to the neoclassical rational choice model render such decisions irrational (and hence anomalous facts) and subject to corrective action.

A general concern is that in the case of the US, the decline in manufacturing and the growth of retailing and services, and the endemic trade deficit leads to a strong emphasis on private consumption to keep the economy running. As household debt has risen to unprecedented levels, there are concerns regarding the sustainability of the debt-fueled private consumption model. "Seventy percent of US economic activity depends on consumerism," Harvey (2010: 107) reports. Crotty (2009) adds that consumption as a percentage of GDP was 63 percent in 1980, 67 percent in 1998, and 70 percent in 2008. As part of the global economic superpower, Montgomerie (2009: 3) writes, US households "act as consumers-of-last-resort for almost all globally produced consumer goods." As real wages have been stagnant since the 1970s and real family income growth has been slow, "rising household spending was increasingly driven by the combined effects of rising debt and the increase in household wealth created by stock market and housing booms" (Crotty, 2009: 576). Unless the stock exchange rises and private homes become more valuable, there is no real source for increased consumption, and consequently the only remaining resort is debt-based spending. Needless to say, policy-makers need to be concerned about the level of household debt, especially in periods of economic downturns and slumping housing markets.

THE ACTORS OF THE FINACIALIZED ECONOMY

Social Explanations for the Finance Market Expansion

While Crotty's (2009) concept of a new finance market architecture, including a variety of new practices, policies, and mechanisms, is one key explanation for the institutional shift and the emergence of new institutional logics in the global finance markets, there are other stories to be told emphasizing the deinstitutionalization in the domain of finance. Mizruchi (2013, 2010), drawing on an sociological institutional theory framework, speaks of the shift from managerial capitalism of the society of organizations to the investor capitalism of the ownership society as an institutional change wherein the old "corporate elites" of the American society lost its position as the leading group owning, managing, and overseeing the economic system (a view of social processes indebted to for example, Vilfredo Pareto's *The Rise and Fall of Elites* [first published in 1901]). In the period after 1980, what would historically have been treated as violations of the anti-trust legislation became widely accepted in the new economic regime. In combination with the assault on the unions and the labor movement, widely treated as a collectivist movement and a thinly veiled form of socialism on American soil, and the restructuring of the finance industry, including the marginalization of the commercial banks, the principal tool for the economic control of American business of the elites, the new pro-business policy opened up for new professional groups to advance their positions (Mizruchi, 2010: 123). While this system of economic and corporate elites dominating American industry was patriarchal and conservative, it still served to stabilize the economy. As Mizruchi points out, the period after 1980 has been characterized by financial and economic instabilities:

> From the end of the Great Depression until the mid-1980s, the American financial system experienced not a single episode that might be termed a "crisis." The stock market had its ups and downs to be sure, in 1974 losing nearly 50 percent of its value within a brief period. But there were no bubbles or abrupt collapses resembling 1929, or 1907, or 1893. (Mizruchi, 2010: 130)

In addition, the decline of the American manufacturing industry, the backbone of the American economy in the interwar period and the site for the organized labor movement, added to the institutional change (Bluestone and Harrison, 1982): in the 1980s one-third of the 500 largest manufacturing firms disappeared (Mizruchi, 2010: 132). Rather than making a career as a manager in the manufacturing industry, becoming a government official, or pursuing a career in the sciences, the best and the brightest dreamed of becoming Wall Street finance industry workers, the safest and most effective bet on making the first million dollars before age 30 in the new regime of value creation and value extraction (Mizruchi, 2010: 127). Says Mizruchi (2010):

> [P]ower had shifted to the financial community. But this community was not the small group of leading, old-line New York commercial banks, as in the earlier years. Rather the financial community was now a mélange of professional investors, working in the service of institutional stockbrokers, financial analysts. hedge-fund managers, and arbitrageurs. (Mizruchi, 2010: 132)

The new economic elite did not rely on controlling major corporations directly, but made finance market control the principle for extracting value from non-financial industries. The medium- to long-term effects were that the traditional corporate elites and their "old money" were succeeded by the new professional class of finance industry workers. While the traditional elites were oriented towards compromising and bargaining, and by and large accepted the unions as a legitimate speaking partner, the new regime rendered such practices and organizations irrelevant as they were treated, theoretically as well as practically, as disturbing factors that interfered with efficient market transactions. In a way, the new pro-business and policy and its reliance on free-market ideologies downplayed the role of humans as markets per se and were given the authority to determine what has a value and what is rendered viable in the new finance-based economy. Not even the old elites could anticipate and counteract such institutional changes, Mizruchi (2010) concludes.

The New Professional Knowledge Workers: The Expanded Role of Economists and the Growth of Finance Theory

If the "old" corporate elites lost their authority and their position in the era of financialization, who were the new groups emerging to fill this void, to successfully advance their positions? "The idea that the power elite is comprised of capitalists and captains of industry now seem antiquated – knowledge workers who redefine corporate efficiency were the initiators and biggest beneficiaries of these changes," Dobbin and Zorn

(2005: 181) respond. The economists are the first group of professional knowledge workers to have advanced their positions during the last four decades. Being originally a relatively small group of technical experts on economic systems and their regulation, economists have during the last decades quadrupled as a proportion of university-based academic researchers, from around 0.5 percent to 2 percent of the academy (Fourcade, 2006, 2009). In addition to the sheer growth in numbers, economists have entrenched a position where they claim they have the answers to an expanding number of questions. "For better and for worse, we now live in an era in which economists have become our most intellectual philosophers, and when decisions made or advised by economistic technocrats have broad and palpable influence on the practice of our everyday lives," Burgin (2012: 155) writes. This new category of professionals, equipped with generic neoclassical economic theories being general enough to explain virtually everything under the sun as they included a set of elementary analytical categories, comprising "incentives," "information," choice," "utility," and so on, served as technocratic experts in both governments and international organizations. These organizations, including the IMF (Chwieroth, 2010; Chorev and Babb, 2009), The World Bank (Griffin, 2009; Neu et al., 2006), and the WTO (Chorev, 2005), implemented, enforced, and controlled what was known as "the Washington Consensus," a set of policies aimed at advancing free-market capitalism (Babb, 2013). It is no wonder that the international ranking of economists and economic theorists is heavily dominated by Anglo-American researchers, the home-turf of free-market thinking: of the top 100 economists in the world, 88 percent work in the US and 10 percent in the UK (Peet, 2007: 63). By any standard, the case of the economists is exemplary of how professional mobilization can translate into jurisdictional claims and accompanying authority and privileges.

For its critics, such entrenched positions are primarily derived from political changes rather than the ability to present a credible analytical framework enabling accurate predictions. That is, economists' stories about the virtues of free-market capitalism struck a chord among elite groups that were ready to buy what they sold, namely a theory abstract enough to effectively evade any criticism on the basis of empirical data, yet concrete enough to be comprehended by non-technical experts and thus capable of influencing policy-making (see for example, Blyth, 2002: 11). Critics of neoclassic economic theory, both inside and outside of the profession, frequently stress the disciplinary assumptions regarding market efficiency as being poorly supported by empirical data and aligned with everyday experience. "Economics is supposed to be a predictive science, yet many of the key predictions of neoclassical economics can easily be rejected," Stiglitz (2010: 245) suggests, himself being at the very core of the discipline. Stiglitz continues: "[e]conomics had moved – more than economists would like to think – from being a scientific discipline into becoming free-market capitalism's biggest cheerleader" (Stiglitz, 2010: 238). When for example, the global financial system collapsed in 2008, economists claimed they were not part of the debacle and that their neoclassic theories were still accurate and to be trusted, while in fact there is ample evidence of these very same economists being deeply involved in the organization of the markets that apparently failed: "[e]conomists did not simply come up with some speculative ideas; they helped run many of the institutions, both public and private, that ended up being central to the inception and playing out of the crisis" (Mirowski, 2013: 181).

In this story about the collapse of the finance markets, one particular branch of neoclassic economic theory, finance theory, is of particular interest. Only quite recently has modern finance "[a]cquired the reputation of economic necessity and scientific respectability" (De Goede, 2005: ix); less than two centuries ago, De Goede (2005: ix) says, finance "[s]tood condemned as irreputable gambling and fraud." Of central importance for the legitimacy and respectability of this professional field was what Hacking (1990) colorfully names "the taming of chance" – the ability to develop calculative practices that rendered risk a manageable entity (Ailon, 2014). In the era of managerial capitalism, running smoothly for most of the twentieth century until at least the early 1970s, finance or "money management" was more or less an uneventful, craft-based vocation that did not "[r]ely on rigorous theories, analytical tools and techniques" (Lounsbury and Crumley, 2007: 999):

> Prior to the 1960s, most of the articles published in finance journals tended to be descriptive and relied on ordinary language to communicate their conclusions and reasoning. Research results did not require a highly specialized academic training to be understood, and practitioners in financial institutions could, and did, contribute to the *Journal of Finance*. (Whitley, 1986: 172)

Harvard Business School's courses in investment had low prestige in the 1950s (MacKenzie, 2006: 261), but that was prior to the development of finance theory. The development of finance theory as a specific branch within neoclassic economic theory is a vast subject not to be covered in detail here, but it is tightly bound up with mathematization of the economics profession. Whitley (1986) stresses the World War II period and its successful application of mathematics to develop control systems that established mathematics as the principal tool for social science analysis:

> The high prestige of the natural sciences after the Second World War, and the success of applied mathematics in dealing with military problems during it,

encouraged the widespread belief in the late 1940s and 1950s that science could
be applied to managerial and business problems and science research into these
problems should be supported. (Whitley, 1986: 171)

The development of cybernetics as a generalized theoretical framework
for the mathematical control of technological, and, thereafter, biological and social systems (Wiener, 1948) displaced mechanical engineering
as the predominant *episteme*, and the publication of works such as John
von Neumann and Oskar Morgenstern's *Theory of Games and Economic
Behavior* (1947) just after the war, established a new standard for economic theorizing and formalization. The work produced in the 1960s and
1970s in finance theory effectively combined mathematical modeling, formalization, and large data sets, and this contributed to the development
of a formal theory of finance. Today, after more than 50 years of finance
theory development, the discipline effectively combines, Whitley (1986:
174) argues, academic styles of reasoning and practical knowledge: "[a]s a
system of intellectual novelty production, the study of finance has become
highly organized around a particular style of research and analysis drawn
from orthodox, neo-classical economics, with strong boundaries between
academically significant work and everyday, lay, knowledge." While
persistent critics of neoclassical economic theory such as Pierre Bourdieu
(2005: 13) speaks of the *morbus mathematicus* of economics, its "mathematical sickness" in cases where relatively trivial conditions and choices
being formalized into mathematical models, in the case of finance theory,
based on the continuous production of numerical inscriptions and quanta,
may be justified.

Despite such criticism, MacKenzie (2006: 245) emphasizes how "a good
finance theory" is in fact capable of helping its user to capture larger
empirical materials than is cognitively possible for most individuals; good
finance theories are thus heuristics of practical value in the everyday
work in finance markets (see for example, Pryke, 2010): "[t]o develop a
'good' finance-theory model required extensive, imaginative bricolage or
tinkering . . . it also required deployment of the theorist's crucial skill: the
capacity to find 'good abstractions'" (MacKenzie, 2006: 245). However,
calculative practices, for instance in the form of "standards" that maintain
an "objective and technical veneer," are adjusted to previous standards,
agreements, and institutional conditions, and consequently there is "ample
room for politics and power struggles to surface" (Lovell, 2014: 266). The
outcome is often that "processes of calculation" do not have to be so much
accurate as they need to provide market participants with "something
they can follow," and that "fit with other parts of the system" (Lovell,
2014: 279). It is, with Herbert Simon's phrase, the *bounded rationality* of

finance market actors that justifies the development of finance theory: "[p]art of the significance of the performativity of economics arises from the fact that individual human beings tend to have quite limited powers of memory, information-processes, and calculation" (MacKenzie, 2006: 265). In addition to the capacity to restructure large amounts of data into patterns and ratios, there is also a "linguistic component" in finance theory, MacKenzie (2006: 250) claims: "[a] second way in which finance theory has been incorporated into the infrastructure of financial markets is linguistic. The theory offers a way of talking about markets, especially about markets whose complexity might otherwise be baffling." A "good finance theory" is thus helpful in structuring and bringing order to what are seemingly chaotic movements in finance markets.

Despite economists' and finance theorists' proclivity towards portraying themselves as rigorous scientists in the Newtonian tradition, making the mathematical modeling one of the principal vehicles for instituting prestige in the activities, studies of practical finance market work stresses how the work is more interpretative and attending to all kinds of market information rather than being strictly calculative. Beunza and Stark (2004) stress how finance industry workers engineer their everyday work by using various technologies, tools, and algorithms to be able to calculate what assets to hold and what to sell. Zaloom's (2006, 2003) ethnographic work of finance industry workers shows that finance traders quickly learn that *"numbers tell very little"* (Zaloom, 2003: 261, original emphasis). Instead, Zaloom (2003: 270) proposes, finance traders become what she calls *informational entrepreneurs* being able to effectively interpret qualitative market information including government announcements and what Zaloom refers to as "market chatter," a variety of weak signals circulating in the community of finance traders. In Zaloom's (2006) account, the use of numbers and mathematics is of key importance for portraying finance markets and the finance industry as being a rational and transparent activity, but in practice, the role of numerics and mathematics are integrated into wider professional practices and everyday judgment, that is, rationalities that extend outside of the narrower domain of calculative practices:

> The ideals of information systems designers and financial exchange managers fit neatly with familiar narratives of progressive rationalization . . . Numbers operate as critical materials of rationalization but they are not always used as the systems designers intended. Traders who use financial technologies do not perceive numbers as objective descriptions of supply and demand. In both pit and screen formats, traders find a patterned logic in the movement of market numbers by identifying competition around whom they generate specific strategies. (Zaloom, 2006: 159)

A quite substantial corpus of literature in what has been called "the social study of finance" examine these social and cultural elements of an industry that is keen on portraying itself as being rationally structured on the basis of mathematical modeling and calculative practices (for example, Svetlova, 2012; Pryke, 2010; Preda, 2009a, 2009b; Knorr Cetina and Grimpe, 2008; MacKenzie, 2006; Preda, 2006; Knorr Cetina and Preda, 2005).

Taken together, the decline of elites provided new possibilities for economists to advance their jurisdictional claims and to portray for example, markets and economic action as being both determined by and captured by the economic models and theorems of neoclassical economic theory. In this general professional advancement, finance theorists represented the perhaps most pure application of mathematical modeling to understand the functioning of finance markets, serving to further justify the deregulation of finance markets and markets *tout court* in the era of financialization. The era of financialization is in many ways the reign of economists, and more specifically, economists subscribing to the neoclassic doctrine. The latest thrust in the colonialization of neoclassic economic theory is perhaps the idea of "neuroeconomics" (Schüll and Zaloom, 2011) the study of for example, economic decision-making on the basis of neurology research, the translation of the cybernetic program into life science research (Rose and Abi-Rached, 2013; Pickering, 2010). This entering into the human brain and its mind-boggling complexity is in line with the reductionist epistemology favored by neoclassic economic theory – a form of neurological gaze on economic behavior – but controversies and debates surround neurology research (Pickersgill, 2011; Changeux, 2004; Dumit, 2004) possibly preventing any useful contributions from such a neuroeconomics program.

Shifting Roles Inside the Firm

While economists managed to advance their professional positions in society at large, offering policy-makers and the wider public an analytical framework that appeared to be both theoretically solid and practically useful, there was a similar shift taking place inside organizations. Many of these changes are accounted for in detail in Part II of this volume, but here we can account for some of the jurisdictional struggles in the era of financialization. Of particular interest in this setting is how managers trained in finance theory in business schools gradually displaced managers trained in for example, engineering and the sciences. Fligstein's (1987) seminal article portrays this shift as an "interorganizational power struggle" that took place when the "new view of the corporation" as a bundle of financial assets was established (see also Fligstein, 1990). For this new group of managers, organic growth of the firm, increased market shares, or even long-term stability – managerial virtues *par preférénce* in the regime of managerial capitalism – were no longer favored managerial objectives; instead the ability to extract economic value from the assets became the priority of decision-makers:

> The pioneers of this new strategy were trained in finance and accounting. Their views were not shaped by the necessities of production or the desire to sell more products. Instead, they focused on the corporation as a collection of assets that could and should be manipulated in increase short-term result. (Fligstein, 1990: 226)

Zorn (2004) is critical of this view, the "power struggle perspective" as a dramatic event played out in executives boardrooms, and suggests that the advancement of the role of Chief Financial Officers (CFOs) were more gradual and represents a long-term shift in corporate governance. Zorn (2004: 346) studied 429 large, public American corporations over the 1963–2000 period and found that in the beginning of the observation interval, none of the firms had a CFO, while in the year 2000, "more than 80 percent did." Taking a legal framework explanation (see for example, Sutton et al., 1994; Edelman, 1992; Baron, Dobbin, and Jennings, 1986; Commons, 1924), Zorn (2004: 349) suggests that it was changes in the regulatory framework prescribing more detailed earnings-reporting, especially after 1978, that popularized the CFO solution. The more prominent role of the CFO was therefore the outcome from a passage in the Celler-Kefauver Act of 1950, leading to finance managers displacing "experts in sales at the helm of the largest corporations" (Zorn, 2004: 349). When the first wave of hostile takeover occurred in the first half of the 1980s, these CFOs were already in place in the large corporations.

As detailed in Chapter 2, by the early 1980s, during the early phases of the Reagan presidency, the inflow of capital to the American economy and the relaxing of finance market control in combination with the low price-per-earnings ratio in major stock-listed companies unleashed a wave of the new finance market innovation *leveraged buyout takeovers*. Schneper and Guillén (2004: 263) define a hostile takeover bid as "[a] corporate acquisition that is actively opposed by the target firm's incumbent management or board of directors." Schneper and Guillén (2004: 263) also remark that there are quite divergent views among both scholars and policy-makers regarding the role of takeovers: "hostile takeovers continue to be hailed by some as an effective way to discipline managers and maximize shareholder wealth but are bedeviled by others as one of the worst manifestations of 'predatory' capitalism." These activities and financial operations served to quite instantly "deinstitutionalize" the until then popular conglomerate firm (Davis et al., 1994). During this period of time, the role of the CFOs and finance theory trained CEOs was further accentuated. The US Celler-Kefauver Act of 1950 had made vertical integration "suspect" (Zorn et al., 2005: 283) and therefore so-called "portfolio theories" and "portfolio planning" prescribing were fashionable managerial practices and techniques in the 1970s: "[b]y the end of the 1970s, 45% of the Fortune 500 had adopted these portfolio planning techniques" (Zorn et al., 2005: 283). These models prescribed that conglomerate firms should own loosely integrated businesses to balance risk over the economic cycle, but the new liberalized regulatory framework and the supply of capital rather served to put these conglomerate firms at risk in the new regime. In the 1983–1988 period, there was a sharp growth in hostile takeover bids (Zorn et al., 2005: 273, Figure 13.1). While agency theorists such as Michael C. Jensen (1993) (see Chapter 4) argued that the hostile takeover bids served to discipline managers and to eliminate the least successful companies from the market through divestment – a form of economic Darwinism assuming that the weak are bound to perish – Davis and Stout's (1992) study of takeover activities reveals an entirely different pattern than that predicted by agency theorists. Rather than targeting poorly managed companies, takeover bids were aiming for companies with low debt and otherwise competing successfully in their markets. In other words, as Davis and Stout (1992: 626) make clear, the idea that takeover bids serve to discipline "poorly performing managers" can only be maintained if one has a faith in low debt as being indicative of incompetent management. Instead of acting like some kind of virus that keeps the population healthy through the elimination of the weakest, takeover bids served a less beneficial role for the aggregated economic system, that is, to restructure well-managed and solid American companies for the benefit of a smaller group of investors. The long-term effects of takeover bids was that CEOs and other decision-makers had to pay careful attention to how the finance markets valued their stocks, as a too low valuation would make the company susceptible to leveraged buyout activities. For Davis and Stout (1992: 630) this shift in policy represents no less than a "managerial counterrevolution," a decisive step towards the investor capitalism (Useem, 1996) of the era of financialization:

> The stability of corporate control was undermined by the construction of a takeover market for large firms, and the financial model of the corporation has been largely institutionalized, but the redefinition of the corporation is not a fait accompli, and the bases of power of corporate players have not been completely eroded. The passage of a raft of antitakeover laws by state governments and the subsequent standstill of the takeover market demonstrates the effectiveness of the managerial counterrevolution. (Davis and Stout, 1992: 630)

As the portfolio planning models and the conglomerate form fell from grace, new managerial concepts and virtues were advanced. Business school professors now advocated a "core competencies" view of the firm (for example, Prahalad and Hamel, 1990) wherein one, and only one, key competence should be effectively exploited (Zorn et al., 2005: 283). From Japan and the manufacturing industry and more specifically the Toyota production system (Liker, 2004; Cusumano, 1985), the idea of *lean production* was imported, a term coined in a global automotive industry research program coordinated from MIT in the 1980s (Womack et al., 1990). The term lean production was fashionable throughout the 1990s and was subject to intense scholarly research and debates in the period (for example, Delbridge, 1998; Berggren, 1994), and in the new millennium the concept made a "second coming" under the shorter label *lean* – this time now claimed to be applicable outside of the domain of manufacturing proper.

Changes in policy, aimed at restoring "economic freedom" and promoting pro-business, free-market competitive capitalism thus translated into a shift from the until then predominant managerial capitalism to an investor capitalism wherein finance theory trained executives and directors were increasingly overseeing corporations whose targeted goals were no longer moderate economic growth and stability but the capacity to extract value from the corporate assets to benefit capital owners. The "managerial counterrevolution" that Davis and Stout (1992) speak of therefore represents a deep-seated institutional shift in competitive capitalism.

SUMMARY AND CONCLUSIONS

The growth of the global finance industry and finance market includes the convergence of a variety of activities and social events, including the inflow of foreign capital into the US following the new inflation-fighting policies of the Federal Reserve chairman Paul Volcker in the late 1970s, the development of a finance theory from within the neoclassic economic theory framework (beginning in the late 1950s), the new "pro-business" policies enacted by both Republican and Democratic presidents in the US, the growth of a new category of professional knowledge workers in the finance industry, the restructuring of the banking sector, and the creation of a new finance market architecture including many new financial assets being traded on an increasingly global and deregulated finance market. All these events and occurrences have contributed to the creation of the dominance of the finance industry wherein capital is increasingly concentrated in a handful of finance institutions, especially after the 2008 events when the American finance industry was reconsolidated. These shifts have undoubtedly been beneficial for finance industry actors, today controlling extensive financial resources and being generously compensated for their work. But financialization also coincides with stagnating economic growth, increased state, company and household debt, growing economic inequality, and not the least, of particular relevance for the study of the financialization of the firm, the decline of managerial capitalism and the subsequent prominence of investor capitalism. That is, the mid- to long-term effects of financialization are subject to much debate and discussion.

In Part II of this volume, the focus shifts from the theoretical, political, and regulatory changes in the 1970s and the following decades to the practices enacted by firms and companies to respond to changes in the environment. Part II addresses the financialization of the firm in Chapters 4 through 6 examines changes in corporate governance, management control, and in everyday working life.

PART II

Analyzing the mediating discourses

4. Corporate governance and financialization

INTRODUCTION

One of the most significant changes in the firm in the era of financialization concerns corporate governance, how the economic value generated in the firm is distributed between the firm's various constituencies. While the regime of managerial capitalism enacted the firm as a socially embedded legal entity that needs to consider and effectively handle a number of social, economic, and legal relationships, the new regime of corporate governance treats the firm as a bundle of legal contracts that specify the rights to claim the economic value generated. As the new corporate governance model regards the market as the supreme processor of information in the form of market prices, it is the shareholders, being exclusively concerned with how much economic value that can be extracted from the firm, that most effectively should allocate the economic resources in the economy. While the previous regime of managerial capitalism was based on a socioeconomic model leaving room for politics and negotiations and took into account a variety of social interests and relations, the new regime of investor capitalism is directed towards the more narrow issues of value creation and value extraction. As will be discussed in this chapter, this distinction between the classic corporate governance model, emphasizing the institutional embeddedness of the firm, and the novel finance theory-based model that refuses to recognize any social considerations beyond the sheer accumulation and distribution of the economic of value generated in the firm, leads to a new theory of the firm. Needless to say, this radical shift in policy has not been devoid of controversy and discussion, and in this chapter the underlying theories and assumptions of the new corporate governance model will be examined. In addition, some of the externalities derived from this finance theory model will be reviewed.

SOCIOLOGICAL AND FINANCE THEORY VIEWS OF CORPORATE GOVERNANCE

Corporate governance means different things for economists and sociologists. For the sociologically minded scholar, "[c]orporate governance is concerned with the *institutions* that influence how business corporations allocate resources and returns" (O'Sullivan, 2000: 1, emphasis added); for economists, the term denotes a "set of mechanisms through which outside investors protect themselves against expropriation by the insiders" (La Porta et al., 2000: 4). For sociologists like Fligstein and Choo (2005: 63), stressing an institutional view, corporate governance include three elements: (1) *corporate law* that defines the legal vehicle by which property rights are organized; (2) *financial market regulation* that sets the rules for how firms obtain capital for their operations and that specifies the various relations between finance market actors and debtors and creditors, owners and managers; and (3) *labor law* that "[d]efines how labor contracts will operate in a particular society" (Fligstein and Choo, 2005: 63). For economists, eager to cut down on assumptions and unnecessary complexity, only the finance market relations are truly valid as financial worth can be calculated on the basis of market operations, preferably unbiased by laws and regulations For sociologists, corporate governance practice is the outcome from a historical and political process carefully balancing many different stakeholders' interests (Gourevitch and Shinn, 2005; Roe, 2003; Roy, 1997). For economists, corporate governance is largely a matter of establishing governance principles to stimulate capital accumulation and efficiency. "[S]ystems of corporate governance result from political and historical processes rather than from efficient solutions to the functional needs of the owners of capital who seek to maximize profits for themselves," Fligstein and Choo (2005: 66) suggest, pointing at the fault line between the economic sociology view and neoclassical economic theory view of corporate governance.

THE AGENCY THEORY VIEW OF CORPORATE GOVERNANCE: THE PRIMACY SHAREHOLDER VALUE CREATION

Jensen and Meckling's (1976) much-cited paper (building on Alchian and Demsetz, 1972), is written in the "theory of the firm" tradition (Moe, 1984), including for instance Ronald Coase's ([1937] 1991) transaction costs theory and Berle and Means ([1934] 1991) seminal account on the relationship between *principals* (for example, owners) and *agents* (for example, salaried managers and directors), and enacts the firm as a bundle of legal contracts. The CEO, the workers, the shareholders, and regulatory agencies are a number of stakeholders that have different expectations of the firm depending on their "investment" in its activities. Workers sell their labor for a fixed or semi-fixed salary, and the CEO is often, at least today, compensated by a combination of salaries, bonuses, and other forms of finance market-based assets. The state and government expect the firm to provide work opportunities and income tax. This is a general analytical model of the firm. However, the so-called agency theory model being developed by US economist Michael C. Jensen (1993, 1986), first at Rochester University and thereafter at Harvard Business School, suggests that corporate governance also needs to take into account the externalities being produced by the legal contracts (for an overview, see Shapiro, 2005). For instance, owners of a publicly owned company need to be ensured that the salaried CEO, the top management team, and the board of directors are acting in accordance with their interests. It may be that the CEO wants to accumulate economic resources in the firm to be able to live through an economic recession, and therefore the amount of capital stored up and not being distributed in the form of for example, dividends, historically the standard approach for listed companies to transfer economic value to their shareholders, may be a source of dispute. The CEO would claim that an internal stock of finance capital would secure the long-term survival of the firm, while shareholders may argue that these risks are overrated and that the shareholders should be able to take the benefit of the capital generated immediately, and in case of an economic downturn that threatens the firm's long-term survival, there are always opportunities for raising new money or to increase the debt of the firm. In the case of divergent beliefs regarding the management of the firm and/or the use of its accumulated finance capital, there are, agency theorists argue, *agency costs*, the principal's (the owners) total costs for monitoring the agent's (the CEO and the board of directors) activities.

So far, agency theory can be easily accepted by a variety of economic analysts and actors, but there may be cases of controversies between owners and managers. In the next step, however, Jensen (1993, 1986) argues that agency costs are not emerging only occasionally, but instead agency costs are persistently produced and accumulate over time in firms as CEOs and managers are anxious to secure their own positions and interests. For instance, in the 1970s, American firms were fond of developing large-scale conglomerates of loosely coupled businesses to be able to spread risks over time and to buffer the effects of any downturn in the economy. Anti-trust laws prohibited horizontal integration and therefore CEOs were increasingly managing portfolios of firms operating in different industries. In addition, management scholars and economic advisers recommended so-called *portfolio strategies* leading to a more stable but also, agency theorists claim, a less efficient economy. In Jensen's (1993) view, these conglomerates were comfortable sites for internal management careers but they did little to add value to the shareholders buying the stocks of these aggregates of firms. In his view, this absorption of what he calls the *free cash flow* or *residual cash flow* prevents capital from being reallocated to industries with high-growth potential and to support the entrepreneurial function of the capitalist economic system, and therefore much economic value was squandered by the CEOs and directors managing these conglomerates. Such a statement demands some more explanation as it both deviates from common-sense beliefs and more conventional economic theory and management writing, assuming that CEOs and other executives are wholeheartedly committed to the task of generating economic value. If they are not committed, they would have a problem to survive in markets with harsh competition, especially in mature or declining industries. In the agency theory model advocated by Jensen, the free cash flow plays a key role:

> Free cash flow is cash in excess of that required to fund all projects that have positive net present values when discounted at the relevant cost of capital. Conflicts of interest between shareholders and managers over payout policies are especially severe when the organization generates substantial free cash flow. The problem is how to motivate managers to disgorge the cash rather than investing it at below the cost of capital or wasting it on organizational inefficiencies. (Jensen, 1986: 323)

In addition to the idea of a certain stock of capital being generated in the firm, Jensen's theory presupposes that managers are unwilling to distribute this residual cash flow to the shareholders. Worse still, they are quite often investing this capital in projects and activities not generating any additional residual cash flow for the shareholders: "managers with unused borrowing power and large free cash flows are more likely to undertake low-benefit or even value-destroying mergers," Jensen (1986: 328) declares. These two propositions, the idea of a free cash flow that shareholders formally contract for, and systematic managerial negligence (operationalized as increased agency costs, the owners' cost for monitoring managers), lead Jensen to the conclusion that the most effective way to reduce agency costs and hence to improve the overall efficiency of an economic system relying on publicly owned firms, is that firms should enact shareholder value creation policies. That is, rather than reinvesting the free cash flow in the firm or the conglomerate, the free cash flow should be transferred to the shareholders; firms should thus primarily serve the role to enrich the owners of stock, not to serve a wider set of stakeholders or take on additional social responsibilities as such directives would demand that managers should handle poorly aligned or even opposing objectives, Jensen claims. This corporate governance model in turn relies on the assumption of finance market efficiency and its corollary, the ability of stock prices to fully reflect managerial efficiency:

> A fundamental premise underlying the market for corporate control is the existence of a high positive correlation between corporate managerial efficiency and the market price of shares of that company. As an existing company is poorly managed – in the sense of not making as great a return for the shareholders as could be accomplished – the market price of the shares declines relative to the shares of other companies in the same industry or relative to the market as a whole. (Manne, 1965: 112)

Jensen is a faithful believer of the EMH, but as we will see, there is no robust evidence of such efficiency in market prices as there are many financial and accounting activities that determine the reported value of the firm. In addition, the agency theory-based shareholder value creation policy also assumes that the state and the government should reduce the taxation of capital income, and it is noteworthy that the popularity of shareholder value policies coincides with the reduction of capital taxation. In other words, if there are any efficiency gains from distributing the free cash in the form of dividends over other corporate governance practices, it is closely bound up with government policies that share this commitment to shareholder enrichment. This co-production of agency theory and policy underline the performativity of agency theory and shareholder value creation: the theory became "true" (or at least "truer") as everyone acted in accordance with the beliefs and assumptions underlying the theoretical model, that is, the belief in the efficiency of free-market transactions.

According to Hart (1995: 686), such free-market policies are closely related to the University of Chicago economic theory praising the efficiency of competitive capitalism and disqualifying government interventions into supposedly self-regulating markets. In this view, there is no need for any detailed corporate law as such legal framework would only intervene into self-correcting markets: "[a]ccording to the Chicago view, then, there is no need for statutory corporate governance rules. In fact statutory rules are almost certain to be counterproductive since they will limit the founders' ability to tailor corporate governance to their own individual circumstances" (Hart, 1995: 686).

The crux is that Jensen and other protagonists of shareholder value policies need to convince others who are less assured about the virtues of the market, and more recently Jensen has debated with proponents of stakeholder theory (for example, Keay, 2011; Brickson, 2005; Schneper and Guillén, 2004; Hillman and Kiem, 2001) who suggest that firms need to pay attention to a number of different constituencies. Jensen (2002) rejects such claims as what fundamentally violates beliefs in efficient markets and what imposes additional and unnecessary complexities when monitoring agency costs. For Jensen (2002: 237), stakeholder theory is "[f]undamentally flawed because it violates the proposition that any organization must have a single-value objective as a precursor to purposeful or rational behavior." Jensen (2002: 237) continues: "firms that adopt stakeholder theory will be handicapped in the competition for survival because, as a basis for action, stakeholders politicizes the corporation, and leaves its managers empowered to exercise their own preferences in spending the firm's resources." Jensen (2002: 237) here speaks of "enlightened value maximization," a somewhat pompous term to denote that it is the shareholders and no one else that should benefit from the economic value generated in the firm. "Multiple objectives is no objective" Jensen (2002: 238) announces: "[m]aximizing the total market value of the firm . . . is one objective function that will resolve the tradeoff problem among multiple constituencies" (Jensen, 2002: 239). At the very heart of this position lies the idea that shareholders (the "financial claimants" in the quote below) are the only legitimate beneficiaries of the free cash flow as that is precisely what they have contracted for, and the central proposition that financial markets are more effective than managers in allocating resources. Therefore, any deviation from the path of shareholder value creation will lead to a decline in efficiency:

> With no criteria for performance, managers cannot be evaluated in any principled way. Therefore, stakeholder theory plays into the hands of self-interested managers allowing them to pursue their own interests at the expense of society and the firm's financial claimants. It allows managers and directors to invest their favorite projects that destroy firm-value whatever they are (the environment, art, cities, medical research) without having to justify the value destruction. (Jensen, 2002: 242)

In summary, Jensen rejects stakeholder theory as being unable to address both the legal problem of who contracts the right to the free cash flow and the question of how to reduce agency costs. Proponents of stakeholder theory, conversely, respond that it is not the case that shareholders are granted the exclusive right to the free cash flow, and add that agency theory both grossly overrates agency costs in firms and that markets are not as efficient as postulated in the neoclassical economic theory literature.

CRITIQUE OF AGENCY THEORY

The critique of agency theory and its solution to the minimization of agency costs, the shareholder value policy, can be separated into two streams of literature. A conceptual literature criticizing the assumptions made in agency theory, and empirical studies examining whether the recommendations derived from agency theory stand up well to empirical testing. In the following, these two bodies of text will be reviewed.

Bratton and Wachter (2010), two legal scholars, criticize agency theory for assuming that agency costs are always stable and for failing to address how corporate law is designed to secure the interests of owners. First, Bratton and Wachter (2010) argue that the claim made by agency theorists, that "shareholder empowerment will cause agency costs to decline" implies that the present corporate governance systems "leave big money on the table," a "counterintuitive" proposition, Bratton and Wachter (2010: 675) say. In brief, this assumption holds that "managers will systematically fail to maximize value in predictable ways. They will favor conservative, low-leverage capital structures, misinvest excess cash in suboptimal projects, fail to reduce excess operating costs, and resist premium sales of control" (Bratton and Wachter, 2010: 676). In competitive capitalism, firms with such poorly functioning managerial decision-making would not be able to survive the competition for very long, and therefore the agency theory proposition about ineffective and opportunistic behavior on the part of executives is not credible. As Fligstein and Choo (2005: 66) remark, economies not adhering to the agency theory recipe for the reduction of agency costs would demonstrate slower growth than the economies that do, if this proposition was correct. Such evidence has not been provided to date.

Second, Bratton and Wachter (2010) argue that there is a constant strive towards better finance market information and transparency, something that is ignored in the agency theory model: "[t]he information gaps between those inside and outside of the corporation has narrowed, due in part to stricter mandatory disclosure requirements and in part to more liquid markets and larger sector of information intermediaries" (Bratton and Wachter, 2010: 668). This transparency makes it easier for shareholders and other constituencies to assess the firm's financial performance and to make the decision whether the stock should be acquired or sold. The increased liquidity of financial assets and the enforced market reporting reduces agency costs and provides fewer opportunities for managers to withhold free cash flow from the firm's various stakeholders.

Third, Bratton and Wachter (2010: 666–667) point at the belief in stock prices as being an "objective and accurate measure" of firm value as being a faulty assumption. This critique supports Manne's (1965:

112) argument that agency theory assumes a "high positive correlation between corporate managerial efficiency and the market price of shares of that company." Unfortunately, the EMH being the bedrock of the shareholder value-based control of managers fails to stand up to empirical tests – financial markets are "not strong-form efficient," Bratton and Wachter (2010: 696) argue. Instead, information asymmetries are "real" and empirical studies "confirm this point beyond doubt," for instance by showing that managers "who trade in the corporation's shares earn abnormally high returns." In other words, there is no robust data that support the assumption that stock prices indicate underlying managerial or organizational efficiency.

These three critiques target internal inconsistencies of agency theory, and Ireland (2010) adds that agency theory despite all the talk about efficiency in the allocation of capital is primarily concerned about securing the interests of one particular group of constituencies, the owners of stock. In Ireland's (2010: 838) view, the corporate legal form was already from the beginning the outcome from the dominance of rentier investors, and the shareholder value policy is yet another attempt to claim an increasingly larger share of the economic value generated in firms: "[t]he no-obligation, no-responsibility, no-liability nature of corporate shares permits their owners – of their institutional representatives – to enjoy income rights without needing to worry about how the dividends are generated," Ireland (2010: 845) argues. In this view, agency theory is not so much about being "credible" and standing up well to empirical tests as it is a thinly veiled attempt to further strengthen the interests of rentier investors, already favored by limited liabilities legislation (Djelic and Bothello, 2013).

The Robustness of the Shareholders-are-the-residual-claimants Argument

Rock (2013: 1910), a legal scholar, argues that the US economic system has shifted from "a management-centric" to a "shareholder-centric" system, and that there is "reason to believe" that managers and directors today largely "think like shareholders." One of the reasons for this change is that the composition of institutional holdings has changed: assets have shifted from "corporate defined-benefit pension funds," historically being very passive owners, to mutual funds being managed by fund managers being "much more willing to support shareholder activism" (Rock, 2013: 1922). "Institutional shareholders in particular enjoy more influence over corporate boards today than at any other time in American business history, and executives are far more focused on keeping share prices high," Stout (2013: 2004) claims.

Agency theorists claim that shareholders contract for the right to the residual cash flow, but such claims are unsubstantiated by corporate law, Stout (2013: 2005) argues "[a]s a legal matter, directors are not agents subject to shareholder's control; nor do shareholders own corporations, which are legal entities that 'own' themselves; nor are shareholders the sole residual claimants of functioning public companies, although they can come close to that status in insolvent firms."[1]

This criticism of agency theory and its shareholder value creation model reveals a major flaw in agency theory as the statement that shareholders "own the right to the residual cash flow" is not substantiated by corporate law. Stout (2013) makes clear that this is both an inaccurate and misleading view, not grounded in corporate law:

> The shareholders-are-the-residual-claimants argument has its roots in bankruptcy law . . . It is not accurate to treat shareholders as the sole residual claimants in a company that is not insolvent. In fact, outside the bankruptcy context, it is highly misleading to suggest that shareholders are legally entitled to receive each and every penny of corporate profit left over after the fixed claims of other stakeholders have been paid. (Stout, 2013: 2013)

Contrary to the agency theory view that shareholders contract for the right to the residual cash flow and that executives and directors are agents acting on behalf of the owners, corporate law grants much authority decision to executives and directors:

> Shareholders' rights turn out to be illusory. Executives and directors own a fiduciary duty of loyalty to the corporation that bars them from using their corporate position to enrich themselves at the firm's expense. But thanks to the business judgment rule, unconflicted directors remain legally free to pursue almost any other goal. Directors can safely donate corporate funds to charity; reject profitable business strategies that might harm the community; refuse risky projects that benefit shareholders and creditors' expense; fend off hostile takeover bids in order to protect the interests of employees or the community, and refuse to declare dividends even when shareholders demand them. Contrary to the principal agent, shareholders in public companies cannot successfully sue directors simply because those directors place other stakeholders' or society's interest above shareholders' own. (Stout, 2012: 44)

---

[1] Stout (2012: 37–44) identifies "three mistaken assumptions" in agency theory: (1) that shareholders "own corporations;" (2) that shareholders are legitimate "residual claimants;" and, (3) that shareholders are "principals" and directors "their agents." These three propositions constitute agency theory while they lack support in corporate law, that is, they are either a form of wishful thinking or signal a belief in the need for future changes in corporate law on basis of normative declarations.

In Stout's view, it is the EMH, widely popular in the 1980s but today "[l]argely discredited both empirically and theoretically" (Stout, 2013: 2018),[2] that led both economists and legal experts to believe that they themselves and market-based actors (that is, mutual funds managers) would be in a better position than professional managers to know where to invest the residual cash flow:

> [E]conomic analysis led many legal experts to conclude that academics had better insight into how to run businesses than businesspeople themselves; that the voluntary contractual arrangements of atomized individuals were inferior to mandatory governance rules imposed by reformers and regulators; and that uniform, 'one size fits all' practices produced better corporate governance than diverse, individualized arrangements. (Stout, 2013: 2007)[3]

This view, that armchair thinking wins over practical professional experience is a curious assumption given the otherwise strong belief in the rationality of the market and in how the unforgiving markets of competitive capitalism effectively discipline market actors including professional managers and directors. In addition to the ignorance of legal matters,

---

[2] Rock (2013: 1916) points out that agency costs, the key theoretical construct in agency theory and its shareholder value model, can "rarely be observed directly." Instead, the best evidence adduced for significant agency costs has been the premiums paid in "change-in-control transactions" and, in particular, those paid in management buyouts. That is, the EMH once again comes in handy for agency theorists, enabling them to claim that if the market always by definition prices assets correctly, then premiums from buyouts must be evidence of accumulated agency costs. But as Stout (2013: 2008) explains, "today, it is widely understood that stock market prices can deviate significantly from underlying value and that shares in diversified conglomerates often trade at a discount that does not necessarily reflect diminished operating performance" (see also Prechel and Morris, 2010, on the effects of recent legislation including the Gramm-Leach-Bliley Act and the Commodity Futures Modernization Act and how it justifies the transfer of economic resources within the multilayer subsidiary form). Seen in this view, in the post-EMH era, agency costs remain a most precarious notion, especially in relationship to other forms of systemic risks in the financial system, for example, the excessive risk-taking and malfeasance demonstrated by finance industry actors in the 2000–2007 period in the US.

[3] From an institutional theory perspective, agency theorist Jensen conducts something similar to what Edelman et al. (2001) refer to as the "managerialization of law," but with the important difference that Jensen restrains managerial decision-making and authority. One may therefore speak of the "financialization of law" as finance market actors being favored by a novel interpretation of law. As law is often broad and ambiguous in its attempt to formally accommodate a variety of particularities and interests, organizations often rely on lawyers and consultants to interpret the intentions of the law (Edelman et al., 2001: 1595). In this process of communicating and translating law, the original legal text is, Edelman et al. (2001: 1595) argue, "filtered through a variety of lenses – and colored by different professional backgrounds, training, and interests." This leads to an adjustment of law to managerial objectives and traditional prerogatives – "the infusion of law with managerial values" (Edelman et al., 2001: 1599) – that in various ways reframe the law as a managerial resource.

while agency theorists are eager to address agency costs derived from the relationship between managers and shareholders, there are in fact two additional categories of agency costs that are regulated by corporate law: (1) agency costs derived from the interests of *controlling* and *non-controlling shareholders*;[4] and (2) agency costs derived from the interests of *shareholders* and *creditors* (Rock, 2013: 1910). In the present, shareholder value creation regime, creditors in particular are disfavored as "there is a tension between the way creditors would like boards to run firms and the way shareholders would like boards to run firms" (Stout, 2013: 2011). "[I]ncentivizing managers to think like shareholders intensifies the shareholder-creditor problem," Rock (2013: 1935) adds. The creditors' position as a principal holding legal rights to residual cash flow is by and large overlooked by agency theorists. Stout (2013) points at some of the detrimental effects of a far-driven shareholder value regime that one-sidedly benefits the shareholders over creditors and others principals:

> [S]takeholders rationally distrust dispensed shareholders who can personally profit from threatening to expropriate or destroy the value of stakeholders' specific interests. This makes it harder for shareholder-focused public corporations to attract dedicated employees, loyal customers, cooperative suppliers, and support from local employees. Shifting public corporations from the managerial model to the shareholder-centric model thus can produce a one-time increase in 'shareholder wealth,' while simultaneously eroding public corporations' long-term ability to generate profits, just as fishing with dynamite produces a one-time increase in catch size while eroding long-term fishing returns. (Stout, 2013: 2016)

In addition to divergences between corporate law and the agency theory view, Stout (2012) points at an additional consequence of agency theory, that of the creation of loud and demanding shareholders that are profoundly unattractive owners for corporations. That is, corporations' willingness to "have public investors at all" may be affected when a strict agency corporate governance policy is implemented (Stout, 2012: 54). This

---

[4] As Belloc (2013: 864–865) notices, the general assumption made in agency theory that shareholders "share a single economic goal" is nowadays inaccurate: instead, individual shareholders, Belloc argues, "[o]ften have conflicts of interest with other shareholders arising from other relationships with the firm, from their investments in derivatives or securities of other corporations and from their investments in other parts of the corporation's capital structure." Studies reveal that an emphasis on "minority shareholder protection" in corporate law may encourage "opportunistic action" played by small activist shareholders, pursuing other goals than the majority of the shareholders (Belloc, 2013: 866). Belloc (2013: 867) thus calls for more extensive research on the "dark side of shareholder protection" that critically questions the assumption that all shareholders have a common interest in improving corporate performance.

is not a hairsplitting issue, as agency theory may in fact contribute to the decline of the public firm as an institution in competitive capitalism. In the US, between 1997 and 2009, "[t]he number of public companies listed on stock exchange has declined by 39 percent in absolute terms, and by a whopping 53 percent when adjusted for GDP growth," Stout (2012: 54) writes. In summary, agency theory and its claim that shareholders hold the legal right is unsubstantiated outside of the more specific case of insolvent firms filing for bankruptcy. Therefore, besides being theoretically incredible and empirically unsubstantiated, agency theory and its shareholder value solution to agency costs are also ignorant of corporate law and its objective to minimize not only one but three categories of agency costs.

Djelic and Bothello (2013) address the implications of corporate law and examine the genealogy of the concept of *limited liability* of central importance in corporate law. Since the nineteenth century, limited liability is institutionalized as no longer being "a rare privilege," but instead becoming "the undisputed regime of responsibility in contemporary capitalism" (Djelic and Bothello, 2013: 590). Limited liability is a legal concept in commercial and corporate law to indicate that a person is personally liable – "in the context of a given venture" – only to a "fixed amount" (Djelic and Bothello, 2013: 599). The institutionalization of limited liability in standard contracts leads to the encouragement of risk-taking – in turn, in its ideal case, leading to innovation and growth – while at the same time, Djelic and Bothello (2013) argue, *moral hazard* has been built into the legal contact. The legal term *limited liability* is therefore Janus-faced, both enabling new opportunities but also creating new concerns that demand further regulatory control and legislation or that induce additional costs. Limited liability is thus the inscription of "deresponsibilization" into the contract, leading to a situation where "individuals would take more risks precisely because they could reap rewards without having to bear the full costs" (Djelic and Bothello, 2013: 607). More specifically, Djelic and Bothello (2013) stress three forms of moral hazard derived from limited liabilities, and here cited at length:

> We argue that these entries in particular contain a triple layer of institutionalized limited liability, which profoundly inscribed moral hazard at the heart of the system. First, shareholders benefit from liability fixed only to their initial investment. Second, managers enjoy limited liability in the sense that they do not bear the full costs associated with unfavorable performance. The magnitude of investment managed by financial institutions is immense, with the potential for very large gains ... A third layer of limited liability, for main financial firms, comes with the institutionalized 'lender of last resort' facility, where large financial institutions will be protected from the most severe effects during crises. It is easy to understand why, with these three layers of insurance-like protection, all actors in the system are incentivized to take more risks. In

such a context, de-responsibilization is not an individual moral failure; rather, it is a general systemic failure. (Djelic and Bothello, 2013: 608)

Similar to Ireland (2010) but unlike agency theorists such as Jensen (1993), Djelic and Bothello (2013) do not regard the shareholders' claim to the right to the free cash flow as being justified neither by "natural rights," nor on basis of the contract they have (implicitly) signed when buying stocks in a company. Instead, the legal contract inscribing the limited liability mechanism needs to be questioned as it encourages risk-taking while it provides "structural protection" from the costs of "risky behaviors and decisions" (Djelic and Bothello, 2013: 609). "This systematic protection is now deeply ingrained and institutionalized within contemporary (financial) capitalism," Djelic and Bothello (2013: 609) conclude.

Given these the critiques of the consistencies of the agency theory framework and its emphasis on shareholder value creation, it is surprising how influential agency theory has been in prescribing corporate governance practices and protocols (Rock, 2013; Dobbin and Jung, 2010). Daily et al. (2003) argue that it is after all the very simplicity of the model that makes it appealing, but they also call for new alternative corporate governance models:

> The popularity of agency theory in governance research is likely due to two factors. First, it is an extremely simply theory, in which large corporations are reduced to two participants – managers and shareholders – and the interests of each are assumed to be both clear and consistent. Second, the notion of humans as self-interested and generally unwilling to sacrifice personal interests for the interest of the other is both age old and widespread. (Daily et al., 2003: 372)

By the end of the day, agency theory is little more than yet another free-market argument that makes the assumption that the market is always right, and claiming that financial market actors, constantly operating to assess the value of financial assets including stocks, would be in a better position than managers inside of the firm to determine where to direct the free cash flow. It is, again, the well-known Chicago economics argument in favor of the market as the superior information processor, the external and collective brain that always knows more than the individual actors participating.

EMPIRICAL STUDIES OF THE IMPLICATIONS OF AGENCY THEORY

As agency theory presents a series of propositions regarding how to reduce agency costs and to distribute the free cash flow, one of its merits is that it lends itself to empirical testing. Davis and Stout (1992) examined which companies were exposed to leveraged buyout activities in the 1980s. Based on Jensen's assumption that opportunistic managers squander the free cash flow on ineffective investments that primarily serve to secure their own positions rather than generating rents benefiting the shareholders, Davis and Stout (1992) suggest that agency theory predicts that CEOs and directors recruited from the finance industry would be more effective in creating shareholder value as they can be assumed to share a belief in finance market efficiency. In their empirical study, Davis and Stout (1992: 626) found on the contrary that "[n]either having a bank executive on the board nor control of a significant block of stock by a bank affected this risk [of takeover]." A board of directors being recruited from the outside and from the finance industry did not make any difference. In addition, also contradicting agency theory, firms that had a CEO recruited from the finance industry *increased* rather than reduce the risk of a takeover:

> [H]aving a finance CEO significantly increased the risk of becoming a take-over target . . . This suggests that finance CEOs, rather than being particularly skilled at running the firm to serve shareholder interests, were carriers of a conception of control that no longer met their own standards of keeping their share price up. (Davis and Stout, 1992: 627)

Similar results were reported by Dalton et al. (1999: 679) who tested the agency theory proposition "that effective boards will be largely comprised of independent, outside directors." Contradicting the proposition, there was no correlation found between the composition of the board of directors and firm performance, indicating that outside directors do not serve the role to discipline managers as predicted by agency theory. Bhagat and Black (2002) conducted a similar study, using the agency theory as their analytical model. A review of the literature suggests that four studies conducted in the US found no evidence of improved performance in the case of independent boards of directors, and studies in Australia, Singapore, and the UK reported similar findings. In four studies, companies with independent directors reported *worse* performances (Bhagat and Black, 2002: 236). Bhagat and Black (2002: 240) used a sample of 205 randomly sampled boards in 1988, and 934 firms in 1991 to test the hypothesis that independent board of directors are capable of performing better than companies having recruited directors internally. The results were daunting from an agency theory view: "[w]e find a reasonably strong *inverse* correlation between firm performance in the recent past and board independence. However, there is no evidence that greater board independence leads to improved firm performance, if anything, there are hints that greater board independence may impair firm performance" (Bhagat and Black, 2002: 263).

However, there were indications of independent directors holding "significant stock positions" being able to make a difference, while other independent directors were not (Bhagat and Black, 2002: 266), a result that seems reasonable given the widespread concern for individual return on investment. "This evidence suggests that the conventional wisdom on the importance of board independence lacks empirical support," Bhagat and Black (2002: 233) summarize.

Similar findings are reported by Davis and Robbins (2005), who studied samples of 647, 691, 691, and 822 firms over the years 1982, 1986, 1990, 1994 respectively, on how they recruited CEOs and "central directors" – directors with particular skills and experiences of relevance for the company. Davis and Robbins (2005: 291) found that firms that outperform their industry are somewhat better able to recruit CEOs and central directors, but found no evidence that "boards composed of these individuals enhance subsequent performance." In other words, Davis and Robbins (2005: 291) conclude, "board composition appears to be an effect of performance, not a cause." In conflict with the agency theory view, Davis and Robbins (2005: 310) therefore suggest that "boards are social institutions first, positioning the firm in a larger network that influences what information it gets and what kind of normative pressures it is susceptible to." In other words, the correlation between the director's background and firm performance is insignificant.

The Social Embeddedness View

In addition to the testing of the role of CEOs and directors, a series of studies from an organization theory perspective, a theoretical framing of the firm that is less focused on financial performance and more concerned with its "social embeddedness" (Davis and Stout, 1992: 612), that is, its ability to maintain meaningful relations with various stakeholders in the firm's milieu, have been published. Westphal and Clement (2008) studied how CEOs seek to influence finance market analysts' reporting on the firm's financial status and performance to counteract unfavorable news. The study is arguably a test of the market efficiency hypothesis as it does not assume that information is always already available in the pricing of assets as there are possibly opportunities for actors to intervene in the reporting of such financial information. As suggested by Davis and Stout (1992), the study assumes a social embeddedness view as financial analysts are dependent on the access to firm executives and experts to be able to make their assessments of the firm's financial performance and to make predictions about future performance. CEOs, conversely, are dependent on positive reports to be able to maintain the stock price at a desired level, one of their principal performance indicators. These mutual dependencies can easily lead to a situation where the two professional groups may compromise their professional domains of jurisdiction. Westphal and Clement (2008: 888) thus speak of "executive favor rendering" in cases where CEOs reward financial analysts who issue reports that avoid negative assessments by giving them better access to the company:

> Executive favor rendering significantly reduced the propensity for analysts to downgrade a firm's stock in response to the announcement of relatively low earnings or diversifying acquisitions. Thus, it appears that analysts tend to reciprocate executive favors by maintaining their stock recommendations for the executive's firm despite the release of negative or controversial information about the firm. (Westphal and Clement, 2008: 888)

Executive favor rendering is beneficial for both the CEO and the finance market analyst, but their mutual interdependencies violate the belief in efficient markets as some information may be withheld or reported in less negative terms to cause less harm for the firm when market actors evaluate the stock. In their empirical study, Westphal and Clement (2008: 888–889) found that "[a]nalysts who downgraded a firm's stock elicit negative reciprocity from the firm's executives, in the form of diminished favor rendering and reduced personal access to top executives at the downgraded firm." In addition, such events tended to create an awareness of the costs of issuing negative reports among financial analysts: "analysts who were aware of another analyst's loss of favor or access to executives after downgrading a focal firm were less likely to subsequently downgrade the firm in response to the disclosure of relatively low earnings or a diversifying acquisition" (Westphal and Clement, 2008: 889). Such social exchanges between company representatives and financial analysts are perfectly understandable from a social embeddedness perspective, and are accommodated by a sociological understanding of the market as a social accomplishment. Within the neoclassic free-market framework, this practice indicates a deviation from the efficient market model: "An implication of our findings is that microsocial factors in manager-analyst relationships, by reducing the objectivity of security analysts' stock recommendation, may ultimately compromise corporate control and financial market efficiency" (Westphal and Clement, 2008: 890). While agency theory regards managerial opportunism as primarily being directed towards the withholding of free cash flow from shareholders, the theory does not predict that there are other forms of opportunistic behavior, for example, that the CEO may act opportunistically on the shareholders' behalf. As the finance market evaluation is always right, such practices are, *ex hypothesi*, not possible. Agency theory thus fails to take into account how CEOs and other company representatives can manipulate market information reporting.

Futhermore, Westphal and Bednar (2008: 62) demonstrate that in firms with a high degree of institutional ownership (that is, the owners being pension funds, large insurance companies, and so on), CEOs are "[l]ikely to engage in persuasion and ingratiation tactics to deter representatives of institutional investors from using their ownership power to the detriment of CEOs' interests." That is, institutional owners are expected to discipline and monitor the CEO to act in accordance with the owners' interests, agency theory predicts, while in fact the CEO in many cases manages to influence these directors to accept the CEO's decisions. "Our theory and supportive findings suggests that CEOs' interpersonal influence behavior provides an alternative source of influence in manager-shareholder relationships," Westphal and Bednar (2008: 63) summarize their research findings. Finally, Westphal and Graebner (2010: 34–35) studied how CEOs facing "less optimistic earnings forecasts and less positive stock recommendations" were able to increase the visibility of the independence of their board of directors for external constituents "without actually increasing their boards' tendency to control management." When being unfavorably graded by finance market analysts, CEOs had to demonstrate that the board of directors are independently overseeing and monitoring the CEOs work, whereas in fact the CEOs' ability to act remains stable and is concealed for external constituencies. This maneuver can be viewed, under certain circumstances, Westphal and Graebner (2010: 36) propose, as an "act of impression management." Also in this case, CEOs are able to defend and maintain executive autonomy. Unfortunately, such activities bias the market information being of central importance for the effectiveness of finance markets as there is a difference between the board's position *de jure* and *de facto* positions:

> These results support our contention that corporate leaders can successfully manage the impression of external constituents about the governance of their firms by engaging in communications that frames board behavior in terms of central normative prescription of the agency logic of governance, while making visible changes in board composition that *appear* to lend credence to their claims, but that are decoupled from actual board behavior. (Westphal and Graebner, 2010: 35)

All these research results are pointing at thorny problems in the agency theory framework: if the board of directors and the finance market analysts check on managerial opportunism, why are the CEOs capable of manipulating both market finance actors and the board of directors in their own favor? However, as this new "managerial opportunism" serves to defend favorable stock prices evaluations and to reduce the effects of negative assessments, this opportunism benefits shareholders and potentially increases the free cash flow, and therefore such activities may be more tolerable for agency theorists in comparison to the deadly sin of withholding the free cash flow from the owners of stock. Under all circumstances, empirical studies point at the theoretical inconsistency of agency theory, its inability to predict outcomes, and its failure to stand up to empirical testing. Numerous studies show how "social dynamics" can "compromise market efficiency" (Zajac and Westphal, 2004: 434).

Davis and Stout (1992): 627 summarize the empirical tests of agency theory, saying that the theory "fares rather poorly as an empirical theory, despite its imposing status as normative theory" and add that "the foundations of agency theory as an empirical theory is weak." More specifically, they continue, "agency theorists seriously misconstrue the extent to which boards can be seen as vigilant monitors looking out for their shareholder principals—if anything, boards' interest are much more closely tied to those of managers." Therefore, as its stands, agency theory "does not provide a credible alternative theory of organizations" (Davis and Stout, 1992: 627). The question is then, why should shareholder value maximization, the normative core of agency theory, be regarded as the most effective control of managers when most other things being predicted by agency theorists have failed to stand up to empirical tests? In addition, if the argument that the finance market is always pricing financial assets correctly, the axiom of agency theory and its shareholder value framework, then there are further issues to critically examine, for instance the stock repurchases that firms undertake on a regular basis.

THE CONUNDRUM OF STOCK REPURCHASES IN EFFICIENT MARKETS

Stock repurchases and stock repurchase announcements are among the most puzzling financial operations in companies for agency theorists. Stock repurchase is not a marginal phenomenon but is a widespread and commonplace technique for manipulating stock prices. "In 1987, repurchases amounted to 1.6% of average market capitalization, and total payout amounted to 3.8%; in 2007, repurchases amounted to 4.6%, and total payout amounted to 6.3%. The dollar amount of annual repurchases increased eighteen-fold from 1987 to the peak year of 2007," Bratton and Wachter (2010: 686) write. Tabb puts the uses of capital to repurchase stock against other uses of this capital, for example, R&D: "[f]rom 2007 through 2008, 438 companies in the S&P 500 [Standard & Poor] stock index spent $2.4 trillions on stock buybacks. Leading high-tech companies, such as Microsoft, IBM and Intel, spent more on stock buybacks than on research and development" (Tabb, 2012: 49).

Also after the 2008 finance market collapse, stock purchases have been widely used:

> In the decade 2001–2010, S&P 500 [Standard & Poor] companies expended £3 trillion on buybacks. They quadrupled from ~$300 [million] per company in 2003 to over £1.2 billion per company in 2007 before declining sharply in the financial crisis of 2008 and 2009. Since then, stock buybacks, have rebounded, averaging ~$800 among S&P 500 companies in 2011 and 2012. (Lazonick and Mazzucato, 2013: 1114)

Apparently, using the free cash flow to repurchase the firm's own stock is an attractive solution to the control of the stock price for CEOs and directors, but it discredits the financial market's ability to price the stock and therefore undermine the accuracy of the principal assumption of the underlying theory. There are a number of proposed explanations that aim to shed some light on stock repurchases. Dittmar (2000) offers five different hypotheses that provide alternative explanations for this practice: (1) the *excess capital hypothesis*, which assumes that the excess capital generated in the firm is most effectively plowed down in raising the stock price rather than being invested in productive resources or distributed to stakeholders; (2) the *undervaluation hypothesis*, which suggests that firms repurchase their stocks in cases such as when the CEO and the directors believe the stock is undervalued in the market, that is, insiders believe they know more about the "substantial value" of the stock than the market actors; (3) the *optimal leverage ratio hypothesis*, which suggests that firms strive to have an optimal debt-to-capital ratio, and in order to reduce the capital stocks are repurchased; (4) the *management incentives hypothesis*, which proposes that CEOs and directors being awarded on basis of their ability to maintain the value of the stock at a certain price level choose to actively influence the stock price by using the firm's free cash flow to repurchase its own stock; and (5) the *takeover deterrence hypothesis*, which postulates that firms with undervalued stocks are more susceptible to takeover activities and therefore the CEOs need to keep the stock price at a high level.

Regardless of which hypothesis is explaining most of the variance in the sample, stock repurchases, like paying dividends, is one channel to distribute capital to shareholders (Dittmar, 2000: 333). Grullon and Ikenberry (2000: 31) notice that it was not until the early 1980s that corporations began adopting stock repurchase programs on a wider scale. Such evidence further mystifies the stock purchase practice as financial markets were deregulated in the 1980s *precisely because* they were understood by policy-makers, informed by the recent finance theory developed in economics departments, as effective mechanisms for pricing assets. Why then would stock repurchases grow in importance at the same time as allegedly more effective pricing mechanisms were instituted? Grullon and Ikenberry (2000: 34) present some data: "total corporate payouts in share repurchase programs during the period 1972–1983 amounted to less than 4.5% of total earnings. Over the period 1984 to 1998, this same ratio exceeded 25%." The new practice was enabled by the relaxing of the rules regarding stock repurchases in the period. In 1982, the US Securities and Exchange Commission (US SEC) adopted *Rule 10b-18* reducing the "ambiguities" regarding stock repurchases (Grullon and Ikenberry, 2000: 34). This new regulatory framework enabled the expansion of stock repurchases: "in the five-year period between 1995 and 1999, U.S. corporations announced intentions to repurchase roughly $750 billion worth of stock. Moreover, in 1998 – and for the first time in history – U.S. corporations distributed more cash to investors through share repurchases than through cash dividends" (Grullon and Ikenberry, 2000: 31).

For some reason, firms preferred to transfer its free cash flow to its shareholders less in the form of dividends and more as stock repurchases after 1982: "the average dividend payout-ratio [in the US] fell from 22.3% in 1974 to 13.8% in 1998, while the average purchase payout ratio increased from 3.7% to 13.6% during the same period" (Grullon and Ikenberry, 2000: 34). The question is: why this change in preferences from dividends to high-stock price evaluations?

Dittmar's (2000: 333) empirical study shows somewhat unsurprisingly that "firms repurchase stock to take advantage of potential undervaluation throughout the sample period." Since stock repurchase programs, as Grullon and Ikenberry (2000: 46) write, "give managers a valuable, and relatively inexpensive, option to repurchase stock," CEOs and directors can easily and at low cost intervene in the market evaluation of the stock. Dittmar (2000) also found that large firms are the "dominant repurchasers," also being a counterintuitive finding as the stocks of larger firms are more frequently traded and therefore these stocks are, if markets are capable of efficiently pricing financial assets (which they are assumed to do), "less likely to be misvalued" (Dittmar, 2000: 333). Despite such concerns, Dittmar (2000) found support for the *excess capital*, the *optimal leverage*, the *undervaluation*, and the *takeover deterrence* hypotheses. That is, all explanations for stock repurchases with the notable exception of the *management incentives hypothesis* were supported. This is again surprising as that would be the most intuitively credible explanation for these practices as managers are often compensated on the basis of their ability to maintain the stock price at a high level. "Preserving the stock price may be of particular interest when management holds stock options," Dittmar (2000: 335) claims. Grullon and Ikenberry (2000: 34) stress that stock purchase activity coincides with the more widespread use of stock option compensation packages for executives in the 1990s. Executives therefore have incentives to reduce or even eliminate dividends entirely and to distribute the free cash flow to shareholders in the form of stock repurchases (Grullon and Ikenberry, 2000: 34). Regardless of such plausible connections between individual incentives and firms' stock repurchasing programs, Dittmar (2000: 348) grants no particular importance to the *management incentives hypothesis*, and instead she suggests that "since the motives are not mutually exclusive and multiple motives are significant, it is possible that firms repurchase stock for several reasons" (Dittmar, 2000: 348). In other words, stock repurchases are not being given a unified explanation in Dittmar's (2000) study but are on the contrary made on the basis of a variety of reasons. However, it is clear that the US regulatory bodies have reduced the costs for using stock repurchases, and have opened up for a low-cost, low-risk method to influence the stock price valuation.

Kahle (2002: 260) argues that previous studies have found that repurchase programs are undertaken to accomplish two objectives: (1) to "signal undervaluation to investors;" and (2) to "return free cash to shareholders." In Kahle's view, these two theories fail to explain the "sudden and drastic increase" in repurchases in the 1990s, and therefore she proposes that one possible explanation is the increased use of stock options to compensate "not just management but all employees in the firm" (Kahle, 2002: 260). Kahle's research findings support the proposition that changes in compensation policy is the driver of stock repurchasing announcements and programs: "[i]n the 1990s, stock options have encouraged firms to repurchase shares both to maximize managerial wealth, since repurchases do not affect the value of managerial options but dividends do, and to fund increasingly prevalent employee stock option programs" (Kahle, 2002: 260). These results are consistent with the *management incentives hypothesis*. However, Kahle also remarks that the finance market has learned to recognize this function of stock repurchasing announcements as "[t]he announcement return to repurchasing firm is significantly lower for firms with large numbers of employee stock options" (Kahle, 2002: 260). The finance market here serves a stabilizing role in assessing the value of the stock. As opposed to Kahle (2002), Baker et al.'s (2003) study, based on a survey retrieved from 194 firms announcing stock repurchases, supports precisely the undervaluation and signaling hypotheses criticized by Kahle (2002). As Baker et al. (2003: 484) comment, studies of stock repurchases "[h]ave been subject to numerous, and often conflicting interpretations," and it remains complicated to discriminate between the different drivers of stock repurchasing programs and their announcements.

Farre-Mensa et al.'s (2014) review of the payout policy literature makes clear that much of the literature of the twentieth century that focused on the effects of taxes or on the choice between dividends and repurchases was mistaken inasmuch as taxes "[d]o not seem to be a first-order explanation for the observed variation in payout, especially at the aggregate level" (Farre-Mensa et al., 2014: 17.3). Among what Farre-Mensa et al. (2014) refer to as "traditional motivation for payouts" (that is, theoretical explanations), the agency theory view that firms should use payouts to reduce potential overinvestment by management dominates firm policy. Still, while agency theory may normatively make the claim that generous payout policies discipline managers, it fails to explain the shift in payout policy from dividends to stock repurchases. The theory that executives want to signal to the market that it prices the stock inaccurately (that is, a conjecture based on the *undervaluation hypothesis*) cannot accommodate the fact that the market reaction to repurchase announcements is "not semi-strong form efficient" (Farre-Mensa et al., 2014: 17.3), that is, there is too much "noise" in the signal to effectively communicate with market actors through open-market repurchase announcements. Farre-Mensa et al. (2014) observe two changes in how firms distribute earnings: (1) there is a sharp growth in payout (between 1970 and 2012, US firms' aggregate dividends grew from $70 billion to $258 billion in real 2012 dollars); and (2) there is a shift from dividends to repurchases ("[d]ividends fell from 66.5% in 1978 to 20.8% in 1999" [Farre-Mensa et al., 2014: 17.5]). These two changes can be explained on the basis of the design of managers' compensation contracts, Farre-Mensa et al. (2014: 17.3) suggest: : "[i]f executives' compensation depends on earnings per share (EPS), a measure that, all else equal, decreases in the number of shares outstanding, they are more likely to repurchase stock rather than pay out capital through dividends." Farre-Mensa et al. (2014: 17.52) notice that "[e]xecutive compensation are often based (explicitly or implicitly) on EPS," and therefore executives have a strong personal incentive to use the free cash flow to repurchase stock. That is, the agency theory explanation for repurchases, is "not precise and detailed enough to guide empirical research" (Farre-Mensa et al., 2014: 17.51) as agency theory suggests that *markets* discipline managers, not their compensation packages, and therefore individual incentives are theoretically insignificant. In addition, the other favorite neoclassical explanation, that government and taxes bias well-functioning markets and thus create incentives to repurchase stock, predicts payout policy poorly (Farre-Mensa et al., 2014: 17.50). Evidence suggests the contrary, that the *more* markets are deregulated, the *more* stock is repurchased. That is, the predominant, instrumental theories of payout policy assuming that: (1) finance market control effectively discipline managers (agency theory); and (2) such forms of control demands free markets (anti-statist theories on taxation) are inaccurate. Instead, Farre-Mensa et al. (2014: 17.52) conclude, "At the forefront are explanations that investigate the interaction between payouts and compensation of both executives and rank-and-file employees." In this recent authoritative review of the literature, the *management incentives hypothesis*, downplayed by for example, Dittmar (2000), is given much explanatory value in the "eco-system view" on payout policy that Farre-Mensa et al. (2014: 17.52) advocate.

Regardless of the officially declared and informal rationales for stock repurchases, for the critics of stock repurchase practices, the free cash flow being transferred to the shareholders could have been used more wisely as for example, investment in R&D or human resources. For instance, among the finance market firms that were bailed out by the federal government in the fall of 2008 in the TARP, many firms had engaged in stock purchases in the 2000–2007 period, including Citigroup ($41.8 billion repurchases in 2000–2007), Goldman Sachs ($30.1 billion), Wells Fargo ($21.2 billion), Merrill Lynch ($21.0 billion), Morgan Stanley ($19.1 billion), American Express ($17.6 billion) and U.S. Bancorp ($12.3 billion) (Lazonick, 2010: 696). "Allocated differently, the trillions spent on buybacks in the past decades could have helped stabilize the economy," Lazonick (2010: 696) claims. "Financial incentives in a host of ways have reduced the U.S. ability to efficiently produce goods and services and to create well-paying jobs outside of finance," Tabb (2012: 49–50) suggests, sharing Lazonick's (2010) view of the detrimental role of stock repurchases. "[T]he increase in stock buybacks is consistent with agency theory, but not with the idea of the firm as the 'locus of innovation,'" Milberg and Winkler (2010: 290) add. In addition, stock repurchases are commonly justified on the basis of the argument that stocks are "undervalued" – per se a curious statement for free-market protagonists – but as Lazonick and Mazzucato (2013: 1115) point out, this "signaling argument" only "works one way" as the very same CEOs and directors are not likely to signal to the market that they believe the company's shares are *overvalued* by selling the stock. These practices indicate that economic incentives and compensation packages may serve a role in stock repurchases that is larger than for example, Dittmar (2000) admits.

CRITIQUE OF SHAREHOLDER VALUE POLICIES

It is not unfair to make the claim that agency theory, in turn based on the firm belief in the efficiency of free-market finance assets pricing, serves as the underlying theoretical framework that justifies shareholder value creation as the predominant corporate governance principle. Shareholder value policies, however, have been subject to detailed analysis in the economic sociology and management literature. This criticism focuses on: (1) the rationale for implementing corporate governance policies that are based on principals and agents having shared interest while ignoring other stakeholders; and (2) the long-term effect of performance indicators enacted by the finance market actor. These two arguments will be discussed in the following.

Shareholder Value as Corporate Governance Policy

Corporate governance is the theory and practice of how to ensure that the firm survives over time through an effective allocation of resources and a continuous adaptation to various interests and expectations in the firm's milieu. While corporate law and the regulatory framework developed over decades or even centuries have carefully sought to balance various interests, the more recent financialization of corporate governance in the form of an exclusive concern for shareholder enrichment represents a break with this tradition of policy-making. While Berle and Means ([1934] 1991) examined the separation of ownership and the execution of managerial work, they were not only concerned with the managers' lack of accountability to investors, but the "lack of accountability to society in general" (Mizruchi, 2004: 581). Today, the predominant shareholder value policy short-circuits all the firm's social relations except the relationship with the finance market actors. As Dobbin and Jung (2010: 38) remark, these finance market actors are not so much individual stockholders as they are fund managers and other institutional investors, themselves being compensated on the basis of their performance vis-à-vis the market index:

> Fund managers controlled over 60% of the shares in the average firm in our sample by 2005, up from 20% in 1970, and so they increasingly determined stock price. Executive interests were thus not aligned with the long-term interest of shareholders so much as with the short-term interest of institutional fund managers. (Dobbin and Jung, 2010: 38)

As a consequence, Deutschmann (2011: 358) suggests, managers are today not so much considered as "skilled professionals" as they are "agents of shareholder value maximization." Therefore, "increasing the value of the investor's portfolio by leveraged buyouts, stock repurchases, mergers and acquisitions became a first priority of business strategy" (Deutschmann, 2011: 358). Commentators have remarked that Alfred Sloan's memoir *My Years with General Motors*, one of the most well-known accounts of managerial work in the era of managerial capitalism, includes no references to finance markets when particular decisions were made. Today, the situation would be entirely different, if nothing else, as Deutschmann (2011: 358) says, "as bonuses and options for managers were largely coupled to share prices, they would benefit from rising share prices too." The financialization of the economy has penetrated all spheres of society to the point where the *distance* between principals and agents is less of a concern in comparison to the *absence* of such distances that would indicate that these two categories of actors represent different social roles and objectives. In other words, in the era of financialization, the principal and agent positions, central to the development of a professional managerial class from the end of the nineteenth century, are today folded into one another; they are agents that share the predicament to be responsive to finance market expectations.

The Long-term Effect of Shareholder Value

Another issue being addressed in the literature is how a long-term reliance on shareholder value creation affects the economy and society. Froud et al. (2000: 108) suggest that the very idea of shareholder value creation as a legitimate and sustainable corporate governance principle is based on a fallacy as it assumes that *all firms* can perform better than any other firm by distributing more free cash flow, and that firms that fail to report high valuations are not economically viable. This simplistic proposition serves to obscure the central point that "management actions and corporate positions that work to deliver shareholder value for some firms will not work for all," Froud et al. (2000: 108) argue. Instead, corporate successes within one sector are in some cases "achieved at the expense of failures elsewhere." In addition, in other cases, the management actions or performance of successful firms "rest on special case advantages which cannot be copied or will not produce equally large benefits for all who imitate" (Froud et al., 2000: 108). The valuation and commensuration of firm effectiveness on the basis of stock prices is in other words ignoring local industry conditions and specific factor prices. Given the neoclassic economic theory's marginal interest for what happens inside of the firm (O'Sullivan, 2000), such ignorance is not surprising. In addition to theoretical fallacies, there are reasons to be concerned about the long-term consequences of a shareholder value policy for industry. Shareholder value creation encourages managers to shift from a governance policy that emphasizes reinvestment of the free cash flow in productive capital that in turn generates further rents and cash flow, to a "downsize and distribute" policy (Lazonick and O'Sullivan, 2000: 17): "[u]nder the new regime, top managers downsize the corporations they control, with a particular emphasis on cutting the size of the labor forces they employ, in an attempt to increase the return on equity," Lazonick and O'Sullivan (2000: 18) argue. Workforce downsizing, Guthrie and Datta (2008: 118) formulate, "has a deleterious effect on firm performance," and such value extraction strategies are short-sighted.

There is ample empirical evidence that suggests that the popularity of the shareholder value ideology coincides with the loss of hundreds of thousands of well-paid blue-collar jobs in the American economy: "[b]etween 1979 and 1983, the number of people employed in the economy as a whole increased by 377,000 or 0.4 percent, while employment in durable goods manufacturing – which supplied most of the well-paid and stable blue-collar jobs – declined by 2,023,000 or 15.9 per cent" (Lazonick and O'Sullivan, 2000: 18–19). In order to boost earnings and stock prices, the easiest way is to cut costs; investing in R&D activities and further market expansion is a more costly and risky strategy, and therefore shareholder enrichment is not so much the outcome of a more efficient allocation of capital as suggested by agency theorists as it is the reduction of costs, primarily through layoff of blue-collar workers. Although there were other factors influencing industry's effectiveness in the 1980s and 1990s, including the computerization of the workplace in the 1990s, the opening up of new markets as the Soviet Bloc collapsed at the end of the 1980s, combined with the general political project to reduce the role of trade unions, the blue-collar worker community pulled the shortest straw: "[a]lthough de-unionization and computerization were going on in the U.S. economy well before the 1980s, the implementation of shareholder value tactics pushed these processes forward," Fligstein and Shin (2007: 419) write. Fligstein and Shin go on to say (2007: 420), "[m]aximizing shareholder value and to minimize the importance of employees is a not-so-veiled way to increase profits by reducing the power of workers." Fligstein and Shin's (2007: 420) results show, they argue, that "the efforts to make more profits were focused on using mergers, layoffs, and computer technologies to reorganize and remove unionized labor forces." Brockman et al. (2007) provide evidence that CEOs were compensated on the basis of their reduction of salaried workers, testifying to the shareholder value policy's role in eliminating blue-collar work in the American economy. In studying 229 layoff announcements, Brockman et al. (2007: 101) show that: (1) total pay to the CEO increased by 22.8 percent the year after the layoff; (2) layoff results in higher CEO compensation that persists over time; and (3) layoffs create higher shareholder value. As CEOs were compensated on the basis of decisions that increased shareholder value, lay-off decisions led to a growth in individual compensation of the CEOs making such decisions: "total compensation is 22.8% higher the year after the layoffs, and this increase also continues. These results suggest that CEOs who make layoff decisions are rewarded with higher compensation levels that persist" (Brockman et al., 2007: 117).

Stockhammer (2004) demonstrates that financialization correlates with a decline in accumulation of capital in the non-financial sector, evidence that supports the view that shareholder value enrichment has been unfavorable for sustainable economic growth: "[m]aximizing shareholder value undercut . . . the basis of productive growth long central to economic expansion" (Tabb, 2012: 55). In addition to the shareholder value policy, Milberg and Winkler (2010) emphasize the effects of *offshoring*, another popular strategy for increasing shareholder value. By moving production facilities to low-cost countries, in many cases with lower degrees of unionization and weaker regulatory frameworks, and offering other cost benefits such as tax reductions when investing in industrial districts in for example, South-East Asia, offshoring has supported the financialization of the non-finance sector by "[r]aising profits and by reducing the need for domestic reinvestment in those profits, freeing earnings for the purchase of financial assets and raising shareholder returns" (Milberg and Winkler, 2010: 276). In the 1970s, beginning in Japan and then spreading across East Asia, increased investment in manufacturing eventually brought chronic excess production capacity and lowered the rate of return on manufacturing and services investment (Milberg, 2008: 423). The consequences were that the net worth of financial corporations "rose steadily" relative to the net worth of non-financial corporations, and that traditionally non-financial firms started to act like financial holding companies, leading to financial services and financial investments creating a higher proportion of the manufacturing companies' revenues (Milberg, 2008: 423–424). This in turn increased the money supply in the US economy. On average, the inflation rate in the US economy has been around 2 percent in the mid-1990s–2006 period, while during the same period, "money supply growth rose by over 7 per cent per annum" (Milberg, 2008: 428). Studies of offshoring strategies suggest that around 40 percent calculated costs savings are needed to break even, and there is empirical evidence of 50 to 60 percent costs savings. If one postulates a 40 percent cost saving, that would translate into 2.8 percent of national income, "a substantial magnitude in relation to the corporate profit share on income that was around 10 per cent in 2006" (Milberg, 2008: 431). In other words, "[o]ffshoring has a statistically significant and positive relation to profits," Milberg (2008: 430) concludes.

The financial benefits of offshoring are visible in the US trade deficits: in 2005–2007, the US trade deficit was US$700 billion annually, whereas China alone accounts for US$256 billion. The US$700 billion trade deficit represents more than 6 percent of GDP (Milberg, 2008: 440). Moreover, the import from low-cost countries to the US more than doubled over 26 years, from less than 3 percent in 1980 to 7 percent of GDP in 2006 (Milberg, 2008: 426). However, all the benefits of offshoring were not equally distributed. According to offshoring theory, the social gains (defined as a shift in the Pareto curve) derived from the restructuring of global value chains "depends on the compensation of losers by winners" (Milberg, 2008: 428). A study published by the IMF in 2006 reveals that offshoring is a "small, but nonetheless negative and significant factor" in the determination of the labor share of income for a group of OECD countries (Milberg, 2008: 431). Complemented by statistics regarding dividend payments and stock repurchases from the early 1980s to 2006 demonstrate that in the early 1980s, around 20 percent of internal funds in the non-financial corporate sector were used for these purposes (that is, to create value for the shareholder), while by 2006, 90 percent were (Milberg, 2008: 436–437). Blue-collar workers thus received less economic compensation after offshoring and global value chain strategies had been implemented. In addition they suffered devastating job losses; shareholders, in contrast, could benefit from the financial and economic gains from exploiting the regional differences in production factor prices. The creation of global value chains has increased what Milberg (2008: 421) calls a "reverse capital flow," from low-wage countries to industrialized countries, and this in turn further reinforces the process of financialization. Still, Milberg (2006) does not suggest that financialization "caused" globalized production systems, or vice versa, but rather the two processes are co-produced and mutually reinforcing:

> Financialization has encouraged a restructuring of production, with firms narrowing their scope to core competencies . . . The point is not that globalized production triggered financialization, but that global production strategies have helped to sustain financialization. Sustainability in terms of profits and international capital flows is not synonymous with social sustainability. And we have seen that social conflict created as a result of the interdependence of financialization and global value chain governance: large increases in income inequality. (Milberg, 2008: 446–447)

There are also wider economic implications from the creation of global production systems: as much production capital has moved outside of the

American economy, US corporations are today less capable of taking on the role as what can boost and stabilize the economy in periods of recession, Milberg and Winkler (2010) argue:

> [F]inancialization and globalization have reinforced each other for the US corporations and, despite the corporate sector's contribution to national savings over the past decade, the offshoring-financialization linkage reduces the capacity of non-financial corporations to act as a driver of the recovery from the non-economic crisis that emerged in 2008. Having moved into core competence beginning in the early 1990s as part of the financialization process, US corporations are today ill-equipped to serve as the driver of economic recovery. (Milberg and Winkler, 2010: 276)

The effects of finance-motivated "globalization" in the form of offshoring served to both accumulate further capital in the finance industry and to undermine the political instrument widely used in the Keynesian economic model, to stimulate economic growth by targeting labor-intensive industries and initiate public investments.

These shifts in corporate governance were again coinciding with changes in the finance markets. As Dobbin and Zorn (2005: 188) say, the "the conventional wisdom ca. 1980 was that if an investor did not like the way a firm was managed, she could vote with her feet, moving her money elsewhere." After the financed markets were deregulated, the institutional investors modified their relationship with executives and the boards of directors and "came to believe that it made more sense to reform management than to sell off stock" (Dobbin and Zorn, 2005: 188). This new finance industry actor strategy created a new market for CEOs (Khurana, 2002) that served to destabilize one of the central pillars of the present regime of managerial capitalism, that of the CEO and a board of directors that identified more with the firm than with the finance industry and the finance market:

> During the neoliberal era changes occurred within large corporations. Under regulated capitalism the CEO was traditionally promoted from within, from high-level managers who had spent their careers with the company. Attaining the CEO position was normally the last step before retirement, and CEOs strongly identified with the interest of their companies. In the neoliberal era, a market arose for CEOs, which involved hiring them from outside the company. As this became the new norm, the relation between a CEO and the company changed. Now the typical CEO would expect to spend only a few years in a company before arranging a move to a bigger one. (Kotz, 2013: 404–405)

In order to align the interests of institutional investors and executives, pay-for-performance via stock options compensation systems were implemented. Unfortunately, these new ways to compensate executives did not manage to reduce agency costs but served to transform the nature of the problem as executives are today more concerned about finance market evaluations – again, the *principle of self-recursio*n – than with actual accomplishments and possibilities for future income and economic growth (Dobbin and Zorn, 2005: 196). Thus, paying a CEO a fixed salary and a small bonus failed to eliminate agency costs, but opening up for lavish economic compensation including stock options, and bonuses and other benefits did not resolve the problem either, Dobbin and Zorn (2005: 196) argue. Instead, executives engage in an irrational management of earnings and financial market reporting while ignoring other, more long-term oriented performance indicators, or even render them irrelevant.

Agency theory and its shareholder value policy, supposedly being the ultimate check on managerial malfeasance (Dobbin and Jung, 2010: 42), served to justify a new view of the employees, not so much as a skilled workforce adding value to the company through their expertise and commitment, but as a sheer cost that could be reduced without any significant implications for long-term competitiveness. Ho's (2009) ethnography of Wall Street finance industry professionals and their attitude towards American industry offers a glimpse of the life world of these "elite professionals" and how they regard themselves as being given the role to discipline managers: "[i]f you look at the old days," one Wall Street worker told Ho (2009: 130–131), "all the companies were basically fat, dumb, and stupid. [T]hey did not change. They were making [enough] money. The [managers] didn't care. Now, you have Wall Street with all their shareholders . . . You can't just be dumb, fat, and happy . . . Wall Street is definitely making a much more efficient corporate America." Such accounts of finance industry professionals provide no indication of these finance market actors seeing any social roles or objectives beyond their more narrow focus on generating wealth for their employers and themselves.

In this Hobbesian *Weltanschauung*, the economy is a battlefield and individuals failing to compete over stable and well-paid jobs are no victims of circumstances and political and economic decisions beyond their control, but are guilty of making "ineffective" human capital investments. In addition, these "elite professionals" did not have any concerns regarding how they participate in transferring wealth from multiple corporate stakeholders to capital owners (Ho, 2009: 140). While managers are *ex hypothesi* treated as opportunistic and rent-seeking actors that needs to be disciplined by finance market control, no such worries have been addressed on the part of the finance market actors themselves, despite overwhelming evidence of the highly controversial and risky practices being unearthed in the events of 2008.

THE FINANCIALIZATION OF CORPORATE GOVERNANCE

Historically speaking, corporate governance regimes have been embedded in social and political interests, and therefore the principal solution to governance problems have been a combination of legislation and the state being active in discounting risks and creating markets that private actors benefit from (Roy, 1997). As Hilt (2014: 8.5) writes, from the mid to late nineteenth century, corporations were instituted as contracts between both the incorporators and the state:

> For a business to become a corporation, the state has to pass a law, and the contents of that law – the corporation's charter – were the outcome of a negotiation between the incorporators and the state government. The formation of early corporations was not merely a contracting process among the incorporators; it was also a contract between the incorporators and the state. (Hilt, 2014: 8.5)

Hilt (2014) argues that much corporate governance literature makes the wrong assumption about the historical development of corporate law and other corporate government practices when envisaging a "simple, linear trajectory" in the modern American legal system. Much research in the field ignores or overlooks historical controversies and conflicts pertaining to the governance of corporations and downplays the role of politics in the creation of the American corporation (Hilt, 2014: 8.18):

> Much of this research that concluded that the Berle & Means view of early corporate governance is simply incorrect. Evidence of substantial corporate governance problems has been found among early American companies. Although the average size of public corporations certainly grew over time, the evolution of American corporate governance has not followed a simple, linear trajectory, beginning with small, well-governed organizations in which shareholders participated actively and eventually ending with large poorly governed organizations with absentee owners and opportunity managers. (Hilt, 2014: 8.3)

The gradual emergence of corporate law, carefully designed to balance various social interests, was in the early 1980s and thereafter challenged by another corporate governance regime based on the idea that finance markets would be capable of reconciling various interests and reducing agency costs by leaving to the finance market actors to price financial assets including company stocks. In an economic sociology view, the shift in corporate governance from legal to market-based control represented a new institutional logic. At the heart of this shift lies a concern not so much for economic stability, and (within reasonable limits) economic equality, as for the *efficiency* of the economy. After 1980, economic efficiency has been pitted against social stability (a proposition that can be substantiated by the presence of the sharp growth in finance market crises after 1980: see Blinder, 2013; Gorton, 2010; Fox, 2009; Black, 2005; Partnoy, 2003), but when agency theorists accuse managers of acting opportunistically to ensure corporate stability, such a critique relies on the efficiency logic rather than the institutional logic of corporate law as the primary corporate governance resource. As Roe (2003) remarks, managerial agency costs come in "two flavors": "[o]ne, machinations that translate value to the managers – 'stealing' – corporate law seeks to control. But the other – 'shirking,' or pursuing goals other than shareholder value – corporate law largely leaves alone" (Roe, 2003: 163). As Roe further adds, standard corporate law prescribes no liability at all for "mistakes, absent fraud or conflict of interest," but this is in fact where the largest agency costs are found. That is, Roe (2003) suggests, where corporate laws is needed the most, it remains silent. But corporate law was not originally designed and enacted to prevent "mistakes" but to secure stable and easily understood rules of the game (Roy, 1997), and therefore it is curious that agency theorists and proponents of shareholder value policies turn a blind eye to the historical view of corporate governance as being the outcome of the work to eliminate problems today widely overcome and therefore essentially forgotten.

As Shleifer and Vishny (1997) remark, the contracts regulating the relationship between managers and investors, first, cannot "require too much interpretation if they are to be enforced by outside courts" (Shleifer and Vishny, 1997: 737), and therefore corporate law can never fully accommodate how managerial mistakes should be punished; second, practically speaking, many investors are too small and too poorly informed to be able to "exercise even the control rights that they actually have" (Shleifer and Vishny, 1997: 737). That is, agency theorists may claim that corporate law is ineffective in curbing managerial opportunism, but they both ignore the historical record of corporate law and its institutional logic and the practical difficulties to interpret and enforce legal contracts. In addition, agency theory assumes opportunistic behavior on the part of some actors (for example, executives) but not others (for example, finance market traders). In summary, therefore, the corporate governance ticket provided by agency theory is both theoretically incredible and inconsistent and stands up poorly to empirical testing. Such facts make the suspicion that agency theory's popularity is to be explained on the basis of ideological beliefs and political preferences, and more specifically the widespread idea that free markets (and the finance market in particular) are the most effective mechanism for allocating resources in the economy. A theory that is neither consistent nor capable of surviving empirical tests would have few chances to be spread widely and influence practices and policy-making unless it was backed by strong ideological beliefs and/or financial funding (Kogut and Macpherson, 2011; Blyth, 2002). The history of the triumph of agency theory and its corollary, the shareholder value creation policy, is thus an exemplary case of what Michel Foucault (1980: 131) speaks of as the *political economy of truth*; truth is not a matter of factual evidence as much as it is discursively produced and non-discursively enacted in actual practices and material conditions. Truth is therefore contingent on social, economic, and political conditions.

SUMMARY AND CONCLUSIONS

The literature on corporate governance suggests that all economies need to institute laws and regulations that specify how ownership right, labor relations, and the right to the economic value generated are to be distributed between different organizational stakeholders. Prior to the era of financialization, the corporate governance system in most Western economies was designed to strike a balance between a variety of stakeholders including the owners, the state, the salaried workers, and so on, and the system was based on the idea that social stability and economic equality were desirable societal outcomes and indicators of good governance. In the era of financialization, the new institutional logic emphasizing efficiency has gradually displaced the previous logic, and for example, agency theorists have accused managers of shirking and acting opportunistically to secure their own interests. Proposing a shareholder value creation model as the solution to the minimization of agency costs, the costs involved in the owner's monitoring of the executives, agency theorists already assumed that: (1) finance markets are capable of effectively pricing financial assets on the basis of underlying factual conditions; and (2) that such effective finance markets are already in place. In making these assumptions, agency theory served both to manifest a theoretical proposition (the idea of market efficiency) and to performatively justify the deregulation of the finance market to accomplish these forms of allegedly superior "markets for managerial control" (Manne, 1965). The shift from the institutional logic of social and economic stability to economic efficiency was thus both the goal and the vehicle for the advancement of shareholder value enrichment policies as a legitimate corporate governance method. In the era of financialization, this combination of ideological beliefs, engaged storytelling (for example, the narrative of managers squandering the free cash flow), and weakly justified assumptions all present in the case of the advancement of agency theory is indicative of how favored scenarios and preferences and storytelling are bound up and not always easily disentangled.

5. Managerial control, auditing, and accountability

INTRODUCTION

In 1978, Pfeffer and Salancik published their influential *The External Control of Organizations*, a treatise wherein they elaborated on the idea that all organizations are bound up with its environment and need to effectively manage these external relations to thrive and survive. Then again, organizations cannot effectively respond to all impulses and stimuli from the outside but must rather, as Daft and Weick (1984) put it, *enact* their own environment, that is, determine what environmental factors to recognize and respond to. As part of this external control of the corporation, Pfeffer and Salancik (1978) introduced the concept of *external standards*, meaning the performance parameters being used to evaluate the organization's performance that are commonly established outside of the firm. Say Pfeffer and Salancik (1978):

> The most important aspects of [external standards] is that the acceptability of the organization and its activities is ultimately judged by those outside the organization ... This does not imply that the organization is at the mercy of outsiders. The organization can and do manipulate, influence and create acceptability for itself and its activities. (Pfeffer and Salancik, 1978: 11)

Albeit being written in the decade of great economic turbulence and at the very threshold of the new regime of financialization beginning in the 1980s, Pfeffer and Salancik (1978) here anticipate what Michael Power (1996) would refer to as the *audit explosion*, the sharp growth in auditing practices in the new regime of managerial control. Seemingly paradoxical, as the finance markets have been stipulated to price assets correctly given their ability to accommodate all available information, the shareholder value policy being implemented broadly in the 1980s was accompanied by a new set of management control mechanisms being located *outside* of the firm. Therefore, after 1980 there has been a strong reliance on various "technologies of objectivity,"[1] in Porter's (1994: 198), apt formulation, to control and monitor organizations. These technologies of objectivity include auditing procedures, credit ratings, new forms of accounting, and so on, and have been heavily oriented towards quantitative data. Porter (1994: 227) uses the expression "mania for quantification" to capture this, if not blind, at least a passionate belief in the ability to capture underlying continuous events in discrete representations and quanta. This new "politics of precision" (Porter, 1995: 191) has a long-term history, beginning in the mid-nineteenth century when government, state bureaucracy, and scientific work became more developed and demanded that the community could accept and trust the knowledge produced and reported by such institutions (Allen, 2012; Keevers et al., 2012; Hummel, 2006; Desrosière, 1998; Wise, 1995; Hacking, 1990; Kula, 1986). However, as Porter (1995: 191–192) stresses, this politics of precision has less to do with the production of "objective data" as much as it is a mechanism for building trust and legitimacy for both the institutions per se, and for the auditors and other issuers of such data themselves. Instead, the production of data and the widespread use of technologies of objectivity must be understood as a far-reaching institutional shift in the domain of governance and regulation. One of the paradoxes of this new regime of governance and control is that while it on the one hand is based on the assumption that there needs to be full transparency in the activities, decision-makers and regulators are on the other hand very much inclined to make decisions on basis of what Porter (2012) refers to as "thin descriptions" (alluding to Oxford philosopher Gilbert Ryle's, 1971, term "thick descriptions," developed into a research method concept by anthropologist Clifford Geertz, 1973):

> Why, in the world of business and administration, are lengthy reports with all their uncertainties circulated among underlings, while the "executive summary," purged of ambiguity and detail, goes to the people at the top? Thinness is, if not the natural state of things, an appealing modern project. It beguiles us with its terse, muscular economy. (Porter, 2012: 212)

One of the explanations for this preference for what is thinly rather than thickly described is what Herbert Simon (1957) speaks of as *bounded rationality*, the cognitive and temporal limits for the decision-making process in organizations that favor the one-dimensional and linear over the multidimensional, the straightforward message over the ambiguous, and what is more easily understood over what would demand more complex considerations. This chapter will address the forms of external

---

[1] On the concept of objectivity, see Daston and Galison (2007) and Megill (1994), and the literature on specific forms of objectivity including *disciplinary objectivity* (Timmermans, 2008, *regulatory objectivity* (Cambrosio et al., 2006), and *pragmatic objectivity* (Hogle, 2009).

The financialization of the firm

control that have been developed and implemented in the period where internal managerial control has become less credible in the case of salaried managers who are expected to act in accordance with their own interests.

The chapter stresses how audits and credit ratings are on the one hand portrayed as being systematic and structured reviews of the firm, while on the other hand in practice these concepts are riddled by inconsistencies, lack of regulatory coherence, moral hazards, and at the bottom line are based on the belief in the market as still being the site where the value of the firm or any other financial asset is ultimately determined. The new regulatory practices and forms of external control of the firm are based on a calculative worldview and the assumption that mathematical representation and quanta are capable of objectively capturing underlying qualities (for an overview, see Zelizer, 2007; Callon et al., 2007; MacKenzie, 2006; Preda, 2006; Smelser and Swedberg, 2005; Knorr Cetina and Preda, 2005; Beunza and Stark, 2004; Swedberg, 2004; Trigilia, 2002). Like any other social and economic practice, the external control of the corporation is a human accomplishment, influenced and structured on the basis of various political and economic objects and demands, and consequently not even the most mathematized and scientific ways of reporting audits and ratings are shielded from criticism, especially not during periods of economic turbulence and scandals of the magnitude caused by for example, the Enron bankruptcy in 2001.

THE MARKET FOR MANAGEMENT CONTROL

The Concept of Auditing

In the era of financialization, audits have become one of the backbone governance procedures. The audit as a modality of what Miller (2001) refers to as a *technology of governance* is based on two principles: (1) it is executed by externally located professional auditors; and (2) it is based on a specific set of calculative practices and accompanying numerical representations (for example, key performance indicators, KPIs). As for example, agency theorists have argued that professional managers are not to be trusted as they are always at risk of squandering the firm's profits, its free cash flow, then one way to discipline managers is to use audits. While this line of reasoning is not complicated to follow, there are still some concerns among accounting researchers how well audits serve this role given the social, cultural, and political embedding of the calculative practices constituting audits. Power (1997: 28) here speaks of "the deep epistemological obscurity of auditing," and address what he refers to as "auditability" as being "not just a natural property of economic transactions," nor simply "a function of the quality of evidence which exists in the environment within which auditing operates," but as the *active construction* of the legitimacy of the knowledge and expertise involved in accomplishing the audit and the outcome, the factual information reported. That is, while audits are brought into firms and organizations under the aegis of objectivity and the auditors' professional autonomy, in practice such values held in esteem are complicated to uphold and maintain as auditors are also anxious to preserve their legitimacy and not to discourage paying clients from commissioning further audits. In other words, the alleged purity of mathematized accounts of underlying assets and processes are easily mingled with all-too-human interests.

In addition, Power (1996: 302) remarks, audits *have performative qualities*, that is, they are more *prescriptive* than *descriptive*, and in the case of criticism being issued in the auditor's report, managerial practices are likely to be modified accordingly to meet future expectations: "[f]ar from being a by-product of management systems structures, 'auditability' becomes, in the absence of specific standards of performance, their constitutive ideal," Power (1996: 302) writes. Moreover, the very idea of auditing as being based on some neutral Archimedian fixed point, a "view from nowhere" in Nagel's (1986) memorable phrasing, is not easily justified. Instead, Power (1996: 305) suggests, "verifiability" and "auditability" are less properties of things in themselves and more of a function of the "institutional credibility of experts." The audit per se and its procedures and routines are never isolated from the practices of the professionals conducting the work, and therefore the credibility of the professionals remains a key issue. Once again, the distinction between inside and outside, externality and interiority being of key importance for the legitimacy of the audit work is porous and fluid: "[e]xpertise is in general a peculiar mixture of internal (epistemic) an external (institutional) validity in which the 'how' and the 'who' of that expertise are deeply interrelated" (Power, 1996: 307). As a consequence, audit procedures are not so much a unified apparatus that provides an objective gaze and a neutral review of the firm's activities as they purport to do, but instead audits are better understood as a patchwork consisting of loosely coupled procedures, tools, and calculative practices:

[C]oncepts of evidence, observation, experiment, testability and replication are far from being stable elements which can be utilized to explicate audit practice. They are themselves the product of processes which mark out them, often competitive, jurisdictions of knowledge-producing communities. Making things auditable is a constant and precarious project of a system of knowledge which must reproduce itself and sustain its institutional role from a diverse assemblage of routines, practices and economic constraints. (Power, 1996: 312)

Given the epistemological instability of audits, one may wonder how and why such procedures are being implemented on a broad scale in the era of financialization. Being based on fluid and shifting practices rather than being stable accounts of underlying firm activities, there are still some benefits from using audits. For Power (1997), audits grant *institutional legitimacy* in economies characterized by ambiguities and a shortage of information and accompanying costs to acquire and interpret such information. At the same time, Power (1997) suggests, audits are more like symptoms indicating underlying institutional changes than the effective solution to managerial control problems:

> [T]he audit explosion reflects a distinctive response to the need to process risk. Auditing threatens to become a cosmetic practice which hides real risks and replaces it with the financial risk faced by auditors themselves. Where the audit process is defensively legalized there is a risk of relying too heavily on an industry of empty comfort certificates. The audit society is society that endangers itself because if it invests too heavily in the shallow rituals of verification at the expense of other forms of organizational intelligence. In providing a lens for regulatory thought and action audits threatens to become a form of learned ignorance. (Power, 1997: 123)

As being portrayed as "rituals of verification" or "a new form of image management," audits are in Power's (1997) account not really in the position to minimize agency costs and eliminate other management control issues. Whether this thesis, being not well tuned with auditing companies' marketing materials, is true or not can fortunately be empirically studied. In the next section a few examples of audits in industry will be examined in some detail.

The international regulation of audits

Humphrey et al. (2009) examine how the international market for audits is regulated and subject to forms of professional and legislative control, and they identify three categories of actors playing a role in determining audit services. First, there is the International Federation of Accountants (IFAC) including a variety of accounting and auditing professional interest organizations representing the interests of the community of accountants and auditors. Second, there are international regulators including agencies such as The World Bank and IMF, having the political objective to ensure political and economic stability in the world economy. Third, there are the large multinational audit firms, including "the Big Four" – Ernst & Young, Deloitte, KPMG and PriceWaterhouseCooper (Humphrey et al., 2009: 813). The "Big Four" accounting firms, serving over 7,200 partners in their networks including "the vast majority of the

world's largest companies" (Humphrey et al., 2009: 813), are therefore
of great importance for the actual auditing work and the reports issued.
In Humphrey et al.'s (2009: 815) view, what they refer to as the "global
audit regulatory arena" is dynamic and subject to continuous change as
it engages a variety of organizations, notably the IFAC member bodies,
which competes over influence and voice. For instance, after the 2008
finance market meltdown there is evidence of activities that seek to both
restore the legitimacy and credibility of the audit industry and to challenge
the status quo (Humphrey et al., 2009: 821). In addition, the many bankruptcies following the events of 2008 have resulted in a number of legal
cases against auditors, in many ways changing the face of the industry
and leading to a higher degree of external and internal control over how
audits are conducted and reported. One example of such legal action is the
liquidators of the failed subprime lender New Century, who filed a US$1
billion lawsuit against the firm's auditor, KPMG, for "allegedly conducting 'reckless and grossly negligent audits' that failed to reveal the lender's
financial problems" (Humphrey et al., 2009: 821). Humphrey et al. (2009:
819) argue that audit reports often reveal relatively little information
regarding how the audits were conducted, and it is therefore complicated
to understand on what basis statements and declarations regarding the
firm's financial and operational status are made:

> The reader is given no substantive insight as to how such inconsistency [identi-
> fied] was evaluated or tested by the external auditor. The standard external
> audit report is not helpful in this regard, being full of general, standardized
> statements on the role and limitations of the audits and containing little about
> the specific work undertaken and findings obtained by auditors. (Humphrey et
> al., 2009: 819)

Such criticism has been endemic in the post-2008 literature, stressing that
auditing was perhaps not the ultimate external check on managerial malfeasance. Instead, the auditors and the auditee share many interests and
have joint concerns (Thornburn and Roberts, 2008; Robson et al., 2007).

Studies of audits in the era of financialization
Kipnis (2008) argues that audits are not so much a practice that has been
developed within a neoliberal regime of accumulation but as a generalized
model based on what Kipnis calls *calculability*, in turn being based on
"universality numeracy" – a trust in numbers" (Porter, 1995) so central
to modernization and industrialization. "Any form of large-scale society
with a division of labor requires means of calculating how the fruits
of labor should be divided," Kipnis (2008: 283) says. In addition, with
modernization and its particular form of economic accumulation called

industrialization comes the increased distance between different social groups and communities. Such distances often translate into *distrust*, in turn being the *raison d'être* for constructing the audit. Audits are thus the effects of increased distrust, but rather than solving such concerns, Kipnis (2008: 283) suggests, they are "likely to be exacerbated in the audit process." That is, audits demand further audit, in turn leading to new practices and activities to cover up activities that are not fully justified according to audit standards, and therefore they lead to various unintended consequences. Kipnis (2008) views audits as a social practice that is thus creating its own momentum that further calls for more structural forms of control:

> Audits and the cultural dynamics they engender are increasing in frequency around the world for a variety of reasons, including industrialization, the rising prevalence of numeracy, and, most importantly, the imagined (but not usually actual) benefits that governing agents believe can be derived from measuring the performance of those who are governed. (Kipnis, 2008: 286)

One of the key concerns regarding audits is then what can be practically accomplished for both stakeholders outside of the firm, and for managers and other decision-makers inside the firm. Free et al. (2009: 120) suggest that audits, like any practice include both *programmatic* (that is, normative) and *technological* (that is, operational) elements and argues that there is only a loose coupling between "the level of programmatic appeal," and "the level of audit practice." As a consequence, the very audit output, the written report, is fairly complicated to understand for the outside analyst as statements are based on opaque routines and methodologies. What is presented to the audience is "field data" being produced on the basis of a "collection of negotiated and highly adapted pragmatic routines," carefully developed to "add credibility to the rankings," but still too obscure to decode for audiences having limited insight into the statistical methods used by the auditor (Free et al., 2009: 137). The legitimacy of the data is thus imposed upon rather than recognized by the audience. Audits thus signal the firm's willingness to be treated as a legitimate actor in the economy and the industry in question, but they do little to reduce the management control problem being a major headache for for example, agency theorists demonstrating very low trust for professional managers. In some cases, audits thus play quite a harmless role of being an instance of impression management as suggested by Power (1997), whereas in other cases the epistemological porosity of audits may cause major harm in the economic and financial system.

Sikka (2009) examines the role of audits and auditors in the era of financialization, and consistent with Power's (1997, 1996) view, Sikka

(2009: 868) argues that the legitimacy of audits is based on their claims to be in the position to construct "independent, objective, true, and fair accounts of corporate affairs." In addition, these "fair accounts" are of great value for a series of market actors and stakeholders including investors, employees, citizens, and the state as they enable "the management of risk." However, Sikka (2009: 868) questions whether such claims can be justified as the measures used in audits including revenues, costs, assets, liabilities, and profits are both "technically" and "politically" determined. In the era of financialization, an abundance of credit has bred "excessive risk-taking" in combination with corporate restructurings and the relaxing of regulatory control, especially in the US (Sikka, 2009: 868–869). In such a milieu, characterized by fluxes and changes, crises and collapses, fraud and moral hazard, auditors' claim of neutrality become precarious. If nothing else, the events of 2008 testify to Sikka's skeptical view as allegedly independent auditors failed to identify and communicate the excessive risks taken by finance market actors: "distressed financial enterprises, whether in the UK, US, Germany, Iceland, The Netherlands, France, or Switzerland, received unqualified audit opinions on their financial statements published immediately prior to the public declaration of financial difficulties" (Sikka, 2009: 869). For Sikka (2009), these embarrassing events for a variety of actors are not unfortunate and isolated events but are indicative of the close bonds and connections across the auditor and auditee boundary: "[t]raditionalists have often claimed that external audit adds credibility to financial statements. . . . The difficulty with such a hypothesis is that the current financial crisis [in 2008] shows that markets and significant others were not comforted by unqualified audit opinions issued by major auditing firms" (Sikka, 2009: 871).

That is, the entire auditing business relies on the legitimacy of the external auditor providing a systematic check on executives and board of directors, but when the reports issued fail to address major challenges and risks facing the audited firm, such legitimacy erodes. For Sikka the "market for management control" (Manne, 1965) conceived of by agency theorists are riddled by internal contradictions and systemic failures. For instance, the market-based system for external control of the firm relies on the firms being audited paying fees for this service, thereby creating bonds between auditor and auditee that may compromise an independent and freestanding analysis. The audit firms are thus, first, capitalist enterprises paid for their services and the claim to conduct independent assessments is impaired by the economic transactions between the two categories of firms (Sikka, 2009: 872).

Second, auditors may, more or less consciously and tactually, expand their role in the economic system and withhold information that may disrupt the economic system, an event that would potentially undermine their future income: "[a]uditors may be reluctant to qualify bank accounts for fear of creating panic or jeopardizing their liability position," Sikka (2009: 871) argues. Third, Sikka (2009) questions the integrity and/or competence of auditors as they failed to predict the collapse of the financial market in 2008 as they favored the "unpredictability thesis" to explain this event. For Sikka (2009: 871), this explanation is not credible given the long series of bubbles and crises in the financial markets during the last three decades in for example, Latin America, Sweden, Norway, and Japan. Fourth and finally, Sikka point at frauds and other forms of behavior that are not flattering for organizations that are given the responsibility to regulate and control market actors: "[a]uditing firms have shown increasingly willingness to violate laws, regulations and assist their clients to publish flattering financial statements" (Sikka, 2009: 871). These four issues and concerns pertaining to the expansion (or the "explosion" that Michael Power speaks of) of auditing practice indicate that rather than being the solution to management control problems, so central to the neoclassic economic theory and its dismissive view of the firm and anything managerial, auditing may be part of the problem. "Audit systems are self-perpetuating, consuming increasing amounts of resources, and insensitive to their own unintended, dysfunctional and immeasurable side-effects," McGivern and Ferlie (2007: 1363) propose.

Market information asymmetries and their consequences
The backbone theory for the expansion of finance markets and their more lenient regulatory control is the idea of efficient markets. Despite being an intriguing thesis, the EMH has been poorly supported by empirical evidence and there are many studies published that question the idea that prices are always, informationally speaking, correct. For instance, Hayward and Boeker (1998) found that securities analysts tended to rate their own bank's clients' securities higher than those issued by other companies. The explanation for this divergence from what the EMH predicts is to be found in the bounded rationality and practical limitations in the analysts' work, Hayward and Boeker (1998) suggest: "[a]nalysts' ratings, like other forms of professional advice, are based on highly ambiguous, uncertain, and limited information. While analysts may act rationally, such rationality is bounded by their limited time, localized search for information, and political and social constraints" (Hayward and Boeker, 1998: 16).

Zuckerman (1999) studied how securities analysts classified different assets and found that the assets of firms not really being able to fit neatly into the existing classificatory system were rated lower than the assets of firms that did fit. Zuckerman (1999: 1429) points at the need for firms competing in finance markets to develop network contacts with securities analysts. That is, rather than finance markets pricing assets on the basis of available public information, there is room for social relations to influence the classificatory system being used when rating financial assets: "[a]rmies of interpreters and prognosticators are present on Wall Street because they fill an important social purpose: they help investors make sense of the dizzying array of possible investments. No such investment has a clear value, and the struggle to anticipate future prices never ends" (Zuckerman, 1999: 1431).

For management scholars and economic sociologists, not being disciplined to believe in the robustness of the neoclassic economic theory frameworks, the EMH is not solid enough to justify the belief that financial markets are fully rational (that is, act consistently) and capable of correcting themselves. The presence of CRAs is also indicative of the need for the "armies of interpreters and prognosticators" that serve as what Carruthers and Stinchcome (1999) call "market-makers" – professional analysts and commentators that help the market run smoother. The presence of CRAs is thus more in line with what has been called *information economics* (Greenwald and Stiglitz, 1986), a branch within neoclassic economic theory, associated with economists such as George Akerlof and Joseph Stiglitz. In information economics, there is never any perfectly functioning distribution of information in the market. Instead, certain actors control information that enables them to generate higher rents than other actors. Unless information is unevenly distributed, it would not be possible to "beat the index." However, this view does not imply that markets are to be treated as "imperfect" as markets are by definition the site where informational resources are exchanges and traded as part of the pricing process:

> [R]eferring to economies with incomplete markets and imperfect information as 'imperfect' seem to be wrong. We do not refer to economies in which inputs are required to produce outputs as "imperfect"; and the costs of obtaining information and running markets are no less real costs that the other forms of production costs. (Greenwald and Stiglitz, 1986: 259)

In information economics, "information costs" are recognized, while in the EMH, there are *ex hypothesi* no such information costs; they would be an anomaly. As a consequence, in the information economics view, there is a need for various market actors to "signal" their underlying value and their intentions to act tactically and strategically to receive a fair market rating and market evaluation. Greenwald and Stiglitz (1986: 259) summarize their argument:

There is not a complete set of markets; information is imperfect; the commodities sold in any market are not homogeneous in all relevant respects; it is
costly to ascertain differences among the items; individuals do not get paid on
a piece rate basis, and there is an element of insurance (implicit or explicit) in
almost all contractual arrangements, in labor, in capital, a product markets. In
virtually all markets there are important instances of signaling and screening.
(Greenwald and Stiglitz, 1986: 259)

In this view of the market, there is a need for skilled assessment of the
financial assets being issued and traded, and therefore CRAs are given
quite a prominent infrastructural role in finance markets.

The role of CRAs

A CRA is defined as "[a] company that assesses the debt instruments
(bond and other securities) issued by firms or governments and assigns
'credit ratings' to these instruments based on the likelihood that the debt
will be repaid" (Rom, 2009: 640). In serving this role, CRAs fit into the
specific capitalist knowledge structure of the market as market participants treat the CRAs as being "endogenous (rather than exogenous) to
global finance" (Sinclair, 2005: 60). That is, market actors see CRAs
as legitimate rather than "imposed entities" (Sinclair, 2005: 60). At the
same time, as Rom (2009: 641) puts it, CRAs are "odd beasts" as they
are "private firms with public purposes" – a fact that is indicated by the
term *agency* rather than the perhaps more appropriate term *firm*. CRAs
are "[f]ully private in terms of ownership, employees and, in general, revenues," Rom (2009: 641) writes. The fact that CRAs are licensed by the US
Securities and Exchange Commission (US SEC), and in practice enjoy a
monopoly situation (Friedman and Kraus, 2012: 2) is frequently pointed
out as a curious feature of the governance structure. Worse still, the CRAs
including the "Big Three" of Standard & Poor, Moody's, and Fitch are
dependent on the fees from the companies and market actors that issue
financial assets. This "issuer-pays" principle is frequently criticized for creating a moral hazard problem in the very governance model: "[t]he change
to the 'issuer pay' business model opened the door to potential conflict of
interest: a rating agency might shade its rating upward so as to command
a higher fee or forestall the issuer from taking its business to a different
rating firm" (White, 2009: 392–393).

For instance, the reluctance of the CRAs to downgrade their ratings
has been linked to their issuer-pays business model, given that that downgrades are "likely to displease issuers" (White, 2013: 109). This system
is often justified on the basis of the need for the CRAs to maintain and
reproduce its "reputational capital," that is, it is assumed that if the CRAs
fail to issue reports that accurately predict the value of financial assets

being issued, the CRAs will suffer indirectly as they would lose their clients' trust. This idea is indicative of the widespread belief in the finance markets' capacity to regulate themselves and the idea that private interest grounded in economic incentives is always more effective in regulating markets than professional control executed by for example, governmental agencies. This assumption is not endorsed offhand by everyone. Partnoy (1999: 630) suggests that the "reputational capital" thesis, portraying credit rating as "a competitive, reputation-driven business," wherein agencies will survive only "to the extent they are accurate and reliable in assessing the credit risks of borrowers," cannot be justified on the basis of empirical data as faulty predictions are not of necessity being punished by the market actors. In addition, the constructed monopoly of the "Big Three" CRAs translates into both the growing size of these companies and the quite hefty profits margin, indicative of a not entirely efficient market for credit rating services. Partnoy (1999) here contrasts the relatively undifferentiated services provided by the CRAs, and their profits margin (calculated to 29 percent by Partnoy): "[d]espite the fact that there are no obvious interpretative techniques unique to rating agencies, it is undeniably true that rating agency profit margins are high" (Partnoy, 1999: 655). In the 2002–2006 period, the "boom years" of financialization (Bolton et al., 2012: 86), the profit levels increased dramatically in the CRAs, and for example, Moody's profits "tripled between 2002 and 2006" (Bolton et al., 2012: 85). The question is then: what role do the CRAs play in finance markets? Several commentators suggest that the rating of financial assets being issued is by no means a matter of superior calculative practices or the access to unique finance market data; instead, credit rating is a relatively standardized procedure that nevertheless is a lucrative business for the agencies being granted the license to operate in the market.

Sinclair (2005: 61) suggests that "rating is not a technical activity it is thought popularly to be." Instead, he continues, it is "highly indeterminate, qualitative, and judgment laden." As a consequence, credit rating is, first and foremost, about "[c]reating an interpretation of the world and about routine production of practical judgment based on interpretations" (Sinclair, 2005: 61). This work being paid for by the finance market actors is thus very much a traditional professional domain of expertise including subjective assessment and professional judgment. While substantial amounts of quantitative data are used in the analysis, there is always room for "considered opinion," Rom (2009: 641) suggests. Partnoy (1999: 660) refers to calculations indicating that 75 percent of the "rating process" being based on statistical information and equations," while 25 percent is "subjective." Sinclair (2005) here remarks that there is a divergence between the orthodox view of credit rating as being a "synchronic-rationalist" procedure, based on strict calculative practices, and the "diachronic-constructivist" view based on professional judgment. The divergence between these views represents the differences in what role instrumental rationality plays. For orthodox commentators, credit ratings play a vital role in upholding markets' efficiency, while the heterodox view stresses the CRAs' favored role as being protected by their licenses from the US Securities and Exchange Commission and how that translates into substantial levels of profit. If nothing else, as Partnoy (1999: 649) remarks, from the mid-1970s, in the early phases of financialization, "rating agencies have exploded in size" and today the CRAs are more influential and powerful than ever despite the facts that they issue basically the same information as they did in the 1930s. To put it in orthodox terms, the utility function has shifted for credit ratings after the mid-1970s, and therefore market participants are willing to pay for the rating of the assets being issued.

Despite the growth of the credit rating market, there is a series of concerns regarding the work of for example, Standard & Poor and Moody's. First, for many users of credit rating services, the service provided is opaque and non-transparent:

> Many users of credit ratings are frustrated by what they refer to as the almost-total mystery surrounding analyst meetings, as well as follow-up and monitoring communications. It is predictable that users of credit ratings would demand more information than CRAs willingly disclose, because the disclosed information is available to the public at no charge, while the CRAs incur disclosure costs. (Frost, 2007: 476)

As Frost (2007) points out, if CRAs are capable of capitalizing on informational asymmetries, they would have low incentives to disclose their work procedures and practices, and the monopoly license does little to help to solve such concerns. Second, some of the CRAs, being American companies, are from time to time criticized as one Frankfurt banker puts it (Sinclair, 2005: 133), for their "colonial attitude" and for frequently failing to take into account "[t]he special characteristics in European accounting, disclosure and management practice." There is always a risk that market actors issuing finance assets are punished for working in a regulatory and governance setting differing from the "baseline" US case. Third, there is ample evidence of credit ratings not being "socially neutral" but reflecting "processes of judgment that tends to produce socially partial policy on the bond issuer's part, other things being equal" (Sinclair, 2005: 117).

Given that these preferences and beliefs are built into the infrastructure of the national and global finance markets, scholars have tried to theorize what role the credit ratings actually play in constituting finance markets. Partnoy (1999: 683) proposes that credit ratings are valuable not so much because they issue valuable and accurate information but because they grant issuers "regulatory licenses." To grant regulatory licenses here denotes the right to determine standards of what Polillo (2011: 438) refers to as *creditworthiness*, the "set of rules and criteria that delineate the boundary between those who are worthy of holding a particular currency and those who are not." Polillo (2011: 438) adds that the very concept of creditworthiness is institutionalized through "moral authority," the "elaboration and setting of moral categories of worth that draw on membership and solidarity," and consequently the right to grant regulatory licenses is grounded in the ability to carefully adhere to certain professional standards and norms. "Creditworthiness may thus be conceptualized as a system of incorporating distinctions that already exists outside of the banking system, between individuals worthy of particular kinds of instruments and those unworthy of them," Polillo (2011: 444) says (see for example, Mizruchi et al., 2006, 2011; Mizruchi and Brewster, 2001). This view on CRAs would be able to explain the increase in importance of CRAs in both the period of the 1930s, and from the period beginning in the mid-1970s:

> Credit rating agencies have not survived for six decades because they produce credible and accurate information. They have not maintained good reputation based on the informational content of their credit ratings. Instead, the credit rating agencies have thrived, profited, and become exceedingly powerful because they have begun selling regulatory licenses, *i.e.*, the right to be in compliance with regulation. Credit ratings are an excellent example of how *not* to privatize a regulatory function. (Partnoy, 1999: 713–714)

In other words, CRAs represent the finance market actors' own preference for how they want to be regulated. *En bref*, the CRAs represent a fairly idiosyncratic form of endogenous market control that disqualifies governmental interventions into markets that by the end of the day are assumed to price assets efficiently. The question remains still whether this system, despite its puzzling inconsistencies (for example, state-granted monopolies, above-normal profit margins, and a series of beliefs and preferences translating into the credit ratings) does the job well or not? That is, are the credit ratings accurate and/or do they help the market for financial assets run smoothly?

Rating financial assets: some empirical evidence
"Prediction is difficult, especially about the future," the noted Danish physicist Niels Bohr claimed (cited in Rona-Tas and Hiss, 2010: 121). Yet predictions are precisely what economists and finance market actors try to

make on an industrial basis (Breslau, 2013; Reichmann, 2013). In financial markets, predictions about the future were certainly not becoming easier by the introduction of increasingly complex derivate instruments and assets in the period after 1980. Prior to the Great Financialization, CRAs had earned the general reputation in the 1980s and 1990s of employing "tough-minded analysts" that were to be feared by issuers, rather than being entities that could be "swayed by issuers" (White, 2013: 102). This status as autonomous and morally incorruptible entities in the finance industry would be complicated to maintain in the new millennium. Bolton et al. (2012: 86) argue that there is a widespread "suspicion" that "rating standards had been relaxed during the boom years." In fact, Bolton et al. (2012: 86) propose a "substantial ratings inflation" in the 2002–2006 period. This proposition is supported by Cornaggia and Cornaggia's (2013: 2265) findings, suggesting, first, that the issuer-pays business model is in conflict with "rating quality": "we conclude that Moody's relatively uninformative ratings result from conflicts of interest in the issuer-pays model." Second, increased competition among CRAs as prescribed by policy-makers do not show any evidence of counteracting the effects of the issuer-pays business model: "when [new] entrants are compensated by issuers (like incumbents), competitors potentially lowers rating quality," Cornaggia and Cornaggia (2013: 2265) summarize their findings.

Despite the "illiquidity" of the new financial assets including MBSs/ Residential Mortgage-Backed Securities (RMBSs) and CDOs, especially considering their lack of historical record and time series that would possibly enable predictions, Rom (2009) stresses that the CRAs played a key role in legitimating the new financial assets, in particular assets related to the development of a subprime housing mortgage market in the US. Fueled by "cheap credit, relaxed lending standards, novel loans, and strong appreciation in home values," a growing number of "subprime borrowers" obtained home mortgages, and the mortgage markets grew enormously in the first years of the new millennium (Rom, 2009: 640). To discount risks and extract value from this specific financial asset, these mortgages were sold by the lenders to investment banks, which in turn "bundled them" into increasingly sophisticated securities. Investors had confidence in these MBSs and the rationality of the underlying financial engineering as CRAs "put their seal of approval on them, indicating that the securities were 'investment grade'" (Rom, 2009: 640).

Between 2002 and 2007, the revenues for RMBSs and (CDOs, two instruments developed to extract economic value from the underlying housing market, grew by "[a]n *average* of more than 100 percent annually; CDO revenues more than *tripled* annually" (Rom, 2009: 647). As these new financial assets were more complex and opaque than "were 'plain-vanilla' corporate debt and government loans," many investors were inclined to rely on "third-party assurances" (White, 2013: 105). Unfortunately, the CRA's ratings of these new financial assets "turned out to be quite optimistic," especially for the securities that were issued and rated during the 2005–2007 period, when the growth in housing prices was slowing down and "the average quality of mortgages had deteriorated even from the looser standards of the early 2000s" (White, 2013: 105). As White (2013: 104) notices, between 1997 and 2006, the S&P/Case-Shiller Index of home prices rose by ~125 percent whereas the US Consumer Price Index rose by only 28 percent, and by the early 2000s, there was a "a widespread belief that housing prices could only go up":

> [A]s of June 30, 2009, 90% of the collateralized debt obligations (CDOs) that were issued between 2005 and 2007 and were rated AAA by S&P had been downgraded, with 80% graded below investment grade; even the more simple MBS that were issued during those years and were originally rated AAA, 63% had been downgraded, with 52% downgraded below investment grade. (White, 2013: 105)

By the end of the 2005–2007 period, when the rate of "subprime delinquencies" (that is, mortgage loan holders being 90 days or more behind in repayment) and foreclosures tripled in the 2005–2007 period, these new financial assets became, as the finance market and government officials themselves phrased it, "toxic." By May 2008, only few months before the finance market collapse, "about one-fourth of subprime mortgage loans were delinquent or in foreclosure" (Rom, 2009: 644). As an immediate consequence, Rom (2009: 644) writes, "the tsunami of downgrades devastated the credit markets and the CRAs' credibility."

Rather than blaming the government for encouraging the development of the subprime housing mortgage market, or for indicating that poor regulatory frameworks were the key explanatory factor for the collapse of the finance market (Mirowski, 2013), Rom (2009) follows the more mainstream path and addresses the role of the CRAs in failing to accurately rate the RMBSs and CDOs: "[w]ith the rise of the subprime market, it appears that the CRAs became much more ignorant, in several ways. First, the raters had little knowledge about the historical performance of subprime loans – indeed, there was relatively little history to guide them" (Rom, 2009: 646).

Rom continues, pointing at two alternative explanations, both equally unflattering for the CRAs: "[f]or the subprime market, were the CRAs *naively* or *willfully* ignorant? If the former is true, the CRAs simply did not understand the risks they were assessing; this speaks ill of the CRAs competence. If the latter is true, the CRAs lacked integrity" (Rom, 2009:

647, original emphasis). The three large CRAs have been seen as having played a "major role in the financial crisis itself," White (2013: 105) summarizes. The question is: why were the CRAs willing to gamble with their solid reputation as free-standing entities?

Previous studies of credit ratings in the 1997–1998 period suggest that CRAs may "deviate considerably and negatively from objective decision-making criteria" (Vaaler and McNamara, 2004: 689), a finding that suggests that CRAs are more likely, in Rom's parlance (2009), to act willfully than being naively ignorant. Clark and Newell (2013) present an institutional perspective on the CRAs' role in the subprime market debacle and propose a behavioral model wherein there is evidence of what Clark and Newell (2013: 20) call a "complicit decoupling" between assets and the ratings issued. While rating agencies are based on the premise that they provide "expert, objective and neutral information," this role can be sidelined in cases where the CRAs and the issuing firm can "trust each other to collude" (Clark and Newell, 2013: 20). Such situations "typically occur gradually" (Clark and Newell, 2013: 20). and are therefore very complicated to handle by regulators. In the institutional theory framework, if decoupling occurs and is revealed to third parties, the legitimacy of the organizations is harmed, and at times puts the organizations' survival at risk (as in for example, the cases of Enron and Lehman Brothers); but in the case of complicit decoupling, "it is not in the interest of the multiple players in a vast interconnected field to fully repair the practices – too many are benefiting too handsomely" (Clark and Newell, 2013: 20). Faulty and inaccurate credit ratings are therefore no longer a practical problem as even inadequate information issued serves the role of what Partnoy (1999: 683) speaks of as "regulatory licenses" and what Clark and Newell (2013: 21) refer to as "a measure of legitimacy." The long-term effect of this gradual complicit collusion is that the market information is skewed and there is a strategic and tactic reporting of inaccurate information that in one way or another that harms market efficiency and increases transaction costs:

> [R]ather than PSRs [Professional Service Raters, that is, CRAs] serving the generally accepted policing role, they morphed over time into engaging in tacit collusion with the corporate issuers they rate so that the ratings have become gradually decoupled. Over time, the PSRs and the corporations they were rating and this, together with allowances from government regulations, opened up for the opportunity for inter-organizational collusions that led to complicit decoupling and, ultimately, the misleading of mainstream investors. (Clark and Newell, 2013: 23)

In Rom's (2009) and Clark and Newell's (2013) accounts, credit raters acted willfully to benefit their own and their paying clients' interests. In acting accordingly, they also performatively undermined market efficiency by issuing inadequate ratings. There is thus a fair share of irony in that the market actors themselves, rather than the regulatory agencies, made reliable information more costly to access and thus increased transaction costs in the finance markets. For orthodox proponents of free-market doctrines, such self-interested strategic action poses a pedagogic challenge to explain to individuals not sharing their commitment to markets.

Mathis et al. (2009) suggest that there is a crucial need for changing the business model of CRAs, while at the same time they fail to see how this is to be accomplished. First of all, a regime of "public supervision" of the CRAs "seems difficult and counterproductive," and making them legally liable for their (inaccurate) ratings would "probably kill the business" (Mathis et al., 2009: 669). In addition, it is unlikely that it is practically possible to back down from the "issuer-pays" business model due to free-riding problems and information leakage (Mathis et al., 2009: 669). This leaves Mathis et al. (2009) with the dour conclusion that there is a need for a reform regarding finance assets rating, while at the same time the rating of assets is today embedded in a thick texture of economic, legal, regulatory, and social relations that are difficult to disentangle. As White (2013) summarizes, despite their key role in fabricating the finance industry collapse and the following Great Recession, CRAs may still have reinforced their position in the ecology of the financialized capitalism:

> There is a deep irony embedded in the current trend of CRA regulation: Although the regulation is an expression of public unhappiness over the role of the major CRAs have played in the financial crisis and in Europe, a likely consequence of this regulation is that the major CRAs could become even more important in the market for creditworthiness information. This is because the regulation will make it more difficult for smaller firms to survive and for new entrants with new ideas to challenge the major CRAs. (White, 2013: 118)

This account suggests that the CRAs will continue to play a significant role also in the future.

More market-based control: the Sarbanes-Oxley Act

As the case of rating agencies suggests, markets are not self-regulatory and market actors themselves do not effectively even out the inconsistencies in the market; instead, market actors are likely to be part of the market efficiency problem. The mind-boggling inconsistencies in financial reporting in the case of the much-celebrated energy company Enron is a key example of how the US political system in fact recognized the need for some kind of regulatory framework regardless of all the infected talk about "pro-business" or "anti-business" across party lines. Both auditing and CRAs are regulatory, market-based solutions to managerial control problems, and the so-called Sarbanes-Oxley Act of 2002 (often referred to with the acronym SOX) is yet another example, critical commentators such as Soederberg (2008) claim, of how regulatory agencies grant market actors the license to control themselves. As the case of Enron and several other cases reveal, many auditing firms executing a final check on managers and the board of directors had in fact dual roles in their client firms, being both regulators and advisers:

> As auditors, they play a quasi-regulatory role as a watchdog, responsible for assuring third parties that the financial statements present a true and fair picture of the banks' financial condition. As financial advisors, it appears that the same forms may have assisted the financial services industry in designing the structured investment vehicles that enabled them to move operations off the industry's balance sheet, effectively ensuring that the banking industry's financial statement did not reflect the full extent of risk and leverage within the financial system. (Arnold, 2009: 807)

As Robson et al. (2007: 417) demonstrate, for the audit firms, the growth in revenues does not come from the audits per se but from the "expansion of non-audit services." Between 1992 and 2001, the percentage of audit fees declined from 81 percent to 21 percent of total fees; non-audit fees, in comparison, increased from 19 percent to 79 percent (Robson et al., 2007: 417, Table 2). In the same period, the ratio of non-audit fees to audit fees changed from 0.2 to 1 in 1992 to 3.7 to 1 in 2001 (Robson et al., 2007: 417, Table 1). These figures are interpreted quite straightforwardly by Robson et al. (2007: 421): "large firms treat audit as the gateway to the supply of the more diverse and financially rewarding non-audit services to the client." Just like major American automotive companies no longer make their profits from selling cars but from providing financial services, audit firms do not make their earnings from audits but from non-audit activities. InSOX, these relations were to be scrutinized and disentangled: "[t]he Sarbanes-Oxley Act prohibits a registered public accounting firm from performing certain non-audit services for a public company, client for whom it performs financial statement audits" (Robson et al., 2007: 431–432). Against this the background of these changing relations between auditing firms and clients, the SOX is perhaps best understood, as Cullinan (2004: 862) puts it, "as a legislative set-back for the accounting profession after a number of years in which the U.S. Congress was quite sympathetic to the interests of the accounting profession."

Thornburg and Robert's (2008: 233) study of the role of Political Action Committees in paying economic contributions to members of the US Congress demonstrates that professional accountants donated

US$15,354,056 to "federal candidates during the 2000 election cycle," while "spending $21,777,432 on lobbying" – a ratio of 1.4 to 1. Of these members of Congress, Republican candidates received twice as much as Democrats. In addition, accountants gave "[s]ignificantly greater contributions to incumbent legislators who were members on committees having jurisdiction over SOX" (Thornburg and Robert, 2008: 245). This analysis shows, by and large, that political contributions "flow disproportionally" from the US public accounting profession to pro-business legislators and members of powerful committees "[h]aving jurisdiction over matters relevant to the economic welfare of its members" (Thornburg and Robert, 2008: 245). This pattern of contributions, Thornburg and Robert (2008: 245) claim, suggests that "[p]olitical strategies focus more on interests of business and its members more than the interests of the broader public." Or, expressed in somewhat more lenient terms, "[t]he US public accounting profession's political activity is in keeping with its public interest pledge, but only to the extent that what is best for business and the profession is also best for the public at large" (Thornburg and Robert, 2008: 246).

Despite such ambitions to sort out and separate what had become a very complicated patchwork of exchanges and relations, not all commentators are happy with outcomes in terms of the regulatory quality. Soederberg (2008: 666) suggests that instead of implementing "state-led regulations" to protect society from the "irrational behavior of market forces," the government responds by opening up for additional market-based solutions to regulatory control, including SOX and its directives. Also Centeno and Cohen (2012: 321) share this view, arguing that SOX or "anything that emerged after the financial crisis" did little to "stem the tide of financial innovations that ultimately helped fuel the boom and eventual market collapse in 2008." SOX is in these accounts a relatively ineffective attempt to try to impose regulatory control on financial markets, as the governance work was essentially left to the market actors themselves. As a consequence, SOX did play a relatively marginal role in counteracting the events of 2008.

SUMMARY AND CONCLUSION

The expansion of finance markets and the increased influence of the finance industry in combination with the new enactment of the firm as a bundle of financial resources, in turn based on the suspicion that professional managers induce agency costs, there has been a shift in the control of the corporation from the boardrooms to external organizations that issue reports and recommendations on the basis of audits and credit ratings. Underlying this new governance model, especially in the US but being of relevance for most OECD countries and developed economies, is the idea that finance markets are superior to any other mechanisms in pricing assets and allocating capital to high-growth and high-rent industries and markets. This theoretical position is unfortunately not always accompanied by substantial empirical evidence testifying to the assumed innate rationality of markets; instead, there is ample evidence of inaccurate information being issued by for example, rating agencies. In the era of financialization, there is less reliance on professional managerial expertise and more of a "trust in numbers" issued by licensed CRAs. However, one must not be too ready to draw the conclusion that calculative practices and audits and credit ratings as such are useless on the basis of these inconsistencies. Such practices are in most cases "doing the job" and work effectively to capture underlying assets and resources when executed professionally. However putting blind faith in these practices and in the people that are doing the work under the auspices of market efficiency of necessity to produce a robust governance model will not solve the problem. Under all conditions, numbers, ratios, quanta, and KPIs have been given an increasingly higher weight in the governance model, and therefore there is a need to critically examine not only these auditing and rating practices but also to discuss what actors should be given the authority and the license to issue these reports and statements.

6. The financialization of working life

INTRODUCTION

The era of financialization, the period beginning around 1980, has coincided with or been part of a series of social, cultural, economic, and institutional changes in society. The Keynesian economics model of the welfare state, what at times is referred to as "embedded liberalism," exemplified by the Social Democratic Scandinavian welfare state of low unemployment, low economic inequality, and a combination of market economy and planned economic production, have been subject to reform. The many changes during the last three and a half decades are both caused by and contributed to new attitudes towards work life and private life, and social theorists have been ready to provide an explanatory framework for the new social order and to provide empirical evidence of the changes that have taken place. For instance, the Polish-British sociologist Zygmunt Bauman has in a series of texts explored the concept of "liquidity" as being a root metaphor for everyday life in late modernity (Bauman, 2005, 2000). In Bauman's view, the modernity that was developed in the era of the industrial revolution beginning at the end of the eighteenth century in Britain, was characterized by immutable, solid, large-scale technological systems including the railway, the telegraph system, the building of infrastructures and sewage systems, and so on. This is a world of materiality and the immediate presence of physical objects. In the late modern era, the period of *liquid modernity*, Bauman (2000) suggests, these immutable structures are gradually displaced by more invisible and weightless information flows and digital objects as the vehicles of the social and economic systems. Such resources are better understood as being "fluids" rather than solid objects; Bauman (2000) says:

> Fluids travel easily. They "flow", "spill", "run out", "splash", "pour over", "leak", "flood", "spray", "drip", "seep", "ooze", unlike solids, they are not easily stopped – they pass around some obstacles, dissolve some others and bore or soak their way through others still. From the meaning with solids they emerge unscathed, while the solids they have met, if they stay solid, are changed – get moist or drenched. The extraordinary mobility of fluids is what associated them with the idea of "lightness." (Bauman, 2000: 2)

In addition, Bauman (2000) proposes, profit sources in the economic markets have moved from the ability to produce to one that capitalizes on *ideas* rather than material resources. In contrast to the production of material objects, dependent on the people hired or engaged in replicating material objects, the economic value extracted from such ideas is dependent on a number of people that are attracted as buyers, clients, and consumers: "[w]hen it comes to making the ideas profitable, the objects of competition are the consumers, not the producers. No wonder that the present-day engagement of capital is primarily with the consumers," Bauman (2000: 151) writes. More empirically oriented social theorists such as Ronald Inglehart have stressed that the present era is characterized by "post-materialist" preferences, that is, people prefer more leisure time to high pay and have expectations of their jobs as being beyond a mere source of income (Inglehart, 1997; Inglehart and Norris, 2009). "In the last several decades the proportion wanting such 'interesting work' has increased from 43.7% in 1989 to 51.0% in 1990 to 56.8% in 2006, a trend line that at least suggests a rising supply of creative labor," Liu and Grusky (2013: 1338) write. At the same time as life in late modernity has opened up new expectations and new beliefs and norms, there is also, as Lipovetsky (2005) examines, a growing anxiety regarding the future. If life and the economy become increasingly liquid (in an ontological sense) as being more fluid, fluxing, and changing, it is also more complicated to monitor and control, not only for policy-makers and regulatory bodies, but also for individuals. In the era of financialization in late modernity, what Anthony Giddens (1990) refers to as "ontological certainty" is gradually undermined and displaced by a more uncertain and precarious life situation. It is perhaps paradoxical, that the more economic wealth that is produced, the measure of all things in free-market capitalism, the less solid the foundation of this society seems.

Lipovetsky (2005: 35) proposes that the narrative of progress dominating the welfare state has today lost much of its credibility, and instead there is a strong emphasis on the *present*. In this society, obsessed with innovation and novelty, there is evidence of what Lipovetsky (2005: 35) calls "accelerated obsolescence" – new goods and services are becoming outmoded and antiquated at an increasingly higher pace. This anxiety for the future in combination with a consumerist culture propelled by the financialization of the economy leads to what Lipovetsky (2005: 40) refers to as a "paradoxical combination of frivolity and anxiety, euphoria and vulnerability, playfulness and dread." While life in the welfare state era was characterized by gradual changes and relatively good opportunities for making predictions about one's own life chances based on education and career choices, today there is a constant sense of being exposed to the ups and downs of the global economic system.

The era of financialization of late modernity is also the period when the sheer accumulation of wealth and economic capital has reached unprecedented levels, while at the same time economic inequality grows in many so-called advanced democratic economies. Brady et al. (2013) examine the level of the "working poor" in the US, perhaps the most advanced economy in terms of the degree of financialization of the economy, and report that in comparison to unemployment, averaging at only 3.4 percent in the US population in the 1974–2004 period, the working poor averaged 10.4 percent in the period (Brady et al., 2013: 873). There is evidence that no less than 61 percent of the officially poor families in the US contain an employed person (Brady et al., 2013: 873). Still, there is a relatively limited concern in the political quarter for the inability of certain groups to live off their salaried work income. In the welfare state, the political objective to provide full employment was based on the proposition that a full day's work and full day's pay should guarantee a decent standard of living, but recent political programs have emphasized that it is the market, not political bodies and trade unions, that should determine the economic worth of salaried work.

Jacobs and Myers (2014) suggest that Reagan's defeat of the Professional Air Traffic Controllers Organization (PATCO) strike in 1981 in many ways represents the starting point for new labor relations in the US, taking a less benign view of the unions. Reagan's efforts to curb unionism was an "[a]lmost unmatched postwar anti-union triumph" (Jacobs and Myers, 2014: 755), and it had a great symbolic value in signaling to the business community that the new administration would tolerate employers in the US by-passing existing labor relations rules and that they would not be punished for such action: "Reagan's aversion for labor implied that this administration might not curb [novel employer practices] even then they were illegal" (Jacobs and Myers, 2014: 755). Reporting empirical data, Jacobs and Myers (2014: 767) show that "reductions in union strength" caused by the new policies, endorsed first by Reagan and later "neoliberal administrations" including that of the Democratic President Bill Clinton served to accelerate inequality after 1981: "[i]n the 12 years before Reagan's presidency, from 1970 to 1981, inequality grew by 4.53 percent, but it expanded by 11.2 percent in 12 Reagan-Bush years from 1982 to 1993, or by 2.5 times as much" (Jacobs and Myers, 2014: 767). The stern anti-unionist policies, initiated and institutionalized by the Reagan Administration, is thus one significant change in the labor relations in the era of financialization, strongly contributing to increased economic inequality. "In countries with high unionization, inequality and poverty are lower and wages are higher," Brady et al. (2013: 873) write; "[f]or a standard deviation increase in unionization, the odds of constant working poverty decline by a factor of 1.19" (Brady et al., 2013: 883). In Fichtenbaum's (2011: 806) calculations, covering the period 1997 to 2006, labor's share of income declined by 3.6 points. In the same period, the percentage of the workforce "covered by collective bargaining in manufacturing declined by 4.8 percentage points" (Fichtenbaum, 2011: 795). More specifically, the decline in unionization between 1997 and 2006 explains between 10 and 16 percent of the decline in labor's share of income. Taken together, the era of financialization and the accumulation of economic wealth have provided opportunities for very few to become extremely wealthy, while for the majority the prospects are less favorable while the uncertainties remain. For a smaller but significant group, mostly composed of minorities, uneducated groups, the disabled, and women, salaried work is not even providing for the most basic needs, and in for example, the US, around 50 million people are today dependent on food stamps and coupons from the state to make ends meet.

This chapter of the book discusses how the financialization of the firm affects the workplace and the work conditions in the firm. While Chapter 4 addressed corporate governance, how the firm handles social, economic and legal relations in its environment, and Chapter 5 discussed how managerial control and oversight has been moved to external auditing organizations and rating agencies, this chapter is examining the internal organization of the firm and its human resource management practices in the era of financialization.

THE ENTERPRISING SELF IN THE FINANCIALIZED EVERYDAY LIFE

If a neoliberal market ideology is the principal driver of financialization (Palley, 2013), then Gershon's (2011) concept of the "neoliberal self" as a subject-position being well tuned to expectations on enterprising capacities in the era of financialization is a useful theoretical construct. As opposed to welfare state ideologies and practices, where "collective solutions" to "individual problems" were favored, in the financialized, neoliberal economy, the classic liberal view of the individual, first formalized by John Locke as being based on the individual's right to their own bodies and their capacities to labor, is given a central role. These capacities are sold in the market and consequently, it is the individual that needs to be held responsible for various outcomes from the attempt to compete in the market (Gershon, 2011: 539). This enactment of the "market-self" implies that "market rationalities" become the predominant mechanism for regulating a series of social relations: this concept of agency requires,

Gershon (2011: 539) proposes, "a reflexive stance in which people are subjects to themselves – a collection of processes to be managed." In other words, the enterprising market-self is based on individuals skillfully being their own self-reflexive managers and creating their own resources and alliances. For Mirowski (2013) this implies a "fragmentation of the self" (see also Sennett, 1998), being "simultaneously a product to be sold, a walking advertisement, a manager or her résumé, a biographer of her rationales, and an entrepreneur of her possibilities" (Mirowski, 2013: 108). In a way, the individual is split into the roles of subject, object, and spectator, Mirowski (2013) says.

In addition to the individualist orientation of the enterprising self, Gershon (2011) adds, there is also a risk factor involved in being an enterprising individual, the *sine qua non* of the neoliberal, financialized economy, and there is always a premium for the capacity to anticipate and cope with risk: "[a]ccording to the neoliberal perspective, to prosper, one must engage with risk. All neoliberal social strategies center on this. Managing risk frames how neoliberal agents are oriented toward the future" (Gershon, 2011: 540). Neoliberal intellectuals frequently speak of economic freedom as a greater virtue than political freedom, but this freedom is always defined in the negative as being the absence of state-based regulatory control and governmental interventions into free markets. Gershon (2011) suggests that rather than equating freedom with "choice" (as in Milton Friedman's, [1962] 2002, declaration), it would be more apt to say that "neoliberalism equates freedom with the ability to act on one's own calculations." This negative freedom is "inevitably unstable" as in a capitalist economic regime, "calculating to one's advantage is too frequently also calculating to someone else's disadvantage" (Gershon, 2011: 540). The consequence is that the individual cannot expect any collectivist solutions to individual problems, and therefore decisions to invest in so-called human capital (for example, education and training) are strictly a personal responsibility. In this respect, every man is in fact an island, only connected to all others through various market-based transactions and exchanges. But at the same time, all activities are precarious as the capitalist economic system is in a constant flux and change. At the end of the day, in the era of the neoliberal, financialized everyday life, subject-formation and identities are of necessity based on a calculative worldview and the capacity to make individual decisions. The problem is that in terms of being a *general enactment* of the self, and not just being the ideal in certain professional communities (for example, in the finance industry), most individuals "[l]ack financial literacy and generally cannot make sensible choices" (Froud et al., 2007: 340). This is turn easily leads to endless educational campaigns where individuals are trained and informed to be able to for example, manage their pension funds and to make balanced investment choices when buying homes. Such individualized economic choices, arguably based on limited insight into the operations of the global finance markets, also need to be regulated by central bank policies, making formal declarations regarding for example, homeowners' willingness to pay their loans and keep their savings at optimal levels. In other words, everyday life in the neoliberal, financialized economy is a matter of constantly optimizing and fine-tuning one's individual career choices and investments to avoid being outpaced by the market: "[a] hypercompetitive world such as this requires constant attention to opportunity and vigilance as to potential threats. There is nowhere to hide, and no moment of respire from the voice mail while the pasta is cooking and compose e-mails while the baby naps" (Martin, 2002: 36).

In the neoliberal, financialized economy, the price for economic freedom is the constant worry for the future and the continuous management of one's self and individual assets, both tangible and intangible. In a way, it is the site of the Hobbesian *bellum omnium contra omnes*; it is a return to a pre-civilized human society.

Perhaps this strong individualist orientation is no more conspicuous than in the case of individual professional entrepreneurs being outsourced and laid-off from major companies during the last the decades of the "slimming of operations" in the pursuit of shareholder value creation. As demonstrated by Vallas and Prener (2012: 345, Figure 5), during the boom years in 1997–2000 and 2004–2008 (until the Great Recession hit), there was an increase in the number of books published that shared the theme of praising entrepreneurship and enterprising activities and that portrayed work in large, bureaucratic organizations as being dull, uncreative, and basically unable to provide possibilities for self-fulfillment. In this literature (for example, Pink, 2001), Vallas and Prener (2012: 347) suggest, the worker's self is redefined as "commercializable product," and one of the consequences of this literature is that it "[i]nduces employees to embrace a critique of the very bureaucratic structures that had previously sheltered them from precarity." In this view, the entrepreneurship literature serves to normalize and idealize insecure work and treat it as liberating and "fun" (Neff, 2013). Lane (2010) studied information technology professionals in the Dallas, Texas, computer industry cluster – the so-called "Silicon Prairie" – and saw the tendency of these former employed professionals creating "a company of one" – individual professional service firms employing only one enterprising individual. Fortunately, these self-employing entrepreneurs (in the favored contemporary vocabulary) did not regard themselves as losers in the battle over work opportunities but rather enacted themselves as individuals being able to cast off outmoded images of "the organization man" who "foolishly looked to paternalistic employers to provide them with job security and financial stability" (Lane, 2010: 9). In contrast, the computer industry workers saw themselves as entrepreneurial agents engaged in the "constant labor of defining, improving and marketing 'the brand called you'" (Lane, 2010: 9). The entrepreneurs in Lane's study had thus accommodated the neoliberal, financialized image of the enterprising self and put this model into practice, including creating a critical distance to previously widespread beliefs regarding privileges, rights, and benefits: while the organization men of managerial capitalism regarded hard work and self-sacrifice as "the key to occupational success" (Lane, 2010: 47), today's white-collar workers and meritocratic individualists argue that being "a loyal employee, or even a talented employee, is not enough to guarantee success in today's hyper-competitive economy." At times, the collectivist solutions to both social and individual problems of the welfare state preceding the financialized economy was treated with contempt and addressed in moralist tones. For instance, one executive interviewed by Lane (2012: 51) declares, "[t]o give my employees job security would be to disempower them and to relieve them of the responsibility that they need to feel their own success." In the neoliberal, financialized economy, we are all expected to create our own successes; that is, in its essence, our economic freedom.

Hochschild (2012) examines another feature of the financialized economy, that of how everyday life of Americans starts to resemble corporations inasmuch as there is an increased use of various services and professional help to organize, structure, and handle, what was previously part of the intimate life of the family sphere. Today, there is an enormous supply of family and household services including everything from wedding planners and cleaning services to personal coaches and "friendship-relations managers" that help stressed out parents and spouses organize their lives. Similar to companies analyzing what services they need to keep in-house and what they need to outsource and buy from market actors and suppliers, the home has become something like an enterprise where "quality time" with the family is prioritized over tedious routine work such as cleaning and doing the laundry. The sharp growth of such services creates job opportunities for less privileged groups, but also serves to re-establish an interwar period servant culture where an army of service workers, often paid low salaries and with few benefits, take over the household work from the more privileged but busy professional workers (Dwyer, 2013). Everyday life in the financialized economy is composed of a curious blend of anxiety and comfort, of hard work and intense competition and the ability to take advantage of (if competing successfully) the fruits of one's very own, personal labor.

PERFORMANCE, REWARDS, AND COMPENSATIONS

Shift in Economic Compensation in the US Economy: Who Benefits and Who Wins the "Pay Game"?

The ethics of economic compensation

Proponents of free-market capitalism regard economic inequalities as either being a necessary evil in an unforgiving economic milieu beyond the full control and governance of any policy-makers, or, which is a more radical standpoint, treat economic inequality per se as being indicative of a vital and dynamic economic system. The Goldman International Vice Chairman Brian Griffiths, a former adviser of Margaret Thatcher, defended this latter standpoint in 2009, saying, "[w]e have to tolerate the inequality as a way to achieve greater prosperity and opportunity for all" (cited in Mandis, 2013: 236). The recurrent declaration of free-market protagonists, that economic inequality is the price that unfortunately needs to be paid to enable economic growth, is repeated time and again regardless of the empirical robustness of the proposition. As the economist Michał Kalecki (1943) wrote during the war years, the discipline of the workforce tends to be more appreciated by business leaders than increased profits:

> [T]he rise in wage rates resulting from the stronger bargaining power of the workers is less likely to reduce profits than to increase prices, and thus affects adversely only the *rentier* interests. But "discipline in the factories" and "political stability" are more appreciated by the business leaders than profits. Their class instinct tells them that lasting full employment is unsound from their point of view and that unemployment is an integral part of the "normal" capitalist system. (Kalecki, 1943: 326)

The ethics of discipline and the ideological conviction that economic inequality is at the bottom line a necessary sacrifice to secure a vital economy taken aside, the substantial theory that economic inequality drives growth is not supported by empirical data. Thewissen (2014: 567) shows that increased inequality does not lead to growth. In addition, labor market flexibility, defined as industrial relations reform that increases discrimination between "core workers," employed on the basis of long-term contracts, and "peripheral workers," hired on short-term contracts, and their respective economic compensation, has insignificant or negative consequences for innovation, a principal predictor for long-term economic growth (Kleinknecht et al., 2014). Kleinknecht et al. (2014: 1210) refer to a study that sampled 19 OECD countries for the 1960–2004) period, suggesting that "a 1% lower wage increase will result in a lower growth of labor productivity by 0.33–0.39%." Moreover, in their own analysis of data from the Netherlands, they distinguish between two categories of innovation: the first is *entrepreneurial innovation*, the so-called "garage model" where *de novo* entrepreneurs develop new technologies eventually leading to new industries; and the second, the *"routinized" model of innovation* where innovation activities are located in R&D departments in traditional corporations and industries (Kleinknecht et al., 2014: 1208). The data reveal that "coefficients of temporary workers" are insignificant for the former category of innovation work while it is significantly negative for the latter category (Kleinknecht et al., 2014: 1213). Interestingly, increased flexibility also in top management teams, where executives and directors come and go at a higher pace, is also negative for long-term performance in companies, Messersmith et al. (2014: 788) suggest: "[f]irms with a stable group of executives may be better able to develop both an appropriate firm-level strategy and the necessary organizational capabilities and culture to support and effectively implement this strategy." Policies, regardless of their moral and ethical grounding, that actively encourage and promote economic inequality, or, more directly, labor market flexibility, may thus hinder rather than promote economic growth, these studies suggest.

For free-market protagonists that subscribe to a free-market ideology, the presence of economic inequality is neither puzzling nor particularly worrisome, Mirowski (2013) suggests. For them, economic inequality is not so much an "unfortunate by-product of capitalism" but is on the contrary "a necessary functional characteristic of an ideal market system," serving to discipline market actors (preferably as many as practically possible as markets expand into new domains) and to coordinate actions and serving as the "strongest motor forces for progress" (Mirowski, 2013: 63). Therefore, free-market protagonists believe that people should be "encouraged to envy and emulate the rich," while demands for equality, in contrast, are "merely the sour grapes of the losers" (Mirowski, 2013: 56). Mirowski's (2013) overly cynical view of the proponents of free-market capitalism may not hold true for more moderate and mainstream groups. Beyond the hard core of libertarian economists in the University of Chicago economics tradition, there is actually quite a bit of concern for inequality; but the neoliberal and neoconservative dogma gaining a foothold in American politics is that attempts by the state to counteract growing economic inequality inevitably lead to new and more severe economic crises (Mirowski, 2013: 63). Consequently, these economic advisers suggest a laissez-faire policy where politicians should "wait and see" how the market evens out the economic inequalities, and if that is not the case, it would be the individual themselves failing to live up to market expectations on expertise or servility that is to blame, not the market. Needless to say, such a political agenda has not been widely embraced outside of the US, even if there is a tendency today, in countries like Sweden with a strong public support for the welfare state, to think of poverty and unemployment as being individual failures rather than social concerns and responsibilities. Under all conditions, regardless of whether one takes a laissez-faire position or have hopes that the welfare state will handle the economic inequalities, the distribution of economic resources as the compensation for work become a key mechanism located inside the firm.

The separation of productivity growth and economic compensation

The economic sociologist Viviana Zelizer (2011) points at three forms of "monetary payment":

> [T]hree possible ways of organizing monetary payment of any kind: as *compensation* (direct exchange), as *entitlement* (the right to a share), and as *gift* (one person's voluntary bestowal on another). Money as compensation implies an equal exchange of value and a certain distance, contingency, bargaining, and accountability among parties. Money as an entitlement implies strong claims to power and autonomy by the recipient. Money as gift implies subordination and arbitrariness. (Zelizer, 2011: 136–137, original emphasis)

When examining economic compensation, it is possible to examine both the aggregate economic statistics and to review how individual professional, industry-based, or even minority groups are benefiting from the pay game. In the following, the analysis starts on the aggregated level. Wolff (2003: 451) examined the aggregated profitability in the US economy between 1947 and 1997 and found that "[t]he net profit in US manufacturing shows a very similar trend to that of the total economy, first falling from a peak at 32.3% in 1953 to a low point of 8.3% in 1983 and then recovering, in part, to 15.9% in 1997." What is interesting to observe is the shift in compensation in the form of salaries in the period. Between 1947 and 1979 real wages grew, on average, at the same rate as labor productivity, while after 1979, real wages rose more slowly than labor productivity (Wolff, 2003: 451). Wolff (2003: 451) therefore found that over the entire period, "labour productivity gains outstripped those of mean compensation (a ratio of 2.19 versus 1.96)." Until the end of the 1970s, the salaried workers were, to simplify things a bit, "paid for their performance," while after 1979 other compensation metrics apply. Weil (2014: 16) reports a similar pattern on the basis of more recent data: "[r]eal wages for median workers . . . grew by only 0.5% between 2000 and 2012. Median hourly compensation (wages plus benefits) grew by only 4%. Yet productivity (measured as output of goods and services per hour worked) rose by over 23% in the period." Also in the longer perspective, the divergence between productivity growth and wages is salient: "[b]etween 1979 and 2007 productivity rose by 80%. Over the same period, however, average hourly wages increased by only 7% and average hourly compensation (wages plus benefit) increased by 8%" (Weil, 2014: 281). To explain these changes, Wolff (2003: 496) refers to "structural changes" including the shift towards "labour intensive sevices" that caused the rate of profits to fall. Recently, after 2008, this structural change can be observed in the disappearance of mid-wage occupations and the growth of lower wage occupations. In the US, lower wage occupations grew 2.7 times as fast as mid-wage and high-wage occupations during the Great Recession, US Bureau of Labor Statistics data reveals (Weil, 2014: 284): Lower wage occupations "constituted 21% of employment losses but 58% of employment growth coming out of the recession," whereas mid wage occupations "accounted for 60% of losses but only 22% of the employment growth" (Weil, 2014: 284). Over the 2003–2013 period (that is, including the period prior to the finance market collapse), "lower-wage occupations grew by 8.7% and high-wage occupations by 6.6%, but mid-wage occupations actually declined by 7.3%" (Weil, 2014: 284). In other words, while high-wage occupations appear to be relatively stable, mid-wage occupations, the bulk of middle-class jobs, are displaced by lower wage occupations in the US economy.

Another structural, explanatory factor would be the shift in the balance between "capital and labor" in the period after 1979, characterized by the decline of labor unions and the labor movement more generally:

> [A] reasonable presumption might be that an equal division of power between capital and labour should lead to real wage's increasing at about the same rate as overall labour productivity. If wages increase more slowly, we might suspect that the balance in power has shifted towards capital, and conversely . . . One must conclude that economic and political power shifted in favour of capital, beginning in the early 1980s. (Wolff, 2003: 497)

Such research findings and interpretations of the causes of the findings have been shared by other researchers, including Vidal (2013) speaking about lower pay and insecure jobs in the "post-Fordist" economic regime. Today, one-third of the jobs are what Vidal (2013: 605) refers to as "low-autonomy jobs" and these jobs are "increasingly unable to provide decent living standards of the workers that fill these positions." Estimates from the US Bureau of Labor Statistics predict that "7 of the top 10 occupations projected to generate the most jobs by 2020 are low-wage service and laborer jobs" (Bernhardt, 2012: 355), making this category of occupations the principal source of new job creation in the US.

Kristal (2013: 362) presents US data for the 1969–2007 period and she explains the shift in compensation on the basis of what she refers to as "class-biased technological change." First, Kristal (2013: 363) remarks that wages and salaries account for only around half of the total income generated in the US economy, a fact that testifies to the financialization of economy. Kristal (2013: 365) also claims that this value generated is not "class-neutral," as there are capital-owning classes that are the primary beneficiaries of these economic values generated. Regarding the distribution of economic value in the form of income, Kristal (2013) confirms Wolff's (2003) evidence of an increased divergence between productivity and compensation after the mid-1970s (even though Wolff uses 1979 as the year ending the first period). After 1973, economic inequality has grown both on the basis of lower compensation and the increased values generated in the finance industry, benefiting a more limited number of Americans: "[a]lthough productivity grew 80.4 percent between 1972 and 2011, expanding total income, average hourly compensation, which includes the pay to CEOs, increased only 39.2 percent and – even more strikingly, the median worker's hourly compensation grew just by 10.7 percent" (Kristal, 2013: 383). In order to explain this shift in policy regarding how the fruits of the productivity gains are shared between organizational constituencies, Kristal (2013: 377) points at computerization and the declining bargaining power of workers in the period where the trade unions lost ground on the basis of new political agendas and policies: "[i]n particular, waning unionization, which led to the erosion of rank-and-file workers' bargaining power, was the main force behind the decline in labor's share" Kristal (2013: 378) concludes. Bernhardt (2012) adds that the "low-wage problem" in the US lies in the internal organization and regulation of the domestic service industries,[1] where employers

---

[1] One of the most widespread explanations for the downward pressure of wages in neoclassical economic theory framework is the effects of "globalization," leading to the downward pressure on worker's compensation when counties and regions with lower production factors costs are able to compete on the global market, but as Madrick (2012: 323) remarks, "low-end work, is mostly labor-intensive services that are not subject to foreign competition." In addition, the low-wage and increased economic inequality problems have not escalated to the same levels in Europe, as many European economies, despite being subject to the same changing technologies (for example, computerization) and global competition as the Anglo-American economies, have developed "strong safety nets and institutionalized practices" that stabilize the economy and counteract economic inequality (Madrick, 2012: 323). In the US, in contrast, beginning in the Reagan presidency, the tendency is to rely on job creation through tax reforms. Unfortunately, in the period 2001 to 2007, before the Great Recession struck, the period where the George W. Bush Administration launched a substantial tax reform, "the rate of job growth was lower than any other recovery and expansion since World War II. Furthermore, GDP growth was slower than in any recession" (Madrick, 2012: 322). What critics refer to as "trickle-down economics" (for example, Quiggin, 2010: Chapter 4), justifying tax cuts on the basis of their ability to boost economic activity, apparently does little to create jobs and stimulate economic growth.

are outsourcing these services to create financial flexibility, and to create a "legal distance between themselves and their employees" (Bernhardt, 2012: 360), a tendency that is facilitated by the "withdrawal of government's hand in the labor market."

Structural changes in the labor market and the workplace

Weil (2014) speaks about the financialized firm as a "fissured workplace" wherein individual workers are no longer representing the brand and the firm that the customer encounters, but are contracted service workers being hired by another subcontractor firm. For instance, in 1960, most of the hotel employees worked for the brand that appeared over the hotel entrance, but today more than 80 percent of the staff are employed by "hotel franchisees" and supervised by separate management companies that "bear no relation to the brand name of the property where they work" (Weil, 2014: 7). As the workplace and the work processes are fractured into a series of separate activities that can be handled by contracted suppliers, a service firm such as a hotel is no longer one, single unified workplace under the management and supervision of one, single employer but becomes an aggregate of isolated processes, each being defined by a contract. Weil (2014) defines two principal drivers of this process: one being the pressure from "capital markets" to treat service firms in particular as a bundle of contracts and the activities to be carried out as specified by the contract; the other being "technological changes" (that is, digital media) that have created new ways of "designing and monitoring the work of other parties, inside and outside of the corporation" (Weil, 2014: 44). There are many consequences of the fissured workplace, but one prominent effect is the downward pressure on wages for service workers being contracted to conduct for example, hotel reception work. In Weil's (2014: 91) account, the fissured workplace is not yet another name for subcontracting, outsourcing, or offshoring, and it does not solely arise from "lead companies" (firms being at the top of the pyramid, e.g., hotel chains such as Hilton or Marriott) seeking to "avoid payment of private or socially required benefits." Instead, the fissured workplace reflects a "fundamental restructuring of business organizations": "[e]mployment decisions arise from a careful and ongoing balancing act by lead companies and the subsequent behaviors of the many smaller companies operating beneath them" (Weil, 2014: 91–92). Unfortunately, regardless of such "careful balancing acts," there are externalities – "the failure of private parties to fully weight the social costs of their actions" (Weil, 2014: 92) – that these lead companies can escape carrying the costs for.

In addition to the new attitudes and norms towards employees in this new low-wage, low-autonomy labor market regime, there is also weaker monitoring and enforcement of labor market laws. Between 1980 and 2002, "the number of federal wage and hour inspectors declined by 31% and the number of enforcement actions fell by 61%; by contrast, the civilian labor force grew 51% during the same period," Bernhardt (2012: 362) writes. In 1975, OSHA, the US Occupational Safety and Health Administration, employed a total of 2,435 staff responsible for the safety and health of 67.8 million workers at more than 3.9 million establishments. In 2010, the agency employed about the same number of staff (2,335), but they were now overseeing double the number of workers (128.6 million) and establishments (8.8 million) (Bernhardt, 2012: 362). Studies report that this regulatory neglect and new managerial practices such as subcontracting and outsourcing of non-strategic services have contributed to a situation where low-wage workers can no longer trust that labor market laws are followed or enforced. A study of more than 4,000 workers in low-wage industries in Chicago, Los Angeles, and New York reported that 26 percent had been paid "less than the minimum wage in the preceding week, 76% had been underpaid for their overtime hours, and 70% did not receive any pay at all when they came in early or stayed late after their shift" (Bernhardt, 2012: 361). Worse still, Bernhardt (2012: 361) continues, of the respondents who complained about their working conditions, "43% experienced illegal retaliation from their employers or supervisor." Also the economic valuation of the health and safety of this category of workers is comparatively low as the maximum fine for a serious OSHA violation is US$7,000 and US$70,000 for a willful violation, a significantly smaller sum than for example, fines up to US$250,000 per day for violations of the Clean Water Act (Bernhardt, 2012: 363). No longer protected by trade unions, or the agencies enforcing labor market law, low-autonomy and low-wage workers endure a problematic situation where there is a more limited political interest regarding their economic compensation, health, and safety among employers, policy-making bodies, and in political quarters.

Liu and Grusky (2013) add to the complexity of the argument regarding where compensations are channeled, and examine what kind of jobs are better paid in the new economic regime. Liu and Grusky (2013) found that it is not always the case that only high levels of education are rewarded. Instead, it is jobs that demand what Liu and Grusky (2013: 1332) calls "analytical skills" including "synthesis, critical thinking, and deductive and inductive reasoning" that have been best compensated: "a standard deviation of analytical skill raised wages by 10.4% in 1980 and 17.5% in 2010, an increase in payout that is far in excess of that observed for any of the other workplace skills" (Liu and Grusky, 2013: 1338). In their discussion of the research findings, Liu and Grusky (2013) criticize the idea that it is exogenous changes including technological shifts (for example, the computerization of the 1990s) that explains the shift in compensation; such shifts are not capable of explaining differences in compensation. In addition, the widespread belief that "cognitive skills," primarily acquired in tertiary education, are well compensated should be abandoned, Liu and Grusky (2013) claim. As a consequence, Liu and Grusky (2013) speak of a "skill-biased institutional change" in the economy as the principal explanatory factor for differences in economic compensations: "[t]he growing demand for analytical labor reflects the accelerating 'creative destruction' of modern capitalism and the associated premium on innovation, problem solving, and rapid response to changing market conditions. These institutional changes would not appear to be simple reactions to technical change" (Liu and Grusky, 2013: 1368–1369).

Returning to the issue of financialization, Lin and Tomaskovic-Devey (2013: 1289) point out that "elite workers" now constitute "a significant fraction of the highest-income population" (see also Dore, 2008, regarding the case of the UK). Consistent with the analysis of Wolff (2003) and Kristal (2013), Lin and Tomaskovic-Devey (2013: 1291) emphasize that income distribution "[r]eflect the relative bargaining and claim-making power of actors in a given organizational and environmental context." Examining the role of the financialization rather than *technological* or *institutional* changes as the driver of new income distribution, Lin and Tomaskovic-Devey, 2013: 1306) found that a 1 percent increase in the "reliance on financial income" is associated with "between a 0.9% and a 3.7% decrease in labor's share in the long run." Again, the 1990s' computerization wave is referred to as an important technological shift, but this new technology is unable to explain all of the changes in income. Instead, Lin and Tomaskovic-Devey (2013: 1317) suggest that financialization is co-produced with the weakening of workers' bargaining power at the same time as it "encourages managers to avoid investments in production," two factors that undermine well-paid and stable jobs in the US economy. Lin and Tomaskovic-Devey (2013) summarize their findings:

> [F]inancialization of the U.S. economy at its core is a system of redistribution that privileges a limited set of actors. In addition to the growing income transfer into the finance sector . . . the increasing reliance on income through financial channels restructured the social relations and the income dynamics in the nonfinance sector. Substituting production and sales investment with financial investment decoupled the generation of surplus from production, strengthening owners' and elite workers' negotiating power against other workers, The result was a structural and cultural exclusion of the general workforce from revenue-generating and compensation-setting processes. (Lin and Tomaskovic-Devey, 2013: 1310)

In summary, the series of studies show that in the financialized economy, workers get a smaller share of the productivity growth. The winners in the pay game are highly skilled elite workers (Lin and Tomaskovic-Devey, 2013), demonstrating analytical skills (Liu and Grusky, 2013). The losers in the pay game are the individuals occupying low-autonomy jobs and being reliant on collective bargaining. In addition, economic inequality is not only caused by a shift in income distribution but also on the basis of the economic value transferred from industry to capital owners. As indicated by Piketty (2014) and Piketty and Saez, (2003), the lion's share of these incomes primarily benefit the top 1 percent or even the 0.1 percent income earners in the US economy.

In the next section, the economic compensation of CEOs and directors will be examined in some detail to see whether these professional workers have benefited from the financialization of the economy.

The Compensation of CEOs and Directors

Studies of executive compensation suggest that firm size rather than performance or any other measure is the most important predictor for CEO pay, but these data do not explain shifts in compensation policy over time. Fortunately, there is a quite substantial literature both reporting income data for these groups and theorizing the shift in compensation during the last few decades.

Tosi et al. (2000: 305) remark that "studies on executive pay as a control mechanism are remarkably inconsistent not only with theory but also with each other," that is, there is no real solid empirical evidence or robust theoretical framework explaining the level of CEOs' economic compensation. In their meta-analysis of studies of CEO compensation, Tosi et al. (2000: 329) found that "[i]ndicators of firm size, taken together, explain almost nine times the amount of variance of total CEO pay than the most highly correlated performance measure." In contrast to what is often believed among both researchers and the public, and what at times is advanced by the CEO community itself as a justification for generous compensation, there is only very limited empirical support for performance-based compensation: "[c]hanges in firm performance account for only 4% of the variance in CEO pay, while exchanges in firm size account for 5% of the variance of CEO pay" (Tosi et al., 2000: 329). That is, statistically speaking, it is better to be a mediocre CEO of a large firm than to be a highly efficient CEO in a smaller firm from an economic compensation perspective. These findings are intuitively easy to understand as large firms with higher turnover have the capacity to carry larger executive compensation costs: "[t]he size of the average S&P 500 company means that even generous U.S. executive compensation packages accounts for only a small percentage of sales and profits" (Erturk et al., 2007: 67). For example, in 2002, average pre-tax profits of the S&P 500 group of firms amounted to just over $900 billion, and "total executive compensation" were no higher than "0.2 or 0.3 percent of sales, which translates into no more than 5 percent of pre-tax profits" (Erturk et al., 2007: 67).

Bebchuk and Grinstein (2005) examine the 1993–2003 period, the real "take-off phase" for the financialization of the economy, and find that the 2003 CEO levels of compensation exceeded the levels predicted by the 1993 regression by 115 percent. These findings were statically significant on the 1 percent level. Commonly, executives are compensated on the basis of stock options and of other forms of financial assets, and often a significant share of the growth in compensation derives from the ability to increase shareholder value – a performance that also benefits the executives. When checking against the growth of the firms and their performance, Bebchuk and Grinstein (2005: 291) find that the log of equity-based compensation increased by 1.347 for the CEO and by 1.468 for the top executives. Even though the equity-based compensation peaked in 2000 by the burst of the information technology bubble, cash-based compensation has continued to trend upwards during Bebchuk and Grinstein's (2005) entire study period. These changes cannot be explained on the basis of any observable, objective changes in the firms being managed. Instead, much of the increased compensation remains to be explained: "changes in size and performance can explain only 66 per cent of the total 166 increase, or about 40 per cent of the total increase, with 60 per cent of the total increase remaining unexplained" (Bebchuk and Grinstein, 2005: 287). Based on these statistically solid results including the control of the effect of firm's being larger and/or more profitable than in 1993, Bebchuk and Grinstein (2005: 289) conclude, "[t]he relationship between pay and firm attributes has changed substantially during the period under consideration." That is, executives are, *ceteris paribus*, more generously compensated in 2003 than they were in 1993. "[C]ompensation levels increased far beyond what can be attributed to changes in size and performance," Bebchuk and Grinstein (2005: 286) contend.

Lord and Saito (2010) report that the median levels of "total real annual CEO compensation" more than doubled from US$1.18 million in 1994 to US$2.80 million in 2007 (in real 1994 dollars) (Lord and Saito, 2010: 43). Just as Bebchuk and Grinstein (2005) remark, Lord and Saito (2010: 43) point at the "brief decline" in total CEO compensation following the market crash in 2000, while after this event, the "real total compensation has risen again significantly in most industries." DiPrete et al. (2010) provide additional executive compensation data: "[a]djusted for inflation, the median salary/bonus increased from 1993 through 2006 by 40%, whereas the mean increased 58%. Adjusted for inflation, the median total compensation went from $1.6 million to $3.2 million, a 106% increase, whereas the means increased by 116%" (DiPrete et al., 2010: 1687).

Suárez (2014: 74) found that while executive pay grew by an average of less than 1 percent a year in the 1950s and 1960s, between 1998 and 2007, the average was 10 percent a year. More importantly, Suárez (2014) reports that the attempt of the political system to limit the growth of executive pay has primarily led to "symbolic policies," incapable of accomplishing a real change. It is therefore noteworthy that after the two recession years of 2008 and 2009 with declining levels of CEO compensation, US CEO pay rose by 28 percent in 2010 and 15 percent in 2011 (Suárez, 2014: 92). Apparently, the political system that failed to regulate executive pay in the 1930s also failed in the 2008–2011 period: "[r]emarkably, the executive pay-setting process has remained relatively stable in spite of the fact that it has been seen as a 'problem' since the emergence of the modern corporation in the early twentieth century," Suárez (2014: 82) summarizes.

In contrast to these studies, data reported by Hall and Liebman (1998: 667) from the 1993–1994 period, arguably at the beginning of the period of increased economic compensation for executives, there is, despite the finding that "CEOs have enjoyed larger gains in compensation, both in absolute terms and relative to most other highly paid groups" (Hall and Liebman, 1998: 667), there is still a "positive correlation" between CEO compensation and performance. The data reported by Bebchuk and Grinstein (2005), Lord and Saito (2010), DiPrete et al. (2010), and Suárez (2014) (but not supported by Hall and Liebman, 1998) suggest that there has been an institutional shift in corporate governance practice inasmuch as executives are today, *ceteris paribus*, substantially more generously compensated for their work than they were in the early 1990s. Executives, in many ways directly involved in determining their compensation even though legally speaking the decision is done by the board of directors, have thus been the winners in the pay game. Most other groups have received substantially lower real economic compensation in the period, but executives have been successful in advancing their interests. Why and how this has been accomplished is yet to be theoretically explained as there are few structural changes in industry that neither clarifies nor justifies these new compensation schemes.

At the Heart of Finance: Economic Compensation on Wall Street

When it comes to economic compensation, there are few contestants that can stand up against the finance industry workers themselves, the centrally located actors in the financialized economy. Sorkin (2009) reports that in 2007, the year when the financial crisis became a pressing concern, finance industry workers still benefited from US$53 billion in total compensation. The year before, in 2006, Wall Street paid out US$62 billion in compensation (Freeman, 2010: 167). At Goldman Sachs, ranked at the top of the five leading brokerages at the onset of the 2008 crisis, accounted for US$20 billion of that 2007 total. That sum amounted to more than US$661,000 in compensation per employee, and the CEO of Goldman Sachs, Lloyd Blankfein, alone "took home $68 million" (Sorkin, 2009: 4). Perhaps even more surprisingly, during the entire 2008 financial collapse, bonuses remained at this remarkable level. In the second half of 2007, Wall Street investment banks lost over US$11 billion, but the impact on the bonuses was modest: the average bonus fell only 4.7 percent (Crotty, 2009: 564). In the *annus horribilis* of 2008, when the global financial system was on the verge of collapsing and was only saved by the state – in a truly collectivist rescue activity orchestrated by the US government and governments elsewhere – the Wall Street compensation was still over US$18 billion, roughly the same as it was in the boom year of 2004 (Crotty, 2009: 564). During the financial crisis, it also became evident that the semantics of the term "bonus" had been modified and meant no longer "compensation for performance," but was used to denote an inherited privilege being paid under all conditions (that is, a *gift* in Viviana Zelizer's, 2011: 136–137, use of the term).[2] In Merrill Lynch, one of the leading Wall Street financial institutions, about 700 employees received bonuses in excess of US$1 billion from a total bonus pool of US$3.6 billion in 2008, all this despite the fact that the firm lost US$27 billion in this particular year (Crotty, 2009: 565). Among these beneficiaries, the top four recipients alone received a total of US$212 million, while the top 14 received US$249 million (Crotty, 2009: 565). In the two major bankruptcies during the 2007–2008 period, Bear Stearns and Lehman Brothers, the CEOs of Bear Stearns and Lehman Brothers received cash flows from bonuses and equity sales of about US$388 million and US$523 million in a conservative estimate, respectively; the top executive team "[o]btained aggregate cash

---

[2] As Spector and Spital (2011: 327) points out, research on the role of bonuses in executive compensation packages provides "little empirical support for the assumption that more money for executives drives improved company performance." Such findings support the view that bonuses are gifts rather than compensation for performance. The "gift-quality" of bonuses thus derives from: (1) empirical studies reporting weak or non-existing correlations between bonuses and performance; (2) the empirical fact that bonuses are paid also when companies report losses (and in this case and in for example, the instance of Enron, Watkins, 2003: 122, even when corporations are on the verge of bankruptcy or *de facto* being bankrupt).

flows of about $1,462 million and $1,014 million, respectively" (Bebchuk et al., 2010: 19–20). This was a most generous compensation for the CEOs and top management teams that conspicuously failed to do the job they were paid to do, to ensure the interests of shareholders and (in the case of the less orthodox governance model) other stakeholders.

The perhaps most spectacular example of corporate plundering was the case of AIG (American Investment Group), one of the most archetypal finance industry companies in the era of financialization. In 2008, when AIG's Financial Products Division lost US$40.4 billion and received US$180 billion in the corporation from the US government and being owned by the government by 80 percent, the 377 members of the division were awarded a total of US $220 million in bonuses for 2008, corresponding to an average of over US$500,000 per employee. Seven AIG employees received "more than US$2 million each" (Crotty, 2009: 565). In 2009, in the midst of the costly rescue activities, AIG announced on March 14, that it would pay bonuses amounting to US$168 million to its Financial Products Division. Barofsky (2012: 138) recalls that this announcement "triggered an explosion of outrage" in Washington DC: "[t]axpayers had put up $170 billion (including $40 billion from TARP) to keep AIG collapse from precipitating a meltdown of the global financial system, and now the executives from the division that had caused its ruin were going to be paid lavishly" (Barofsky, 2012: 138). Most people, not sharing a strong commitment to the idea that free markets are superior in pricing assets and thus adequately compensating valuable skills and know-how, would think of these levels of compensation – especially given the incompetent work conducted and the levels of risk-taking in the operations by these millionaire finance industry workers – as unjust. Again, facts stand without adequate explanation or theoretical framing beyond the sheer idea that markets always price assets correctly. Whether the finance industry, claiming an increasingly larger share of the profits generated in other industries and therefore amassing enormous sums of capital, have the right to reward itself with economic compensations at these levels remain both a policy issue and a moral question. A managerial question would then be: is the reliance on equity-based compensation of managers an efficient corporate governance principle? We now turn to that question.

Long-Term Effects of High-pay Policies

The agency theory model assumes a form of "ownership society" where the ownership of stock is widespread and includes a number of capital owners, operating within different time horizons and on the basis of different "risk utility functions" – if this is not the case, the efficiency hypothesis would fail as all capital owners would favor the same investment objects, leading to an overvaluation of certain financial assets while starving other industries and companies of capital. In addition, corporate governance policy that rewards managers distributing the free cash flow commonly pays a premium for risk-taking. In contrast, managers who are paid to secure long-term survival and stability of the firm – executives being "paid like bureaucrats," in Jensen and Murphy's (1990) formulation (cf. Hall and Liebman, 1998) – are less prone to jeopardize the shareholders' and creditors' resources. This places a premium of risk-taking that in turn leads to higher risk taking than would otherwise be justified. The new compensation system "encouraged executives to take risks" and to increase short-term stock evaluations, but there were no checks on or punishment for declines which thus encouraged "reckless risk-taking" (Dobbin and Jung, 2010: 37). For executives, there was "only an upside."

Sanders and Hambrick (2007) studied how executives being compensated by stock options assess risks and how this view affects their performance. To start, Sanders and Hambrick (2007: 1057, original emphasis) define risk as "*the degree to which potential outcomes associated with a decision are consequential, vary widely and include the possibility of extreme loss.*" To compensate executives for their work through stock option packages is generally treated as a method to, as prescribed in agency theory, "ameliorate problems of shirking by aligning CEO payoffs with shareholder payoff" (Sanders and Hambrick, 2007: 1060). When aligning the interests of CEOs and shareholders (but no other stakeholders, to be noticed), opportunism on the part of the CEOs is curbed, the theory predicts. In addition, the use of stock options rather than direct bonuses in cash is argued to help overcome "the problem of shortsightedness" (Sanders and Hambrick, 2007: 1060). Another benefit is that stock options would encourage the CEOs to take greater risks on behalf of the shareholders. Rather than recruiting CEOs with an administrative attitude towards their work, shareholders want a tiger at the helm, willing to take risks and bring back higher levels of free cash flow to capital owners, the theory assumes. These three rationales are jointly justifying the use of stock options in the compensation package.

In their empirical research work, Sanders and Hambrick (2007: 1073) found, as predicted by the theory, that the CEOs who were paid in stock options, invested more aggressively in "major investment categories" – R&D, capital spending, and acquisitions (as well as in an aggregate index of all three). Unfortunately, unpredicted by agency theory, Sanders and Hambrick (2007: 1073) found that the CEOs making such high-risks decisions and pursuing high-risk strategies tended to "generate more big losses than big gains" (as measured both by market and accounting metrics), and that their "ratio of big losses to big gains was greater than the corresponding ratios for CEOs who derived less of their pay from stock options" (Sanders and Hambrick, 2007: 1073). Using a baseball vocabulary popular with US business school researchers and management writers, Sanders and Hambrick (2007: 1073) conclude that the CEOs compensated with stock options "[s]trike out much more often than they hit home runs" (see also Djelic and Bothello, 2013).

These findings are brought back to examine the consistency and empirical relevance of the agency theory and its shareholder value model. In this case, agency theory poorly predicts the outcome from the compensation package design, and it fails to propose a corporate governance model that effectively balances various objectives and demands: "[w]hat agency theorists did not envision," Sanders and Hambrick (2007: 1073–1074) write, "was that the extreme performance delivered by option-loaded CEOs was more likely to be in the form of big losses than big gains. Investors – not even risk-neutral investors – would not have desired this outcome." The agency theory model of corporate governance is designed to reward "money-making" (Dobbin and Jung, 2010: 36), but it acts little and poorly to theorize the externalities of such a model. For instance, the premium on risks may work satisfyingly in growth markets and in the upward movement in the economic cycle, but when the economy turns sour, there are few regulatory mechanisms to handle economic decline and falling levels of profit. In summary, risk-taking is overcompensated and it also fails to reduce the agency costs that in the first place justified the reliance on finance market-based control of executives (Dobbin and Zorn, 2005: 196). More generally speaking, while the agency theory model is easily understood and perhaps also functioning in a few cases under some very specific conditions (in for example, high-income, stagnating industries with few new growth investment opportunities, being at the early stage of an upward movement in the economic cycle), it is arguably too simplistic and empirically unsubstantiated to provide a credible, long-term solution to management control and corporate governance problems. If nothing else, the significant sharp growth in economic compensation of executives and their following preference for risk-taking remain a mystery from a theoretical perspective: "[t]hat the executives had the incentive – and the tools – to design compensation packages that benefited them at the expense of others seems abundantly clear. What still is a mystery is why shareholders didn't recognize this," Stiglitz (2010: 154) writes. Apparently, the market for management control is yet in its infancy and executive communities can still determine their own compensation.

Beyond the Executive Board Room: Performance-reward Systems in the Era of Financialization

In the era of financialization, the firm is enacted as first a bundle of legal contracts that specifies what rights the contractor is entitled to, and second, what various forms of compensation the different contractors are entitled to depending on what role they play in the firm's value creation practices. For the co-workers, the salaried workforce, the performance-reward system was previously based on bargaining between the employer and labor representatives, the trade unions as in the case of Scandinavian countries, or between the employer and individual employees. In that way, the salary and other benefits and rights were very much part of a legal process anchored in negotiated social relations. In some industries and professional areas, especially professional work being based on the institution of private practices and bureaus (for example, medical doctors and jurists running their own small clinics and businesses), there is a more direct relationship between the income and the performance-reward system. As the era of financialization has been dominated by a preference for free-market solutions over negotiations and bargaining, there is a tendency that a larger group of salaried workers are compensated on the basis of their individual contributions to the employers' economic performance. For instance, in many professional fields including engineering work, management consulting, legal services, and many expert-based domains of work, so-called "billable hours" have been used for a long period of time. Yakura (2002) examines the use of billable hours as a performance-reward system that, formally speaking, in many ways is both transparent and based on individual contributions and ultimately market-based evaluations of individual work. In Yakura's (2002) account, much of the value of the system of billable hours pay derives from the fact that it is based on uniform calculative practices that are easily understood by all co-workers: "[b]illing systems help to legitimate the value of consulting services by assigning uniform dollar rates to the hours billed. Billing practices ensure that the consulting services have uniform value, even where the realities belie that uniformity. They rely on the assumption that time is money" (Yakura, 2002: 1077).

The equation "time equals money," Benjamin Franklin's famous dictum, thus lies at the very heart of the billable hours-based performance-reward system. In addition, the billable hours system enables management of the consulting firm studied by Yakura (2002) to monitor the workload of the co-workers as the billing system generated a variety of monthly issued reports that were used in a variety of settings. The statistics regarding both pay and workload could also be easily aggregated for different projects, work groups, departments, and, if needed, different offices and branches (Yakura, 2002: 1090). Management was in other words using the billable hours system as both a performance-reward system *and* a management control system (Castilla and Benard, 2010; Castilla, 2008). The system also had a few weaknesses including the rewarding of performance on the individual level, and what Espeland and Sauder (2007) call *reactivity*, the tendency of the consultants to act opportunistically to enhance their own performance and compensation. This remains the Achilles' heel of the billable hours system, that the co-workers are more concerned with their individual pay than with the department's or the firm's aggregated performance.

Alvehus and Spicer (2012) speak explicitly about the use of a billable hours system in an accounting firm as a form of "financialization of working life," and their study reveals some of the externalities of the otherwise transparent performance-reward system. Alvehus and Spicer (2012) identify a number of undesirable effects from the billable hours system. First, the billable hours system did not really take into account all the costs involved in producing a service as some of the less experienced accountants tended to devalue their own work by not billing the full time worked. As reporting billable hours is a "question of self-evaluation and judgment" (Alvehus and Spicer, 2012: 501), some of the costs, perhaps mostly carried by the individual co-worker, never surfaced. Second, the use of billable hours is part of a general shift from professional work as being a civic profession to what Brint (1994: 11) calls "expert professionalism." Expert professionalism denotes expertise that, despite its professional jurisdiction, are valued and priced on the basis of the same market mechanisms and the "more hard-nosed market-oriented logic" (Alvehus and Spicer, 2012: 506) as any other form of expertise. Professionals are thus expected to sell their expertise on the market, and they are salaried in accordance with how market actors value and price their offerings. Third, Alvehus and Spicer (2012: 507) argue, the billable hours system creates a notion of time that is "only vaguely related to the clock time or to the experience of time." "An hour worked" is not always "an hour billed" and as the accountants become more skilled and experienced, they learn the hard way how to navigate the system and how to muddle through the process of avoiding projects with low-rent potentials and how to make use of "less costly colleagues," that is, newly recruited assistants, to let them do some of the routine work. While such tactical maneuvers are reasonable given the design of the system and how it encourages and rewards a concern for individual pay, it also opens up for a form of "internal labor market" that some people are perhaps more skilled in mastering than others. In other words, in the classic Marxist model of the exploitation of labor, it is the capital-owners that withhold the economic value generated from the workers, but in the billable hours system, there is also a risk that colleagues are exploiting one another's work. This represents an entirely new managerial logic wherein the free-market ideology is internalized on the individual level (Neff, 2013), not only as a generalized ideology but as an everyday life practice that needs to be skillfully executed to secure adequate compensation: "[t]he result is that working life was experienced as one large market that should be skillfully negotiated in order to reap the benefits. This suggests that not only have we seen the financialization of the economy and firms: we have also seen the financialization of workplace control" (Alvehus and Spicer, 2012: 507).

Law firms have a long tradition in letting their co-workers quite independently serve a stock of clients (Gorman and Kmec, 2009; Flood, 2007). These firms are themselves at the center of the financialized economy, as most financial transactions and operations are accompanied by juridical services such as formal contracts, Faulconbridge and Muzio (2009: 641) argue: "thanks to their central role in lubricating financial markets and activities from currency trading and the work of hedge funds, to mergers and acquisitions and the financial restructuring of transnational corporations." Not surprisingly, law firms have reported an "extraordinary increase in profitability" (Faulconbridge and Muzio, 2009: 641) as they have not only been able to generate more clients and work opportunities but also to raise their fees for their services. These law firms have used the so-called PEP model, *Profits per Equity Partner*, to measure its profitability, a model that is tightly bound up with the market evaluation of an individual jurist's performance and work. The large law firms are often privately owned and use a very hierarchical and meritocratic partnering system where financially viable and enterprising co-workers can make an internal career in the firm and eventually could become a partner. When achieving this goal, they would be entitled to a share of the aggregated profit of the firm.

Faulconbridge and Muzio (2009: 642) suggest that the "rise to pre-eminence" of PEP model is a consequence of a management logic that is similar to the shareholder value model. The measure of shareholder value creation is based on a variety of methods being developed by management consulting and accounting firms, including concepts such as Economic Value Added (EVA™), Market Added Value (MVA), Total Shareholder Return (TSR), and Cash Flow Return on Investment (CFROI) (Faulconbridge and Muzio, 2009: 643). Law firms, having their own traditions and institutionalized practices, quite distinct from the field of management consulting, have still been thoroughly penetrated by financial management practices as the for example, PEP model is implemented on a broad basis, Faulconbridge and Muzio (2009: 647) argue. In their view, the large law firms are today part of the finance industry as they have refocused their expertise on the most profitable areas of work, that is, to support and assist the globalization of the finance industry: "large law firms . . . have re-focused on a limited array of practice areas, such as capital markets and especially work associated with derivatives and 'exotic' financial products, which are closest to the logic and operations of 'finance capitalism' and which offers some of the more handsome financial rewards" (Faulconbridge and Muzio, 2009: 649).

The PEP model performance-reward system is thus closely aligned with a financialized logic making economic value extraction a central feature (Faulconbridge and Muzio, 2009: 651): "[t]he rule of the game of the financialized law firm is . . . simple: increase the number of people who bake the cake (the number of salaried lawyers) whilst stabilizing or reducing the number of people who can share the cake (the number of equity partners)" (Faulconbridge and Muzio, 2009: 651).

To maximize the economic value generated, not entirely unlike a Ponzi scheme, the partners at the top of the firm benefit from recruiting many assistants at the bottom who are more moderately compensated for their work. As a consequence, Faulconbridge and Muzio (2009: 651) suggest, "[a]n increase in associate numbers, and therefore, growing leverage ratios throughout the 1993–2003 period . . . coincides with gradual improvement of PEP." Similar to the points made by Alvehus and Spicer (2012), the financialized and individualized performance-reward model opens up for an internal labor market where the lesser paid co-workers are at risk of receiving lower compensation for the economic value they generate than is formally justified, and consequently for example, younger employees and women (still paid less than men) are the most vulnerable groups in the PEP model. Faulconbridge and Muzio (2009) summarize their research findings and remark that the economic value generated in large law firms is not only a matter of increased demand, more skilled professionals, and more efficient markets for legal services, but there is also a factor of financial engineering and managerial manipulation involved to be able to present the firm as successful and profitable:

> The extraordinary increase in profitability of large and global corporate law firms recorded . . . over the past decade are not only the result of firms generating more and more demand for the work and charging ever higher fees for their services . . . that spike in profitability are also the result of a process of financialization that has re-engineered law firms to make them appear to be ever more profitable and successful. (Faulconbridge and Muzio, 2009: 641–642)

In summary, in the era of financialization, the performance-reward system based on billable hours, originally developed among enterprising professionals that served in markets through private practices and bureaus, have gradually penetrated industries where collaborative work and information and knowledge sharing is not only needed but vital for the long-term competitiveness and survival of the firm. As individual compensation boils down to the amount that can be billed to clients, there are some undesirable effects of this new performance-reward system including opportunistic behavior to benefit individual compensation and the tendency to exploit new entrants to the profession and lower paid co-workers. Kotz (2013) addresses the consequences of this new human resource management practice, favoring individual benefits and therefore putting the collective contributions at risk:

> Under neoliberal capitalism, market principles and relations began to penetrate inside enterprises. In some sectors company officials' pay was tied to what they could demonstrate in the way of individually generated profits. Instead of a cooperative team of high-level officials, company officials began to resemble a competing group of individuals, each striving to maximize his or her own income without regard for the effects on the long-term performance of the company. (Kotz, 2013: 405)

In a way, the individualized and financialized performance-reward system is the triumph of free-market ideology as the distinction between market and hierarchy (Coase, [1937] 1991; Williamson, 1975) become porous and cease to make a practical difference: markets are now "everywhere," also inside organizations. These organizations have historically served as safe havens where economic value could be created on the basis of other logics than just the strict market-based valuation of skills and know-how. In other words, the calculative practices of the finance industry and the finance market have been enacted as a generalized model, based on the virtues of transparency, valuation, and commensuration, that suits all kinds of social activities.

THE FIRM AS A BUNDLE OF FINANCIAL ASSETS

Introduction

As has been repeated a number of times in this volume, the enactment of the firm as a bundle of financial assets has led to finance market minded managers taking on executive positions in firms and organizations. This new cadre of managers in turn ensures that the firm is regarded in favorable terms among finance market analysts and actors. In addition to the executives and directors inside the firm, located in the formal corporate

governance structure, there are finance market actors such as securities analysts that serve to prescribe managerial practices for the firms
they rate (Nicolai et al., 2010). For instance, the term "core competencies," popularized by Prahalad and Hamel (1990) in the early 1990s, an
idea that was part of a general institutional shift that put an end to the
previously widespread portfolio management models being preached
by business school professors and management consulting firms in the
1960s and 1970s (Zorn et al., 2005; Davis and Greve, 1997; Davis et al.,
1994), has been advocated by securities analysis firms. Nicolai et al.(2010:
182) suggest that "[a]nalysts play an important role in the management
fashion-setting process," while it remains unclear what more precise role
they play, for example, whether analysts act as "originators, facilitators,
or mediators of such fashions." In Nicolai et al.'s (2010: 184) view, it
is not entirely positive that securities analysts, being experts in pricing
financial assets, are taking on this role as corporate advisers, to "[d]efine
appropriate behavior and contributions to the institutionalization of new
practices." Such practices make "capital market-oriented companies"
more susceptible to the spread of fashionable management concepts than
for example, family-owned businesses (Nicolai et al., 2010: 184). If securities analysts are prone to prescribe the same management concepts for
all firms they rate, there are also greater risks for inadequate or poorly
functioning management concepts to be spread at a higher rate than they
would otherwise.

Nicolai et al.'s (2010) research findings are indicative of the tendency
to manage the firm "from the outside" as there are certain constituencies
including managers in major funds that have a lot to gain from influencing managerial behavior and decision-making. In addition, the idea of
the firm as a bundle of financial assets also nourishes a view of the firm
as not being based on synergies and what strategic management theorists
refer to as *causal ambiguities* (for example, Wilcox King and Zeithelm,
2000; Reed and DeFillippi, 1990). Instead, a mechanistic view of the firm
is taken wherein every single component of the firm can be exchanged or
eliminated at low cost. The underlying idea is that intangible resources in
particular, including for example, intellectual property rights (IPRs) and
brands, are modalities of capital – capital-not-yet-being-actualized.

Willmott (2010: 519) makes a connection between the recent interests
in brands and financialization, which he defines as "[a] contemporary
drive to subordinate and reconstitute all forms of economic activity –
consumption as well as production – in relation to its financial relevance
and significance." In the era of financialization, branding and "brandiza-
tion" are playing a key role as a "[f]unctional means of differentiating
products or services, increasing product recognition and reputation and

thereby securing or gaining market share" (Willmott, 2010: 522). Brands are intangible assets but nonetheless they are "increasingly important," Willmott (2010: 525) suggests, in the valuation of companies. This enactment of brands as a vehicle for economic value creation and extraction leads inevitably to the research question whether "[c]apital invested in branding can produce a higher rate of return than the equivalent investment in the production of goods and services" (Willmott, 2010: 525). Such a question is complicated to explain without taking into account the broader socioeconomic and institutional setting wherein brands are introduced and "managed." In the era of financialization, there is a strong belief that brands *per se*, rather than being merely *icons* (in Charles Sanders Peirce's, 1991, use of the term), symbols connected to underlying qualities and capacities, are capable of generating economic rents. Willmott (2010) exemplifies with the case of the CEO of the Korean conglomerate Samsung which in 2007 made the declaration that it had raised the "brand value" of the firm from US$15 billion in 2005 to US$16.1 billion in 2006 (Willmott, 2010: 531). Regardless of whether such claims can be substantiated, the Samsung CEO's statement is indicative of the strategic and tactic importance of brand value in the financialized economy where value is self-recurrently defined. If nothing else, it is telling of the escalating degree of intangible resources in firms, now being at an 80 percent level in the Standard & Poor 500 companies group (Pagano and Rossi, 2009).

Intellectual Property Rights and the Dangers of Over-Propertization

Given that the financialization of the economy is based on the idea of free-market efficiency, the strong focus on the virtues of IPRs and the legal protection of intangible assets is counterintuitive. As Sell (2003: 6) notices, the bundling of "free trade arguments" and the insistence on the stricter legal enforcement of property rights is a curious and seemingly contradictory operation. In the previous regime, IPRs were seen as "a necessary evil" and what is at odds with free trade, but today IPRs are one of the principal assets of the financialized firm. For Sell (2003: 28), the present regime of legal protection of intellectual properties has swung too far in the other direction, and today constitutes an impediment for the exploitation of new ideas and research findings: "[w]hile endorsing IP-rights in principle, believing that they are both necessary and important, I maintain that the balance between private rights and public access has shifted too far in favour of private rights at the expense of the public weal." Commentators like Mirowski (2011: 114) speaks of "the egregious fortification of IP" as being a major challenge for the economy in the future as virtually all new research findings are surrounded by dense legal protection. In terms of

being an empirical phenomenon, there are many studies testifying to the
sheer growth of patents:

> The last two decades saw a vast increase in patents. The United States Patent
> and Trademark Office (USPTO) granted 76,748 patents in 1985, 107,124 in
> 1991, and 221,437 in 2002. A similar development happened in Europe. There
> were 42,957 applicants for patents in 1985, 60,148 in 1991 and 110,640 in 2002
> at the European Patent Office (EPO) ... From 1990 to 2000, the number of
> patents granted in biotechnology rose 15 percent a year at the USPTO and 10.5
> percent at the EPO. (Zeller, 2008: 93–94)

Also in the university setting, originally developed as intellectual centers
conducting research beyond short-term private interests, Powell and
Snellman (2004: 204) report an eightfold increase in university patents
in the period 1976–1998, testifying to an institutional shift from science
as a "communal resource" in Robert Merton's (1973) use of the term, to
the university as a rent-seeking actor anxious to protect its intellectual
properties. One of the researchers participating in the research work that
was subject to Stanford University's patenting of the recombinant DNA
developed by Stanley N. Cohen and Herbert W. Boyer at the University of
California at San Francisco, objected to this shift:

> 'I don't want to sign a letter saying that I was just another laboratory worker,'
> commented a University of Michigan professor to nature in 1980 when the
> now famous recombinant DNA patents were under scrutiny ... The patent-
> ing process, which required disclaimers on the patenting application from co-
> authors and other scientists that they were not investors, contravened scientific
> conventions of dissemination and credit. (Colyvas and Powell, 2007: 222)

Stanley N. Cohen admitted that he had not "dreamed of the notion of
patenting this" (cited in Smith Hughes, 2001: 548), and Herbert W. Boyer
experienced personal hostility for his participation in the two universities'
work to orchestrate institutional changes that would help them capitalize on commercial opportunities derived from the research in the field of
molecular biology (Smith Hughes, 2001: 558).

Owen-Smith (2006) addresses how the historical distinction between the
university's production of publications and industry's filing of patents has
today become blurred. Both publications and patents serve as "markers of
accomplishments" and "means to disseminate information," Owen-Smith
(2006: 70) argues. The term *ownership* is applicable in both cases, but there
are major differences that need to be recognized and properly understood.
In the case of publications, the academic researchers' privilege and prerog-
ative, "ownership" is translated into reputation and rewards derived from
others' uses of an author's findings. That is, Owen-Smith (2006: 70) says,

articles have no presumption of "exclusivity." In contrast, propriety ownership conveys a bundle of rights. First, what Owen-Smith (2006: 70) calls *excludability*, "the right to prevents others' use of your property," and second, *appropriability*, "the right to capture economic returns from the use of your property." These two rights are operating along lines diverging from the "ownership" accruing from publications, and therefore the shift from publications to patents represents a new regime of university-based research and rent-seeking. Previously, Owen-Smith (2006: 70–71) writes, "publications were the territory of academics, and patents were concentrated to industry," but in the new regime, these boundaries are porous and fluid. While there is enthusiasm in certain quarters regarding the new role of the university (for example, Berman, 2012, who speaks of universities as veritable "economic engines" in the present period), there are others that are deeply concerned about the deinstitutionalization of the university system (Lorenz, 2012; Mirowski, 2011; Stevens et al., 2008; Khurana, 2007; Washburn, 2005; Apple, 2004; Bok, 2002). One of the drivers for this change has been, some commentators argue, the shift in funding from university endowments to major foundations being operated on the basis of business principles and therefore demanding adequate returns on investment in basic research work: "[t]he large foundations were . . . carrying business methods and managerial values from the world of large corporations into academic science," Kohler (1991: 396, cited in Mirowski, 2011: 102) suggests.

While universities and their patenting activities may be one specific case being of great interest per se, it is the legal protection of firm's R&D work that creates barriers for the full exploitation of research findings, several scholars suggest. Boldrin and Levine (2004) are strongly critical of how IPRs are being granted in the present era, leading to what they refer to as an "over-propertization" of intangible resources: "[i]In fact intellectual property may be damaging for innovation, growth, and overall social welfare; the monopoly profits generated by intellectual property have played, and still play, a much more secondary role than is commonly believed in determining the rate and pace of economic progress" (Boldrin and Levine, 2004: 328).

The expansion of IPRs is based, Boldrin and Levine (2004: 329) argue, on the faulty presumption that new ideas have a "near-zero marginal costs of reproducing and distributing them," which in turn would lead to a situation, in the absence of robust property rights, where "there will be no output of new ideas." This syllogism is based on the assumption that novel thinking is easily acquired and put into operations that in turn generate rents, but this assumption is neither theoretically credible, nor supported by empirical data: "[g]iven the huge literature on technology transfer, there is no mystery in the fact that it is costly to transfer productive knowledge. The mystery is: why do conventional economic theories of innovation ignore this fact?," Boldrin and Levine (2004: 333) write.

Zeller (2008: 93–94) takes this line of argument further and proposes that the "explosive expansion of intellectual property monopolies" is not so much the effect of technological breakthrough as the consequence of "far-reaching economic and institutional changes linked to the emergence of a finance dominated accumulation regime." This regime, for instance in the field of life sciences and in the specific branch of biotech, is on the one hand based on public R&D expenditure "effectuated by governments and their educational systems" (Zeller, 2008: 101–102), while on the other hand, based on the "private appropriation" of the research findings, in many cases encouraged by governments. The matrix of openness/closure and private/public in life science venturing thus represents a new regime of knowledge production and rent-seeking anchored in financialization, Zeller (2008: 106) suggests: "[t]he regime of intellectual property monopolies in the context of finance-dominated accumulation regime impedes potentials for innovation and favors an enormous squandering of human and material resources." This provocative statement regarding the externalities of patenting demands some further explanation. In Zeller's (2008) view, IPRs are designed to enable risk-taking and the production of new know-how that can be transformed into new products and commodities. Paired with a free-market ideology with its emphasis on free trade and the unregulated flow of capital across national borders, IPRs are supposed to constitute the infrastructure of the high-growth, innovative economy where productive resources are put to their best use. Seen in an international perspective, this new legal environment works poorly. "In 1993, only ten countries accounted for 84 percent of worldwide research and development expenditure and collected more than 90 percent of the cross-border license fees," Zeller (2008: 109) writes. In 2001, the situation was basically the same: "[c]ompanies in the capitalist metropolises received 97 percent of the license payments in 2001. This corresponds to 71 billion USD every year" (Zeller, 2008: 109). In practice, then, IPRs serve to protect the interests of firms and actors located in the capitalist centers and there are few opportunities for, for example, countries with low patenting activity to benefit from new knowledge. In addition, Pagano and Rossi (2009: 670) write, the very idea of "patentability" has gradually expanded, and now virtually everything under the sun can be subject to IPRs, a tendency that further ossifies economic activities as actors that increasingly tread ground that is criss-crossed with legal rights. As detailed by Calvert (2008) and Bonaccorsi et al. (2011), patent laws were originally developed to help engineers protect their mechanical inventions from being copied, but in today's advanced life science research, the original patent laws addressing artifacts and devices are in cases poorly suited to handle the abstract biological pathways and mechanisms that are filed for legal protection.

The Two Forms of Private Equity Investment

Investing in existing business activities: private equity buyouts

While many companies in advanced capitalists economies are so-called *public companies*, traded on the stock exchange and open for anyone to buy shares, there is also a substantial private equity market in the era of financialization. To simplify a quite complex issue, one can say that private equity investments appear in two forms: as *buyout activities* and as *venture capital investment*. The buyout activities normally involve a much larger stock of capital than venture capital investment. Buyout investment denotes the process wherein private equity investors and often a management team pool their own money together with debt finance to buy the shares of a company from its current owners. The owners are paid a premium above the market price as an incentive to sell their shares. After a certain time, the private equity investors resell the company and distribute the divestment gains to their business partners and keep their share of the profit (Bacon et al., 2010: 1344). Venture capital investment is investment in small and growing firms that have the potential to develop a new product or service. The private equity investors supplying venture capital make their profit from selling the company on what is commonly addressed as an *exit market*, that is, larger, multinational companies willing to acquire the skills, competence, and above all the IPRs of the start-up firm. While venture capital investment is by and large treated as a business activity that rests on expertise and the capacity to anticipate and predict the future value of the start-up firm, its know-how, and IPRs, buyout activities are at times seen in a less favorable light (Bacon et al., 2010). For instance, numerous commentators and union representatives argue that buyout activities easily rest on what Rodrigues and Child (2010: 1331, Table 1) call an "extraction strategy" rather than a "renewal strategy," that is, the new private equity-based owners do not take a long-term perspective on the firms they own but are instead focusing on maximizing the value that can be extracted from the future sale of the firm. Bacon et al. (2010) argue that these risks are exaggerated on the basis of survey research data. Contrary to buyout activities leading to firms being slimmed down to extract value benefiting finance market actors, Bacon et al. (2010) report four empirical findings: (1) private equity investors do not intervene into existing industrial relations issues, that is, unions are not treated

differently in the new regime; (2) rather than extracting value from the firm
through cost reductions, many private equity firms increase the value of
their investment by "focusing on customer service and developing highly
trained and experienced personnel" (Bacon et al., 2010: 1362); (3) rather
than reducing the number of jobs, most private equity buyouts create jobs,
further creating a positive climate for economic activities; and (4) private
equity buyouts are more welcome than the alternative of closure or sale
to a competitor with a "non-union culture" (Bacon et al., 2010: 1362).
Despite these concerns regarding the research design of the study,[3] Bacon
et al.'s (2010) research still indicates that buyout activities are not necessarily, as critics at times assume, short-term and value extraction-oriented. In
order to create a value in the companies invested in, the new owners must
assure that they oversee well-functioning operations; operations riddled by
conflicts as such poorly managed activities would prevent future investors
from buying the company, the functionalist explanation proposes.

Investing for renewal: venture capital
At least until the mid-1970s, universities have served as public institutions that conduct basic research on basis of research grants from state-
controlled funds and foundations. By the late 1960s, universities realized
that there was great economic potential in research findings, and that
they would benefit from being able to patent these research findings. The
changes in the regulatory control of basic research work and the advancement of the university as a rent-seeking actor, sharing many interests with
any company, represents a gradual and stepwise shift in institutional logic.
The passing of the Bayh-Dole Act in 1980 is commonly portrayed as a
major event in establishing a new role for the university as an economic
actor in its own right (Grimaldi et al., 2011; Mazzoleni, 2011; Berman,
2008; Rafferty, 2008; Mowery and Ziedonis, 2002). "[U]niversity-based
science efforts are now linked to industry ... [and] government agencies are playing an increasingly central role in managing and facilitating
the process of technological development," Block and Keller (2009: 463)
write, emphasizing the key role of basic research in the national and
regional innovation system. For the proponents of the new role of the
university (for example, Berman, 2012), the new regulatory regime enables
fruitful collaboration across the university-industry border, benefiting

---

[3] Bacon et al.'s (2010) study is unfortunately based on the belief that managers are in the
best position to answer questions regarding the new owners and the implication for the
company. This design is particularly problematic when it comes to trade union activities
and influence that would demand a freestanding response from trade union representatives,
not salaried managers.

both economic growth and, in the case of for example, life sciences, the development of new therapies and research methods. For critics, the new situation is more complicated as private enterprises are given the right to exploit publicly funded research, indicating a transfer of economic value from a public to a private domain. Pitts-Taylor (2010: 642) uses the term *biomediated capitalism*, and Cooper (2008: 10) makes a connection between a free-market neoliberalism agenda and the increased activities to exploit public basic research work through the vehicle of private enterprises. In Cooper's view, the free-market ideology, successfully advanced by neoliberal and neoconservative intellectuals, is the primus motor behind the shift in institutional logic from public research as a common good to privately owned assets protected by IPRs.

Regardless of what view is taken, there is a strong tendency to translate basic research findings into both IPRs and start-up companies that in turn are supposed to either grow organically or to produce research findings and/or products that have an economic value for certain market actors. In other words, life sciences in particular are increasingly conceived of as business ventures and are being valued in terms of how much financial capital such new start-ups and ventures will initially require and eventually how much economic value can be extracted from the initial investment made by for example, a venture capital firm or a state-controlled innovation agency. In short, basic life science research is financialized.

This financialized, generic business venture model is not only applicable to basic research findings and start-up firms but is also of relevance for Big Pharma, the multinational pharmaceutical industry. The pharmaceutical industry today generates high amounts of cash flow but is still dependent on finance market assessments and funding to maintain its activities, Andersson et al. (2010) argue. In addition, in order to secure future cash flow, financing further R&D work and maintaining high levels of shareholder value creation, approvals from the US Food and Drug Administration (USFDA) and similar national regulatory bodies are of vital importance. These dependencies on both finance markets and regulatory authorities in combination with the complexities in predicting what new drugs will make it to the market, that is, being able to demonstrate adequate levels of efficacy and safety in the eyes of expert regulators, leads to new drug development as having, Andersson et al. (2010: 640) suggest, "Casino-like features" (see also Sinn, 2010). There are so many factors to consider when it comes to the decision of what new candidate drugs to select for further clinical testing that it becomes difficult to decide where to invest the R&D money. "The chances of success of an early-stage drug are unpredictable and financial loss is the most likely outcome," Andersson et al. (2010: 640) remark (see also Gleadle et al., 2014). As will be discussed below, this seemingly stochastic variance in outcomes, the distribution between "hits and misses" is also a major concern in venture capital investment in life science venturing. This condition leads to the paradoxical situation where the "financialized start-up firm" – that is, the principal rationale for investing in a specific start-up firm derives from the estimate of how much value can theoretically be extracted from the investment – is frequently being starved of capital. The outcome is that most developed economies are struggling to supply venture capital investment to what Joseph Schumpeter ([1928] 1991a: 65–66) speaks of as the "entrepreneurial function" of competitive capitalism.

Venture capital and innovation
Venture capital firms invest in life science ventures in order to extract economic value from their investment. Therefore, new therapies are favored but life science start-ups are more likely to acquire an economic value prior to the registering of new therapies if they are bought by a major pharmaceutical or medical technology firm or can license their IPRs, making the venture capital investment quite a complex procedure. The term *venture capital* was first used by the American chemical company DuPont, and was officially introduced into the economic vocabulary in a *Wall Street Journal* editorial on January 13, 1938 (Kenney, 2011: 1686). Venture capital is defined accordingly: "[t]he process of external equity finance by professional investors in a new or young (that is, early stage) company to create new assets for the primary purpose of reaping substantial economic gains through a market flotation [initial public offering, IPO] or trade sale" (BCVA-NESTA, cited in Hopkins et al., 2013: 907). For the proponents of what we here can call the venture capital model of life science venturing, venture capitalists provide expertise and extended network contacts to start-up firms, often with only limited managerial competence and commercial human resources. Samila and Sorenson (2010: 1350) represent such a view: "venture capitalists provide more than mere funding for innovation. These professionals screen ideas and inventions to determine which have the greatest market potential, help to connect inventors to make business-minded individual, and advise the companies in which they invest" (Samila and Sorenson, 2010: 1350). "Venture capitalists provide legal, financial, and strategic advice, and help to connect entrepreneurs to talent, buyers and suppliers," Samila and Sorenson (2010: 1350) add. In conducting this work, venture capital investors, Samila and Sorenson (2010: 1350) claim, "[h]elp to improve the entrepreneurial abilities not only of the few that they fund but also of the larger community in which they reside." That is, Samila and Sorenson (2010: 1349) take an "ecosystem view" on venture capital investors,

suggesting that analysts need to examine the entire ecosystem wherein venture capital firms operate, including the role of "government, educational institutions, and industry play complementary roles." As a corollary from this, venture capital investors operate primarily on a regional level as they often confront "[d]ifficulties that investors in more mature companies do not" (Samila and Sorenson, 2010: 1351), including intricate national regulatory systems, idiosyncratic corporate law, and various bureaucratic procedures and routines demanding expertise and local knowledge. The exception from this are cases of *syndicated investment* when venture capital firms co-invest with other venture capital firms with detailed understanding of the local setting (Deli and Santhanakrishnan, 2010; Kogut et al., 2007; Wright and Lockett, 2003; Sorenson and Stuart, 2001).

A quite significant literature seeks to verify a positive relation between venture capital investment and the degree of patenting in an economy to underline the economic value of venture capital firms. Kertum and Lerner (2000: 674) suggest that "venture capital is associated with a substantial increase in patenting." In addition, they regard venture capital as the driver of economic growth rather than it being its foremost effect: "[T]he results suggests that venture funding does have a strong positive impact on innovation . . . a dollar of venture capital appears to be about three times more potent in stimulating patenting than a dollar of traditional R&D" (Kertum and Lerner, 2000: 675). In their history of the triumph of venture capital investment, there was a dramatic increase of venture capital in the late 1970s and early 1980s (Kertum and Lerner, 2000: 676), but this inflow of capital did not translate into increasing patenting activity on a short-term basis. Instead, patenting declined from the early 1970s to the mid-1980s, but thereafter it "rose sharply" (Kertum and Lerner, 2000: 678). Macroeconomic changes and the Federal Reserve's high-interest policy in the 1980s arguably played a role here, but Kertum and Lerner (2000) offer little explanation for the increased interest in venture capital investment in the period. For instance, by the late 1970s, there were institutional and regulatory changes in the finance markets that benefited the development of a venture capital market: "[t]he funding for venture capital has come mainly from US pension funds and insurance companies. Since 1979 they have been allowed to include some high-risk investments in their portfolios and by the late 1990s held $1 of venture capital for every $100 of public traded equity" (Feng et al., 2001: 499).

Nevertheless, the changes in terms of capital supply were significant: by 1984, Gorman and Sahlman (1989: 231) write, "in excess of $4.5 billion of new capital was committed to the industry, an amount of over six times greater than the amount committed in 1980."

Despite intense scholarly interests for venture capital and venture capital investors (Leyshon and Thrift, 2007: 102), there are critical discussions regarding the efficacy of venture capital investment. On average, venture capital funds write off 75.3 percent of their investments (Hochberg et al., 2007: 262), which means that rents derive from a small subset of portfolio companies. While investments that lead to no significant rent for the venture capital investor may still benefit the economy at large, there is always a risk of overinvestment in start-up firms. For instance, in the mid-1980s, returns on venture capital investment declined, arguably on the basis of the entry of inexperienced venture capitalists, squandering capital in ventures with limited potential (Gompers and Lerner, 2001: 149). As demonstrated by Rider and Swaminathan (2012: 178), the presence of such inexperienced or unqualified venture capitalist investors may be quite significant as a large percentage of venture capital firms "raised only one fund." The consequence is that venture capital investment, often treated in neoclassic economic theory as a "pure form" of capital investment in the high-growth sectors constituting the entrepreneurial core of competitive capitalism, is made with less precision than is widely assumed: "entrepreneurs and institutional investors might mistakenly infer that the market for venture capital is more munificent than it actually is at any given point in time," Rider and Swaminathan (2012: 178) conclude. The high risks of venture capital investments reduce the aggregated return on capital invested. As a consequence, venture capital is only available for a very, very small group of "elite start-up firms" controlling the right resources and skills and with favorable market prospects being valued by venture capital investors:

> VC is an extremely expensive source of risk capital for the investee firm, only suitable for a tiny minority of firms, and VCs are demanding investors . . . who can only operate when exit routes are available and place intense pressure on their investee forms to increase in value during a short period. (Hopkins et al., 2013: 908)

In life sciences, time and again portrayed as a knowledge-intensive, high-growth industry, based on unique scientific and clinical know-how and skills – the "perfect match" for venture capital investment by any formal standard – remain a field being starved of venture capital as the immense complexities of the human biological system make the inevitable and costly clinical trials very much an unpredictable activity whose outcomes can mercilessly and momentarily sweep away the market value of a firm (Burrill, 2012). In addition to the sheer complexity involved in the research work and the difficulties this entails for the approval process, there are today fewer exit opportunities for venture capitalists as multinational pharmaceutical and medical technology companies become more conservative investors. Previously, start-up firms demonstrating clinical data that indicate good efficacy and safety of the new therapy were frequently acquired by the major firms in the field, but today a shortage of capital has shrunk the exit market for venture capital investors:

> Ventures investors are no longer willing or able to fund companies with an indefinite exit. Instead, they are waiting later to fund companies, building exits into their investments from the start, and looking to innovative technologies other than therapeutics that can address medical and healthcare system needs, but provide a more predictable path to revenue. (Burrill, 2012: 5)

In addition, in the life sciences, regardless of what free-market proponents of venture capital investments like Lerner (2009) say, the government and the state have large roles to play in funding the underlying basic research and in orchestrating the development of entrepreneurial activities in academic life science research (Keller and Block, 2013). In the life sciences, there are intricate and dense relations between public sector activities and private capital investment, not always fully recognized by mainstream venture capital researchers.

In summary, venture capital investment is based on the idea of private equity effectively being able to exploit the market opportunities based on expertise and market experience. At the same time, venture capital is dependent on the government and the state, both making initial large-scale investment in basic research and in discounting many of the risks involved in venture capital investment, making a private-public collaboration the *sine qua non* of venture capital markets. For the proponents of venture capital, this specific form of private equity investment is what propels the entrepreneurial function of competitive capitalism, while for critics, it is playing only a most marginal role in selecting the most profitable ventures from a stock of public investment in research activities. Under all conditions, the venture capital model is strongly reliant on the image of the firm as a bundle of financial assets that can be used to extract economic value, and the venture capital investment model is therefore granted high prestige in the era of financialization. Not only do venture capital investors serve to exploit the market opportunities created by public investment, they do also (in a smaller number of cases) generate wealth for themselves and their partners. Venture capital investors thus embody two praised virtues of competitive capitalism, that of renewal and capital accumulation.

SUMMARY AND CONCLUSIONS

While Chapter 4 examined corporate governance practices, paying specific attention to the rights and responsibilities of organizational stakeholders, and Chapter 5 detailed how managerial control has been located outside of the firm, in auditing companies and rating agencies, this chapter addresses how the financialized firm structure organizes its resources in accordance with the predominant view of the firm as a bundle of financial assets and accompanying juridical contracts. First of all, employees are today treated as enterprising and entrepreneurial subjects, paid on the basis of their human capital investments and their ability to create wealth for their employer. As a consequence, compensation becomes no longer based on collective bargaining but on the individual's promotion of oneself within an increasingly competitive sphere. Studies of economic compensation point at increasingly higher pay for CEOs, directors, and finance market actors, while the real wages for many income groups have stagnated over the last decades. In addition, the day-to-day work activities are increasingly structured in accordance with a generalized finance market model wherein each employee's individual contribution to the creation of economic value is monitored and assessed. This economic compensation regime creates an "internal finance market" that opens up for and rewards behaviors that may counteract collaborative efforts. Moreover, in the new view of the firm, resources such as IPRs, brands, and know-how generate economic value. Venture capital investors, for instance, play the role of pricing such resources and thus serve to supply finance capital to entrepreneurs creating tomorrow's companies and employers. Taken together, the financialization of the economy and the firm has led to substantial changes in how firms are managed and how they are understood not so much as organizations embedded in social relationships but as financial assets that hold the promise to generate economic value.

7. Concluding remarks: the financialized firm and its implication

INTRODUCTION

> Economic ideas provide agents with an interpretative framework, which describes and accounts for the workings of the economy by defining its constitutive elements and 'proper' (and therefore 'improper') interrelations. Economic ideas provide agents with both scientific and a normative account of the existing economy and polity, and a vision that specifies how these elements *should* be constructed. That is, economic ideas also act as blueprints of new institutions. In sum, ideas allow agents to reduce uncertainty, propose a particular solution to a moment of crisis, and empower agents to resolve that crisis by constructing new institutions in line with these new ideas.
>
> Mark Blyth (2002: 11)

When the communist economies in Eastern and central Europe collapsed at the end of the 1980s, after a long process of gradual decline of the planned economic regime of accumulation, Western Center–Right intellectuals were ready to boldly announce that market liberalism has once and for all defeated not only communism and socialism in the Marxist-Leninist tradition, but *all other* conceivable economic systems. Market liberalism and its institutions (at times referred to with the term the Washington consensus) was now, at the end of history, treated as the only credible, vital politico-economic system. Whether such prophecies will be fulfilled remain to be seen, but there is precious little that indicates a robustness of the present politico-economic system given the decline in economic growth, increased economic inequality, and the high levels of debt produced in the incumbent system. Market liberals and social democrats both denounced authoritarian societies based on Marxist doctrines. Social democrats, in particular, were the first and most persistent critics of communism and were in many countries the *de facto* "shock absorbers" counteracting a radicalization of the labor community through social reforms. But the mistake the market liberals, neoliberals, neoconservatives, and others celebrating what they regarded as the triumph of free-market capitalism was to think that capitalism would be able to regulate itself: such a model ignored or vastly underrated the social embedding of capital and the role of the sovereign state. As Martin (2014: 26) says, in today's economic system, capital in the form of currency is "ephemeral and cosmetic," but the underlying mechanism of "credit accounts and clearing" is "the essence of money":

> [T]he official paraphernalia of banks and credit cards and solemnly printed notes with unforgeable insignia is not what is essential to money. All of that can disappear and yet money still remains: a system of credit and debt, ceaselessly expanding and contracting like a beating heart, sustaining the circulation of trade. (Martin, 2014: 28)

Capital as the mechanism that regulate social relations based on credit is the lifeblood of capitalism, its cause and effect, its maid and its master; it is what both circulates and what remains the solid foundation of the present economic regime. Capital is not so much the mere exchange medium of the capitalist economic system as it is, in Aristotelian terms, its *substance*. In contrast, for free-market protagonists such as Friedrich von Hayek and Milton Friedman, it is the *market*, the locus where all information pertaining to the circulation of capital is assembled, integrated, and visualized as prices, that is the principal site for capital circulation and accumulation (see also Fourcade and Healy, 2007; Hirschman, 1982, 1977). For Hayek and Friedman, the market is a Platonist *chora*, the primordial site that precedes everything else, that which, "lacking any substance or identity of its own, falls in between the ideal and the material" (Grosz, 2001: 91) – the very *ursprung* of all economic activities. Regardless whether the analysis of capital (*qua* money, that is, credit) or the market should dominate the analysis of the financialization of the economy and the firm, there are predominant economic ideas[1] (Blyth, 2002) that structure the work to build institutions, to negotiate regulatory frameworks and legal frameworks, and to implement managerial practices that effectively render the firm as a bundle of financial assets:

> Without theories of how economic, political, and social worlds work – theories that vary among groups and over time – it will not often be clear that what

---

[1] In the policy literature, what Blyth (2002: 11) speaks of as *ideas* denotes a variety of cognitive resources that structure and provide coherence to abstract policy-making, including what Schmidt (2008: 306–307) speaks of as *cognitive ideas* and *normative ideas*, or what Campbell (2002: 27) refers to as *cognitive paradigms* or *frames*. The literature thus proposes a series of competing and/or complementing terms, but in this setting, the term *idea* proposed by Blyth (2002) is used. Berman and Milanes-Reyes (2013) discuss one such "economic idea," the Laffer curve, being a central model in the Reaganomics program, as being one such inherently fluid and changing idea that served many purposes over time in policy-making, beginning (for some) as a theoretical proposition regarding taxation and economic growth and ending (for some) as a form of joke or an indication of the failed economic policy of the Reagan Administration.

policy options will help advance one's interests, and thus what actions one should take. These theories, moreover, are not absolute truths, but can be contingent, evolving, and the product of larger worldviews. (Berman and Pagnucco, 2010: 366)

Economic ideas thus always represent interests and beliefs, regardless of whether they are advanced as substantiated and empirically verified theories and propositions, or if they are policy recommendations issued by think tanks and lobbyist groups, making it complicated to turn a blind eye to the social and political processes accompanying all institutionalization processes.

A substantial literature, not the least in economic sociology, has criticized the neoclassic economic theory corpus for the ontologization of the market, the inscription of certain universal and irreducible qualities onto this site of exchanges. In an economic sociology view, markets are the accomplishments of humans, technologies, regulatory and legal frameworks, and scripts and practices being aligned and coordinated to enable transactions over time and space; markets are never "always already in place" but need to be constructed, and a sovereign (the king, the state, and so on) needs to actively discount some of the risks before market transactions and capital accumulation can occur. This is a view that strongly contrasts against the neoclassic view that assumes the presence of markets as a Euclidian axiomatic principle, leading to a marginal interest for the collective efforts to constitute markets. In an economic sociology perspective on markets and their role in competitive capitalism, stressing the importance of market-makers and market-making *per se*, the Marxist and historians' concern for what capital is and how capital can transduce into many different forms become yet another aspect of how human beings jointly define and construct the means necessary to enable economic activities and exchanges. In this view, capital must be understood as what aligns and coordinates a series of activities across individual actors and organizational fields. The study of the financialization of the firm does therefore not primarily rely on the analysis of how capital is one unified resource that is manifested in many places throughout competitive capitalism, but must also examine how a variety of practices and activities are enabled, made legitimate, and generate economic value through their alignment with capital.

In this final chapter, some of the remaining issues to be addressed are highlighted, including some reflections regarding the drivers of the financialization of the economy and the firm. In addition, some theoretical and managerial implications of the financialization of the economy and the firm will be discussed.

DRIVERS OF FINANCIALIZATION: THE POWER ELITE THESIS

Elites in Capitalism

> The goose that lays golden eggs has been considered a most valuable posses-sion. But even more profitable is the privilege of taking the golden eggs laid by somebody else's goose. The investment bankers and their associates now enjoy that privilege. They control the people through the people's own money. If banker's power were commensurate only with their wealth, they would have relatively little influence on American businesses . . . The power and the growth of power of our financial oligarchs comes from wielding the savings and quick capital of others . . . the fetters which bind the people are forged from the people's own gold.
> Louis D. Brandeis ([1914] 1967: 12–13)

> A rich fool is rich; a poor fool is a fool.
> Michel Serres (1982: 229)

Social theorists such as economic sociologists have examined how the political system is influenced by economic interests and more specifically the role of capital owners in shaping political agendas and policy-making (Schifling, 2013, Martin, 2010; Burris, 2001; Jenkins and Eckert, 2000). The literature suggests that while the business community represents diverse interests and at times has faced problems in advocating policies that benefit all industries with different demands, the business community and capital owners have still managed to play a key role in shaping the political agenda in the US, especially after the mid-1970s mobilization of the business community. In contrast, speaking more specifically of organi-zation and management studies, Maclean et al. (2014: 847) remark that the concept of class – here discussed in terms of *social elites* – has "disap-peared" from organization theory (see also Barley, 2007, and Eztion and Davis, 2008), partly due to the absence of "more nuanced class categories grounded in contemporary social and organizational realities." This igno-rance of social class and elites is unfortunate as, Maclean et al. (2014: 847) write, "[s]ocial class plays a persistent role in the selection mechanisms which determine who holds sway in the corporate elite and, ultimately, society at large." In the following, some of the "mechanisms" underlying the financialization of the firm will be examined in more detail.

As Kundera (1988: 127) points out, the concepts of "elitism" and "elitist" appeared in France only in the late 1960s, and for the first time in history, "the very language threw a glare of negativity, even of mis-trust, on the notion of elite." While elite in everyday language denotes the most qualified individuals within a more confined domain of expertise (in for example, the sporting world) or a more general term denoting for example, political, economic, or cultural elites; in a sociological vocabulary elites signifies particular groups that have the capacity to enroll various resources to protect their interests and/or to advance their positions. The everyday word "elite" is also to various degrees used in different languages, and while for example, the French and Americans appear to use elites in a quite casual manner, in egalitarian societies such as in Scandinavia, the word elite is a delicate and politically charged term only used with great care and is therefore primarily used in the sporting world and to characterize for example, certain military operations demanding specialized training. In addition, in a country like Sweden, elites may be tolerated while "elitism," its corollary term, is treated with a great deal of skepticism. These cultural differences taken aside, there is a quite substantial literature that regards the financialization of the economy and the firm as being bound up with elites' mobilization to restore class privileges and the right to control productive resources. At the same time, the era of financialization also served to establish new professional communities and groups that were marginalized or simply not yet existing (for example, hedge fund managers) prior to the expansion of the finance capital base. In the following, these activities leading to financialization will be examined from the perspective of what Charles Wright Mills (1956) referred to as the "power elites."

The term *power* is one of the trickiest and most amorphous terms in the social science vocabulary (see for example, Hindess, 1996; Lukes, 1986), and it is beyond the scope of this volume to review this literature. In this setting, we follow Mills (1959: 40): "'Power', as the term is now generally used in social sciences, has to do with whatever decisions men make about the arrangements under which they live, and about the events which make up the history of that period." In Mills' (1959) view, power elites in society have the capacity to practically influence how decisions are made so that they themselves would benefit from the outcome and the consequences. The very concept of power elites, or, more shortly, elites, is based on the idea of social classes having different abilities to mobilize resources that influence decisions in their favour. The very idea of class, in turn, Dahrendorf (1959: 96) makes clear, is bound up with the idea of "conflict" and "conflict of interests"; these notions are closely aligned with the "heuristic purpose of concept and theory of class." Elites are social classes, and social classes endure a conflictual co-existence, these propositions state. In the history of the modernization of the national state, beginning with the industrialization of the economy in the period from the late eighteenth century in Britain to the mid- to late-nineteenth century in many other parts of continental Europe and Scandinavia, these troubled social relations have been mediated by the development of a political system and a bureaucratic state apparatus, demonstrating a remarkable capacity, in Karl Mannheim's phrasing (cited in Bendix, 1971: 148), "to turn all problems of politics into problems of administration." Consequently, the economic growth and the rise in living standard over the last one and a half centuries are co-evolutionary with the differentiation of a modern state apparatus. This apparatus has been developed and designed to respond to democratic ideals regarding representation, economic equality, and justice, and yet the story of the financialization of the economy and the firm is exemplary in how elites have been able to get their interests recognized and turned into legal and regulatory action. Crouch (2012: 47) is concerned about these changes in the political system, increasingly subsumed under economic interests and arguments. In a free economy, economic wealth can easily be converted into political influence, and private money can be invested in campaigns to influence public opinion, and even to own and control newspapers and other media to support such campaigns. If financialization is defined as the expansion of finance markets, then scholars should be examining the question: how did these changes came about, that is, what resources were mobilized and how were the political and regulatory bodies tuned to the interests of certain groups?

"A society is called capitalist if it entrusts its economic process to the guidance of the private businessman," Schumpeter ([1928] 1991b: 189) states. Few mainstream commentators would question the remarkable advancements made during the last two centuries and their implications for social well-being and the rise in life expectancy rates. However, as Mulholland (2012: 303) says, "the rich always betrays the poor," and consequently capitalism and capitalists needs to be protected against themselves in order to organize a sustainable economy. "Political economies of power and being are fundamentally relational. Power results from relative position in an objectified hierarchical order where the distribution of resources and opportunities favors those at the top," Owen-Smith (2006: 66) writes, underlining how the elite group may take advantage of initial favorable positions. The concern is that in the era of financialization, propelled by free-market economic ideas (Levitt, 2013a, 2013b), the business enterprise becomes "the model for all social relations" (Lazzarato, 2012: 181).

A few historical studies of capitalist economic systems and their decline may shed further light on how economic, political, and social concerns need to be balanced and continually renegotiated to avoid one group getting the upper hand. Expressed in institutional theory terms but also consistent with social exchange theory (Blau, 1964), Yue et al. (2013: 38) say that "managing mutual dependence between social groups is critical for maintaining institutional stability." In their study of the Manhattan banking community, Yue et al. (2013: 39) argue that a "high level of network cohesion" facilitates coordination and "helps elites to better govern private institutions to their group interest." As a consequence, elites have strong incentives to maintain a high level of exclusivity and to "[d]eny the out-groups equal opportunities for participation in an attempt to monopolize institutional benefits" (Yue et al., 2013: 39). At the same time, elites that follow this instinct ignore the fact "that the stability of competitive environments rests on a delicate distributional balance with the out-group [that is, non-elite groups]." When certain groups are excluded for too long as for example, meritocratic systems are overruled by nepotistic systems for the allocation of life chances, social relations and market conditions deteriorate and throw the market into a crisis. Therefore, Yue et al. (2013) suggest, that there needs to be institutions that regulate and control so that at least a minimal degree of equal opportunities can be maintained to avoid institutional instabilities. At the same time, institutional stabilization is "not necessarily an automatic process but rests on ongoing mobilization both within the institutionally advantaged group and between them and other social groups," Yue et al. (2013: 39) argue. In other words, in order to maintain its position as elites, elite groups need to tolerate an inflow of non-elite individuals into their community; such an inflow is not self-organizing as there are strong incentives to protect inherited privileges, and therefore there is a need for securing qualified and informed regulatory bodies that monitor the activities. Yue et al. (2013) here outline a generic model for how elites can benefit from the use of regulatory bodies, and this argument regarding an effective balance between openness and closure can be applied to the case of financialization.

Driver of Financialization: Policy Enforcement

Following Yue et al. (2013), an institutional perspective can be taken to examine the financialization of the firm. Lawrence et al., (2013: 1029) use the term *institutional work*, defined as "[p]urposive action aimed at affecting institutions," to examine changes in organizations. A substantial body of literature suggests that institutional work played a decisive role in advancing the financialization of the economy. Schmidt et al. (2012: 76, original emphasis) use the term "big politics" to understand how actors seek to "formally codify and instiutionalise *political* decisions, values and actions." In operational terms, "big politics" is "institutionalized in obdurate networks of ideologies, elections, parliaments, parties, lobby groups – think tanks, trade unions, mayors, and campaigns" (Schmidt et al., 2012:

76). All these big politics actors are engaged in influencing the regulatory and legislative practices in Washington and other political centers. First, there are examples of how regulatory control is informed by particular interests. The so-called Washington Consensus, dominating world politics from the mid-1980s to the finance market meltdown of 2008, aimed at creating a global regulatory system that enabled stability and provided a framework for the expansion of private enterprises. Mobilizing a combination of international agreement and regulatory bodies including the IMF, the World Trade Organization, and the World Bank as vehicles for implementing and enforcing political objectives, the instituted relations between democratic bodies and regulatory agencies were compromised, Polillo and Guillén (2005) argue. Examining the key idea in the neoliberal policy of an independent central bank (see also Kogut and Macpherson, 2011), representing a "purportedly objective, nonpartisan, disinterested and depoliticized approach to policy making." Polillo and Guillén (2005: 1768) demonstrate how the IMF practically served to promote the policy of the Reagan Administration in the 1980s. IMF programs specified an independent central bank as one of its so-called terms, formal demands for policy changes in the country's political and regulatory system prescribed by the IMF:

> The IMF – the agency in charge of assisting countries in financial difficulty – has increasingly attached certain conditions, including an independent central bank, to its leading agreements. Although IMF has had the authority to demand certain terms as a condition of lending since 1952, the agency's enhanced visibility and stature in global financial affairs started during the Reagan presidency, which marshaled the idea of policy convergence across countries as the most effective way to fight financial turbulence in global markets. The Reagan administration saw in the IMF the institution that could impose and monitor a set of guidelines to ensure "responsible" or "disciplined" economic policy making around the world. (Polillo and Guillén, 2005: 1774)

In the 1980s, the average IMF program included "[t]hree times as many terms as during the previous decade" (Polillo and Guillén, 2005: 1775), indicating how the IMF increasingly enforced free-market policy implementation in the 1980s. Hiatt and Park (2013) present a more recent case, that of the promotion of genetically modified organisms (GMOs) and the role of the US Department of Agriculture, of how industry interest organizations are capable of influencing regulatory agencies and therefore set the agenda for policy-making. Hiatt and Park (2013) suggest that when regulatory agencies are under the threat to lose legitimacy, they rely on the assessment of "prominent third-party actors," but that in turn blurs the distinction between regulators and the industry actors subject to regulatory oversight and control. In Polillo and Guillén's (2005) view, this mobilization of the international regulatory bodies to implement free-market policies creates what at times is called "democratic deficit," as technocratic regulatory agencies populated by non-elected officials over-rule the decision-making of democratically elected bodies:

> The importance of global pressures of a coercive, normative, or mimetic kind when it comes to explaining central bank independence raises tantalizing questions about the constraints that globalization can place on the democratic choice that the citizenry is supposed to be able to exercise over such important matters as the structure and nature of economic policy-making institutions. The very act of granting a group of appointed (not elected) technocrats, independence form political power – that is, from elected representatives or officials – reveals a fundamental tension in the way in which different kinds of issues are handled in modern societies . . . especially monetary policy, have been socially and politically constructed as lying beyond the scope of democratic oversight and control. (Polillo and Guillén, 2005: 1794)

Economic ideas and political mobilization thus leads to the institutionalization of routines and practices.

Legislation, Lobbying, Think Tanks, and Partisan Politics

Also in the case of legislative practices, there is evidence of the presence of private interests that in various ways influence the juridical system and policy-making (Walker and Rea, 2014). In Gershon's (2011: 541) critical account, in the formalist understanding, laws are seen as "neutral media" and thus offer "a universal means through which anyone can negotiate with anyone." This alleged transparency and neutrality of laws makes them an effective technology of governance. In addition, laws are useful for policy-makers and anyone seeking to influence the enactment of law because they have the juridical capacity to "[d]efine entities as equal, or at least commensurate, despite wide disparities in size and internal organization" (Gershon, 2011: 540). That is, law applies to any social actor, large as well as small, rich and poor. In contrast, economic sociologists regard law as what is "closely connected to the notion of order," and therefore law is bound up with the power elites' activities to shape and inform the legislative process (Swedberg, 2003: 7). Therefore, in this view, "law can be seen as one of the many weapons in the arsenal of power, similar to physical coercion" (Swedberg, 2003: 7). In addition, the normative assumption made in some domains of legal studies, that "a decision by the state automatically translates into a law, and that this law is automatically followed" (Swedberg, 2003: 6), is not subscribed to by economic sociologists. Instead, they assume that the relationship between law, regulation, and social practices demonstrate relatively complex causal relations including unintended and unanticipated consequences of legislation (for an extended argument on the basis of institutional theory perspective, see Edelman, 1992, 1990; Edelman et al., 2001, 2011; Edelman and Suchman, 1997).

Given the ability of laws to conceal and obscure various political interests (regardless of the economic sociology view), it is no wonder that elites operate to influence legislation to advance their interests. First of all, since the early 1970s, there has been a sharp growth in the establishment of think tanks that serve to provide expertise, knowledge, and policy recommendations in US political systems. While there were 62 think tanks in 1945, today there are around 1,400 think tanks in the US (Medvetz, 2012: 33). Especially after 1977, there is a steep growth of the use of the concept "think tank" in American newspapers (Medvetz, 2012: 123, Figure 3.5. For the case of the UK, see James, 1993), testifying to the build-up of novel institutions serving to critically question traditional academic research work. Lowry (1999: 759) here speaks about a "market for private foundation patronage," wherein the foundations financing think tanks seek "purposive benefits" (Lowry, 1999: 760) – "fiscally conservative/ libertarian organizations dominate the state-based think tank phenomenon in America," Leeson et al. (2012: 62) note. Dye (1978) spoke already in the late 1970s of "oligarchic tendencies" in the policy-making process, and ever since this tendency has been accentuated.

Financed by private financiers and funds, these think tanks are based on the ability to claim for themselves "a kind of mediating role in the social structure," a position in turn based on the capacity to "establish a mixture of resources captured from other fields" (Medvetz, 2012: 178). Being dependent on financing from external sources, access to political bodies and decision-making communities, and good contacts with media, think tanks are constructing their authority on the basis of their ability to integrate these otherwise distinctively separated fields. When orchestrating this integration, think tanks paradoxically advance its own claim to expertise and pose "acutely adequate basic questions about the meaning of the term 'expertise' itself and its value in modern societies" at the same time (Medvetz, 2012: 178). Think tanks thus both purport to represent robust and solid know-how and expertise, while at the same time they seek to disqualify and undermine other sources of such know-how and expertise, most noteworthy traditional, autonomous academic research. The influence and growth of think tanks is thus indicative of the decline of the authority of autonomous scientific production as such, Medvetz (2012) suggests:

> [T]he formation of the space of think tanks – a system of knowledge production inhabited by experts whose success depends on a strategy of self-subordination

to political, bureaucratic, and media demand (a self-subordination that is nearly invisible because it is carried out willingly by the most political experts) – is symptomatic of the *de-autonomization* of the scientific field. For all the variation in their orientation in the ethos of scientific production, and for all of the fuzziness surrounding them, think tanks must therefore be examined in the context of growing threats to the autonomy of science itself. (Medvetz, 2012: 178–179, original emphasis)

In addition, think tanks can serve as a hybrid form of knowledge production because it suits the actors in the political system, providing them with the opportunity to pledge allegiance to systematic, scientific inquiry as a source of legitimate input material in policy-making processes, while at the same time they are free to choose from a larger stock of know-how and experts:

While American politicians cannot always dismiss scientific entirely, the presence of large stable, and internally differentiated think tank universe allows them to "shop" for policy expertise to support their pre-held views and thus to pit multiple forms of expertise against one another. Thus, when autonomously produced social scientific knowledge does not suit their purposes, politicians can always count on the assistance of policy experts willing to lend the stamp of scientific or technical credibility to their views. (Medvetz, 2012: 179)

For instance, one think tank policy expert emphasized that think tanks serve as what Medvetz (2010) refers to as "political aides" by their ability to boil down complex aggregates of data and theory to practical, operable information and advice: "[t]hese economists like to build their models that have nothing to do with the real world and that's one of the reasons I think the think tanks have risen. [Think tanks] are more interested in talking about what the real world is" (Think tank policy expert, cited in Medvetz, 2010: 559).

In this novel institutional setting, where pseudo-academic expertise is advanced as being peer-reviewed and procedurally qualified while in fact being commissioned – perhaps not in terms of details but certainly in terms of its wider politico-economic outlook – by the financiers, the status, prestige and not the least the autonomy of systematic knowledge production is at stake, Medvetz (2012) proposes:

[T]he growth of think tanks over the last forty years has played a pivotal role in undermining the relevance of autonomously produced social scientific knowledge in the United States by fortifying a system of social relations that relegates its producers to the margins of public debate. To the degree that think tanks arrogate for themselves a central role in the policy-making process, they effectively limit the range of options available to more autonomous intellectuals, or those less willing to tailor their work to the demands of moneyed sponsors and politicians. (Medvetz, 2012: 225)

The consequences are that economic ideas may be given a heavier weight than their empirical support would grant them in a more autonomous regime of scientific inquiry. Economic ideas are advanced in a hybridized field where political interests, financing considerations, and media attention all contribute to the shaping and the interpretation of relevant data and particular ideas.

Second, related to the steep growth in think tanks, there are numerous lobbyists operating in Washington and other global decision-making centers, working tenaciously to twist the legislation in the favor of their clients. "In 1971, only 1975 firms had registered lobbyists in Washington, but by 1982, 2,445 did," Hacker and Pierson (2010: 176) write. Ever since, the group of professional knowledge workers of lobbyists has grown exponentially in proportion. As Barley (2007: 202) proposes, "In our republic, people are now separated from their representatives by an asteroid belt of organizations, and among the most powerful of these are corporations and their trade associates." For instance, on October 1, 2009, *The Guardian* reported (cited in Crouch, 2012: 67), "US health insurance firms, hospitals and pharmaceutical corporations deployed six lobbyists for each member of Congress and spent $380 million campaigning against the ['Obamacare' health care reform] policy." The public health care system, being a political objective to reform for decades in US politics, was widely branded as a form of "socialism" among the Republican Party representatives, and apparently their claims were backed by significant economic interests.[2] These lobbyists not only approached politicians but state agency representatives were also targeted. For instance, a former chairman of the US SEC, the government's most important agency for controlling and regulating the finance market, recalled the fierce attempts to influence the decision-making:

> During my seven and a half years in Washington ... nothing astonished me more than witnessing the powerful special interest groups in full swing when they thought a proposed rule or a piece of legislation might hurt them, giving nary a thought to how the proposal might help the investing public ... Individual investors, with no organized labor or trade association to represent their view in Washington, never knew what hit them. (Former SEC chief Arthur Levitt, cited in Hacker and Pierson, 2010: 187)

---

[2] Vidal et al. (2010: 3735) report that the average weighted revenue per lobbyist/year was $349,000 for the "subgroup of congressional staffers" they examined. This figure is in line with reported salaries for lobbyists. Based on such figures, one may calculate the annual amount of money spent on lobbyists in Washington and possibly also trace the money trails financing such advisory services.

Concluding remarks 213

Lobbyists are professional knowledge workers hired to influence political decision-making, and therefore their role in the political system is still relatively distinct albeit still controversial and hotly debated. Especially the close relations between the political system and the lobbyist industry are problematic from a democratic perspective:

> One hundred and thirty former members of Congress are lobbyists . . . lobbying employs nearly half of the politicians and Congressional aides who return to the private sector when they leave Congress, and salaries have raised to about $300,000 a year for well-connected Congressional aides who 'move downtown' from Capitol Hill to K Street (were lobbying, lawyers, and think tanks congregate). (Peet, 2011: 395)

In addition to lobbyists, members of Congress and senators play a key role in the political process to advance new legislation. The Texas Republican Senator Phil Gramm was a central figure in the elimination of the 1933 Glass-Steagall Act, regulating finance markets in 1999. Gramm's political career was based on donations from corporate benefactors who approached Gramm with the proposal, Perrow (2010: 318) writes, "to weaken existing regulations that were interfering with their profitability." The Gramm-Leach-Bliley Act of 1999 (The Financial Services Modernization Act) created incentives and opportunities for managers to "inflate parent companies' balance sheets" in firms organized into a multilayer subsidiary form (Prechel and Morris, 2010: 338). "The new law removed the last firewalls among commercial banks, insurance companies, securities firms, and investment banks," Stein (2011: 288) writes. In addition, the 2000 Commodity Futures Modernization Act (CFMA), signed by President Clinton, exempted many financial products like CDSs from government regulation (Stein, 2011: 288). CFMA thus created opportunities for management to "[t]ransfer much of the risk to unsuspecting investors by using complex financial instruments in unregulated equity markets" (Prechel and Morris, 2010: 350). These new legislations, serving to "modernize" and "deregulate" the financial reporting, "[c]reated dependencies, incentives, and opportunities for managers to engage in financial malfeasance" (Prechel and Morris, 2010: 350).

In the 1989–2002 period, Gramm was "the top recipient of campaign contributions from commercial banks and in the top five for donations from Wall Street" (Perrow, 2010: 318). When Gramm left Senate, he had accumulated funds large enough for him to donate US$1 million to "encourage other senators" to pursue his agenda (Perrow, 2010: 318). Senator Gramm's partner Wendy Gramm served a similar decisive role in relaxing finance market control in the 1990s as the chair of the Commodity Futures Trading Commission leading the deregulatory work during the

Bush Sr. administration. The *Wall Street Journal* (November, 12, 1999, cited in Froud et al., 2004: 907) referred to Mrs Gramm as the "Margaret Thatcher of financial regulation." In the last few days before Bill Clinton's inauguration as Democratic President, Mrs Gramm pushed through a series of important decisions regarding the deregulation of financial markets. A few days after Clinton took office, Mrs Gramm resigned from the federal commission and after five more weeks she was appointed to the Enron board and its audit committee. Mrs Gramm's compensation for this work was estimated to be in the range of US$915,000 and US$1.85 million in salary, attendance fees, stock option sales, and dividends from 1993 to 2001 (Froud et al., 2004: 907; see also Partnoy, 2003: Chapter 10). The specific case of Enron is perhaps an outlier but it is still indicative of the way the finance market money is piped into political bodies in Washington:

> [Between 1990 and 2002] it was increasingly hard to find any Texan politician or any senior national politician who had not taken money from Enron ... According to the *Houston Chronicle*, after the collapse, 248 Senators and members of the House of Representatives were involved in committees investigating Enron's collapse of the conduct of Andersen [accounting firm]; 212 of 248 had received donations from one or both companies. (Froud et al., 2004: 905)

It is hard to not think that there must be significant difficulties involved in separating democratic roles and more finance market-oriented assignments for these democratically elected representatives.

Follow the Money

In an attempt to control the influence of money on federal elections after the Watergate scandal, Congress overturned the Tillman Act of 1907 which banned corporate campaign contributions and in 1971, Congress passed the Federal Election Campaign Act legalizing political contributions from capital owners (Prechel and Morris, 2010: 334). As a consequence of the new legislation, capital owners could after 1974 influence political processes in two interrelated ways: (1) by making political contributions to elected politicians; and (2) by hiring lobbyists to "present their agendas to appointed and elected officials" (Prechel and Morris, 2010: 334). Peet (2011) addresses the US political system and its demands for ever-increasing sums of money, especially in the era of financialization and neoliberal policy-making:

> In the last US elections under the Keynesian regime in 1976 and 1980, presidential candidates collectively raised and spent about $175 million per election. As neoliberalism took hold, the cost of election took off. In the most recent US

presidential elections in 2008, candidates raised $1749 million, with the total costs of the election accounting to $5285 millions. (Peet, 2011: 394)

Taken together, this system of fund-raising benefits a very small group of donators:

> Where do you get the dollars from to run the campaign? From people who have billions of dollars. About one-tenth of 1% of the US adult population (231,000 people) donates over $2000 each to political campaigns, and these donations make up 75% of the total contributions; a mere 26,000 people donate 36% of total contributions. This money comes overwhelmingly (74%) from business sources rather than labour (3%). In the past, the Republican Party that most directly and openly supports business interests raised twice as much as the Democratic Party. (Peet, 2011: 394)

The presidency of George W. Bush is an example of a period where political decision-making greatly benefited economic elites. Despite starting two wars in Iraq and Afghanistan, calculated to have cost "at least $1.4 trillion" (Crotty, 2012: 85), Bush implemented a far-reaching tax reform. These tax cuts were formally designed to stimulate the economy but only did so "to a limited extent" (Stiglitz, 2009: 335). Instead, the immediate effects favored the highest income groups: "[d]uring Bush's four-year period of expansion no less than 73% of total income growth accrued to the top 1%" (Palma, 2009: 842, original emphasis). This occurred at the same time as national debt "almost doubled" during the Bush presidency (Tabb, 2012: 31). Just like his neoconservative role model and his father's companion, Ronald Reagan, George W. Bush relied on various neoliberal and neoconservative think tanks to fill advisory and executive positions in the presidential administration (Eztion and Davis, 2008: 161; Smith, 2007: 91–92).

In addition, it is possible to trace more straightforward links between political decisions on Capitol Hill and campaign contributions to individual politicians. Mian et al.(2010) examine the voting behavior in the case of the American Housing Rescue and Foreclosure Prevention Act (AHRFPA) and the Emergency Economic Stabilization Act (EESA) in 2009, two acts aimed at restoring stability in the US economy after the finance industry collapse. The *Wall Street Journal* claimed that the AHRFPA was "[t]he most important piece of housing legislation to come along in a generation" (Mian et al., 2010: 1971), and the EESA was of great importance for the finance industry burdened by the subprime mortgage debacle. Mian et al. (2010: 1969) found that a strong predictor for the voting behavior on the EESA was the "amount of campaign contributions from the financial service industry." As Mian et al. (2010: 1969) remark, this result is consistent with the "anecdotal evidence" that "the financial

The financialization of the firm

industry lobbied heavily to shape the EESA and get it passed." However, it is possible to discriminate between categories of politicians with different career prospects. While voting behavior among politicians running for re-election was "highly sensitive to past campaign contributions" (Mian et al., 2010: 1969), the voting behavior of retiring politicians was "completely insensitive to campaign contributions." Such data indicate a relatively linear relationship between campaign contributions and voting behavior. In addition, voting behavior was affected by the constituents' "mortgage default rate" in different districts and therefore the finance industry campaign contributors increasingly targeted politicians in districts in which there were a "high fraction of subprime borrowers" (Mian et al., 2010: 1997). In order to have the EESA passed, the finance industry supplied campaign funds to politicians not retiring and representing constituents with many subprime residential mortgage holders: "[o]ur results are consistent with the hypothesis that politicians voted in favor of the EESA in part due to special interest campaign contributions from the financial services industry," Mian et al. (2010: 1997) summarize.

The British newspaper *The Observer* (16 June, 2002, cited in Froud et al., 2004: 905) used the term "vending-machine politics" to address the intimate relationships between funding and the political decision-making process, a relationship that was conspicuous during political crises such as the Enron case. Such a political system is based on what political scientists call *clientelism*.[3] "Politically, the lesson of Enron is that business friendly

---

[3] Clientelism is a political system based on "personal, dyadic relationships between individuals" (Hicken, 2011: 291), where favors are exchanged to benefit both parts in the relationship. Lemarchand and Legg (1972: 151) define clientelism as "a personalized and reciprocal relationship between an inferior and a superior, commending unequal resources." Political scientists regard forms of clientelism as a "generic trait of political systems regardless of their stages of development" (Lemarchand and Legg, 1972: 149), that is, it is present in various political systems and appears in many versions. Still, political scientists by and large regard clientelism as a shorthand term for political systems and institutions that are "less than ideal" (Hicken, 2011: 290). In clientel relationships, politicians "support benefits only to individuals or groups that support or promise to support the politicians" (Hicken, 2011: 291); likewise, unless politicians deliver or promise to deliver a valued benefit in return, the client's electoral support is consumed. Clientelism includes not only the distribution of jobs but also "other resources," including "goods, services, decisions, etc." (Hicken, 2011: 295). Despite its presence in political system, clientelism is problematic as "norms of rationality, anonymity, and universalism are largely absent from the patron-client nexus" (Lemarchand and Legg, 1972: 151). Hicken (2011: 302–303) lists a number of negative consequences of clientelism, including (1) its potential to "reverse the standard accountability relationship that is central to democratic theory," (2) its hampering of "the development of the political institutions necessary for democratic development and consolidation," (3) its association with the "politicization of the bureaucracy and is an impediment to the development of a system of administrative control and oversight," and (4) the strong links between clientelism and "corruption or perception of corruption." As Barack Obama reflects in his *The Audacity of Hope*, there is always a risk that campaign

governments, which are amenable to lobbying by individual firms, may not be in the interest of capitalist enterprise in general," Froud et al. (2004: 907) argue. The strong connections between Wall Street finance industry actors and Washington is of great importance when examining how elites can legitimately influence politics. "The US Treasury is typically managed by financial experts on temporary leave from the investment banks, primarily Goldman Sachs," Peet (2011: 394) says. Other commentators confirm the presence of these exchanges between for example, Goldman Sachs, the most powerful finance industry firm, and the political bodies in Washington: "[Goldman Sachs] succeeded by creating an unparalleled nexus between the canyons of Wall Street and the halls of power – a nexus known as 'Government Sachs,'" Cohan (2011: 75) writes (see also Mandis, 2013: 237). It is thus no wonder that the Bush Administration included a former Goldman Sachs chairman, Hank Paulson, as the Treasury Secretary, eventually playing a key role during the financial crisis of 2008 and the implementation of the TARP – a program that greatly benefited many Wall Street actors including Goldman Sachs (Barofsky, 2012; Sorkin, 2009) and that could be seen, in its consequences, as a "government subsidy" (Mian and Sufi, 2014: 183). While the finance industry lost 7.7 percent of its jobs in the 2007–2009 period, the US manufacturing industry lost twice as many (14.6 percent); in the construction industry 31.6 percent of the jobs disappeared (Stein, 2011: 298). Despite permitting lavish bonuses during the years of crisis, finance industry firms such as Goldman Sachs managed to maintain its status and prestige.

Implications and Consequences

By and large, the entire period of financialization of the economy, beginning in the late 1970s, has been characterized by the gradual expansion of the elite's rights to claim the profits collected by and generated in the expanding and increasingly deregulated finance industry. Palley (2013: 5) speaks of financialization as being the most significant effects of a neoliberal shift in policy in American politics, and emphasizes how the balancing of "capital and labour interests" has shifted in post-World War II era:

> Neoliberalism is an ideology of elite interests, and it serves to shift economic power and income from labor to capital. Financialization reinforces this shift and further changes the redistribution of income at a more disaggregated level

---

contributions serve to influence political agendas, more or less consciously and conspicuously: "I know as a consequence of my fund-raising I became more like the wealthy donors I meet" (Barack Obama, cited in Frank, 2012: 181).

by increasing the managers' share of the wage bill, increasing the share of interest income, and increasing the financial sector's share of profit income. (Palley, 2013: 5)

In such accounts, the story of financialization is one of elites mobilizing to secure their own interests at the expense of other groups, in most cases under the banner of increased market efficiency and a more effective allocation of productive resources, allegedly to the "benefit of everyone." Empirical evidence suggests otherwise. As part of the finance market crisis handling policy of the Federal Reserve, the money pumped into the US economy did only to a limited degree benefit those groups that fell below the creditworthiness line calculated by the banking system (commonly calculated in terms of so-called FICO-scores, see Rona-Tas and Hiss, 2010):

> [A] *Wall Street Journal* article reported that cash injections by the Federal Reserve in the aftermath of the 2008 credit crunch have almost exclusively benefited the most creditworthy, because bankers would only lend to people in the higher-scoring brackets . . . "even though we have the greatest monetary policy stimulus in the history of the Fed, we really have not managed to lower the funding costs for a large swath of people," said David Zervos, a bond strategist with Jeffries Inc., a Wall Street investment bank. He called the Fed efforts "monetary policy for rich people." (Fourcade and Healy, 2013: 569)

Based on such evidence, there are several commentators that do not believe this neat win-win argument advanced by the champions of financialization. Says Levitt (2013), taking a quite negative view of the US economy's prospects for the future: "[t]he social and political institutions that sustained the American dream are corrupted and broken. The economy of the U.S. is still the largest in the world, but thirty years of neoliberal policies have severely compromised, if not destroyed, the financial and political institutions which led to its pre-eminence" (Levitt, 2013a: 175).

Mainstream commentators do not endorse such negative views and do not really believe in financialization as a "silent takeover" (Hertz, 2001), but point at the unintended consequences of purposeful action leading to the financialized economy (Krippner, 2011). At least, many of the deregulatory policies being enacted and enforced were after all justified by neoclassical economic theory making the promise that a deregulated and globalized finance market would work better than a national, regulated market. No matter what position one takes, ranging from critical and Marxists theories to more mainstream economics theory and political science models for policy-making, there is little doubt that the financialization of the economy has been shaped by particular elite groups' ability to influence policy-making bodies and communities. "As it currently stands, the financial system benefits very few people, and those few have a vested interest in staving off any reform that could move us away from debt financing. However, we cannot continue down the road of unsustainable debt binges and painful crashes," Mian and Sufi (2014: 186) argue. In contrast, Crouch (2012) suggests that we may now have reached a point of no return where it is hard to stop a self-perpetuating process of escalating financialization, including debt-based consumption and increased economic inequalities. Economic elites have benefited much from the economic inequalities and they strongly oppose a return to the "collectivist solutions" of the post-World War II period and the welfare state model, including redistributive taxation, vital and reform-oriented trade unions, and government regulation. For free-market pundits, such collectivist solutions are not only violating the market efficiency criteria they staunchly defend, it is also an "immoral model" as it undermines the individual's personal responsibilities to enterprise in the market society. That is, the entire vocabulary and worldview of free-market capitalism and the era of financialization has been, at least in part, internalized by a wide variety of social actors and policy-makers. Perhaps it is true, as Levitt (2013a: 175) puts it, that the social and political institutions that sustained the American dream are "corrupted and broken." But such statements are not really helpful in seeking to restore an institutional and regulatory framework that can lower unemployment rates and accomplish reasonable levels of economic equality. It is better to accommodate more straightforward agendas, such as Konzelmann's (2014: 734), saying that "the only effective way forward is a rehabilitation of the economy away from the reliance on financial services and the demotion of finance to its role as the servant of enterprise, not its master."

THEORETICAL AND MANAGERIAL IMPLICATIONS

Implications for Organization Studies

The field of organization studies is often structured into a series of sub-disciplinary discourses wherein finance theory and finance management constitute a particular field of research. Being more oriented towards neo-classical economic theory and consequently using quantitative research methodologies, the finance management literature often examines quite technical details regarding the firm's capital structure or the capital supply of the firm. In addition, the economic sociology literature, the social studies of finance literature (rooted in the sociological tradition of science and technology studies), and the critical management studies literature contributes to the analysis of how finance markets interact with the focal firm and how for example, financial performance metrics tend to be enacted as legitimate and effective ways to institute managerial control. In addition, the accounting literature, grounded in the tradition to examine numerical accounting data and reporting, is well equipped for examining the consequences of the financialization of the firm. In other words, the wide-ranging consequences of the financialization of the economy and the individual firm is best examined and understood on basis of collaborative research efforts across the managerial subdisciplines. Management studies may here contribute to an integrative framework wherein terms such as *institutional work* proposed by institutional theorists (for example, Lawrence et al., 2009) can capture the mobilization of finance industry actors and their protagonists and allies to advance their interests and to strengthen their legitimacy in the field.

Moreover, a research agenda exploring the consequences of financialization needs to both pay attention to reported facts (for example, the levels of economic compensation to CEOs and finance industry professionals), while at the same time anchoring these facts in wider social and economic changes in industry, in policy-making, and in individual firms. Financialization is not only the factual consequences of decisions and policies already made and enacted, but is equally the outcome from the ability to establish vocabularies and conceptual frameworks that shape and inform everyday managerial action. The very idea of shareholder value, based on a loosely coupled theoretical framework including various propositions, assumptions, and declarations in the agency theory literature, is one example of the theoretical and even literary underpinnings of financialization. In addition, the high-flying hypothesis that markets and finance markets in particular are better suited for allocating resources as prices of the assets being traded always already include all information available in the market, has been used to justify and motivate a series of deregulatory policies that eventually proved to be disastrous. Therefore, to entrench the position as a credible spokesperson regarding the nature and the rationality of the market and hierarchies and their various mixed forms is to secure a most influential position. As empirical data and evidence first of all always lag behind what Blyth (2002) calls economic ideas, and, second, as prescribed by the Duhem hypothesis[4] (after the French physicist Pierre Duhem, 1996), empirical data does not always lead to an agreement regarding the falsification of a hypothesis. Therefore, the ability to "tell credible stories" about economic ideas is a very powerful

---

[4] Hacking (1992: 30) defines the Duhem hypothesis accordingly: "[A] theory inconsistent with an observation can always be saved by modifying an auxiliary hypothesis, typically a hypothesis about the working of an instrument such as the telescope."

skill. Such economic ideas may become, if advocated forcefully, the blue-prints of new institutions. As a consequence, the study of the financializa-tion of the firm cannot unfold as a mere accumulation of facts but also needs to examine the beliefs, assumptions, the ideologies, economic ideas, and not the least the mobilization of key political and professional actors that have a stake in portraying the firm as a bundle of financial assets. The study of the financialization of the firm should preferably engage a wide spectra of management scholars and organization theorists.

Implications for Managerial Practice

There are arguably a variety of lessons to the learned for managers from the history of financialization. In one of the most widely circulated quotes (see for example, Blinder, 2013) from the Wall Street executive commu-nity during the 2008 finance market collapse was made by Citigroup CEO Chuck Prince on July 10, 2007, saying, "When the music stops, in terms of liquidity, things will be complicated, but as long as the music is playing, you've got to get up to dance. We're still dancing" (cited in Brunnermeier, 2009: 82). This quote is interesting for many reasons. First of all, it is a rec-ognition of the concern that there are few possibilities for finance industry actors to institute mechanisms of self-reflexivity or self-correction; anyone must submit to and abide by the rules of the game. Actors cannot both play the game and question the rules, and consequently they are up dancing just as long as the music plays. Second and related to the first observation, it is a CEO's surrender of agency, a conspicuous admittance that once you are participating in this game, there is no place to where one can retreat. The finance market has its own pace and momentum and there is no chance of *voice* but only, at best, *exit* (in Hirschman's, 1970, formulation). Both these interpretations indicate a form of fatalist worldview, a recognition of humans as being practically and morally unable to lift themselves outside of the webs of meaning they themselves have created; once you are in, you can never leave, or better still – *if* you leave, you leave forever.

    Speaking about neoliberalism, the politico-economic doctrine that several commentators regard as the driving force of financialization (a proposition here being recognized but not favored over other explana-tions), Peck (2010: 7) suggests that neoliberalism has been "victorious" in the war of ideas since the 1970s, but that these victories always have been "Pyrrhic and partial ones." This is because, Peck (2010: 7) argues, neoliberalism is "cursed" with its "utopian vision" of a free society and a free economy that is ultimately "unrealizable." The "ideological appari-tion" of neoliberal intellectuals such as Friedrich von Hayek of the totally free market is therefore "coupled with the endless frustration borne of the inevitable failure to arrive at this elusive destination" (Peck, 2010: 7). This is the tragedy and the curse of the free-market ideology: it can never effectively overcome the inconsistencies, political bargaining, cognitive limitations, and other forms of all-too-human influences shaping actual markets. The free market becomes a mirage, a dream that can never be fulfilled. As a consequence, free-market protagonists are condemned to endless disappointment as humans and their limitations always interfere and the hopes of additional deregulation of markets will discipline these fierce humans and lead to little more than new disappointment. Ultimately, free-market ideologies result in a form of endemic misanthropy, a position that sides with Thomas Carlyle's derogatory view of economics as the "dismal science" (Doel, 2009; Trigilia, 2002).

La fête continue, Chuck Prince made clear to everyone; until somebody closes down the party and announces that it is time to go home to get some sleep, or the system crumbles from within (as it did in 2008), the dancing goes on. As leading policy-makers including the once venerated chairman Alan Greenspan interpreted all evidence of the music playing for too long and too loudly as being indicative of the sound system being in perfect shape – "rational markets can take care of themselves," was Alan Greenspan's adage (cited by Palma, 2009: 831) – and sounding just fine, and therefore, why not let the dancers enjoy themselves as long as it lasts?

Managers can learn from the history of financialization that "groupthink" (Janis, 1982), cognitive dissonance (Festinger, 1957), bounded rationality (Simon, 1957), and other cognitive and sociocultural limitations are playing a key role in the organization of society and industry, a fact that renders common-sense thinking and integrity useful managerial skills in everyday work in organizations. In addition, abstract economic ideas are powerful resources as they provide guidance and meaning in periods of turmoil and uncertainty. Still, no matter who pays the bill, academic credentials and institutional affiliations are worth preciously little unless theoretical claims made are supported by empirical evidence or at least credible and reasonably easily understood lines of reasoning and arguments. In addition, in contrast to some professionally developed economic ideas, common-sense thinking, otherwise frequently branded as archaic or all-too-practical ways of knowing, benefit from being anchored in what has been called a *moral economy*, "the shared moral notions and belief about justice that form the 'repertoire' . . . for people's thinking" (Sachweh, 2012: 421–422). Common-sense thinking is generally treated as being conservative and skeptical of the new, based on a preference for certainty and continuity, and safely couched in everyday experience and in convictions acquired at an early stage of life. In a society and an economy fully committed to dancing until the music stops, no matter what, such a sober *Weltanschauung* may be of great value as it tends to question the purpose of all the dancing (that is, the one-sided accumulation of financial profits devoid of wider purpose and meaning).

Managers working in corporations can also learn from the era of financialization that finance markets add value by effectively allocating risks and distributing capital resources from those that have cash in excess to those who need capital investment, but they must also learn to question unsubstantiated claims that finance markets and finance industry actors would be better equipped – cognitively, politically, morally – than anyone else regarding what is best for the economy. Neoclassical economic theory is based on the idea of the market being the undisputably most efficient way to structure economic activities and transactions, leading to competition that in turn lowers cost and/or promote more differentiated product or service offerings. Under normal conditions, high levels of profit are treated as indicative of poorly functioning markets, where specific actors have been able to entrench monopoly positions where they can take advantage of above-normal rents and profit levels. In the case of the finance industry, very few mainstream economists, policy-makers, or commentators regard the astronomical levels of profits and economic compensations as being indicative of a poorly functioning market (Crotty, 2008). On the contrary, the orthodox neoclassical economic theory emphasized investment in human capital and the virtues of re-regulatory policies when explaining the above-normal levels of profit in the finance industry. Such explanations derive from the dominant economic ideas of the period.

So, managers working in financialized firms should be aware of the history and consequences of financialization, an insight that may help them navigate in an environment shaped by managerial practices, tools, and methods, more or less closely connected to finacial theories and their prescribed practices.

SUMMARY AND CONCLUSION

When the issue of financialization is brought into discussion, it is easily mistaken for being a critique of capitalism *per se*. Regardless of all its flaws and its inability to by itself distribute economic resources evenly, capitalism remains the most effective economic regime for the accumulation of wealth, and therefore also, when regulated adequately, for securing well-being and economic equality for the largest possible share of the population. As McCloskey (2006: 16, original emphasis) writes in her ardent defense of bourgeoise virtues as being the bedrock of the liberal society and Western-style economies, "The amount of goods and services produced and consumed by the average person on the planet has *risen* since 1800 by a factor of about eight and a half." In addition, Levitt (2013a: 141) stresses that in the relatively short period of two centuries, 1780 to 1980, Western capitalism "achieved a historic fifty-fold increase in world output and seven-fold increase in world population." This economic growth was accomplished by a combination of: technological development; legislation and law enforcement; institutional reform and a differentiated political system; a liberalization of international trade; enterprising and entrepreneurial activities, and the political encouragement thereof; and the effective investment of capital in high-growth industries and sectors; all part of the virtues and benefits listed by the proponents of what Albert Hirschman (1982, 1977) refers to as *doux commerce*, the belief that "commerce was a civilizing agent of considerable power and range" (Hirschman, 1982: 1464; see also Fourcade and Healy, 2007). This regime of competitive capitalism, regardless of the oligopolistic tendencies, is rightly praised for its ability to produce economic growth. At the very heart of this economic expansion and activity lies the liberal idea that every individual has the right to the fruits of one's own labor, the right to capitalize on individually entrenched skills and competencies, and therefore value accumulation is closely bound up with skills or with the ability to bear risks (in for example, the case of money lending). These liberal theorists of British origin, Duggan (2003: 4) argues, "provided a set of metaphors, an organizing narrative, and a moral apologia for capitalism." The field of finance, closely related to mercantile activities and to the production of goods and services, while still being the handling of intangible and highly abstract human resources, were initially not included in such moral apologia but has been counteracted by theological doctrines and common-sense thinking regarding the virtues of hard, manual labor.

In some accounts, there is a distinction made between the "real economy" and the "finance economy," but such distinctions succumb to this century-old distinction between what are respectable economic activities (production, and thereafter also trade) and what is potentially morally questionable (the handing of money in any form), and it also underrates the importance of finance as the lifeblood of capitalist economic systems. As a consequence, the financialization of the firm being examined in this volume is not *per se* a novel view of the corporation as all activities being managed and organized in the corporate form have always to some extent been subject to calculative practices and managerial control in monetary terms. Instead, the financialization of the firm is by and large a shift in corporate governance policy, stressing the benefits and claims of particular stakeholders, most significantly the owner's of stock, a shift from medium-term to long-term to short-term value extraction activities, and the more general assumption that finance industry locales rather than the executive boardrooms are the "natural" site for the allocation of capital resources. In other words, the firm (or any other economic pursuits) has always been financialized – otherwise for example, the Catholic Church would not have to be so concerned about its effects and consequences – but the new, radical view in the era of financialization is that value extraction can be treated as a domain separated from value creation. Finance industry innovations such as increasingly complex securities and other derivate instruments have enabled a leverage and circulation of financial assets that are only loosely coupled with the underlying actual asset (say, a house and the mortgage loans of the homeowner). This disconnection of *value creation* and *value extraction* is the mark of financialization, and it is easy to admit that this trick to create extensive value out of one single asset works as long as the substantial share of the actors believe this is possible. This Ponzi scheme value creation is still untenable over time, a fact that became evident for many policy-makers and commentators by 2008. Competitive capitalism, for better or for worse – to allude to Churchill's statement on democracy – the "least bad" of alternatives regarding economic accumulation, is dependent on finance, but it does not benefit from a finance industry managed by actors who think they are "bigger than the game" and therefore take on the role to discipline managers and decision-makers that do not share its own interests and convictions.

The era of financialization is a period characterized by the advancement of daring but ultimately unsubstantiated hypotheses in neoclassical economic theory regarding the efficiency of market and the advancement of neoliberal and neoconservative doctrines treating elite groups as being unrestrictedly entitled to the fruits of the labor of others, a concern already addressed more than a century ago for progressive liberal commentators such as Louis D. Brandeis ([1914] 1967). These new theories, doctrines, policies, and beliefs – in short, *economic ideas* – have led to a decline in economic growth, increased economic inequality, an enormous accumulation of debt on all levels (household, firm, state), and, in some national economies, a gradual loss of long-term competitiveness as investment in production capital (technology, human resources, and so on) have been given a low priority as the expanding finance markets could secure an easier and safer return on investment elsewhere. For some groups, for example, the American blue-collar worker community and parts of the middle class, the outcomes have been unfavorable. A lack of self-criticism in the discipline of economics and policy-makers' willingness to listen to theoretical arguments at best loosely coupled with empirical data and historical data series in particular, have led to a situation where policy-making is more focused on efficiency and the generation of short-term profit rather than to build a dynamic and vital economy and a sustainable society that benefit the community.

The lesson learned from the last three decades of expansion of the finance market and the finance industry actors' prerogatives and possibilities for generating profits is that it is possible to generate massive amounts of wealth in certain quarters of the economy, but that such wins are mostly someone else's loss; unlike the claims made by the proponents of finance theory and free-market policies, promising that the reign of the finance industry actors would be beneficial for everyone as finance markets were the "brains of capitalism," such claims are today incredible and at best unfulfilled. Proponents of the rationality of the finance industry frequently make references to how smart, bright, and brilliant, both finance theory professors and Wall Street finance industry professionals are (see for example, Mandis, 2013; Cohan, 2011; Ho, 2009), and besides being a tedious self-gratifying gesture being repeated over and over – perhaps this is also an American cultural trait, this conspicuous praise of "the best and the brightest" over recognizing collective accomplishments? – it has the unintended consequence to breed a sense of suspicion among outsiders: if these people are so extraordinarily brilliant and endowed with diplomas from Princeton and Harvard, how come they are so aggressively committed to the sole and the perhaps not-so-noble pursuit of enriching themselves and their employers? In the Western tradition, the Aristotelian conviction that philosophy (that is, intellectual work in the widest sense), not commercial activities, was the more honorable choice for the intellectually gifted has dominated, but such cultural beliefs have now fallen from grace in only a few decades. In the past, heroes of the civil societies were scientists and engineers contributing to society through technological or scientific marvels, politicians or activists standing up for something they believed in, or perhaps even a few sportsmen and sportswomen and a small group of adventurers and discoverers stretching their capacities beyond what was thought to be possible. In the era of financialization, we are told time and time again of *la crème de la crème* of the last generations work for Goldman Sachs et al. to engineer wealth for faceless capital owners and themselves.

A vital, well-managed, and efficient finance industry is of great value and importance for the economic system of competitive capitalism, but such a finance industry must work in collaboration with the wider economic system and recognize political and social objectives beyond the sheer accumulation of capital in the 0.5 percent top income group of the population. The vigorous defense of an unregulated finance market proposed that capital owners would benefit from economic growth by wisely investing their capital in high-growth sectors, that is, to finance the entrepreneurial function of competitive capitalism, but ample evidence suggests that it is the state, already burdened by the externalities of free-market capitalism including increased pauperization, yet informed by economic pundits that it must enact "austere fiscal policies" (Konzelmann, 2014; Schiu, 2014; Blyth, 2013; Lysandrou, 2013), that provides the lion's share of such capital. The romantic and overly rosy view of capital owners, generously sharing their capital with aspiring entrepreneurs simply does not hold water. There are examples of the "super-rich" such as Bill Gates and Richard Branson investing in daring and promising philanthropical projects, but these cases are exceptions to the rule, and they certainly do not put all their assets at stake. In general, rich people prefer to invest where the yield is the highest at a tolerable calculated level of risk.

In order to avoid finishing this volume in a depressing and dreary tone, it can be concluded that the four decades of gradual expansion of finance markets can be treated as a dynamic and highly experimental period of competitive capitalism, where a number of daring hypotheses were given the opportunity to be tested empirically (for example, the free-market experiments orchestrated by the IMF in Latin and South America) and that the outcomes provide material for learning for the coming period. It is always easy to be wise in hindsight, and it may be advisable to follow Krippner's (2011) view that many policy-makers were not fully capable of overseeing and anticipating the consequences of their decisions and policies in the 1970s, 1980s, and 1990s. At the same time, the liberalization of the finance markets and the globalization of capital is beyond doubt bound up with the advancement of economic theories, political doctrines, and political mobilization, so the financialization of the firm is, like is often the case in social and economic systems, the consequence from muddling through political decision in a world beset by cognitive limitations, emergence, and unintended consequences. We should then not be too ready to throw the first stone, while at the same time, it is not meaningful to treat historical events as being mere haphazard outcomes from uncoordinated activities and policy-making. History is made by men and women, but these men and women cannot always be expected to know what the consequences of their actions will be. Therefore, there is a need for scholarly attention to examine these consequences, regardless of whether they were intended or not. That is, one must not forget events like the 2008 financial market collapse, or we may once again find ourselves standing in dumb misery, staring at things happening that were on broad front previously declared to be most unlikely to occur.

Bibliography

Abdelal, Rawi (2007), *Capital Rules: The Construction of the Global Finance*, Cambridge, MA: Harvard University Press.

Aglietta, Michel (2000), Shareholder value and corporate governance: some tricky questions, *Economy and Society*, 29(1): 146–159.

Ailon, Galit (2012), The discursive management of financial risk scandals: the case of Wall Street journal commentaries on LTCM and Enron, *Qualitative Sociology*, 35(3): 251–270.

Ailon, Galit (2014), Financial risk-taking as a sociological gamble: notes on the development of a new social perspective, *Sociology*, 48(3): 606–621.

Akard, Patrick J. (1992), Corporate mobilization and political power: the transformation of U.S. economic policy in the 1970s, *American Sociological Review*, 57(5): 597–615.

Akerlof, George (1970), The market for "lemons": quality uncertainty and the market mechanism, *Quarterly Journal of Economics*, 84(3): 488–500.

Alchian, A. and Demsetz, H. (1972), Production, information costs and economic organization, *American Economic Review*, 62(5): 777–795.

Alderson, Arthur S. and Nielsen, François (2002), Globalization and the great U-turn: income inequality trends in 16 OECD countries, *American Journal of Sociology*, 107(5): 1244–129.

Allen, Douglas W. (2012), *The Institutional Revolution: Measurement and the Economic Emergence of the Modern World*, Chicago and London: University of Chicago Press.

Alvehus, Johan and Spicer, André (2012), Financialization as a strategy of workplace control in professional service firms, *Critical Perspectives on Accounting*, 23(7–8): 497–510.

Amoore, Louise (2011), Data derivatives: on the emergence of a security risk calculus for our times, *Theory, Culture and Society*, 28(6): 24–43.

Andersson, Tord, Gleadle, Pauline, Haslam, Colin and Tsitsianis, Nick (2010), Bio-pharma: a financialized business model, *Critical Perspectives on Accounting*, 21(7): 631–641.

Apple, Michael W. (2004), Creating difference: neo-liberalism, neo-conservatism and the politics of educational reform, *Educational Policy*, 18(1): 12–44.

Aristotle (1998), *Politics*, Indianapolis and Cambridge: Hackett.

Arnold, Patricia J. (2009), Global financial crisis: the challenge to accounting research, *Accounting, Organizations and Society*, 34: 803–809.

Arrighi, Giovanni (2010), *The Long Twentieth Century: Money, Power, and the Origins of Our Times*, 2nd edn, London and New York: Verso.

Asen, Robert (2009), Ideology, materiality, and counterpublicity: William E. Simon and the rise of a conservative counterintelligentsia, *Quarterly Journal of Speech*, 95 (3): 263–288.

Babb, Sarah (2013), The Washington Consensus as transnational policy paradigm: its origins, trajectory and likely successor, *Review of International Political Economy*, 20(2): 268–297.

Bacon, Nick, Wright, Mike, Scholes, Louise and Meuleman, Miguel (2010), Assessing the impact of private equity on industrial relations in Europe, *Human Relations*, 63(9): 1343–1370.

Baker, Dean (2013), Speculation and asset bubbles, in Wolfson, Martin H. and Epstein, Gerald A. (eds), *Handbook of the Political Economy of Financial Crises*, New York and Oxford: Oxford University Press, pp. 47–60.

Baker, H. Kent, Powell, Gary E. and Veit, E. Theodore (2003), Why companies use open-market repurchases: a managerial perspective, *Quarterly Review of Economics and Finance*, 43(3): 483–504.

Barba, Aldo and Pivetti, Massimo (2009), Rising household debt: its causes and macroeconomic implications – a long-period analysis, *Cambridge Journal of Economics*, 33(1): 113–137.

Barley, Stephen R. (2007), Corporations, democracy, and the public good, *Journal of Management Inquiry*, 16: 201–215.

Barofsky, Neil M. (2012), *Bailout: An Inside Account of How Washington Abandoned Main Street While Rescuing Wall Street*, New York: Free Press.

Baron, James N., Dobbin, Frank R. and Jennings, P. Devereaux (1986), War and peace: the evolution of modern personnel administration in U.S. industry, *American Journal of Sociology*, 92: 350–383

Bartolini, Stefano, Bonatti, Luigi and Sarracino Francesco (2014), The Great Recession and the bulimia of US consumers: deep causes and possible ways out, *Cambridge Journal of Economics*, 38(5): 1015–1042.

Batra, Ravi (2005), *Greenspan's Fraud: How Two Decades of his Policies have Undermined the Global Economy*, New York: Palgrave Macmillan.

Bauman, Zygmunt (2000), *Liquid Modernity*, Cambridge: Polity Press.

Bauman, Zygmunt (2005), *Liquid Life*, Cambridge: Polity Press.

Bebchuk, Lucian and Grinstein, Yaniv (2005), The growth of executive pay, *Oxford Review of Economic Policy*, 21(2): 283–303.

Bebchuk, Lucian A., Cohen, Alma and Spamann, Holger (2010), The wages of failure: executive compensation at Bear Stearns and Lehman Brothers, 2000–2008, John M. Olin Center for Law, Economics, and Business discussion paper no. 657, Harvard University.

Becker, Gary S. (1968), Crime and punishment: an economic approach, *Journal of Political Economy*, 76(2): 169–217.

Belloc, Filippo (2013), Law, finance and innovation: the dark side of shareholder protection, *Cambridge Journal of Economics*, 37(4): 863–888.

Bendix, Reinhard (1971), Bureaucracy, in Bendix, Reinhard and Roth, Guenther (eds), *Scholarship and Partisanship: Essays on Max Weber*, Berkeley, Los Angeles and London: University of California Press, pp. 129–155.

Berggren, C. (1994), "Lean production – the end of history?", *Work, Employment, and Society*, Vol. 7, No. 2, pp. 163–188.

Berle, Adolf A. and Means, Gardiner C. ([1934] 1991), *The Modern Corporation and Private Property*, New Brunswick: Transaction Publishers.

Berman, E.P. (2008), Why did universities start patenting? Institution-building and the road to the Bayh-Dole Act, *Social Studies of Science*, 38: 835–871

Berman, Elizabeth Popp (2012), *Creating the Market University: How Academic Science Became an Economic Engine*, Princeton and Oxford: Princeton University Press.

Berman, Elizabeth Popp and Milanes-Reyes, Laura M. (2013), The politicization of knowledge claims: the "Laffer curve" in the U.S. Congress, *Qualitative Sociology*, 36: 53–79.

Berman, Elizabeth Popp and Pagnucco, Nicholas (2010), Economic ideas and the political process: debating tax cuts in the U.S. House of Representatives, 1962–1981, *Politics and Society*, 38(3): 347–372.

Bernhardt, Annette (2012). The role of labor market regulation in rebuilding economic opportunity in the United States, *Work and Occupations*, 39(4): 354–375.

Beunza, Daniel and Stark, David (2004), Tools of the trade: the socio-technology of arbitrage in a Wall Street trading room, *Industrial and Corporate Change*, 13(2): 369–400

Bhagat, Sanjai and Black, Bernard (2002), The non-correlation between board independence and long-term firm performance, *Journal of Corporation Law*, 27: 231–274.

Billig, Michael (2005), *Laughter and Ridicule: Towards Social Critique of Humour*, London, Thousand Oaks and New Delhi: Sage.

Biven, Josh and Shierholz, Heidi (2013), The great recession's impact on jobs, wages, and incomes, in Wolfson, Martin H. and Epstein, Gerald, A. (eds), *Handbook of the Political Economy of Financial Crises*, New York and Oxford: Oxford University Press, pp. 61–94.

Black, William K. (2005), *The Best Way to Rob a Bank is to Own One: How Corporate Executives and Politicians Looted the S&L Industry*, Austin: The University of Texas Press.

Blau, Peter M. (1964), *Power and Exchange in Social Life*, New Brunswick: Transaction Books.

Blinder, Alan S. (2013), *When the Music Stopped: The Financial Crisis, the Response, and the Work Ahead*, New York: Penguin.

Bluestone, Harry and Harrison, Bennett (1982), *Deindustrialization of America: Plant Closings, Community Abandonment, and the Dismantling of Basic Industry*, New York: Basic Books.

Bluhm, Christian and Wagner Christoph (2011) Valuation and risk management of collateralized debt obligations and related securities, *Annual Review in Financial Economics*, 3: 193–222.

Block, Fred (2014), Democratizing finance, *Politics and Society*, 42(1): 3–28.

Block, Fred and Keller, Matthew R. (2009), Where do innovations come from? Transformations in the US economy, 1970–2006, *Socio-Economic Review*, 7(3): 459–483.

Blyth, Mark (2002), *Great Transformations: Economic Ideas and Institutional Change in the Twentieth Century*, New York and Cambridge: Cambridge University Press.

Blyth, Mark (2013), *Austerity: The History of a Dangerous Idea*, Oxford and New York: Oxford University Press.

Bok, Derek (2002), *Universities in the Marketplace: the Commercialization of Higher Education*, Princeton: Princeton University Press.

Boldrin, M. and Levine, D.K. (2004), 2003 Lawrence R. Klein lecture: the case against intellectual monopoly, *International Economic Review*, 45(2): 327–350.

Bolton, Patrick, Freixas, Xavier and Shapiro, Joel (2012), The credit ratings game, *Journal of Finance*, 67(1): 85–112.

Bonaccorsi, Andrea, Calvert, Jane and Joly, Pierre-Benoit (2011), From protecting texts to protecting objects in biotechnology and software: a tale of changes of ontological assumptions in intellectual property protection, *Economy and Society*, 40(4): 611–639.

Bourdieu, Pierre (2005), *The Economic Structures of Society*, Cambridge: Polity Press.

Brady, David, Baker, Regina S. and Finnigan, Ryan (2013), When unionization disappears: state-level unionization and working poverty in the United States, *American Sociological Review*, 78(5): 872–896.

Brandeis, Luois D. ([1914] 1967), *Other People's Money and How the Bankers use it*, New York: Harper Torchbooks.

Bratton, William W. and Levitin, Adam J. (2013), Transactional genealogy of scandal: from Michael Milken to Enron to Goldman Sachs, *Southern California Law Review*, 86: 783–921.

Bratton, William W. and Wachter, Michael L. (2010), The case against shareholder empowerment, *Pennsylvania Law Review*, 160(1): 653–728.

Braudel, Ferdnand, (1980), *On History*, Chicago and London: The University of Chicago Press.

Braudel, Fernand (1992), *The Wheels of Commerce: Civilization & Capitalism 15th–18th Century*, vol. 2, Berkeley and Los Angeles: The University of California Press.

Breslau, Daniel (2013), Designing a market-like entity: economics in the politics of market formation, *Social Studies of Science*, 43(6): 829–851.

Brickson, S.L. (2005) Organizational identity orientation: forging a link between organizational identity and organizations' relations with stakeholders, *Administrative Science Quarterly*, 50: 576–609.

Briggs, Asa and Burke, Peter (2009), *A Social History of the Media: From Gutenberg to the Internet*, Cambridge and Malden: Polity.

Brint, Steven (1994), *In the Age of Experts: The Changing Role of Professionals in Politics and Public Life*, Princeton: Princeton University Press.

Brockman, Jeffrey, Chang, Saeyoung and Rennie, Craig (2007), CEO cash and stock-based compensation changes, layoff decisions, and shareholder value, *Financial Review*, 42: 99–119.

Brunnermeier, Markus K. (2009), Deciphering the liquidity and credit crunch 2007–2008, *Journal of Economic Perspectives*, 23 (1): 77–100.

Bryan, Dick and Rafferty, Michael (2013), Fundamental value: a category in transformation, *Economy and Society*, 42(1): 130–153.

Burckhardt, Jacob ([1860] 1954), *The Civilization of the Renaissance in Italy*, translated by S.G.C. Middlemore, New York: The Modern Library.

Burgin, Angus (2012), *The Great Persuasion: Reinventing Free Markets Since the Depression*, Cambridge: Harvard University Press.

Burrill, G. Steven (2012), Innovating in the new austerity, *Journal of Commercial Biotechnology*, 18: 5–6.

Burris, Val (2001), The two faces of capital: corporations and individual capitalists as political actors *American Sociological Review*, 66(3): 361–381.

Callinicos, Alex (2009), *Bonfire of Illusions: The Twin Crises of Neoliberalism*, Cambridge: Polity.

Callon, Michel, Millo, Yuval and Muniesa, Fabian (eds) (2007), *Market Devices*, Oxford and Malden: Blackwell.

Calomiris, Charles W. and Haber, Stephen H. (2014), *Fragile by Design: The Political Origins of Banking Crises and Scarce Credit*, Princeton and Oxford: Princeton University Press.

Calvert, Jane (2008), The commodification of emergence: systems biology, synthetic biology and intellectual property, *Biosocieties*, 3(4): 383–398.

Cambrosio, Alberto, Keating, Peter, Schlich, Thomas and Weisz, George (2006), Regulatory objectivity and the generation and management of evidence in medicine, *Social Science and Medicine*, 63(1): 189–199.

Campbell, John L. (2002), Ideas, politics, and public policy, *Annual Review of Sociology*, 28: 21–38.

Carruthers, Bruce and Espeland, Wendy (1991), Accounting for rationality; double-entry book-keeping and the rhetoric of economic rationality, *American Journal of Sociology*, 97(1): 31–69.

Carruthers, Bruce G. and Kim, Jeong-Chul (2011), The sociology of finance, *Annual Review of Sociology*, 37: 239–259.

Carruthers, Bruce G. and Stinchcombe, Arthur L. (1999), The social structure of liquidity flexibility, markets and states, *Theory and Society*, 28: 353–382.

Castilla, Emilio J. (2008), Gender, race and meritocracy in organizational careers, *American Journal of Sociology*, 113(6): 1479–1526.

Castilla, Emilio J. and Benard, Stephen (2010), The paradox of meritocracy in organizations, *Administrative Science Quarterly*, 55(4): 543–576.

Centeno, Miguel A. and Cohen Joseph N. (2012), The arc of neoliberalism, *Annual Review of Sociology*, 38: 317–340.

Chandler, Alfred D. (1977), *The Visible Hand: The Managerial Revolution in American Business*, Cambridge: Harvard University Press.

Chandler, Alfred (1984), The emergence of managerial capitalism, *Business History Review*, 58: 473–503.

Changeux, Jean-Pierre (2004), *The Physiology of Truth: Neuroscience and Human Knowledge*, Boston: Belknap Press of Harvard University Press.

Cheng, Ing-Haw and Xiong, Wei (2014), Financialization of commodity markets, *Annual Review in Financial Economics*, 6: 7.1–7.23.

Chorev, N. (2005), The institutional project of neo-liberal globalization: the case of WTO, *Theory and Society*, 34: 317–355.

Chorev, Nitsan and Babb, Sarah (2009), The crisis of neoliberalism and the future of international institutions; a comparison of the IMF and the WTO, *Theory and Society*, 38: 459–484.

Chwieroth, Jeffrey M. (2010), *Capital Ideas: The IMF and the Rise of Financial Liberalization*, Princeton and Oxford: Princeton University Press.

Clark, Cynthia E. and Newell, Sue (2013), Institutional work and complicit decoupling across the U.S. capital markets: the work of rating agencies, *Business Ethics Quarterly*, 23(1): 1–30.

Coase, R.H. ([1937] 1991), The nature of the firm, in Williamson, Oliver E. and Winter, Sidney G. (eds), *The Nature of the Firm: Origin, Evolution, and Development*, New York and Oxford: Oxford University Press.

Cohan, William D. (2011), *Money and Power: How Goldman Sachs came to Rule the World*, London: Allen Lane and New York: Anchor Books.

Colander, David, Goldberg, Michael; Haas, Armin; Juselius, Katarina; Kirman, Alan; Lux, Thomas and Sloth, Brigitte (2009), The financial crisis and the systemic failure of the economics profession, *Critical Review*, 21(2–3): 249–267.

Colyvas, Jeannette A. and Powell, Walter W. (2007), From vulnerable to venerated: the institutionalization of academic entrepreneurship in the life sciences, *Research in the Sociology of Organizations*, 25: 219–259.

Commons, John R. (1924), *Legal Foundations of Capitalism*, New York: Macmillan.

Cooper, Melinda (2008), *Life as Surplus: Biotechnology and Capitalism in the Neoliberal Era*, Seattle and London: The University of Washington Press.

Cornaggio, Jess and Cornaggia, Kimberly J. (2013), Estimating the costs of issuer-paid credit ratings, *Review of Financial Studies*, 26(9): 2229–2269.

Craig, R.J. and Amernic, J.H. (2004), Enron discourse: the rhetoric of a resilient capitalism, *Critical Perspectives on Accounting*, 15(6–7): 813–851.

Crotty, James (2008), If financial market competition is intense, why are financial firm profits so high? Reflections on the current "golden age" of finance, *Competition and Change*, 12(2): 167–183.

Crotty, James (2009), Structural causes of the global financial crisis: a critical assessment of the "new financial architecture", *Cambridge Journal of Economics*, 33(4): 563–580.

Crotty, James (2012), The great austerity war: what caused the US deficit crisis and who should pay to fix it?, *Cambridge Journal of Economics*, 36: 79–104.

Crouch, Colin (2012), *The Strange Non-Death of Neo-Liberalism*, Cambridge: Polity.

Cullinan, Charlie (2004), Enron as a symptom of audit process breakdown: can the Sarbanes-Oxley Act cure the disease?, *Critical Perspectives on Accounting*, 15(6–7): 853–864.

Cusumano, M.A. (1985), *The Japanese Automobile Industry: Technology and Management at Toyota and Nissan*, Cambridge: Harvard University Press.

Daft, Richard L. and Weick, Karl E. (1984), Toward a model of organizations as interpretation systems, *Academy of Management Review*, 9(2): 284–295.

Dahrendorf, Ralf (1959), *Class and Class Conflict in Industrial Society*, London: Routledge and Kegan Paul.

Daily, Catherine M., Dalton, Dan R. and Cannella, Albert A., Jr (2003), Corporate governance: decades of dialogue and data, *The Academy of Management Review*, 28(3): 371–382.

Dalton, Dan R., Daily, Catherine M., Johnson, Jonathan L. and Ellstrand, Alan E. (1999), Number of directors and financial performance: a meta-analysis, *Academy of Management Journal*, 42(6): 674–686.

Daston, Loraine and Galison, Peter (2007), *Objectivity*, New York: Zone Books.

Davis, Gerald and Robbins, Gregory (2005), Nothing but net? Networks and status in corporate governance, in Knorr Cetina, Karin and Preda, Alex (eds), *The Sociology of Financial Markets*, Oxford and New York: Oxford University Press, pp. 290–311.

Davis, Gerald F. (2009), *Managed by the Markets: How Finance Reshaped America*, New York and Oxford: Oxford University Press.

Davis, Gerald F. (2010), After the ownership society: another world is possible, *Research in the Sociology of Organizations*, 30B: 331–356.

Davis Gerald F. and Greve, Henrich R. (1997), Corporate elite networks and governance changes in the 1980s, *American Journal of Sociology*, 103(1): 1–37.

Davis, Gerald F. and Stout, Suzanne K. (1992), Organization theory and the market for corporate control: a dynamic analysis of the characteristics of large takeover targets, 1980–1990, *Administrative Science Quarterly*, 37(4): 605–633

Davis, Gerald F., Diekmann, Kristine A. and Tinsley, Catherine (1994), The decline and fall of the conglomerate firm in the 1980s: the deinstitutionalization of an organization form, *American Sociological Review*, 59: 547–570.

Day, John (1987), *The Medieval Market Economy*, Oxford: Blackwell.

Deeg, Richard (2009), The rise of internal capitalist diversity? Changing patterns of finance and corporate governance in Europe, *Economy and Society*, 38(4): 552–579.

De Goede, M. (2005), *Virtue, Fortune, and Faith: A Genealogy of Finance*, Minneapolis and London: University of Minnesota Press.

Delbridge, Rick (1998), *Life on the Line in Contemporary Manufacturing: The Workplace Experience of Lean Production and the "Japanese Model"*, New York and Oxford: Oxford University Press.

Deli, Daniel N. and Santhanakrishnan, Mukunthan (2010), Syndication in venture capital financing, *The Financial Review*, 45: 557–578.

De Roover, Raymond (1974), The scholastic attitude toward trade and entrepreneurship, in Raymond De Roover, *Banking Business, and Economic Thought in Early Modern Europe: Selected Studies of Raymond de Roover*, edited by Julius Kirshner, Chicago and London: The University of Chicago Press, pp. 336–345.

Desrosière, Alain (1998), *The Politics of Large Numbers: A History of Statistical Reasoning*, translated by Camille Naish, Boston and London: Harvard University Press.

Deutschmann, Christoph (2011), Limits of financialization: sociological analyses of the financial crisis, *European Journal of Sociology*, 52(3): 347–389.

DiPrete, Thomas A., Eirich, Gregory M. and Pittinsky, Matthew (2010), Compensation benchmarking, leapfrogs, and the surge in executive pay, *American Journal of Sociology*, 115(6): 1671–1712.

Dittmar, Amy K. (2000), Why do firms repurchase stock?, *Journal of Business*, 73(3): 331–355.

Djelic, Marie-Louise (2001), *Exporting the American Model*, Oxford and London: Oxford University Press.

Djelic, Marie-Laure and Bothello, Joel (2013), Limited liability and its moral hazard implications: the systemic inscription of instability in contemporary capitalism, *Theory and Society*, 42(6): 589–615.

Dobbin, Frank and Jung, Jiwook (2010), The misapplication of Mr. Michael Jensen: how agency theory brought down the economy and why it might again, *Sociology of Organizations, Volume* 30B: 29–64.

Dobbin, Frank and Zorn, Dirk (2005), Corporate malfeasance and the myth of shareholder value, *Political Power and Social Theory*, 17: 179–198.

Doel, Marcus A. (2009), Miserly thinking/excessful geography: from restricted economy to global financial, crisis, *Environment and Planning D: Society and Space*, 27: 1054–1073,

Dore, Ronald (2008), Financialization of the global economy, *Industrial and Corporate Change*, 17(6): 1097–1112.

Douglas, Mary (1999), Jokes, in *Implicit Meanings: Selected Essays in Anthropology*, London: Routledge.

Drucker, Peter F. (1946), *Concept of the Corporation*, New York: The John Day Company.

Duggan, Lisa (2003), *The Twilight of Equality?: Neoliberalim, Cultural Politics, and the Attack on Democracy*, Boston: Beacon Press.

Duhem, Pierre (1996), *Essays in the History and Philosophy of Science*, translated and edited by Roger Ariew and Peter Barker, Indianapolis and Cambridge: Hackett Publishing.

Dumit, Joseph (2004), *Picturing Personhood: Brain Scans and Biomedical Identity*, Princeton: Princeton University Press.

Dwyer, Rachel E. (2013), The care economy? Gender, economic restructuring, and job polarization in the U.S. labor market, *American Sociological Review*, 78(3): 390–416.

Dye, T.R. (1978), Oligarchic tendencies in national policy-making: the role of the private policy-planning organization, *Journal of Politics*, 40: 309–331.

Edelman, Lauren (1992), Legal ambiguity and symbolic structures: organizational meditation of civil rights law, *American Journal of Sociology*, 97: 1531–1576.

Edelman, Lauren B. (1990), Legal environments and organizational governance: the expansion of due process in the American workplace, *American Journal of Sociology*, 95(6): 1401–1440.

Edelman, Lauren B. and Suchman, Mark C. (1997), The legal environment of organizations, *Annual Review of Sociology*, 23: 479–515.

Edelman, Lauren B., Fuller, Sally Riggs and Mara-Drita, Iona (2001), Diversity rhetoric and the managerialization of law, *American Journal of Sociology*, 106(6): 1589–1641.

Edelman, Lauren B., Krieger, Linda H., Eliason, Scott R., Albiston, Catherine R. and Mellema, Virginia (2011), When organizations rule: judicial deference to institutionalized employment structures, *American Journal of Sociology*, 117(3): 888–954.

Eichengreen, Barry J. (2008), *Globalizing Capital: A History of the International Monetary System*, Princeton: Princeton University Press.

Epstein, Gerald A. (ed.) (2005), *Financialization and the World Economy*, Cheltenham, UK and Northampton, MA, USA: Edward Elgar.

Erturk, Ismail, Froud, Julie, Johal, Sukhdev, Leaver, Adam and Williams, Karel (2007), Against agency: a positional critique, *Economy and Society*, 36(1): 51–77.

Erturk, Ismail, Froud, Julie, Johal, Sukhdev, Leaver, Adam and Williams, Karel (2010), Ownership matters: private equity and the political division of ownership, *Organization*, 17(5): 543–561.

Erturk, Ismail, Froud, Julie, Johal, Sukhdev, Leaver, Adam, and Williams, Karel (2012), Accounting for national success and failure: rethinking the UK case, *Accounting Forum*, 36(1): 5–17.

Espeland, Wendy N. and Sauder, M. (2007), Rankings and reactivity: how public measures recreate social worlds, *American Journal of Sociology*, 113(1): 1–40.

Esposito, Elena (2013), The structures of uncertainty: performativity and unpredictability in economic operations, *Economy and Society*, 42(1): 102–129.

Eztion, Dror and David, Gerald F. Davis (2008), Revolving doors?: A network analysis of corporate officers and US Government Officials, *Journal of Management Inquiry*, 17(3): 157–161.

Fairbrother, Malcolm (2014), Economists, capitalists, and the making of globalization: North American free trade in comparative-historical perspective, *American Journal of Sociology*, 119(5): 1324–1379.

Fama, Eugene F. (1970), Efficient capital markets: a review of theory and empirical work, *Journal of Finance*, 25(2): 383–417.

Farre-Mensa, Joan, Michaely, Roni and Schmalz, Martin (2014), Payout policy, *Annual Review in Financial Economics*, 6: 17.1–17.60.

Faulconbridge, James R. and Muzio, Daniel (2009) The financialization of large law firms: situated discourses and practices of reorganization, *Journal of Economic Geography*, 9(5): 641–661.

Festinger, Leon (1957), *A Theory of Cognitive Dissonance*, Stanford: Stanford University Press

Fichtenbaum, Rudy (2011), Do unions affect labor's share of income: evidence using panel data, *American Journal of Economics and Sociology*, 70(3): 784–810.

Fligstein, Neil (1987), The interorganizational power struggle: rise of financial personnel to top leadership in large corporations, *American Sociological Review*, 52(1): 44–58.

Fligstein, Neil (1990), *The Transformation of Corpotate Control*, Cambridge and London: Harvard University Press.

Fligstein, Neil and Choo, Jennifer (2005), Law and corporate governance, *Annual Review of Law and Social Science*, 1: 61–84.

Fligstein, Neil and Habinek, Jacob (2014), Sucker punched by the invisible hand: the world financial markets and the globalization of the US mortgage crisis, *Socio-Economic Review*, 12(4): 637–665.

Fligstein, Neil and Shin, Taekjin (2007), Shareholder value and the transformation of the U.S. economy, 1984–2000, *Sociological Forum*, 22: 399–424.

Flood, John A. (2007), Lawyers as sanctifiers: the role of elite law firms in international business transactions, *Indiana Journal of Global Legal Studies*, 14(2): 35–66.

Foucault, M. (1980), *Power/Knowledge*, New York: Harvester Wheatsheaf.

Fourcade, Marion (2006), The construction of a global profession: the transnationalization of economics, *American Journal of Sociology*, 112: 145–194.

Fourcade, Marion (2009), *Economists and Societies: Discipline and Profession in the United States, Britain, and France, 1890s to 1990s*, Princeton and London: Princeton University Press.

Fourcade, Marion and Healy, Kieran (2007), Moral views of market society, *Annual Review of Sociology*, 33: 285–311.

Fourcade, Marion and Healy, Kieran (2013), Classification situations: life-chances in the neoliberal era, *Accounting, Organizations and Society*, 38(8): 559–572.

Fox, Justin (2009), *The Myth of the Rational Market: A History of Risk, Reward and Delusion on Wall Street*, New York: HarperCollins.

Frank, Thomas (2000), *One Market Under God: Extreme Capitalism, Market Populism, and the End of Economic Democracy*, New York: Doubleday.

Frank, Thomas (2004), *What's the Matter with America?: The Resistible Rise of the American Right*, London: Secker and Warburg (end edition for the European market).

Frank, Thomas (2012), *Pity the Billionaire: The Hard Times Swindle and the Unlikely Comeback of the Right*, New York: Metropolitan Books/ Henry Holt.

Free, Clinton, Salterio, Steven E. and Shearer, Teri (2009), The construction of auditability: MBA rankings and assurance in practice, *Accounting, Organizations and Society*, 34(1): 119–140.

Freeman, Richard B. (2010), Its financialization!, *International Labour Review*, 149(2): 163–183.

Friedman, Jeffrey and Kraus, Wladimir (2012), *Engineering the Financial Crisis: Systemic Risk and the Failure of Regulation*, Philadelphia: University of Pennsylvania Press.

Friedman, Milton ([1962] 2002), *Capitalism and Freedom*, 4th edn, Chicago and London: The University of Chicago Press.

Frost, Carol Ann (2007), Credit rating agencies in capital markets: a review of research evidence on selected criticisms of the agencies, *Journal of Accounting, Auditing and Finance*, 22(3): 469–492.

Froud, Julie, Leaver, Adam and Williams, Karel (2007), New actors in a financialised economy and the remaking of capitalism, *New Political Economy*, 12(3): 339–347.

Froud, Julie, Haslam, Colin, Johal, Sukhdev and Williams, Karel (2000), Shareholder value and financialization: consultancy promises, management moves, *Economy and Society*, 29(1): 80–110.

Froud, Julie, Johal, Sukhdev, Papazian, Viken and Williams, Karel

(2004), The temptation of Houston: a case study of financialisation, *Critical Perspective on Accounting*, 15(6–7): 885–909.

Gay, Peter (1986), *Weimar Culture: The Outsider as Insider*, New York: Harper and Row.

Geertz, Clifford (1973), *The Interpretation of Cultures*, New York: Basic Books.

Gershon, Ilana (2011), Neolibereal agency, *Current Anthropology*, 52(4): 537–555.

Giddens, Anthony (1990), *The Consequences of Modernity*, Cambridge: Polity Press.

Gleadle, Pauline, Parris, Stuart, Shipman, Alan and Simonetti, Roberto (2014), Restructuring and innovation in pharmaceuticals and biotechs: the impact of financialisation, *Critical Perspectives on Accounting*, 25(1): 67–77.

Glyn, Andrew, Howell, David and Schmitt, John (2006), Labor market reforms: the evidence does not tell the orthodox tale, *Challenge*, 49(2): 5–22.

Gompers, Paul and Lerner, Josh (2001), The venture capital revolution, *Journal of Economic Perspectives*, 15(2): 145–168.

Gorman, Elizabeth H. and Kmec, Julie A. (2009), Hierarchical rank and women's organizational mobility: glass ceilings in corporate law firms, *American Journal of Sociology*, 114(5): 1428–1474.

Gorman, Michael and Sahlman, William A. (1989), What do venture capitalists do?, *Journal of Business Venturing*, 4: 231–248.

Gorton, Gary B. (2010), *Slapped by the Invisible Hand: The Panic of 2007*, New York and Oxford: Oxford University Press.

Gotham, Kevin Fox. (2006), The secondary circuit of capital reconsidered: globalization and the U.S: real estate sector, *American Journal of Sociology*, 112(1): 231–275.

Gourevitch, Peter A. and Shinn, James (2005), *Political Power and Corporate Control: The New Global Politics of Corporate Governance*, Princeton: Princeton University Press.

Graeber, David (2011), *History of Debt: The First 5,000 Years*, New York: Meville House.

Grahame, Kenneth ([1908] 1993), *The Wind in the Willows*, London: Wordsworth.

Gramsci, A. (1971), *Selection from Prison Notebooks*, New York: International Publishers.

Greenwald, Bruce C. and Stiglitz, Joseph E. (1986), Externalities in economies with imperfect information and incomplete markets, *Quarterly Journal of Economics*, 90: 229–264.

Griffin, Penny (2009), *Gendering the World Bank: Neoliberalism and the Gendered Foundation of Global Governance*, New York: Palgrave Macmillan.

Grimaldi, Rosa, Kenney, Martin, Siegel, Donald S. and Wright, Mike (2011), 30 years after Bayh–Dole: reassessing academic entrepreneurship, *Research Policy*, 40: 1045–1057.

Grosz, Elizabeth (2001), *Architecture from the Outside: Essays on Virtual and Real Spaces*, Cambridge: MIT Press.

Grugulis, Irena (2002), Nothing serious? Candidates' use of humour in management training, *Human Relations*, 55(4): 387–406.

Grullon, Gustavo and Ikenberry, David L. (2000), What do we know about stock repurchases?, *Journal of Applied Corporate Finance*, 13(1): 31–51.

Gutherie, James P. and Datta, Deepak K, (2008), Dumb and dumber: the impact of downsizing on firm performance as moderated by industry conditions, *Organization Science*, 19(1): 108–123.

Hacker, Jacob S. and Pierson, Paul (2010), Winner-take-all politics: public policy, political organization, and the precipitous rise of top incomes in the United States, *Politics and Society*, 38(2): 152–204.

Hacking, Ian (1990) *The Taming of Chance*, Cambridge: Cambridge University Press.

Hacking, Ian (1992), The self-vindicating of the laboratory sciences, in Pickering, Andrew (ed.), *Science as Practice and Culture*, Chicago and London: University of Chicago Press.

Haiven, Max (2014), *Cultures of Financialization: Fictitious Capital in Popular Culture and Everyday Life*, Basingstoke: Palgrave Macmillan.

Hall, Brian J. and Liebman, Jeffrey B. (1998), Are CEOs really paid like bureaucrats? *The Quarterly Journal of Economics*, 113(3): 653–691, doi:10.1162/003355398555702.

Hallyn, Fernand ([1987] 1990), *The Poetic Structure of the World: Copernicus and Kepler*, New York: Zone Books.

Hardy, Cynthia and Philips, Nelson (1999), No joking matter: discursive struggle in the Canadian refugee system, *Organization Studies*, 20(1): 1–24.

Harrington, Brooke (2008), *Pop Finance: Investment Clubs and the New Investor Populism*, Princeton and Oxford: Princeton University Press.

Hart, Oliver (1995), Corporate governance: some theory and implications, *The Economic Journal*, 105(430): 678–689.

Hart, Randle J. (2014), The greatest subversive plot in history? The American radical right and anti-UNESCO campaigning, *Sociology*, 48(3): 554–572.

Harvey, David (2010), *The Enigma of Capital and the Crisis of Capitalism*, London: Profile Books.

Hayek, F.A. (1944), *The Road to Serfdom*, Chicago: University of Chicago Press.

Hayek, Friedrich, von (1960), *The Constitution of Liberty*, Chicago and London: University of Chicago Press.

Hayward, Matthew L.A. and Boeker, Warren (1998), Power and conflict of interest in professional firms: evidence from investment banking, *Administrative Science Quarterly*, 43: 1–22.

Healey, Nigel M. (1992), The Thatcher supply-side "miracle": myth or reality?, *American Economist*, 36(1): 7–12.

Hertz, Noreena (2001), *The Silent Takeover: Global Capitalism and the Death of Democracy*, London: Heineman.

Hiatt, Shon R. and Park, Sangchan (2013), Lords of the harvest: third-party influence and regulatory approval of genetically modified organisms, *Academy of Management Journal*, 56(4): 923–944.

Hicken, Allen (2011), Clientelism, *Annual Review of Political Science*, 14: 289–310.

High, Brandon (2009), The recent historiography of American neoconservatism, *The Historical Journal*, 52(2): 475–491.

Hilferding, Rudolf von ([1910] 1981), *Finance Capital: A Study of the Latest Phase of Capitalist Development*, translated by Morris Watnick and Sam Gordoin, London: Routledge and Kegan Paul.

Hillman, Amy J. and Kiem, Gerald D. (2001), Shareholder value, stakeholder management, and social issues: what's the bottom line, *Strategic Management Journal*, 22: 125–139.

Hilt, Eric (2014), History of American corporate governance: law, institutions, and politics, *Annual Review in Financial Economics*, 6: 8.1–8.21.

Himmelstein, Jerome L. (1992), *To the Right: The Transformation of American Conservatism*, Berkeley, Los Angeles and London: University of California Press.

Hindess, Barry (1996), *The Discourse on Power: From Hobbes to Foucault*, Oxford: Blackwell.

Hirschman, Albert O. (1970), *Exit, Voice, and Loyalty*, Cambridge: Harvard University Press.

Hirschman, Albert O. (1977), *The Passions and the Interests*, Princeton: Princeton University Press.

Hirschman, Albert O. (1982), Rival interpretations of market society: civilizing, destructive, or feeble?, *Journal of Economic Literature*, 20: 1463–1484.

Ho, Karen (2009), *Liquidated. An Ethnography of Wall Street*, Durham and London: Duke University Press.

Hochberg, Yael V., Ljungqvist, Alexander and Lu, Yang (2007), Whom you know matters: venture capital networks and investment performance, *Journal of Finance*, 62(1): 251–301.

Hochschild, Arlie Russell (2012), *The Outsourced Self: Intimate Life in Market Times*, New York: Metropolitan Books.

Hogle, Linda F. (2009), Pragmatic objectivity and the standardization of engineered tissues, *Social Studies of Science*, 39: 717–742.

Hopkins, Michael M., Crane, Philippa A., Nightingale, Paul and Baden-Fuller, Charles (2013), Buying big into biotech: scale, financing, and the industrial dynamics of UK biotech, 1980–2009, *Industrial and Corporate Change*, 22(4): 903–952.

Hummel, R.P. (2006), The triumph of numbers: knowledges and the mismeasurement of management, *Administration and Society*, 38(1): 58–78.

Humphrey, Christopher, Loft, Anne and Woods, Margaret (2009), The global audit profession and the international financial architecture: understanding regulatory relationships at a time of financial crisis, *Accounting, Organizations and Society*, 34(6–7): 810–825.

Hyman, Louis (2011), *Debtor Nation: The History of America in Red Ink*, Princeton: Princeton University Press.

Inglehart, Ronald (1997), *Modernization and Postmodernization: Cultural, Economic, and Political Change in 43 Societies*, Princeton: Princeton University Press.

Inglehart, Ronald and Norris, Pippa (2009), *Cosmopolitan Communications: Cultural Diversity in a Globalized World*, Cambridge: Cambridge University Press.

Ireland, Paddy (2010), Limited liability, shareholder rights and the problem of corporate irresponsibility, *Cambridge Journal of Economics*, 34: 837–856.

Jabłecki, Juliusz and Machaj, Mateusz (2009), The regulated meltdown of 2008, *Critical Review*, 21(2–3): 301–328.

Jacobs, David and Myers, Lindsey (2014), Union strength, neoliberalism, and inequality: contingent political analyses of U.S. income differences since 1950, *American Sociological Review*, 79(4): 752–774.

James, Simon (1993), The idea brokers: the impact of think tanks on British government, *Public Administration*.,71(4): 491–506

Janis, Irving L. (1982), *Groupthink: Psychological Studies of Policy Decisions and Fiascoes*, 2nd edn, Boston: Houghton Mifflin.

Jarsulic, Marc (2013), The origins of the U.S. financial crisis of 2007: how a house-price bubble, a credit bubble, and regulatory failure caused the greatest economic disaster since the great depression, in Wolfson, Martin H. and Epstein, Gerald, A. (eds), *Handbook of the Political*

Economy of Financial Crises, New York and Oxford: Oxford University Press, pp. 21–46.

Jenkins, J. Craig and Eckert, Craig M. (2000), The right turn in economic policy: business elites and the new conservative economics, *Sociological Forum*, 15(2): 307–338.

Jensen, M. (1993), The modern industrial revolution, exit, and failure of internal control systems, *Journal of Finance*, 48(3): 831–880.

Jensen, Michael C. (1986), Agency costs of free cash flow, corporate finance, and takeovers, *American Economics Review*, 76(2): 323–329.

Jensen, Michael C. (2002), Value maximization, stakeholder theory, and the corporate objective function, *Business Ethics Quarterly*, 12(2): 235–256.

Jensen, Michael C. and Meckling, William H. (1976), Theory of the firm: managerial behavior, agency costs and ownership structure, *Journal of Financial Economics*, 3(4): 305–360.

Jensen, Michael C. and Murphy, Kevin J. (1990), CEO incentives: it's not how much you pay but how, *Harvard Business Review*, 68(3): 138–149

Jones, Daniel Stedman (2012), *Masters of the Universe: Hayek, Friedman, and the Birth of Neoliberal Politics*, Princeton and Oxford: Princeton University Press.

Jones, Owen (2011), *Chavs: The Demonization of the Working Class*, London: Verso.

Judt, Tony (2010), *Ill Fares the Land: A Treatise on Our Present Discontent*, London: Allen Lane.

Kahle, Kathleen M. (2002), When a buyback isn't a buyback, *Journal of Financial Economics*, 63: 235–261.

Kahle, Kathleen M. and Stulz, René M. (2013), Access to capital investment, and the financial crisis, *Journal of Financial Economics*, 110(2): 280–299.

Kalecki, Michał (1942), A theory of profits, *The Economic Journal*, 52(206/207): 258–267.

Kalecki, Michał (1943), Political aspects of full employment, *Political Quarterly*, 14(4): 322–330.

Kalthoff, Herbert (2005), Practices of calculation. Economic representation and risk management, *Theory, Culture and Society*, 22(2): 69–97.

Keay, Andrew (2011), Moving towards stakeholderism? Constituency statutes, enlightened shareholder value, and more: much ado about little?, *European Business Law Review*, 22: 1–49

Keen, Maurice (1968), *The Penguin Medieval History of Europe*, London: Penguin.

Keevers, Lynne, Treleaven, Lesley, Sykes, Christopher and Darcy,

Michael (2012), Made to measure: taming practices with results-based accountability, *Organization Studies*, 33(1) 97–120.

Keller, Matthew R. and Block, Fred (2013), Explaining the transformation in the US innovation system: the impact of a small government program, *Socio-Economic Review*, 11(4): 629–656.

Kelly, Nathan J. and Enns, Peter K. (2010), Inequality and the dynamics of public opinion: the self-reinforcing link between economic inequality and mass preferences, *American Journal of Political Science*, 54(4): 855–870.

Kenney, Martin (2011), How venture capital became a component of the US national system of innovation, *Industrial and Corporate Change*, 20(6): 1677–1723.

Kertum, Samuel and Lerner, Josh (2000), Assessing the contribution of venture capital to innovation, *RAND Journal of Economics*, 31: 674–692.

Keynes, John Maynard (1953), *The General Theory of Employment, Interest and Money*, New York and London: Harcourt.

Khurana, R. (2002), *Searching for a Corporate Savior: The Irrational Quest for a Charismatic CEO*, Princeton: Princeton University Press.

Khurana, Rakesh (2007), *From Higher Aims to Hired Hands: The Social Transformation of American Business Schools and the Unfulfilled Promise of Management as a Profession*, Princeton: Princeton University Press.

Kinderman, Daniel, (2012), "Free us up so we can be responsible!" The co-evolution of corporate social responsibility and neo-liberalism in the UK, 1977–2010, *Socio-Economic Review*, 10, 29–57.

Kindleberger, Charles P. (2007), *A Financial History of Western Europe*, New York and London: Routledge.

Kipnis, Andrew (2008), Audit cultures: neoliberal governmentality, socialist legacy, or technological governing, *American Ethnologist*, 35(2): 275–289.

Kleinknecht, Alfred, van Schaik, Flore N. and Zhou, Haibo (2014), Is flexible labour good for innovation? Evidence from firm-level data, *Cambridge Journal of Economics*, 38(5): 1207–1219

Knight, Frank H. (1921), *Risk, Uncertainty, and Profit*, Boston and New York: Houghton Mifflin.

Knorr Cetina, Karin and Grimpe, Barbara (2008), Global financial technologies: scoping systems that raise the world, in Pinch, Trevor and Swedberg, Richard (eds), *Living in a Material World: Economic Sociology Meets Science and Technology Studies*, Cambridge and London: MIT Press, pp. 161–189.

Knorr Cetina, Karin and Preda, Alex (eds) (2005), *The Sociology of Financial Markets*, New York and Oxford: Oxford University Press.

Kogut, Bruce and Macpherson, J. Muir (2011), The mobility of economists and the diffusion of policy ideas: the influence of economics on national policies, *Research Policy*, 40: 1307–1320.

Kogut, Bruce, Urso, Pietro and Walker, Gordon (2007), Emergent properties of a new financial market: American venture capital syndication, 1960–2005, *Management Science*, 53: 181–198.

Konzelmann, Suzanne J. (2014), The political economics of austerity, *Cambridge Journal of Economics*, 38 (4): 701–741.

Korczynski, Marek (2011),The dialectical sense of humour: routine joking in a Taylorized factory, *Organization Studies*, 32(10): 1421–1439.

Korpi, Walter and Palme, Joakim (2003), New politics and class politics in the context of austerity and globalization: welfare state regress in 18 Countries, 1975–95, *American Political Science Review*, 97(3): 425–446.

Kotz, David M. (2013), Changes in the postwar global economy and the roots of the financial crisis, in Wolfson, Martin H. and Epstein, Gerald, A. (eds), *Handbook of the Political Economy of Financial Crises*, New York and Oxford: Oxford University Press, pp. 395–410.

Krippner, Greta R. (2005), The financialization of the American economy, *Socio-Economic Review*, 3(2): 173–208.

Krippner, Greta R. (2010), The political economy of financial exuberance, *Research in the Sociology of Organizations*, 30B: 141–173.

Krippner, Greta R. (2011), *Capitalizing on Crisis: The Political Origins of the Rise of Finance*, Cambridge and London: Harvard University Press.

Kristal, Tali (2013), The capitalist machine: computerization, workers' power, and the decline in labor's share within U.S. industries, *American Sociological Review*, 78(3): 361–389.

Kula, Witold (1986), *Measures and Men*, Princeton: Princeton University Press.

Kundera, Milan (1988), *The Art of the Novel*, translated by Linda Asher, New York: Grove Press.

Lakatos, I. (1970), Falsification and the methodology of scientific research programmes, in Lakatos, I. and Musgrave, A. (eds), *Criticism and the Growth of Knowledge*, Cambridge: Cambridge University Press, pp. 91–195.

Lane, Carrie A. (2010), *The Company of One: Neoliberal Faith and the Post-Organizational Man*, Ithaca: Cornell University Press.

Lane, Frederic C. (1973), *Venice: A Maritime Republic*, Baltimore: Johns Hopkins University Press.

Langley, Paul (2008), Financialization and the consumer credit boom, *Competition and Change*, 12(2), 133–147.

Langley, Paul (2013), Anticipating uncertainty, reviving risk? On the stress testing of finance in crisis, *Economy and Society*, 42(1): 51–73.

La Porta, Rafael, Lopez-de-Silanes, Florencio, Shleifer, Andrei and Vishny, Robert (2000), Investor protection and corporate governance, *Journal of Financial Economics*, 58(1–2): 3–27.

Lawrence, Thomas B., Leca, Bernard and Zilber, Tammar B. (2013), Institutional work: current research, new directions and overlooked issues, *Organization Studies*, 34(8): 1023–1033.

Lawrence, Thomas B., Suddaby, Roy and Leca, Bernard (2009), *Institutional Work: Actors and Agency in Institutional Studies of Organization*, Cambridge: Cambridge University Press.

Lazonick, William (2010), Innovative business models and varieties of capitalism: financialization of the U.S. corporation, *Business History Review*, 84: 675–702.

Lazonick, William and Mazzucato, Mariana (2013), The risk-reward nexus in the innovation-inequality relationship: who takes the risks? Who gets the rewards?, *Industrial and Corporate Change*, 22(4): 1093–1128.

Lazonick, William and O'Sullivan, Mary (2000), Maximizing shareholder value: a new ideology for corporate governance, *Economy and Society*, 29(1): 13–35.

Lazzarato, Maurizio (2012), *The Making of Indebted Man*, Los Angeles: Semiotext(e).

Le Goff, Jacques ([1986] 1988), *Your Money or Your Life: Economy and Religion in the Middle Ages*, New York: Zone Books.

Leeson, Peter T., Ryan, Matt E. and Williamson, Claudia R. (2012), Think tanks, *Journal of Comparative Economics*, 40: 62–77.

Lemarchand, Rene and Legg, Keith (1972), Political clientelism and development: a preliminary analysis, *Comparative Politics*, 4(2): 149–178.

Lenglet, Marc (2011), Conflicting codes and codings: how algorithmic trading is reshaping financial regulation, *Theory, Culture and Society*, 28(6): 44–66.

Lépinay, Vincent Antonin (2011), *Codes of Finance: Engineering Derivatives in a Global Bank*, Princeton: Princeton University Press.

Lerner, Josh (2009), *Boulevard of Broken Dreams: Why Public Efforts to Boost Entrepreneurship and Venture Capital Have Failed and What to Do About It*, Princeton and London: Princeton University Press.

Levitt, Kari Polanyi (2013a), From mercantilism to neoliberalism and the financial crisis of 2008, in Levitt, Kari Polanyi (ed.), *From the Great Transformation to the Great Financialization: On Karl Polanyi and Other Essays*, New York: Zed Books, pp. 137–179.

Levitt, Kari Polanyi (2013b), The great financialization of 2008, in Levitt, Kari Polanyi, *From the Great Transformation to the Great Financialization: On Karl Polanyi and Other Essays*, New York: Zed Books, pp. 180–191.

Leyshon, A. and Thrift, N. (2007), The capitalization of almost everything: the future of finance and capitalism, *Theory, Culture, and Society*, 24(7/8): 97–115.

Liker, Jeffrey K. (2004), *The Toyota Way: 14 Management Principles from the World's Greatest Manufacturer*, Cambridge: Harvard Business School Press.

Lin, Ken-Hou and Tomaskovic-Devey, Donald (2013), Financialization and U.S. income inequality, 1970–2008, *American Journal of Sociology*, 118(5): 1284–1329.

Lipovetsky, Gilles (2005), *Hypermodern Times*, translated by Andrew Brown, Cambridge: Polity Press.

Liu, Yujia and Grusky, David B. (2013), The payoff to skill in the third industrial revolution, *American Journal of Sociology*, 118(5): 1330–1374.

Lord, Richard A. and Saito, Yoshie (2010), Trends in CEO compensation and equity holdings for S&P 1500 firms: 1994–2007, *Journal of Applied Finance*, 3(2): 40–56.

Lorenz, Chris (2012), If you're so smart, why are you under surveillance? Universities, neoliberalism, and new public management, *Critical Inquiry*, 38: 599–629.

Lounsbury, Michael and Crumley, Ellen T. (2007), New practice creation: an institutional approach to innovation, *Organization Studies*, 28: 993–1012.

Lovell, Heather (2014), Climate change, markets and standards: the case of financial accounting, *Economy and Society*, 43(2): 260–284.

Lowry, Robert C. (1999), Foundation patronage toward citizen groups and think tanks: who gets grants?, *Journal of Politics*, 61(3): 758–777.

Luhmann, Niklas (2000), *Art as a Social System*, translated by Eva M. Knodt, Stanford: Stanford University Press.

Lukes, Steven (ed.) (1986), *Power*, Oxford: Blackwell.

Lysandrou, Photis (2013), Debt intolerance and the 90 per cent debt threshold: two impossibility theorems, *Economy and Society*, 42(4): 521–542.

Macéus, Karolina Palutko (2014), *Det är jag som äger Carnegie!: Maktspelet om Sveriges mest anrika bank*, Stockholm: Ekerlids.

MacKenzie, Donald (2004), The big, bad wolf and the rational market: portfolio investment, the 1987 crash and the performativity of economics, *Economy and Society*, 33(3): 303–334.

MacKenzie, Donald (2006), *An Engine, Not a Camera: How Financial Models Shape Markets*, Cambridge and London: MIT Press.

MacKenzie, Donald (2012), Knowledge production in financial markets: credit default swaps, the ABX and the subprime crisis, *Economy and Society*, 41(3): 335–359.

MacKenzie, Donald and Pardo-Guerra, Juan Pablo (2014) Insurgent capitalism: island, bricolage and the re-making of finance, *Economy and Society*, 43(2): 153–182.

MacKenzie, Donald and Spears, Taylor (2014a), "The formula that killed Wall Street": the Gaussian copula and modelling practices in investment banking, *Social Studies of Science*, 44(3): 393–417.

MacKenzie, Donald and Spears, Taylor (2014b), "A device for being able to book P&L": the organizational embedding of the Gaussian copula, *Social Studies of Science*, 44(3): 418–440.

Maclean, Mairi, Harvey, Charles and Kling, Gerhard (2014), Pathways to power: class, hyper-agency and the French corporate elite, *Organization Studies*, 35(6): 825–855.

Madrick, Jeff (2011), *Age of Greed: The Triumph of Finance and the Decline of America, 1970 to the Present*, New York: Alfred A. Knopf.

Madrick, Jeff (2012), The deliberate low-wage, high-insecurity economic model, *Work and Occupations*, 39(4): 321–330.

Mandis, Steven G. (2013), *What Happened to Goldman Sachs: An Insider's Story of Organizational Drift and its Unintended Consequences*, Boston and London: Harvard Business Review Press.

Manne, Henry G. (1965), Mergers and the market for corporate control, *Journal of Political Economy*, 73(2): 110–120.

Marron, Donncha (2007) "Lending by numbers": credit scoring and the constitution of risk within American consumer credit, *Economy and Society*, 36(1): 103–133

Martin, Felix (2014), *Money the Unauthorized Biography*, London: Vintage.

Martin, Isaac William (2010), Redistributing toward the rich: strategic policy crafting in the campaign to repeal the sixteenth amendment, 1938–1958, *American Journal Sociology*, 116(1): 1–52.

Martin, Randy (2002), *Financialization of Everyday Life*, Philadelphia: Temple University Press.

Martinez-Moyano, Ignacio J., McCaffrey, David P. and Oliva, Rogelio (2014), Drift and adjustment in organizational rule compliance: explaining the "regulatory pendulum" in financial markets. *Organization Science*, 25(2): 321–338.

Mathis, Jérmôme, McAndrews, James and Rochet, Jean-Charles (2009), Rating the raters: are reputation concerns powerful enough to discipline rating agencies?, *Journal of Monetary Economics*, 56(5): 657–674.

Mazzoleni, Roberto (2011), Before Bayh-Dole: public research funding, patents, and pharmaceutical innovation (1945–1965), *Industrial and Corporate Change*, 20(3): 721–749.

McCloskey, Deirdre N. (2006), *The Bourgeois Virtues: Ethics for an Age of Commerce*, Chicago and London: The University of Chicago Press.

McConnell, John J. and Buser, Stephen A. (2011), The origins and evolution of the market for mortgage-backed securities, *Annual Review in Financial Economics*, 3: 173–192.

McGirr, Lisa (2001), *Suburban Warriors: The Origins of the New American Right*, Princeton: Princeton University Press.

McGivern, Gerry and Ferlie, Ewan (2007), Playing tick-box games: interrelating defences in professional appraisal, *Human Relations*, 60(9): 1361–1385

Medvetz, Thomas (2010), "Public policy is like having a Vaudeville act": languages of duty and difference among think tank-affiliated policy experts, *Qualitative Sociology*, 33: 549–562.

Medvetz, Thomas (2012) *Think Tanks in America*, Chicago and London: University Of Chicago Press.

Megill, Allan (ed.) (1994), *Rethinking Objectivity*, Durham: Duke University Press.

Mehrling, Perry (1999), The vision of Hyman P. Minsky, *Journal of Economic Behavior and Organization*, 39(2): 129–158.

Mehrling, Perry (2011), *The New Lombard Street: How the Fed Became the Dealer of Last Resort*, Princeton and Oxford: Princeton University Press.

Mehta, Judith (2013), The discourse of bounded rationality in academic and policy arenas: pathologising the errant consumer, *Cambridge Journal of Economics*, 37(6): 1243–1261.

Merton, Robert K. (1973), *The Sociology of Science: Theoretical and Empirical Investigations*, edited by Norman W. Storer, Chicago: The University of Chicago Press.

Messersmith, Jake G., Lee, Jeong-Yeon, Guthrie, James P., Ji, Yong-Yeon (2014), Turnover at the top: executive team departures and firm performance, *Organization Science*, 25(3): 776–793.

Mian, Atif and Sufi, Amir (2009), The consequences of mortgage credit expansion: evidence from the U.S. mortgage default crisis, *The Quarterly Journal of Economics*, 124(4): 1449–1496

Mian, Atif and Sufi, Amir (2014), *House of Debt*, Chicago and London: The University of Chicago Press.

Mian, Atif, Sufi, Amir and Trebbi, Francesco (2010), The political economy of the US mortgage default crisis, *The American Economic Review*, 100(5): 1967–1998.

Milberg, William (2008), Shifting sources and uses of profits: sustaining US financialization with global value chains, *Economy and Society*, 37(3): 420–451.

Milberg, William and Winkler, Deborah, (2010), Financialisation and the dynamics of offshoring in the USA, *Cambridge Journal of Economics*, 34: 275–293.

Miller, Peter (2001), Governing by numbers: why calculative practices matter, *Social Research*, 68(2): 379–395.

Millo, Yuval and Mackenzie, Donald (2009), The usefulness of inaccurate models: towards an understanding of the emergence of financial risk management, *Accounting, Organization and Society*, 34: 638–653.

Mills, Charles Wright (1956), *The Power Elite*, New York and Oxford: Oxford University Press.

Mills, Charles Wright (1959), *The Sociological Imagination*, Oxford: Oxford University Press.

Minsky, Hyman P. (1986), *Stabilizing an Unstable Economy: A Twentieth Century Fund Report*, New Haven and London: Yale University Press.

Mirowski, Philip (2005), A revisionist's view of the history of economic thought, *Challenge*, 48(5): 79–94.

Mirowski, Philip (2010), Inherent vice: Minsky, Markomata, and the tendency of markets to undermine themselves, *Journal of Institutional Economics*, 6(4): 415–443.

Mirowski, Philip (2011), *Science-Mart: Privatizing American Science*, Cambridge and London: Harvard University Press.

Mirowski, Philip (2013), *Never Let a Serious Crisis go to Waste: How Neoliberalism Survived the financial meltdown*, New York and London: Verso.

Mizruchi, Mark (2004), Berle and Means revisited: the governance and politics of large U.S. corporations, *Theory and Society*, 33: 519–617.

Mizruchi, Mark S. (2010), The American corporate elites and the historical roots of the financial crisis of 2008, *Research in the Sociology of Organizations*, 30B: 103–139.

Mizruchi, Mark S. (2013), *The Fracturing of the American Corporate Elite*, Cambridge, MA: Harvard University Press.

Mizruchi, Mark S. and Stearns, Linda Brewster (2001), Getting deals done: the use of social networks in bank decision-making, *American Sociological Review*, 66: 647–671

Mizruchi, Mark S. and Stearns, Linda Brewster (2005), Banking and financial markets, in Smelser, Neil J. and Swedberg, Richard (eds), *The Handbook of Economic Sociology*, 2nd edn, Princeton and London: Princeton University Press, pp. 284–306.

Mizruchi, Mark S., Stearns, Linda Brewster and Fleischer, Anne (2011), Getting a bonus: social networks, performance, and reward among commercial bankers, *Organization Science*, 22(1): 42–59.

Mizruchi, Mark S., Stearns, Linda Brewster and Marquis, Christopher

(2006), The conditional nature of embeddedness: a study of borrowing by large U.S. firms, 1973–1994, *American Sociological Review*, 71: 310–333.

Moe, Terry M. (1984), The new economics of organization, *American Journal of Political Science*, 28: 739–777.

Montgomerie, Johnna (2009), The pursuit of (past) happiness?: middle-class indebtedness and American financialisation, *New Political Economy*, 14(1): 1–24.

Mowery, David C. and Ziedonis, Arvide, A. (2002), Academic patent quality before and after the Bayh-Dole act in the United States, *Research Policy*, 31: 399–418.

Mulholland, Marc (2012), *Bougeoisie Liberty and the Politics of Fear: From Absolutism to Neo-conservatism*, New York and Oxford: Oxford University Press.

Nagel, Thomas (1986), *The View From Nowhere*, New York and Oxford: Oxford University Press.

Neff, Gina (2013), *Venture Labor: Work and the Burden of Risk in Innovative Industries*, Cambridge and London: MIT Press.

Neu, Dean, Gomez, Elizabeth Ocampo, Graham, Cameron and Heincke, Monica (2006), "Informing" technologies and the World Bank, *Accounting, Organizations and Society*, 31(7): 635–662.

Neumann, John von and Morgenstern, Oskar (1947), *Theory of Games and Economic Behavior*, Princeton: Princeton University Press.

Nicolai, Alexander T., Schultz, Ann-Christine and Thomas, Thomas W. (2010), What Wall Street wants – exploring the role of security analysts in the evolution and spread of management concepts, *Journal of Management Studies*, 47(1): 162–189.

Nik-Khah, Edward (2014), Neoliberal pharmaceutical science and the Chicago School of Economics, *Social Studies of Science*, 44(4): 489–517.

North, Douglass C. (1991), Institutions, *Journal of Economic Perspectives*, 5(1): 97–112.

North, Douglass C. and Weingast, Barry R. (1989), Constitutions and commitment: the evolution of institutional governing public choice in seventeenth-century England, *The Journal of Economic History*, 49(4): 803–832.

Olson, Mancur (1965), *The Logic of Collective Action*, Cambridge: Harvard University Press.

Onaran, Özlem, Stockhammer, Engelbert and Grafl, Lucas (2011), Financialisation, income distribution and aggregate demand in the USA, *Cambridge Journal of Economics*, 35(4): 637–661.

Orhangazi, Özgür (2008), Financialisation and capital accumulation in the non-financial corporate sector: a theoretical and empirical investigation on the US economy: 1973–2003, *Cambridge Journal of Economics*, 32: 863–886.

Ortmann, Günther (2010), On drifting rules and standards, *Scandinavian Journal of Management*, 26: 204–214.

O'Sullivan, Mary (2000), *Contests for Corporate Control: Corporate Governance and Economic Performance in the United States and Germany*, New York and Oxford: Oxford University Press.

Owen-Smith, Jason (2006), Commercial imbroglios: proprietary science the contemporary university, in Frickell, Scott and Moore, Kelly (eds), *The New Political Sociology of Science: Institutions, Networks and Power*, Madison: The University of Wisconsin Press, pp. 63–90.

Pagano, Ugo and Rossi, Maria Alessandra (2009), The crash of the knowledge economy, *Cambridge Journal of Economics*, 33(4): 665–683.

Palley, Thomas I. (2013), *Financialization: The Economics of Finance Capital Domination*, New York and Basingstoke: Palgrave Macmillan.

Palma, José Gabriel (2009), The revenge of the market on the rentiers: why neo-liberal reports of the end of history turned out to be premature, *Cambridge Journal of Economics*, 33(4): 829–869

Panitch, Leo and Gindin, Sam (2012), *The Making of Global Capitalism: The Political Economy of American Empire*, New York and London: Verso.

Pareto, Vilfredo (1901), *The Rise and Fall of Elites*, New Brunswick: Transaction Publishers.

Partnoy, Frank (1999), The Siskel and Ebert of financial markets?: Two thumbs down for the credit rating agencies, *Washington University Law Quarterly*, 77(3): 619–714.

Partnoy, Frank (2003), *Infectious Greed: How Deceit and Risk Corrupted the Financial Markets*, London: Profile Books.

Peck, Jamie (2010), *Constructions of Neoliberal Reason*, New York and Oxford: Oxford University Press.

Peck, Jamie and Theodore, Nikolas (2000), Work first: workfare and the regulation of contingent labour markets, *Cambridge Journal of Economics*, 24: 119–138.

Peet, Richard (2007), *Geography of Power. The Making of Global Economic Policy*, London and New York. Zed Books.

Peet, Richard (2011), Inequality, crisis and austerity in finance capitalism, *Cambridge Journal of Regions, Economy and Society*, 4(3): 383–399.

Peirce, Charles Sanders (1991), *Peirce on Signs: Writings on Semiotics by Charles Sanders Peirce*, edited by James Hopes, Chapel Hill and London: The University of North Carolina Press.

Peñaloza, Lisa and Barnhart, Michelle (2011), Living U.S. capitalism:

the normalization of credit/debt, *Journal of Consumer Research*, 38(4): 743–763.

Perrow, Charles (2010), The meltdown was not an accident, *Research in the Sociology of Organizations*, 30B: 309–330.

Pfeffer, J. and Salancik, G.R. (1978), *The External Control of Organizations: A Resource Dependence Perspective*, New York: Harper and Row.

Pickering, Andrew (2010), *The Cybernetic Brain: Sketches of Another Future*, Chicago and London: The University of Chicago Press.

Pickersgill, Martyn (2011), Ordering disorder: knowledge production and uncertainty in neuroscience research, *Science as Culture*, 20(1): 71–87.

Piketty, Thomas (2014), *Capital in the Twenty-First Century*, Cambridge: Harvard University Press.

Piketty, Thomas and Saez, Emanuel (2003), Income inequality in the United States, 1913–1998, *Quarterly Journal of Economics*, 118(1): 1–39.

Pink, Daniel H. (2001), *Free Agent Nation: How America's New Independent Workers are Transforming the Way we Live*, New York: Warner Books.

Pitts-Taylor, Victoria (2010). The plastic brain: neoliberalism and the neuronal self, *Health*, 14(6): 635–652.

Pixley, Jocelyn (2012), *Emotions in Finance: Books, Bust, and Uncertainty*, New York and Cambridge: Cambridge University Press.

Polillo, Simone (2011), Money, moral authority, and the politics of creditworthiness, *American Sociological Review*, 76(3): 437–464.

Polillo, Simone and Guillén, Mauro F. (2005), Globalization pressures and the state: the worldwide spread of central bank Independence, *American Journal of Sociology*, 110(6): 1764–1802.

Pontusson, Jonas and Raess, Damian (2012), How (and why) is this time different? The politics of economic crisis in western Europe and the United States, *Annual Review of Political Science*, 15: 13–33.

Poon, Martha (2009), From new deal institutions to capital markets: commercial consumer risk scores and the making of subprime mortgage finance, *Accounting, Organizations and Society*, 34 (5): 654–674.

Porter, Theodore M. (1994), Objectivity as standardization: the rhetoric of impersonality in measurement, statistics, and cost-benefit analysis, in Megill, Allan (ed.), *Rethinking Objectivity*, Durham: Duke University Press, pp. 197–238.

Porter, Theodore M. (1995), *Trust in Numbers: The Pursuit of Objectivity in Science and Public Life*, Princeton: Princeton University Press.

Porter, Theodore M. (2012), Surface and depth in science and science studies, *Osiris*, 27(1): 209–226.

Powell, Walter W. and Snellman, Kaisa (2004), The knowledge economy, *Annual Review of Sociology*, 30: 199–220.

Power, Michael (1996), Making things auditable, *Accounting, Organization, and Society*, 21(2–3): 289–315.

Power, Michael (1997), *The Audit Society: Rituals of Verification*, New York and Oxford: Oxford University Press.

Power, Michael (2013), The apparatus of fraud risk, *Accounting, Organizations and Society*, 39(6–7): 525–543.

Prahalad, C.K. and Hamel, Gary (1990), The core competence of the corporation, *Harvard Business Review*, 68: 79–91

Prechel, Harland (1994), Economic crisis and the centralization of control over the managerial process: corporate restructuring and neo-Fordist decision-making, *American Sociological Review*, 59: 725–745.

Prechel, Harland and Morris, Theresa (2010), The effects of organizational and political embeddedness on financial malfeasance in the largest U.S. corporations: dependence, incentives, and opportunities, *American Sociological Review*, 75(3): 331–354.

Preda, Alex (2006), Socio-technical agency in financial markets: the case of the stock ticker, *Social Studies of Science*, 36: 753–782.

Preda, Alex (2009a), *Information, Knowledge and Economic Life: An Introduction to the Sociology of markets*, New York and Oxford: Oxford University Press.

Preda, Alex (2009b), Brief encounters: calculation and the interaction order of anonymous electronic markets, *Accounting, Organization and Society*, 34: 675–693.

Pryke, Michael (2010), Money's eye: the visual preparation of financial markets, *Economy and Society*, 39(4): 427–459.

Quiggin, John (2010), *Zombie Economics; How Dead Ideas Still Walk Among Us*, Princeton and London: Princeton University Press.

Rafferty, Matthew (2008), The Bayh-Dole act and university research and development, *Research Policy*, 37: 29–40.

Reay, Michael J. (2012), The flexible unity of economics, *American Journal of Sociology*, 118(1): 45–87.

Reay, Mike (2007), Academic knowledge and expert authority in American economics, *Sociological Perspectives*, 50(1): 101–129.

Reddy, Sanjay G. (1996), Claims in expert knowledge and the subversion of democracy, *Economy and Society*, 25(2): 222–254.

Reed, R. and DeFillippi, R.J. (1990), Causal ambiguity: barriers to imitations, and sustainable competitive advantage, *Academy of Management Review*, 15(1): 88–102.

Reichmann, Werner (2013), Epistemic participation: how to produce knowledge about the economic future, *Social Studies of Science*, 43(6): 852–877.

Rider, Christopher I. and Swaminathan, Anand (2012), They just fade away: mortality in the US venture capital industry, *Industrial and Corporate Change*, 21(1): 151–185.

Robson, Keith, Humphrey, Christopher, Khalifa, Rihab and Jones, Julian (2007), Transforming audit technologies: business risk audit methodologies and the audit field, *Accounting, Organizations, and Society*, 32, 409–438.

Rock, Edward A. (2013), Adapting to the new shareholder-centric reality, *University of Pennsylvania Law Review*, 161(7): 1907–1988.

Rodrigues, Suzana B. and Child, John (2010), Private equity, the minimalist organization and the quality of employment relations, *Human Relations*, 63(9): 1321–1342.

Roe, Mark (2003), *Political Determinants of Corporate Governance: Political Context, Corporate Impact*, New York and Oxford: Oxford University Press.

Rom, Mark Carl (2009), The credit rating agencies and the subprime mess: greedy, ignorant, and stressed?, *Public Administration Review*, 69(4): 640–650.

Rona-Tas, Akos and Hiss, Stefanie (2010), The role of ratings in the subprime mortgage crisis: the art of corporate and the science of consumer credit ratings, *Research in the Sociology of Organizations*, 30A: 115–155.

Rose, Nikolas, and Abi-Rached, Joelle M. (2013), *Neuro: The New Brain Sciences and the Management of the Mind*, Princeton and London: Princeton University Press.

Roy, William G. (1997), *Socializing Capital: The Rise of the Large Industrial Corporation in America*, Princeton: Princeton University Press.

Ryle, Gilbert (1971), The thinking of thoughts: what is "le Penseur" doing?, in *Collected Papers*, vol. 1, London: Hutchinson.

Sachweh, Patrick (2012), The moral economy of inequality: popular views on income differentiation, poverty and wealth, *Socio-Economic Review*, 10(3): 419–445.

Samila, Sampsa and Sorenson, Olav (2010), Venture capital as a catalyst to commercialization, *Research Policy*, 39: 1348–1360.

Sanders, Gerard and Hambrick, Donald C. (2007), Swinging for the fences: the effects of CEO stock options on company risk taking and performances, *Academy of Management Journal*, 50(5): 1055–1076.

Sanders, Teela (2004), Controllable laughter: managing sex work through humour, *Sociology*, 38(2): 273–291.

Sarkar, Prabirjit (2013), Does an employment protection law lead to unemployment? A panel data analysis of OECD countries, 1990–2008, *Cambridge Journal of Economics*, 37(6): 1335–1348.

Schifling, Todd (2013), Defense against recession: U.S. business mobilization, 1950–1970, *American Journal Sociology*, 119(1): 1–34.

Schmidt, Robert and Sage, Daniel, Eguchi Toru and Dainty, Andy (2012), Moving architecture and flattening politics: examining adaptability through a narrative of design, *Architectural Research Quarterly*, 16(1): 75–84.

Schmidt, Vivien A. (2008), Discursive institutionalism: the explanatory power of ideas and discourse, *Annual Review of Political Science*, 11: 303–326.

Schneper, William D. and Guillén, Mauro F. (2004), Stakeholder rights and corporate governance: a cross-national study of hostile takeovers, *Administrative Science Quarterly*, 49(2): 263–295.

Schui, Florian (2014), *Austerity: The Great Failure*, New Haven: Yale University Press.

Schüll, Natasha Dow and Zaloom, Caitlin (2011), The shortsighted brain: neuroeconomics and the governance of choice in time, *Social Studies of Science*, 41(4): 515–538.

Schumacher, Ute and Hutchinson, Gladstone (2003), William E. Simon's capacities' approach to liberty: an essay in economic citizenship, *Atlantic Economic Journal*, 31(3): 283–288.

Schumpeter, Joseph A. ([1928] 1991a), *Essays: On Entrepreneurs, Innovations, Business Cycles, and the Evolution of Capitalism*, edited by Richard V. Clemence, New Brunswick and London: Transaction Publishers.

Schumpeter, Joseph A. ([1928] 1991b), Capitalism, in Schumpeter, Joseph A., *Essays: On Entrepreneurs, Innovations, Business Cycles, and the Evolution of Capitalism*, edited by Richard V. Clemence, New Brunswick and London: Transaction Publishers, pp. 189–210.

Seeger, Matthew W. and Ulmer, Robert R. (2003), Explaining Enron: communication and responsible leadership, *Management Communication Quarterly*, 17(1): 58–84.

Sell, Susan K. (2003), *Private Power, Public Law: The Globalization of Intellectual Property Rights*, New York: Cambridge University Press.

Sennett, Richard (1998), *The Corrosion of Character: The Personal Consequences of Work in the new capitalism*, New York and London: W.W. Norton and Company.

Serres, Michel (1982), *The Parasite*, Baltimore: John Hopkins University Press.

Shapiro, Susan P. (2005), Agency theory, *Annual Review of Sociology*, 31: 263–284.Shleifer, Andrei and Vishny, Robert (1997), A survey of corporate governance, *The Journal of Finance*, 52(2): 737–783.

Sikka, Prem (2009), Financial crisis and the silence of the auditors, *Accounting, Organizations and Society*, 34(6–7): 868–873.

Simmel, George ([1900] 1978), *The Philosophy of Money*, London: Routledge and Kegan Paul.Simmons, Beth A., Dobbin, Frank and Garrett, Geoffrey (2008), Introduction. The diffusion of neoliberalism, in Simmons, Beth A., Dobbin, Frank and Garrett, Geoffrey (eds), *The Global Diffusion of Markets and Democracy*, New York and Cambridge: Cambridge University Press, pp. 1–63.

Simon, H.A. (1957), *Models of Man*, New York: Wiley.

Sinclair, T.J. (2005), *The New Masters of Capital; American Bond Rating Agencies and the Politics of Creditworthiness*, Ithaca and London: Cornell University Press.

Singer, David Andrew (2007), *Regulating Capital: Setting Standards for the International Financial System*, Ithaca and London: Cornell University Press.

Sinn, Hans-Werner (2010), *Casino Capitalism: How the Financial Crisis Came About and What Needs to be Done Now*, New York and Oxford: Oxford University Press.

Sissoko, Carolyn (2010), The legal foundation of the financial collapse, *Journal of Financial Economic Policy*, 2(1): 5–34.

Skott, Peter and Ryoo, Soon (2010), Macroeconomic implications of financialisation, *Cambridge Journal of Economics*, 32: 827–862.

Sloan, Alfred P., Jr, (1964), *My Years with General Motors*, New York: Doubleday.Smelser, Neil J. and Swedberg, Richard (2005), *The Handbook of Economic Sociology*, Princeton and London: Princeton University Press.

Smil, Vachlav (2013), *Made in the USA: The Rise and Retreat of American Manufacturing*, Cambridge and London: MIT Press.

Smith, Adam ([1776] 1986), *The Wealth of Nations*, London: Penguin.

Smith, Mark A. (2007), *The Right Talk: How Conservatives Transformed the Great Society into the Economic Society*, Princeton: Princeton University Press.

Smith Hughes, Sally (2001), Making dollars out of DNA: the first major patent in biotechnology and the commercialization of molecular biology, 1974–1980, *Isis*, 92(3): 541–575.

Soederberg, Susanne (2008), A critique of the diagnosis and cure for "Enronitis": the Sarbanes-Oxley act and neoliberal governance of corporate America, *Critical Sociology*, 34(5): 657–680.

Sorenson, Olav and Stuart, Toby E. (2001), Syndication networks and the spatial distribution of venture capital investments, *American Journal of Sociology*, 106(6): 1546–1588.

Sorkin, Andrew Ross (2009), *Too Big to Fail: The Insider Story of How*

Wall Street and Washington Fought to Save the Financial System – and Themselves, New York: Viking.

Sotiropoulos, Dimitris P., Milios, John and Lapatsioras, Spyros (2013), *A Political Economy of Contemporary Capitalism and its Crisis: Demystifying Finance*, London and New York: Routledge.

Spatt, Chester (2014), Security market manipulation, *Annual Review in Financial Economics*, 6: 15.1–15.14.

Spector, Bert and Spital, Frances C. (2011), The ideology of executive bonuses: an historical perspective, *Journal of Management History*, 17(3): 315–331.

Spira, Laura and Page, Michael (2002), Risk management: the reinvention of internal control and the changing role of internal audit, *Accounting, Auditing and Accountability Journal*, 16(4), 640–661.

Stearns, Linda Brewster and Allan, Kenneth D. (1996), Economic behavior in institutional environments: the merger wave of the 1980s, *American Sociological Review*, 61(4): 699–718.

Stein, Judith (2011), *Pivotal Decade: How the United States Traded Factories for Finance in the Seventies*, New Haven: Yale University Press.

Stengers, Isabelle (1997), *Power and Invention: Situating Science*, Minneapolis, and London: University of Minnesota Press.

Stevens, Mitchell L., Armstrong, Elizabeth A. and Arum, Richard (2008), Sieve, incubator, temple, hub: empirical and theoretical advances in the sociology of higher education, *Annual Review of Sociology*, 34: 127–151.

Stiglitz, Joseph E. (2009), The anatomy of murder: who killed America's economy?, *Critical Review*, 21(2–3): 329–340.

Stiglitz, Joseph E. (2010), *Freefall: America, Free Markets, and the Sinking of the World Economy*, New York and London: WW. Norton.

Stockhammer, Engelbert (2004) Financialization and the slowdown of accumulation, *Cambridge Journal of Economics*, 28(5): 719–741.

Stockhammer, Engelbert (2013), Financialization and the global economy, in Wolfson, Martin H. and Epstein, Gerald, A. (eds), *Handbook of the Political Economy of Financial Crises*, New York and Oxford: Oxford University Press, pp. 512–525.

Stout, Lynn A. (2012), *The Shareholder Value Myth: How Putting Shareholders First Harms Investors, Corporations and the Public*, San Francisco: Berrett-Koehler.

Stout, Lynn A. (2013), Toxic side effects of shareholder primacy, *University Pennsylvania Law Review*, 161(7): 2003–2023.

Strahan, Philip E. (2013), Too big to fail: causes, consequences, and policy responses, *Annual Review in Financial Economics*, 5: 43–61.

Styhre, Alexander (2014), *Management and Neoliberalism: Connecting Policies and Practices*, New York and London: Routledge.

Suárez, Sandra L. (2014), Symbolic politics and the regulation of executive compensation: a comparison of the Great Depression and the Great Recession, *Politics and Society*, 42(1): 73–105.

Sutton, John, Dobbin, Frank, Meyer, John W. and Scott, W. Richard (1994), The legalization of the workplace, *American Journal of Sociology*, 99: 994–971.

Svetlova, Ekaterina (2012), On the performative power of financial models, *Economy and Society*, 41(3): 418–434.

Swank, Duane (2008), Tax policy in an era of internationalization: an assessment of a conditional diffusion of the spread of neoliberalism, in Simmons, Beth A., Dobbin, Frank and Garrett, Geoffrey (eds), *The Global Diffusion of Markets and Democracy*, New York and Cambridge: Cambridge University Press, pp. 64–103.

Swedberg, R. (2004), What has been accomplished by economic sociology and where it is heading?, *European Journal of Sociology*, 45(3): 317–330.

Swedberg, Richard (1998), *Max Weber and the Idea of Economic Sociology*, Princeton, NJ: Princeton University Press.

Swedberg, Richard (2003), The case for an economic sociology of law, *Theory and Society*, 32(1): 1–37.

Tabb, William J. (2012), *The Restructuring of Capitalism*, New York: Columbia University Press.

Tabb, William J. (2013), The international spread of financialization, in Wolfson, Martin H. and Epstein, Gerald A. (eds), *Handbook of the Political Economy of Financial Crises*, New York and Oxford: Oxford University Press, pp. 526–539.

Tawney, Richard Henry ([1926] 1998), *Religion and the Rise of Capitalism*, New Brunswick and London: Transaction Publishers.

Taylor, Lance (2010), *Maynard's Revenge: The Collapse of the Free Market Macroeconomics*, Cambridge and London: Harvard University Press.

Terrion, Jenepher Lennox and Ashforth, Blake E. (2002), From "I" to "we": the role of putdown humour and identity in the development of a temporary group, *Human Relations*, 55(1): 55–88.

Thewissen, Stefan (2014), Is it the income distribution or redistribution that affects growth?, *Socio-Economic Review*, 12(3), 545–571.

Thornburg, Steven and Roberts, Robin W. (2008), Money, politics, and the regulation of public accounting services: evidence from the Sarbanes–Oxley Act of 2002, *Accounting, Organizations and Society*, 33(2): 229–248.

Timmermans, Stefan (2008), Professions and their work: do market shelters protect professional interests?, *Work and Occupations*, 35(2): 164–188.

Tomaskovic-Devey, Donald and Lin, Ken-Hou (2011), Income dynamics, economic rents, and the financialization of the U.S. Economy, *American Sociological Review*, 76(4): 538–559.

Tosi, Henry L., Werner, Steve, Katz, Jeffrey P. and Gomez-Mejia, Luis R. (2000), How much does performance matter? A meta-analysis of CEO pay studies, *Journal of Management*, 26(2): 301–339.

Tourish, Dennis and Vatcha, Naheed (2005), Charismatic leadership and corporate cultism at Enron: the elimination of dissent, the promotion of conformity and organizational collapse, *Leadership*, 1(4): 455–480.

Trigilia, Carlo (2002), *Economic Sociology: State, Market, and Society in Modern Capitalism*, Malden: Blackwell.

Troy, Gil (2009), *The Reagan Revolution: A Very Short Introduction*, New York and Oxford: Oxford University Press.

Useem, Michael (1996), *Investor Capitalism*, New York: Basic Books.

Vaaler, Paul M. and McNamara, Gerry (2004), Crisis and competition in expert organizational decision making: credit-rating agencies and their response to turbulence in emerging economies, *Organization Science*, 15(6): 687–703.

Vallas, Steven and Prener, Christopher (2012). Dualism, job polarization, and the social construction of precarious work, *Work and Occupations*, 39(4): 331–353.

Van Arnum, Bradford M. and Naples, Michele I. (2013), Financialization and Income Inequality in the United States, 1967–2010, *American Journal of Economics and Sociology*, 72(5): 1158–1182.

Van der Zwan, Natascha (2014), Making sense of financialization, *Socio-Economic Review*, 12(1): 99–129.

Vaughan, D. (1996), *The Challenger Launch Disaster: Risky Technologies, Culture, a Deviance at NASA*, Chicago: The University of Chicago Press.

Vidal, Jordi Blanes I, Draca, Mirko and Fons-Rosen, Christian (2010), Revolving door lobbyists, *American Economic Review*, 102 (7): 3731–3748.

Vidal, Matt (2013), Low-autonomy work and bad jobs in postfordist capitalism, *Human Relations*, 66(4): 587–612.

Vogel, David (1983), The power of business in America: a re-appraisal, *British Journal of Political Science*, 13(I): 19–43.

Vogel, Steve K. (1996), *Freer Markets, More Rules: Regulatory Reforms in Advanced Industrial Countries*, Ithaca and London: Cornell University Press.

Vollmer, Henrik (2007), How to do more with numbers: elementary stakes, framing, keying, and the three-dimensional character of numerical signs, *Accounting, Organization and Society*, 32: 577–600.

Vollmer, Hendrik, Mennicken, Andrea and Preda, Alex (2009), Tracking the numbers: across accounting and finance, organizations and markets, *Accounting, Organizations and Society*, 34(5): 619–637.

Volscho, Thomas W. and Kelly, Nathan J. (2012), The rise of the super-rich: power resources, taxes, financial markets, the dynamics of the top 1 percent, 1949 to 2008, *American Sociological Review*, 77(5): 679–699.

Walker, Edward T. and Rea, Christopher M. (2014), The political mobilization of firms and industries, *Annual Review in Sociology*, 40: 281–304.

Washburn, Jennifer (2005), *University Inc.: The Corruption of Higher Education*, New York: Basic Books.

Watkins, S. (2003), Former Enron vice president Sherron Watkins on the Enron collapse, *Academy of Management Executive*, 17(4): 199–125.

Weber, Max (1999), *Essays in Economic Sociology*, Richard Swedberg (ed.), Princeton: Princeton University Press.

Weil, David (2014), *The Fissured Workplace: Why Work Became so Bad for so Many and What Can be Done About it*, Cambridge and London: Harvard University Press.

Westphal, James D. and Bednar, Michael K. (2008), The pacification of institutional investors, *Administrative Science Quarterly*, 53(1): 29–72.

Westphal, James D. and Clement, Michael (2008), Sociopolitical dynamics in relations between top managers and security analysts: favor rendering, reciprocity and analyst stock recommendations, *Academy of Management Journal*, 51(5): 873–897.

Westphal, James D. and Graebner, Melissa, E. (2010), A matter of appearance: how corporate leaders manage the impressions of financial analysis about the conducts of their boards, *Academy of Management Journal*, 53(1): 15–44.

Westwood, Robert and Rhodes, Carl (eds) (2007), *Humour, Work and Organization*, New York and London: Routledge.

White, Lawrence J. (2009), The credit-rating agencies and the subprime debacle, *Critical Review*, 21(2–3): 389–399.

White, Lawrence J. (2010), Markets: the credit rating agencies, *Journal of Economic Perspectives*, 24(2): 211–226.

White, Lawrence J. (2013), Credit rating agencies: an overview, *Annual Review in Financial Economics*, 5: 93–122.

Whitley, Richard (1986), The transformation of business finance into financial economics: the role of academic expansion and changes in the U.S. capital markets, *Accounting, Organizations, and Society*, 11: 171–192.

Wiener, Norbert (1948), *Cybernetics, or Control and Communication in the Animal Machine*, New York: John Wiley.

Wilcox King, Adelaide and Zeithelm, Carl P. (2000), Competencies and firm performance: examining the causal ambiguity paradox, *Strategic Management Journal*, 22: 75–99.

Wilkinson, Stephen (2006), *Bodies for Sale: Ethics and Exploitation in the Human Body Trade*, New York and London: Routledge.

Williams, James W. (2013), Regulatory technologies, risky subjects, and financial boundaries: governing "fraud" in the financial markets, *Accounting, Organizations and Society*, 39(67): 544–558.

Williamson, Oliver E. (1975), *Market and Hierarchies*, New York: Free Press.

Willman, Paul, Fenton O'Creevy, Mark P., Nicholson, Nigel and Soane, Emma (2001), Knowing the risks: theory and practice in financial market trading, *Human Relations*, 54(7): 887–910.

Willmott, Hugh (2010), Creating "value" beyond the point of production: branding, financialization and market capitalization, *Organization*, 17: 517–542.

Wise, M. Norton (ed.) (1995), *The Values of Precision*, Princeton: Princeton University Press.

Wisman, Jon D. (2013), Wage stagnation, rising inequality and the financial crisis of 2008, *Cambridge Journal of Economics*, 37(4): 921–945.

Wolfe, Tom (1987), *Bonfires of the Vanities*, New York: Farrar, Straus and Giroux.

Wolff, Edward N. (2003), What's behind the rise in profitability in the US in the 1980s and 1990s? *Cambridge Journal of Economics*, 27(4): 479–499.

Womack, J., Jones, D.T. and Roos, D. (1990), *The Machine That Changed the World*, New York: Macmillan.

Wood, Diana (2002), *Medieval Economic Thought*, New York and Cambridge: Cambridge University Press.

Wright, Mike and Lockett, Andy (2003), The structure and management of alliances: syndication in the venture capital industry, *Journal of Management Studies*, 40(8): 2073–2102.

Yakura, Elaine K. (2002), Billables: the valorization of time in consulting, *American Behavioral Scientist*, 44: 1076–1095.

Young, Ann P. (1999), Rule breaking and a new opportunistic managerialism, *Management Decision*, 37(7): 582–588.

Yue, Lori Qingyuan, Luo, Jiao and Ingram, Paul (2013), The failure of private regulation: elite control and market crises in the Manhattan banking industry, *Administrative Science Quarterly*, 58(1): 37–68.

Zajac, E.J. and Westphal, J.D. (2004) The social construction of stock market value: institutionalization and learning perspectives on stock market reactions, *American Sociological Review*, 69: 433–457.

Zalewski, David A. and Whalen, Charles J. (2010), Financialization and income inequality: a post Keynesian institutionalist analysis, *Journal of Economic Perspectives*, 44(3): 757–777.

Zaloom, Caitlin (2003), Ambiguous numbers: trading technologies and interpretation in financial markets, *American Ethnologist*, 30: 258–272.

Zaloom, Caitlin (2006), *Out of the Pits: Trading and Technology from Chicago to London*, Durham and London: Duke University Press.

Zelizer, Viviana (2007), Pasts and futures of economic sociology, *American Behavioral Scientist*, 50(8): 1056–1069.

Zelizer, Viviana A. (2011), *Economic Lives: How Culture Shapes the Economy*, Princeton and Oxford: Princeton University Press.

Zeller, Christian (2008), From the gene to the globe: extracting rents based on intellectual property monopolies, *Review of International Political Economy*, 15(1): 86–115.

Zorn, Dirk M. (2004), Here a chief, there a chief: the rise of the CFO in the American firm, *American Sociological Review*, 69: 345–364.

Zorn, Dirk, Dobbin, Frank, Dierkes, Julian and Kwok, Man-shan (2005), Managing investors: how financial markets reshaped the American firm, in Knorr Cetina, Karin and Preda, Alex (eds), *The Sociology of Financial Markets*, New York and Oxford: Oxford University Press, pp. 269–289.

Zuckerman, Ezra W. (1999), The categorical imperative: securities analysts and the illegitimacy discount, *American Journal of Sociology*, 104: 1398–1438.

Zuckerman, Ezra W. (2012), Construction, concentration, and(dis)continuities in social valuations, *Annual Review of Sociology*, 38: 223–245.

Index